# STAND OUT

## BUSINESS COMMUNICATION STRATEGIES THAT WORK

D0219143

Cherilyn Boyer | Cheryl Brodersen | Mikel Chertudi
Caitlin Hills | Michael Mandel | Kim Marchesseault
Marisa Michaels | Diza Sauers

**Kendall Hunt**
publishing company

Cover image © Shutterstock.com

www.kendallhunt.com
*Send all inquiries to:*
4050 Westmark Drive
Dubuque, IA 52004-1840

# Table of Contents

# UNIT 3: WRITING STRATEGIES  83

## Chapter 3-4: Document Design    123

# UNIT 4: GRAMMAR    131

## Chapter 4-1: Understanding Grammar    133

## Chapter 4-2: Understanding Punctuation    145

# UNIT 6: PROFESSIONAL PRESENTATIONS   237

# Preface

Our students are curious, insightful, engaged, and conscientious.

They deserve educational resources that are thorough, useful, efficient, and fun.

As business communication educators, we strive to create a resource uniquely tailored to our Millennial and Gen Z student population as they prepare to enter an increasingly globalized and online workforce. This text aligns closely with our own industry-informed, cohesive, and strategically formulated curriculum.

We continuously seek feedback from our students and the employers who hire them to inform our content, approaches, and learning outcomes. This title is a product of a continuous feedback loop. As authors whose primary responsibilities are teaching, we remain in the classroom year-round. As a team, we annually instruct more than 2,000 undergraduates in writing, presentation, interpersonal, and intrapersonal communication skills.

We spend significant time both inside and outside the classroom, teaching, mentoring, and coaching our students to become "workplace ready." We believe in helping our students develop practical skills they can immediately apply. Over the years, we found that not all business communication educational resources shared this depth or sense of urgency.

As an author team with nearly a century of combined teaching experience, we have used our share of textbooks to help us help our students develop these workplace-ready skills. While many of those textbooks had qualities we each liked, none of them fully met our students' needs. After years of working with textbooks we liked but didn't love, we decided the time had come to write our own.

There is no better way to grow as a team than to co-author a book (we could write a whole volume just on this experience!). The textbook you now hold in your hands/are reading on a screen is the result of years of discussions, sharing our content matter expertise, observing each other's teaching, collaborating with employers, arguing with each other, burying the hatchet with each other, and genuinely collaborating every step of the way.

Our students successfully use this title in our own undergraduate courses; we hope you will have similar positive experiences when you use it in yours.

***Stand Out: Business Communication Strategies That Work*** is designed to walk students through the process of determining the right strategy and approach for any given communication scenario. Rather than providing specific formulas or structures for the infinitely diverse situations business communication professionals may encounter during their daily activities, this title empowers students to use their innate critical thinking skills.

As students read through each unit of **Stand Out,** they will discover meaningful concepts that will help them become more credible business writers, presenters, and colleagues. The true-to-life examples and sample exercises will help them develop the critical business skill of agility in the workplace. On a more mechanical level, this textbook includes an ancillary website with additional resources and actual student samples. Students gain a comprehensive understanding of business communication that covers form, function, and strategy.

**Stand Out** concludes with an entire unit of case studies, complete with assignment prompts and student sample responses to those prompts. Rather than hunting for level-appropriate case studies or writing their own, business communication instructors will save time and effort by using these cases in their courses. Even if instructors choose not to assign any of these cases, students have extra opportunities to further explore their business communication skills.

From cover to cover, **Stand Out** empowers students to increase their professional credibility. This textbook inspires students to build the skills that employers frequently complain they lack: written, oral, and interpersonal communications.

We designed this text to be engaging for undergraduate students, with helpful tips for even the most advanced working professionals. We know our students have many competing demands for their time, so we have created this textbook that they actually enjoy reading.

This textbook is dedicated to students; may it help you move forward on your paths to success.

# UNIT 1:
## Communication Foundations

# The Standards for Success

**A**s a faculty, we have spent the past decade speaking with recruiters and teaching business communication to more than 10,000 students—undergraduate business students, MBA candidates, and executives. We have worked with hundreds of recruiters, alumni who have flourished in their various industries, and other colleagues who teach business communication across the world. After studying thousands of business documents, presentations, and scholarly research on the field of business communication, our team documented trends, refined coaching techniques and teaching strategies, and arrived at some best practices and guidelines for coaching leaders as they hone their communication skills.

It probably comes as no surprise to you that distinguishing yourself from the competition stems from your ability to skillfully communicate your knowledge and experiences. For the past decade, communication skills have been in the top five skills most valued by recruiters (NACE, 2014). Whether you are communicating in meetings, presentations, video conferencing, or writing on screens, your ability to manage your message largely reflects on you and "your brand." Effective training in business communication is essential to your development as a business professional.

What have we come to understand about standards and best communication practices through years of training thousands of business professionals? The answer is simple: the practice of effective communication is what weaves an entire organization together. Without communication, an enterprise cannot serve its mission, its customers cannot be served, and its management cannot be effective. While each division of a business is essential to the entire enterprise, the basic principles of communication are what keep the whole organization running. Without communication best practices, cross-functional coordination would not be possible.

When you couple the importance of communication with the recent explosion of technologies, the ravaging effects of globalization, and the acceleration of disruptive industries, suddenly the importance of communication becomes clear. Even if you can find footing in such turbulence, recent data confirms that declining literacy rates and gutted educational systems have had a direct impact on the development and mastery of basic communication skills. Even if your communication skills are well developed, the same may not be said for your colleagues. Learning to work with people at all communication skill levels will help position your organization for success.

# Skills to Succeed in the Business World

Positioning for success requires professional standards. For this book to assist you in your own development, you'll need to understand the pieces—the individual components of the standards—in order to understand how the pieces make up the whole. Each standard represents a key component to successful messaging. This book is designed to help you master the various workplace communication scenarios and tasks you will encounter in the work world. Since every individual has natural strengths and weaknesses, understanding the standards will help you identify what areas you need to improve. As with any set of standards, these are a reflection of common industry practices that will provide you with the ability to move forward and succeed in your chosen field of business. It sounds so simple, and yet it is one of the areas leaders at all levels return to again and again to shore up their training, refine their skill set, and continue to build upon in their own evolution as successful professionals.

In 2008, Tony Wagner published his landmark book, *The Global Achievement Gap*. He caused a furor and sparked a national debate in curricular redesign for American schools to catch up to the needs of the rapidly emerging global "knowledge-based" economy. His book highlighted several key areas that are required for any worker in the 21st century:

- Critical Thinking/Problem Solving
- Collaboration Across Networks/Leading by Influence
- Agility/Adaptability
- Initiative and Entrepreneurial Nature
- Effective Oral and Written Communication Skills
- Accessing and Analyzing Information
- Curiosity and Imagination

Not surprisingly, educators, trainers, and leaders across the country took notice of Wagner's alarming claims. While the rallying cry continues to reinvent the education system, more commonly embraced is the concept that education must align itself with business trends. Our program recognizes and adapts these trends into our programmatic standards so every working professional we partner with will be better equipped to participate in the new global knowledge economy.

# Business Communication Standards

Our standards provide you with the language to name and identify the skills and strategy needed to construct an effective message. When we evaluate written work, presentations, or even group communication efforts (meetings, feedback sessions, video conferencing), we look at the components of critical thinking, logic and reasoning (data), structural coherence, visual strategy, and error interference. Individually, each one of these categories gives you a set of strategies to use to make your messaging stronger; collectively, they pack a wallop.

| CRITICAL THINKING | LOGIC AND REASONING | STRUCTURAL COHERENCE | INFORMATION DESIGN | ERROR INTERFERENCE |
|---|---|---|---|---|
| Audience | Logical units of discourse | Coherent "whole" | Format and channel | Disruptive errors |
| Purpose | Claim or assertion | Internal logic | Visual design | Credibility errors |
| Context | Idea unity and integrity | Section unity and integrity | Readability/Skim | Etiquette errors |
| Frame | Supporting evidence | Transitions | Professionalism | Accent errors |
| Strategic approach | | Language use | | |

# Critical Thinking

Why have employers across the world pushed to recognize critical thinking ability as a key indicator and predictor of employee success? Karen Bruett of Dell Corporation's Strategic Business Development Department sums it up best when she states: "Corporations have changed dramatically in the last 20 years in terms of the way work is organized. Now lots of networks of cross-functional teams work together on specific projects. Work is no longer defined by your specialty; it is defined by the task or problem you and your team are trying to solve. Teams have to figure out the best way to get there—the solution is not prescribed" (Wagner, 2008).

"The biggest challenge for front-line employees is having the critical thinking and problem solving they need to be effective because nobody is there telling them exactly what to do. They have to figure it out" (Wagner, 2008).

Working on teams, sometimes across departments or even physical locations around the globe, requires top-notch communication skills and strategies, and these, in turn, require keen critical thinking skills.

Your success rests in your ability to recognize trends, problems, patterns, and root issues. Rarely does the working world offer a clear, black-and-white set of problems.

Perhaps in some of your academic coursework you have been asked to solve concrete problems. In many instances, these are set up for you to easily understand how to construct or apply a particular formula to arrive at a conclusion. This is seldom the case in the working world.

To clearly articulate a problem statement, you must have a clear understanding of many different (often conflicting) data sets. Only after you have identified these deeper structural issues can you address the real (not perceived) problem at hand. This implies critical thinking skills are measured through the ability to:

- Raise vital questions and problems
- Gather and assess relevant information and effectively interpret it
- Come to well-reasoned conclusions and solutions
- Think within alternative systems of thought
- Recognize assumptions, implications, and practical consequences
- Communicate effectively with others in identifying solutions to complex problems (Paul, 2002)

As you progress through the chapters in this book, we will both revisit and apply how critical thinking is fundamental to every aspect of successful communication.

If you truly consider it, you already use your critical thinking skills without really being aware of them. When you apply for a job and you put the most relevant information that meets the employer's needs in your cover letter, you are thinking critically. When you build a "frame" for your message so that it is easily understood by your particular audience, you are using critical thinking skills. As you determine the true root cause of an issue to then determine recommendations or summarize key conclusions, you are using your critical thinking skills. As you identify the most relevant strategic approach to formulate your message, you are thinking critically.

To write well and to speak eloquently is to witness critical thinking in its most visceral and powerful form. This is why our programmatic standards evaluate our students' critical thinking skills so rigorously: to help them adapt and be agile in their communications.

## Logic and Reasoning

As Tony Wagner identifies, "analyzing and accessing information" is clearly a 21st century skill. Mike Summers, Global Talent Management agent at Cisco, agrees. He states, "There is so much information available that it is almost too much, and if people aren't prepared to process the information effectively it almost freezes them in their steps" (Wagner, 2008). Quite often, when we join the working world, we need to build our own reputation and credibility. We start with a blank slate; you might have come highly recommended, but you haven't proven yourself in your new workplace. One way to build your credibility, and one key indicator of an employee's ability to solve problems, is to demonstrate a solid sense of logic and reasoning in how you present data.

© ImageFlow/Shutterstock.com

**Figure 1**    *"Don't be the Data Dump Guy!"*

**ANALYSIS**

Take a problem or data set and break it down. Examine the pieces, and see how they relate to one another and to the bigger picture (i.e. your bottom line).

**SYNTHESIS**

Look at your analysis. Are there ways to put the pieces back together to create something new, insightful, and original? This is your opportunity to teach your audience something new.

When we build credible messages, we need to include data and information that is both relevant and timely. A message that builds credibility includes relevant information that has been analyzed. Effective communication takes into consideration communicator credibility by always "treating" the data, not merely reporting it.

One of the most common feedback loops we hear about, particularly from recruiters, is the clear preference for applicants who can distinguish themselves by not merely presenting data, but by having a clear understanding of what to DO with the data.

Increasingly, with the overwhelming amount of information available at our fingertips, it is not enough to present a cascading stream of information. This is known as a "data dump." Recruiters look for applicants who can determine what data to include and what to discard. The ability to analyze data also predetermines the ability to find patterns, underlying causes, and root cause issues that might shed new light on the information. Putting the information back together to reveal new patterns is called *synthesis*, and it is a key aspect of your ability to apply logic and reasoning to your message. Being able to group information, present similar units (not compare apples to oranges), and to tease out the key pieces of data most relevant to a specific audience is key to success. Generating a well-crafted message requires that you understand what information to include and, most importantly, what the information signifies to varying audience members.

This is a key component in building and sustaining any message of validity, and it is one critical step in solidifying your success (and reputation) as a savvy professional. It is only through a trustworthy and reliable reputation that you can begin to collaborate across networks, exercise influence, and persuade. Your own professional capital is only as powerful as your ability to build and sustain your credibility.

## Structural Coherence

Have you ever wondered why your eyes glaze over during the middle of a long lecture? Have you ever found yourself using "TL;DR" (Too Long; Didn't Read) as you try to wade through a policy handbook, online diatribe, or posting? Conversely, have you ever hung on a speaker's every word and felt your point of view changing? In the world of work, there are many practices or "secret handshakes" that are used to keep our messages clear, focused, and effective. In a fast-paced world, understanding how to generate a coherent message can make the difference between sealing the deal or losing a job.

Understanding strategic organizational structures is so important that we devote the entire next chapter to mastering the various forms. Strategic organization helps you finesse a resistant audience member or determine the best way to present information to someone who is anticipating or expecting your information. Keeping the Bottom Line on Top (BLOT) is a key standby, and when you understand this is what business professionals are looking for from you as a potential partner, it will become a rule you live by, too. Whether you memorize SBAR (Situation, Background, Analysis, Recommendations) for your next report, or you learn the wily ways of an indirect bad news message, strategically knowing how to organize your message not only helps you finesse a business exchange, but also builds your credibility in the process.

We signal professionalism through the logical coherence of our messages. Structural coherence can be examined on a sentence-by-sentence level, or applied to the construction of an entire message. Much like a Jenga™ tower, each building block needs to be placed precisely and with care to keep the tower—the overall message—standing. Whether you are speaking or writing, the coherence of your message is determined by your capability to shape and match your message according to accepted organizational strategies. Further, a sense of coherence to any message has to do with your ability to bend language to your will. A gifted communicator uses not one word more than is needed per sentence, not one line more than is needed per paragraph, and not one more paragraph than is necessary. Less is more.

## Information Design

One clear outcome of the technological revolution has been to accelerate a communal understanding of visual literacy. We fundamentally understand the concept of "brand," as we are savvy consumers. In fact, social media has made all of us front-line marketing experts, selling products, services, and ideas to our personal networks. We are told to "manage our brand" and to have a savvy sense of "brand awareness." While this is certainly vital to your success as a business professional, you want to heighten your understanding of the basics in visual design and its impact on every aspect of messaging. Not surprisingly, one critical aspect of our standards has to do with understanding the impact of visual strategy. Whether you are improving the "skim" factor and readability of a document or selling your own image in a presentation by how you are dressed and positioned, you are using visual appeal to help convey your message.

**Figure 2**

While there are many books written on the topic of information design, our Unit 6 on professional presentations will provide you with practical approaches for making your work more polished and professional. While visual literacy is rooted in aesthetics, there are some best practices for document design and formatting.

As a business practice, the field of design has been integrated into most business communication channels. The Hichert Partner's International Business Communication Standards (IBCS) includes a comprehensive argument for the necessity of visual design to increase transparency and facilitate better decision making. Their research led them to conclude that strong design and clear communication improve business outcomes through:

i. **Improved quality:** The quality of the deliverables in every process stage will increase. This means more readily understood dashboards, clearer messages in more comprehensible reports, and—ultimately—better decisions.

ii. **Reduced reaction time:** The speed of the overall decision-making process will increase. The delivery time of new dashboards will be shorter, business analysts can answer the questions more quickly, and executives can make sound decisions faster.

iii. **Reduced costs:** Saving time in the delivery of dashboards, in the analysis of data, and in the creation of reports and presentations will reduce costs. But reducing the time executives spend on trying to understand the reports will be the biggest advantage. (Hicher, 2014)

Apparently, a picture is worth a thousand words, but a well-designed business graphic can be translated into bottom line dollars. As we explore and apply these standards in other chapters of this book, we will return to the discussion of how design impacts far more of our credibility, reputation, and reception of our messages than you might think.

## Error Interference

Most of us are afraid of making mistakes: they are embarrassing or can be costly. We lose face and feel as if our credibility has been eroded in some way when we make a mistake. And, to a certain extent, this can actually be the case. Certain types of errors can diminish your credibility with your audience. Knowing how to avoid landmines can go a long way toward saving you some embarrassing moments in the workplace. There is a difference between making a mistake and "failure," but we can train you to be aware of common errors so you can avoid them growing into failures.

In our standards for both written and spoken channels, we distinguish between the types of errors. These errors can manifest anywhere along the communication continuum, and we will conclude each chapter with fatal errors that are easy to avoid in your messaging and communication.

### Disruptive Errors

Disruptive errors are errors that are so egregious that the meaning of your message is completely lost. When you make these disruptive errors, the reader or listener is no longer engaged. Basically, your message gets dumped. In an accelerated and fast-paced business world, errors can be annoying. But a disruptive error is fatal. We have all heard the story about the applicant who misspelled the name of the employer. We've all heard recruiters talk about "reading for an error" so they can reject the application (mostly because there are so many qualified applicants). Or worse, the classic example of a disruptive error, the widely circulated story of the Cisco Fatty. In 2009, a competitive candidate landed a coveted job at Cisco, and on the ride home tweeted a snarky "Cisco just offered me a job! Now I have to weigh the utility of a fatty paycheck against the daily commute to San Jose and hating the work" (Wong, 2009). By the time the candidate got home, the offer had been rescinded. In these instances, a fatal error can cause your cover letter to sit unread, your presentation to be tossed, or your promotion denied.

Disruptive errors can be recognized in unintelligible sentences, omitted words/phrases, unclear pronoun references, wrong words and visuals, inappropriate actions, miscues, erratic behavior, and non-verbal delivery. This type of error tends to make the audience's task more difficult, even intruding on the listening or viewing process. Disruptive errors may cause even deeper problems that interfere with your audience's very understanding of what you are trying to say.

### Credibility Errors

Credibility errors can be recognized in lack of poise and professional confidence in verbal and non-verbal delivery (including appearance and vocal quality). While these do not usually disrupt communication, they tend to reflect negatively on the presenter's credibility, reducing the audience's confidence in not only what you have to say, but also in your ability to say it. These types of errors can be as simple as reading your corporate culture incorrectly (shuffling into a more formal corporate event wearing your favorite jeans and t-shirt), or they can be more serious, like not taking the time to adhere to company-provided templates. Your range of language and ability to adhere to agreed-upon corporate norms can manifest as credibility errors. This type of error can become serious if they cause the audience to judge your character by how frequently they occur or go uncorrected.

**Figure 3** *Your Image Sends Signals*

### Etiquette Errors

Some audiences (but not all) hardly notice etiquette errors, especially if they happen quickly and are passed over uncorrected in the moment. Etiquette errors arise from misjudgment of cultural and contextual expectations, such as levels of formality and familiarity. Etiquette errors can reduce the presenter's credibility, especially with audiences who are concerned about professional image or those who believe that critical thinking is reflected in the observance of protocol and social rules. In written language, these sometimes manifest in the use of emoticons or acronyms (TTFN, OMG, LOL etc.) when the intended audience either wants more formality or has other workplace expectations. The use of slang or vernacular when speaking can initially be considered an etiquette error, but can rapidly escalate into a disruptive error if not corrected.

### Accent Errors

Accent errors rarely interfere with communication, and they usually do not seriously damage your credibility. In writing, these include missing or incorrect articles (a, an, the), wrong prepositions (at, for, by, around, etc.), or incorrect use of idioms. In oral communication these errors are often found in the speech of non-native speakers and are nearly impossible for non-native speakers to correct in the short term. These are often overlooked and ignored by the audience. Accent errors are not to be confused with language usage errors. If language-based issues are grievous enough to eclipse the message, then they are considered disruptive errors regardless of the speaker's native language.

# Application in the Workplace

Once you start to master the standards, you'll notice you can apply them in any number of circumstances to improve communication in the workplace, in relationships, and in online formats. You will start to notice that more people listen when you speak, more of your ideas get bought into, and soon you'll be building a reputation as a skilled communicator. Or as Bill Gates so succinctly says, "I'm a great believer that any tool that enhances communication has profound effects in terms of how people can learn from each other, and how they can achieve the kind of freedoms that they're interested in." In the spirit of making the world a better place, one skillful communicator at a time, we welcome you on your journey to becoming a skillful and strategic communication master.

## PROFESSIONAL INTERPERSONAL COMMUNICATION STANDARDS

| | CRITICAL THINKING | LOGIC AND REASONING | STRUCTURAL COHERENCE | INFORMATION DESIGN | ERROR INTERFERENCE |
|---|---|---|---|---|---|
| **CRITERIA** | • Audience<br>• Purpose<br>• Context<br>• Frame<br>• Strategic approach | • Logical units of discourse<br>• Claim or assertion<br>• Supporting evidence<br>• Information sharing | • Coherent "whole"<br>• Fluency<br>• Internal logic<br>• Team unity & integrity<br>• Language use | • Image management<br>• Professionalism<br>• Delivery | • Disruptive errors<br>• Credibility errors<br>• Etiquette errors<br>• Accent errors |
| **EXCEEDS EXPECTATIONS** | • Demonstrates **leadership** through understanding of audience, purpose, and context; framing problem/project and strategic approach; and the ability to:<br>1. **run effective meetings** with a clear statement of purpose that encompasses the higher view with an articulated position and understanding of task (i.e. decision, information gathering);<br>2. **successfully manage relationships** with other team members, superiors, and subordinates;<br>3. **listen empathically** and respond accordingly to the needs of group and individuals;<br>4. **encourage divergent viewpoints** while maintaining articulated group strategies. | • Demonstrates **exceptional** logic and reasoning by<br>1. **successfully anticipating** multiple team communication styles and flexing accordingly;<br>2. providing **thought leadership** and support through **claims/assertions** that are logically sound, clear, credible, valid, and substantiated;<br>3. **supporting team** efforts with information and data that are accurate, concrete, explicit, relevant (to claims and team interests), well-explained, varied, and engaging;<br>4. **readily sharing information** as appropriate with team members; not withholding information. | • Demonstrates **mastery** of fluency and coherence through<br>1. the **thoughtful** and **complete** communication of ideas;<br>2. **well-structured and guided discussions and meetings** that anticipate team needs and provide & structure;<br>3. **appropriate support** for team (listening, data, conflict management, resolution);<br>4. **accountability and reliability** in all forms of team communication;<br>5. language that is **precise, concise, fluid and well-articulated**. | • Demonstrates **expertise** of information design through<br>1. **optimal** personal presentation & etiquette (polished, poised, professional);<br>2. **sophisticated** and professional interpersonal communication;<br>3. **professional** virtual image management;<br>4. **exceptional** professionalism in written correspondence;<br>5. **ethical** and **authentic** behavior. | • **No etiquette or credibility errors.** Although minimal disruptive or accent errors may be present, no error interference.<br><br>Sophisticated interpersonal skills earmark this individual as fluid and professional. |

| | | | | |
|---|---|---|---|---|
| **MEETS EXPECTATIONS** | • Demonstrates **clear** understanding of lateral and peer leadership through understanding of audience, purpose, and context; framing problem/project and strategic approach; and the ability to:<br>1. **participate mindfully in meetings** with a clear statement of purpose);<br>2. **manage relationships** with other team members, superiors, and subordinates;<br>3. **resolve conflict;**<br>4. **listen well** and respond to the needs of group;<br>5. **encourage divergent viewpoints.** | • Demonstrates **clear** logic and reasoning by<br>1. **understanding own communication style** and flexing accordingly to others needs;<br>2. providing **team support** through **claims/assertions** that are logically sound, clear, credible, valid, and substantiated;<br>3. **supporting team** with information and data that are accurate, concrete, explicit, and relevant;<br>4. **sharing information.** | • Demonstrates **appropriate** fluency and coherence through<br>1. **thorough** and **complete** communication of ideas;<br>2. **ability to** anticipate team needs and help keep team functioning;<br>3. **appropriate support** for team (listening, data, conflict management, resolution);<br>4. **accountability and reliability** in all forms of team communication;<br>5. language that is **appropriate** and professional. | • Demonstrates **professionalism** of information design through<br>1. **appropriate** personal presentation & etiquette (polished, poised, professional);<br>2. **adequate** interpersonal communication skills;<br>3. virtual image management;<br>4. **professionalism** in written correspondence;<br>5. **ethical** behavior. | • **Minor etiquette or credibility errors.** Although minimal disruptive or accent errors may be present, no major error interference.<br>Appropriate interpersonal skills earmark this individual as emerging professional. |
| **DOES NOT MEET EXPECTATIONS** | • Demonstrates **rudimentary** knowledge of lateral and peer leadership through poor understanding of audience, purpose, context, and framing through:<br>1. **erratic** or **unreliable** team participation;<br>2. **poorly managed relationships** with other team members, superiors, and subordinates (dominates, bullies, withdraws);<br>3. **poor** listening skills;<br>4. creates **conflict** and will not address resolution. | • Demonstrates **poor** logic and reasoning through<br>1. **failure** to understanding own communication style and flex according to others needs;<br>2. presents **unsubstantiated,** invalid, or unclear **claims/assertions;**<br>3. **provides team** with unreliable information and data that are inaccurate, and irrelevant;<br>4. **willfully withholds** or **distorts information** to disrupt effective team decision making. | • Demonstrates **lack** of fluency and coherence through<br>1. **disjointed** or incomplete communication of ideas;<br>2. **inability** to anticipate team needs and help keep team functioning;<br>3. **disruptive behavior** interfering with team processes (steers team off course, fails to track information accurately);<br>4. **poor** communication (frequently needs to repeat ideas to be understood). | • Demonstrates **ineffective** information design through<br>1. **inappropriate** personal presentation & etiquette;<br>2. **poor** interpersonal communication skills;<br>3. no virtual image management;<br>4. **unprofessional** written correspondence;<br>5. **unethical** behavior. | • **Errors damage message comprehension and writer credibility.**<br>Individual needs substantial coaching before entering professional arena. |

**Error Interference Definition**

**Disruptive Errors:** Disruptive errors can be recognized in the inability to understand audience or context. Disruptive errors are grievous and damage credibility: severe group dynamics, breach of trust, high levels of conflict, and egregious behavior fall into this category.

**Credibility Errors:** Credibility errors can be recognized in inconsistent performance and the inability to follow-through with team members. Accountability items such as submitted assignments, meeting attendance, and quality of work all effect credibility, and ultimately team performance.

**Etiquette Errors:** Etiquette errors violate group norms and agreed upon practices. These can be simple (talking on your cell phone while in team meetings or surfing the net while conducting group research). They an also manifest when the individual transgresses upon group values (keeping meetings short; punctuality; appropriate tone; respect.) These types of errors are easily overlooked at first, but accumulatively have a toxic effect on group efficacy.

**Accent Errors:** Commonly found in the writing of non-native speakers – (which are nearly impossible for non-native speakers to correct in the short term) – these are often overlooked and ignored by team members in the initial phases of group formation while team members acculturate themselves. Once these become "excuses" for lack of team participation, team members aren't as forgiving and tend to view these as credibility errors.

## PROFESSIONAL PRESENTATION STANDARDS

| | CRITICAL THINKING | LOGIC AND REASONING | STRUCTURAL COHERENCE | INFORMATION DESIGN | ERROR INTERFERENCE |
|---|---|---|---|---|---|
| **CRITERIA** | • Audience<br>• Purpose<br>• Context<br>• Frame<br>• Strategic approach | • Logical units of discourse<br>• Claim or assertion<br>• Idea unity and integrity<br>• Supporting evidence | • Coherent "whole"<br>• Internal logic<br>• Section unity & integrity<br>• Transitions<br>• Language use | • Visual design<br>• Accessibility of information<br>• Professionalism<br>• Delivery | • Disruptive errors<br>• Credibility errors<br>• Etiquette errors<br>• Accent errors |
| **EXCEEDS EXPECTATIONS** | • Demonstrates **sophisticated** understanding of audience, purpose, and context through framing and strategic approach, including, not limited to:<br>1. **purpose** statement that is articulate, coherent, overreaching, encompassing higher view with articulated position and audience task (i.e. decision, information gathering);<br>2. **forecasting** that provides structural cohesion and unity and acknowledges and informs audience of guiding structure;<br>3. **professionalism** that acknowledges relational value and confirms audience status and knowledge base through fluid, conversational, tailored delivery. | • Demonstrates **exceptional** logic and reasoning through<br>1. **claims/assertions** that are logically sound, clear, credible, valid, and substantiated;<br>2. **unity, integrity,** and **thoroughness** of ideas and reasoning provided to support claims and assertions;<br>3. **supporting evidence, information, and data** that are accurate, concrete, explicit, relevant (to claims and audience interests), well-explained, varied, and engaging. | • Demonstrates **integrity** of structural coherence through<br>1. the development of a **meaningful "whole";**<br>2. **well-structured, logical flow** of ideas;<br>3. **cohesive development** within sections (sections can "stand alone");<br>4. **seamless content based** transitions with clear and well signified shifts;<br>5. language that is **precise, concise, fluid and well-articulated.** | • Demonstrates **mastery** of information design through<br>1. **optimal** verbal and nonverbal delivery (polished, poised, professional);<br>2. **sophisticated** visual design strategy;<br>3. compression of complex information into **clear statements and visuals** for rapid intake and maximum impact;<br>4. **enhanced** audience comprehension of complex material through relevant examples and analogies. | • **No etiquette or credibility errors.** Although minimal disruptive or accent errors may be present, no error interference. Presentation is client-ready and professional. |

*(Continued)*

| | MEETS EXPECTATIONS | DOES NOT MEET EXPECTATIONS |
|---|---|---|
| • Demonstrates **clear** understanding of audience, purpose, and context through framing and strategic approach, including, not limited to:<br>1. **purpose** statement that is clear and coherent;<br>2. **forecasting** that provides basic structural unity (often as a list);<br>3. **professionalism** that employs established protocol for specific audience and context. | • Demonstrates **rudimentary** understanding of audience, purpose, and context through framing and strategic approach, including, not limited to:<br>1. **purpose** statement that is awkward or absent;<br>2. **forecasting** that is absent or irrelevant to the message;<br>3. **lack** of professionalism that results in erratic and inappropriate statements or language use. | |
| • Demonstrates **clear** logic and reasoning through<br>1. **claims/assertions** that are explicitly stated, logical and credible;<br>2. **evident ideas and reasoning** provided to support claims and assertions;<br>3. **supporting evidence, information, and data** that are relevant and varied. | • Demonstrates **poor** logic and reasoning through<br>1. **claims/assertions** that are vague, inadequate, unsubstantiated or incomplete;<br>2. **underdeveloped or absent ideas and reasoning** provided to support claims and assertions;<br>3. **insufficient, irrelevant, vague, or absent evidence,** information, and data provided to back claims. | |
| • Demonstrates **clarity** of structural coherence through<br>1. an overall **sense of meaning** evident in the text;<br>2. **general flow** of ideas;<br>3. **clear** section development;<br>4. **effective** transitions;<br>5. **clear** language. | • Demonstrates **lack** of structural coherence through<br>1. **lack of coherence, unity and cohesion** in the text;<br>2. **inconsistent flow** of ideas;<br>3. **erratic** section development;<br>4. design strategies (i.e. lists, visuals) used as **compensation** for lack of cohesion, logic, and meaning;<br>5. **poor** transitions;<br>6. **imprecise, unclear language.** | |
| • Demonstrates **effective** information design through<br>1. **appropriate** verbal and non-verbal delivery (professional);<br>2. **professional** visual design strategy;<br>3. use of common strategies (bullets, headings, graphics) to promote **clarity and comprehension;**<br>4. **improved** audience comprehension through relevant examples. | • Demonstrates **ineffective** information design through<br>1. **inappropriate** verbal and non-verbal delivery;<br>2. **unpolished** visual design strategy;<br>3. interference or absence of **clarity** and **readability** through use of common delivery strategies;<br>4. **audience comprehension** of complex material is **impaired** by visual, verbal, and nonverbal elements. | |
| • **Minimal etiquette or credibility errors.**<br>Although occasional disruptive errors and frequent accent errors may be present, there is no serious error interference.<br>Document needs minimal revision before submission to client. | • **Errors damage message comprehension and writer credibility.**<br>Document needs substantial revision before submission to client. | |

**Error Interference Definition:**

**Disruptive Errors:** Disruptive errors can be recognized in unintelligible sentences, omitted words/phrases, unclear pronoun references, wrong words & visuals, inappropriate actions, miscues, erratic behavior and non-verbal delivery. This type of error tends to make the audience's task more difficult, even intruding on the listening and viewing process. Disruptive errors may also interfere with communication, preventing the audience from comprehending what the writer means.

**Credibility Errors:** Credibility errors can be recognized in lack of poise and professional confidence in verbal and non-verbal delivery (including appearance and vocal quality). While these do not usually disrupt communication they tend to reflect negatively on the presenter's credibility, reducing the audience's confidence in what the presenter has to say. Credibility errors become serious if they cause the audience to judge a presenter's character or management ability by the frequency of mere presence of certain violations of professional expectations.

**Etiquette Errors:** Some audiences (but not all) hardly notice etiquette errors, especially if happening quickly in the moment. Etiquette errors evolve from presenter misjudgment of cultural and contextual expectations, such as levels of formality and familiarity. Etiquette errors can reduce the presenter's credibility, especially with audiences who are concerned about professional image or those who believe that critical thinking is reflected in the observance of protocol and social rules.

**Accent Errors:** Commonly found in the speaking of non-native speakers – (which are nearly impossible for non-native speakers to correct in the short term) – these are often overlooked and ignored by the audience, particularly if they are cognizant of the status of the presenter. Accent errors rarely interfere with communication, and they usually do not seriously damage the writer's credibility. These include missing or incorrect articles, wrong prepositions, or incorrect use of idioms.

## PROFESSIONAL WRITING STANDARDS

| CRITERIA | CRITICAL THINKING | LOGIC AND REASONING | STRUCTURAL COHERENCE | INFORMATION DESIGN | ERROR INTERFERENCE |
|---|---|---|---|---|---|
| | • Audience<br>• Purpose<br>• Context<br>• Frame<br>• Strategic approach | • Logical units of discourse<br>• Claim or assertion<br>• Idea unity and integrity<br>• Supporting evidence | • Coherent "whole"<br>• Internal logic<br>• Transitions<br>• Section unity & integrity<br>• Language use | • Format and channel<br>• Visual design<br>• Readability/accessibility<br>• Professionalism | • Disruptive errors<br>• Credibility errors<br>• Etiquette errors<br>• Accent errors |
| **EXCEEDS EXPECTATIONS** | • Demonstrates **sophisticated** understanding of audience, purpose, and context through framing and strategic approach, including, not limited to:<br>1. **purpose** statement that is articulate, coherent, overreaching, encompassing higher view;<br>2. **forecasting** that provides structural cohesion and unity and acknowledges and informs audience of guiding structure;<br>3. **professionalism** that acknowledges relational value and confirms audience status and knowledge base. | • Demonstrates **exceptional** logic and reasoning through<br>1. **claims/assertions** that are logically sound, clear, credible, valid, and substantiated;<br>2. **unity, integrity**, and **thoroughness** of ideas and reasoning provided to support claims and assertions;<br>3. **supporting evidence, information, and data** that are accurate, concrete, explicit, relevant, well explained, varied, and engaging. | • Demonstrates **integrity** of structural coherence through<br>1. the development of a **meaningful "whole"**;<br>2. **well-structured, logical flow** of ideas;<br>3. **cohesive development** within sections (sections can "stand alone");<br>4. **seamless** transitions;<br>5. **precise, concise, and accurate** language patterns. | • Demonstrates **mastery** of information design through<br>1. **optimal** format and channel choice;<br>2. **sophisticated** visual design strategy;<br>3. compression of complex information into **clear visual patterns** for rapid intake and high skim value;<br>4. **enhanced** reader comprehension of complex material through clear, concise, visual and verbal elements. | • **No etiquette or credibility errors.**<br>Although minimal disruptive or accent errors may be present, no error interference.<br>Document is client—ready and professional. |

*(Continued)*

| | | | | |
|---|---|---|---|---|
| **MEETS EXPECTATIONS** | Demonstrates **clear** understanding of audience, purpose, and context through framing and strategic approach, including, not limited to:<br>1. **purpose** statement that is clear and coherent;<br>2. **forecasting** that provides basic structural unity (often as a list);<br>3. **professionalism** that employs established protocol for specific audience and context. | Demonstrates **clear** logic and reasoning through<br>1. **claims/assertions** that are explicitly stated, logical and credible;<br>2. **evident ideas and reasoning** provided to support claims and assertions;<br>3. **supporting evidence, information, and data** that are relevant and varied. | Demonstrates **clarity** of structural coherence through<br>1. an overall **sense of meaning** evident in the text;<br>2. **general flow** of ideas;<br>3. **clear** section development;<br>4. **effective** transitions;<br>5. **clear** language. | Demonstrates **effective** information design through<br>1. **appropriate** format and channel choice;<br>2. **professional** visual design strategy;<br>3. use of common strategies (bullets, headings, graphics) to promote **clarity and readability;**<br>4. **improved** reader comprehension of complex material through clear, concise, visual and verbal elements. | **Minimal etiquette or credibility errors.** Although occasional disruptive errors and frequent accent errors may be present, there is no serious error interference. Document needs minimal revision before submission to client. |
| **DOES NOT MEET EXPECTATIONS** | Demonstrates **rudimentary** understanding of audience, purpose, and context through framing and strategic approach, including, not limited to:<br>1. **purpose** statement that is awkward or absent;<br>2. **forecasting** that is absent or irrelevant to the message;<br>3. **lack** of professionalism that results in erratic and inappropriate statements or language use. | Demonstrates **poor** logic and reasoning through<br>1. **claims/assertions** that are vague, inadequate, unsubstantiated or incomplete;<br>2. **underdeveloped or absent ideas and reasoning** provided to support claims and assertions;<br>3. **insufficient, irrelevant, vague, or absent evidence,** information, and data provided to back claims. | Demonstrates **lack** of structural coherence through<br>1. **lack of coherence, unity and cohesion** in the text;<br>2. **inconsistent flow** of ideas;<br>3. **erratic** section development;<br>4. design strategies (i.e. lists, visuals) used as **compensation** for lack of cohesion, logic, and meaning;<br>5. **poor** transitions;<br>6. **imprecise, unclear language.** | Demonstrates **ineffective** information design through<br>1. **inappropriate** format and channel choice;<br>2. **unpolished** visual design strategy;<br>3. interference or absence of **clarity and readability** through use of common strategies (bullets, headings, graphics);<br>4. **reader comprehension** of complex materials is **impaired** by visual and verbal elements of the text. | **Errors damage message comprehension and writer credibility.** Document needs substantial revision before submission to client. |

## Error Interference Definition

**Disruptive Errors:** Disruptive errors can be recognized in unintelligible sentences, omitted words/phrases, unclear pronoun references, incorrect verb forms, run-on sentences, or wrong words. This type of error tends to make the reader's task more difficult, even intruding on the reading process. Disruptive errors may also interfere with communication, preventing the reader from comprehending what the writer means.

**Credibility Errors:** Credibility errors can be recognized in faulty subject/verb agreements, some punctuation errors, or spelling errors. While these do not usually disrupt communication, they tend to reflect negatively on the writer's credibility, reducing the readers' confidence in what a writer has to say. Credibility errors become serious if they cause the reader to judge a writer's character or management ability by the frequency of the mere presence of certain violations of Standard English.

**Etiquette Errors:** Many readers (but not all) hardly notice etiquette errors, especially if reading quickly for the moment. Etiquette errors include substituting "I" for "me" after prepositions; misplacing apostrophes (team's /teams'); confusing it's and its; or excessive use of passive voice. However, etiquette errors can reduce the writer's credibility, especially with those readers who are concerned about professional image or those who believe that critical thinking is reflected in the observance of grammar rules.

**Accent Errors:** Commonly found in the writing of non-native speakers – (which are nearly impossible for non-native speakers to correct in the short term) – these are often overlooked and ignored by readers, particularly if they are cognizant of the non-native-speaker status of the writer. Accent errors rarely interfere with communication, and they usually do not seriously damage the writer's credibility. Accent errors include missing or incorrect articles, wrong prepositions, or incorrect use of idioms.

# Strategic Business Communication

Ever wish you knew the secret handshake that would let you win at work? Ever wondered how one salesperson can be so annoying, yet another anticipates exactly what you want or need even if you don't know? Would you know how to send a letter to someone rejecting their candidacy? Denying their claim? Would you draw a complete blank if your boss asked you to write an informational report compiling the data from three different news sites, each one with a slightly different perspective? Wouldn't it be great if you knew the "secret handshake" to allow you to finesse any of these circumstances?

A large part of skillful communication involves audience analysis: understanding the right approach to reach a particular audience, in a specific circumstance, at a given time. While experience is always the best teacher, it is not always the most forgiving. Undoubtedly, life will provide you with many learning moments, but you'll be better equipped to navigate a variety of audiences by learning a variety of strategic approaches. Think of it as learning the secret handshake, a shortcut into your audience's good graces. Our intention is to make you as workplace-ready as possible, and to equip you with the basic knowledge to navigate any scenario that might require a special approach.

If you've ever played sports, then you know that there are certain "plays" that get made—both teams know the play when they see it, and they know how to react and respond. These are rules of engagement. Similarly, if you are a musician, you recognize notation in music that not only tells you how to play, but if you are playing with others (in a quartet, or in a symphony), it also helps you anticipate and know the other players' parts before they are played. You not only know how to respond, but also how to collaborate so you create meaning (music). Understanding when and how to play—the game or melody—is very similar to selecting the right strategy for any workplace messaging you might be asked to create. And, in the same way an athlete or musician learns the proper approach and commits it to muscle memory, you can also learn what organizational strategies are most commonly used and for what specific types of circumstance.

# Strategy Starts with Your Audience

As with most messaging, we start with the audience. Understanding your audience, their positions, values, and circumstances, remains a critical component of successful engagement. A message, no matter how eloquent, must be crafted with a particular audience in mind. Therefore, an effective communication strategy requires forethought and careful planning. Part of this process involves identifying the audiences with whom you wish to communicate and tailoring your messages to meet the needs of each particular group. In business, we call these different groups *stakeholders*. Think of them as various players on a team; each one of them has a particular function or relationship to the central mission. If you needed to explain a botched play, you wouldn't speak the same way to an angry coach as you would to a vivacious cheerleader—the messages, the approach, and probably the content would be very different. Still, they are stakeholders because they are invested in the outcome of the game, and your message still needs to be delivered. Accordingly, you would need to adapt your strategy to accommodate each one of their sets of needs.

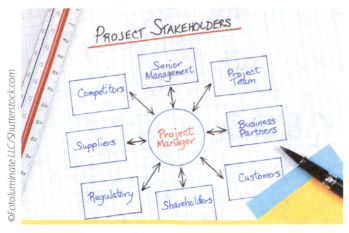

©Fotoluminate LLC/Shutterstock.com

**Figure 1**    *Know your stakeholders*

In the business world, your stakeholders are the people or groups affected by your organization's performance. Generally, they have something to lose or gain by your company's activities, and often, stakeholders can influence the success or failure of your projects, ventures, or events. From an organizational perspective, tailored communication is not only wise, but vital to your survival.

A need for strategic messaging usually arises from exigency; that is, a situation or event that calls for audience engagement. These situations are innumerable and range from circumstances like new product launches, to corporate mergers, or changes in leadership or policy. It's important to remember that you have both internal and external audiences: the stakeholders within your organization, and those who don't work for the company, but have some kind of monetary, emotional, or practical interest in the situation at hand. As you develop a stakeholder or audience analysis for purposes of communication, you may consider factors like stakeholders' levels of influence, or the timing and channels in which messages should be sent. These elements will help you further refine your message once you've chosen a strategic approach. In order to select the appropriate strategy, first determine the correct channel for your message.

## Reaching Your Audience

In an omni-channel world, knowing the right channel to reach your audience can sometimes determine if your message is received at all. Knowing how your audience prefers to receive information is critical to the success of your message. Your boss might not want you to text her at all hours. Your co-worker might insist you post your collaborations on Google Docs. Your mother might not want to hear from you on Facebook. A co-worker needing a new job might want you to ping them on LinkedIn. And sometimes, people even pick up the phone and talk to one another. You'll want to be sure you select the right channel for your message.

Choosing the optimal channel and format for your communication demonstrates that you understand whom you're talking to. The channel refers to the medium by which the message is transmitted. Are you making a phone call, collaborating via Google Docs, presenting to a large crowd in a hotel banquet hall, or sitting down across a conference table from someone in a more intimate setting?

The format refers to the type of message or document that you are sending. What format is the most appropriate for the purpose, audience, and occasion? The two tables below can help you make some of these important decisions.

| VERBAL MESSAGES | FORMAL | INFORMAL |
|---|---|---|
| Internal | Formal presentation or seminar<br><br>Formal virtual/remote presentation (i.e. conference call or video conference) | Informal presentation<br><br>Informal virtual/remote presentation (e.g. conference call, Apple FaceTime, Google Hangout, etc.) |
| External | Formal presentation or seminar<br><br>Formal virtual/remote presentation | |

| WRITTEN MESSAGES | FORMAL | INFORMAL |
|---|---|---|
| Internal | Formal report<br>Contractual letter | Informal report<br>Memorandum<br>Email<br>Text/Instant Message |
| External | Formal report<br>Formal letter | Email<br>Hand-written correspondence |

**Table 1** *Message Format*

Each channel has its benefits and drawbacks. As you select your channel, be sure to consider critical elements such as whether or not you are creating a permanent record.

How rich is the channel? Face-to-face communication is the richest because you can read so many nonverbal cues. How much feedback do you need? Is your client angry? Does your message contain unpleasant information? Is the receiver expecting to hear from you? How much control do you need over your message? All of these variables are taken into consideration as you determine the best way to reach your audience.

## CHANNEL SELECTION CONSIDERATIONS

Richness vs. leanness

Need for interpretation (ambiguity)

Speed of establishing contact

Immediacy of feedback

Cost

Amount of information conveyed

Permanent record

Control over message

# Establishing the Purpose of Your Communication

If you're presenting information to someone, chances are you're doing one of three things: you're informing them about something, persuading them to do something, or delivering bad news. Keep in mind, these categories are not always mutually exclusive. In fact, you may see some overlap. For instance, a bad news message may contain a persuasive appeal like a special offer or consolation gift. These nuances become more apparent as you gain experience messaging.

Generally, you should be able to identify your message as informative (positive or neutral), informative (negative), or persuasive. Once you have done so, you can build the most appropriate strategy for your purpose.

# Determining Your Strategic Approach

Based on your experience as a communicator, you have probably encountered this choice before: is it best to present your core message up front, or to reveal it later in the conversation or document? Your ability to choose the appropriate approach is a reflection of your communication competence. The way in which you convey a particular message, is intimately linked to your audience's perceptions of you and your message. Therefore, the choice between direct or indirect is more about effectiveness than it is about style. The tables below provide the basic approach for direct and indirect messages.

## DIRECT MESSAGE

```
_____
_____
Bottom Line On Top
_____
_____
_____
_____
_____
_____
```

## INDIRECT MESSAGE

```
_____
_____
_____
_____
_____
_____
Bottom Line On Bottom
_____
```

| DIRECT MESSAGES | INFORM (POSITIVE OR NEUTRAL) | INFORM (NEGATIVE/BAD NEWS) | PERSUADE |
|---|---|---|---|
| **Introduction** | **Frame and Forecast**<br>• Frame for your audience<br>• State your purpose<br>• Forecast information | **Establish Rapport and Reveal the Bad News**<br>• Briefly establish rapport<br>• Present negative news | **Frame and Forecast**<br>• Frame for your audience<br>• State your purpose——present the request<br>• Forecast information |
| **Body** | **Present the Key Points of Your Message**<br>• Include data relevant to your purpose<br>• Group concepts into logical main points<br>• Articulate your findings<br>• Use readability strategies——headings, bullet points, tables, charts, etc. (if appropriate) | **Present the Reasons**<br>• Explain reasons and causes<br>• Be clear and specific, if appropriate.<br>• Recognize audience needs | **Position and Present Rationale**<br>• Explain reasoning<br>• Anticipate reader's potential points of resistance and counter with credible facts that matter to them. |
| **Conclusion** | **Restate Key Points and Invite Future Contact**<br>• Summarize<br>• Invite inquiry | **Close with Goodwill**<br>• Demonstrate appreciation<br>• Manage future contact | **Restate Request and Call Audience to Action**<br>• Call to action<br>• Make action convenient and immediate for reader with needed contact information and next steps |

Table 2

| INDIRECT MESSAGES | INFORM (NEGATIVE/BAD NEWS) | PERSUADE |
|---|---|---|
| **Introduction** | Start with a **Buffer**<br>• Present relevant, neutral ideas: common ground, shared accomplishments, expressions of appreciation, etc.<br>• Transition to next paragraph | **Align/Attention**<br>Align your goals with the reader and get their attention using the following:<br>• Provide common ground<br>• Highlight established relationship |
| **Body** | Provide **Reasons** for bad news<br>• Facts, analysis, outcomes and/or information<br>Present **Bad News**<br>• Reveal after reasons<br>• Limit space dedicated to revealing the bad news.<br>• Find a silver lining (if appropriate) | **Interest/Information**<br>• Create a sense of interest by offering relevant information<br>**Direct Benefits**<br>• Show reader benefits to their taking the proposed action<br>**Deflection**<br>• Anticipate reader's resistance and counter with credible facts |
| **Conclusion** | • Reference silver lining, if applicable<br>• Close with **Goodwill** | **Call to Action**<br>• Present the request (ask)<br>• Make action convenient and immediate for reader and include necessary contact information and next steps |

Table 3

Direct messages place the bottom line on top (BLOT). This means that the most important information is concisely presented early on, and clearly arranged throughout the message. There are many advantages to using the direct approach. It decreases the likelihood of misunderstanding and can save your listeners or readers time. In a culture where time is often equated with money, people grow impatient if they have to hunt for meaningful content. Further, the direct message design, when used in a written correspondence, provides readers with an easy-to-navigate reference document. Despite its utilitarian appeal and intuitive design, a direct approach won't always serve your purposes.

Enter the indirect approach, used when a blunt, front-loaded message simply won't do. The indirect approach places the bottom line on or near the bottom (BLOB) of your message. It's wise to use an indirect approach when you need to provide readers and listeners with some logical or emotional preparation before you present the bottom line. For instance, you may attract more consumers if you first describe your fair and sustainable production process before revealing the higher-than-average price point. By offering a bit of background, your audience may be more receptive to your product.

No two situations are exactly alike, so you will often choose your approach at the intersection of purpose and audience. Though it may appear that some purposes are always best suited for either the direct or indirect approach, it's important to look both ways before making your decision.

Once you identify your purpose and approach, you can craft your message for success. Below are some examples of direct and indirect strategies for neutral and positive informational, negative or bad news informational, and persuasive messages.

# Communicating to Inform: Positive or Neutral News

## The Direct Approach: Inform (Positive and Neutral)

Positive and neutral messages aim to convey information clearly and concisely. It would be challenging, if not impossible, to achieve this objective through an indirect approach. Whether solicited or unsolicited, these messages are almost always direct. This is because neutral and positive messages are those met with little or no resistance. Therefore, there is no need to ease your way into your bottom line. In fact, doing so will probably frustrate your audience members. Routine informational messages should reflect an interest in sharing refined, well-organized information free of ambiguity and unnecessary clutter. How can you develop a message that is succinct and visually appealing? You start with a clear, concise introduction.

## Introduction

### #1 Provide a Frame for your Audience

Just as a storyteller establishes the setting of a story, you should provide the context of your message. Offer a very brief background statement that prepares the audience for your information and describes their role in the communication. If your message is solicited, meaning someone has asked for information, you might reference his or her request: "As requested, I attended this week's budget meeting and noted changes relevant to our department."

If the message is unsolicited, you may need an additional sentence or two to contextualize the information. "We strive to provide all departments with information pertinent to their functions. As a member of our organization's facilities management team, you will receive monthly memos regarding our ongoing renovation plans. This is the first memo in a series of 12, as we estimate the project will take one calendar year."

You can often enhance the "setting" with a "what's in it for you" (WIIFY) statement. How is this information relevant to your audience, and how might it benefit them? "This information will help you avoid potentially inconvenient building closures and allow you to plan your workdays more effectively." A WIIFY further develops context by explaining how the audience can use, even benefit from your information. We sometimes refer to the WIIFY as the bottom line—what you want your audience to know or do after reading your message.

By creating a context for your message, you limit confusion and paint an appropriate backdrop for your purpose and forecast statements. It's important to note that these elements sometimes overlap. For instance, the second example above provides context, and it fulfills a second critical element of the introduction: the purpose statement.

## #2 State Your Purpose

Your purpose statement should communicate the function of the message. "This memo contains an overview of the three construction projects slated for this month." Or, "The purpose of this meeting is to establish new timelines for product release." You should always assume the burden of establishing a clear purpose at the start of any information exchange. The purpose defines your intention for writing.

## #3 Forecast Information

Give your audience a preview of the content to come. You have already addressed the what and why elements of your message and your forecast should describe how you will present the information. For instance, you might say, "Below, you'll find a summary of each renovation, in chronological order: the gymnasium, the graduate computer lab, and west campus parking lot." By mapping the remainder of your message, you help your audience process and retain the information that follows. Make a habit of forecasting the major points of a direct message. If you've forecasted effectively, your audience will have little trouble navigating the body of your document.

# Body

## Present the Key Points of Your Message

Whether speaking or writing, the body of a message should be organized into several main ideas; these are the items presented in your forecast, and they should appear in the order introduced. Grouping your information will help your audience make sense of the message, and if done in written form, will present a user-friendly, high-skim, easily-referenced document. Think carefully about the designation of your main points. The building closures example lends itself to a fairly simple layout, as logically, three building closures fall into three distinct areas of information. Main points don't always emerge so effortlessly. Often, you need to gather, interpret, and refine groups of information into a few points. When summarizing data or large amounts of information, you need to think critically about how to treat your points. It requires that you survey and filter the information to

- Identify data relevant to your purpose
- Exclude superfluous information
- Interpret themes, trends, and implications
- Group concepts into logical main points
- Identify relationships between main points
- Articulate your findings

Coherently organizing the data you include in your message will make the information you present more accessible for your audience to follow and understand.

## Conclusion

### *Provide a Summary*

**CONCLUSION**

The conclusion of a direct informational message should summarize the information and close on a cordial note.

Just as you forecasted, or previewed the message in your introduction, you should summarize these points in your conclusion. This is the time to restate your ideas and bottom line, not to add information or further develop the content in the body section. Conclude your written or oral message with friendly sentiment and/or an invitation for further communication.

The Direct Informational Approach is a succinct and highly organized approach. Most business audiences are already attuned to this organizational strategy and will anticipate finding information in the appropriate place. This is particularly true in more formal documents such as proposals and reports. Unit 3 provides you with more detail on how to write these types of documents.

# The Informational Message: It's Usually Best to Be Direct

Positive and neutral messages are best delivered in a straightforward fashion. There are rare occasions in which communicators may delay disclosing good news until later in a message. This could add an element of suspense, surprise, or excitement to an announcement, and it might be appropriate for certain types of live events. However, such events are few and far between, so consider the indirect neutral or positive message approach as rhetorical unicorns; both are rare for good reason.

# Communicating to Inform: Negative or Bad News

## The Direct Approach: Inform (Negative–Bad News)

Sometimes, a situation calls for a direct, immediate message. Imagine a car company needing to inform the public about a critical product recall, or a food chain needing to warn consumers of contaminated ingredients; time is of the essence, and clarity is essential. In this instance, the audience needs the information delivered directly.

## Introduction

### Establish Rapport

**Pulling off the Band-Aid**

The introduction of a direct negative informational message must present the bad news.

Begin your message with a cordial introductory sentence or greeting. Use a "you" attitude, but keep the lead-in brief, and get down to business. This helps win the audience to your side, even if just a little, before you drop your bombshell.

### Present Negative News

State the reason for your communication. In this case, you will present the bad news.

## Body

### State the Reasons or Causes

Explain the reasons for the negative news. Offer your audience an account explaining the reason or cause for the negative news. Avoid making disparaging remarks or denying responsibility. It is usually best to be as dispassionate as possible here. Think of the old *Dragnet* tagline: "just the facts."

### Explain Details

It may be appropriate to explain the details of the negative event or message. If you have information that might benefit the audience, you can share this in the body of your message.

Show the audience that you recognize their needs, and appreciate the impact your negative news has on their lives. It is crucial that you do this with sincerity.

> **DIRECT BAD NEWS: DO IT RIGHT!**
> 1. Establish Rapport (use the You Attitude)
> 2. State the Bad News (pull off the Band-Aid!)
> 3. Explain the Reasons (causes, etc.)
> 4. Close with Goodwill (play nice)

## Conclusion

### Close with Goodwill

Conclude a direct bad news message with a message of goodwill. This should include an invitation for future interaction.

# The Indirect Approach: Inform (Negative–Bad News)

The world of business is full of ventures, triumphs, and failures. Though we try our best to avoid the latter, delivering negative news is a skill critical to competent professional communication. When dealing with unfortunate, but non-life-threatening news, communicators may benefit from taking an indirect approach. This eases your audience into the message preparing them emotionally and logically for the bottom line. Though an audience might expect an immediate and direct notification of danger, indirect messages are often more effective for conveying bad news, especially when that audience is resistant or hostile.

## Introduction

**BUFFER**

The introduction of an indirect negative informational message provides a buffer.

### Start with a Buffer

A buffer is a statement that establishes common ground with your audience and may communicate appreciation, understanding, or praise for your audience. It should be relevant and sincere in nature. Don't become effusive in a buffer; indicate the topic at hand while you align yourself with your reader. For example, if you have to close down a franchise but want your customer base to continue to frequent your other franchises which are further away, you might say, "Like you, we've always been committed to going the extra mile to make sure we get it right at Happy Burger." You've now aligned yourself with your audience and appealed to their sense of "going the distance" to get what they want. With alignment, you are ready to move forward with your message.

## Body

**EXPLAIN YOUR REASONS, THEN STATE BAD NEWS**

The body of an indirect negative informational message explains the reason for the bad news before the negative bottom line.

### Offer Reasons

In an indirect negative news message, present the reasons or causes before you reveal the unpleasant bottom line. If you do this well, your reader sees how this bad news naturally follows the reason. In effect, priming the reader for the bad news to come can lessen its shock or disappointing effects.

### State the Negative News

Once you have created some common ground and prepared the audience for the unfortunate news, you must reveal the news itself. Be clear, but don't dwell on this news nor offer unnecessary details. If possible, minimize the bad news with a silver lining. For example, you may point out that the inconvenience of a franchise closure means larger dining space at the newer, bigger Happy Burger.

## Conclusion

### Close with Goodwill

Once you have prepared your audience and delivered the bad news, close your message with goodwill. You may reference the silver lining, and if you are willing, you may invite future communication. "Thank you for supporting Happy Burger, your family-friendly neighborhood restaurant. We appreciate your patience and look forward to serving you our award-winning burgers for years to come." The conclusion is brief, positive, and respectful in tone. The bad news message, especially when indirect, demonstrates a unique challenge for communicators. It requires a sincere understanding of the situation and audience, and the ability to honestly address the matter at hand in a way that maintains a positive sender/receiver relationship. Like bad news messages, persuasive messages require their own strategic approach.

# Communicating to Persuade

The art of persuasion is an ancient one. Dating back to Aristotle, the line of argument, or the act of persuasion, is familiar to most of us. Any time you take a position and try to convince someone to change their mind, you are engaging in the dark arts of persuasion. Unlike the informational approach, where your primary objective is to shape and present data, when you enter into a persuasive strategy, you are actively trying to convince or advocate. This is where things start to get a little complicated.

Logos, Pathos, and Ethos were Aristotle's words for identifying persuasive appeals.

In contemporary business speak, these are still readily used, just under different names. Did you know the more credibility you have, the more you will be able to persuade an audience? Ethos is essentially another word to describe the credibility of both you and your argument. Without credibility, you won't be believed. In a 24/7 news cycle, we are inundated with information. For your argument to be convincing, you'll need to leverage a credible set of evidence that is relevant to the audience and the case you are making.

Your ability to appeal to logic (Logos) is critical to creating a persuasive case. The type of logic and reasoning you apply to your argument deepens its appeal. Howard Gardner (2006) provides seven "levers" that are highly convincing. Why pull your sled uphill when you can start at the top and zoom down? When you select data, use the levers persuade your audience.

With data in place and a sense of credibility, you're ready to appeal to your audience's emotions and values. As a savvy consumer, you are probably highly aware when a marketing campaign appeals to your emotions. How does Apple produce all those "feels" around a product? Simple. They appeal to a consumer's emotions—loyalty, jealousy, competition. When you have a strong emotional attachment that convinces you to purchase a product you probably don't even really need, you are succumbing to an emotional appeal.

When you put all the appeals together, you'll find that you have a substantial and powerful platform to convince an audience of your position. Your logical structure (another form of Logos) will support your ability to build and sustain your claims. In this instance, a strategic structural approach helps you to build a persuasive message. You can do this using a direct or indirect approach.

## CLASSIC APPEALS

The classic appeals are heuristic categories to help you frame your message and structure your evidence. Use them to appeal to your audience through familiar cultural frameworks.

**Ethos (authority):** Establish credibility

**Pathos (emotion):** Appeal to values and beliefs through emotional connection

**Logos (logic/facts):** Appeal to reason through proven facts and logic

## LEVERS

Gardner (2006) identifies seven factors or levers that influence and persuade.

1. **Real world events**— similar "real life" examples
2. **Reason**—logical discourse
3. **Research**—fact-based evidence gathered from credible sources
4. **Resonance**—value or belief-based framing and evidence
5. **Re-description**—multiple and varied representations of similar evidence
6. **Resources/rewards**—audience benefit
7. **Resistance**—reframed rebuttal

# The Direct Approach: Persuade

Direct persuasive messages are most effective when addressing a receptive audience. You may use this approach if receivers are time-deprived, or if you know your audience prefers direct communication. A letter of application (cover letter) is one type of direct persuasive message. We will use a cover letter as an example as we walk through the parts of a direct persuasive message below.

## Introduction

The introduction of a direct persuasive message should state your purpose (present your request). It is best to state your request in the first few sentences of your introduction. Your introduction should also frame the message for your audience and forecast the key points your message will cover.

In a cover letter, you should let the reader know you are writing to apply for the position at the beginning of your document. Your introduction should also provide a frame for your audience by letting the reader know your qualifications or how you could add value to the organization through the position for which you are applying. The final sentence in your introduction should provide a brief overview of the key points you plan to discuss in the message such as your past work experience and professional skills.

## Body

The body of a direct persuasive message should explain or support your request. In the body, offer the audience supporting information, facts, details, or additional explanation to clarify your request or directive. This may include the reasons for your request. If addressing a resistant audience, counter possible points of resistance with credible reasoning. Regardless of audience members' attitudes, you can create interest by highlighting how the proposed action will yield direct, or indirect benefits to the audience. Remember that this section should not include details about how your request will benefit you. In order to persuade the reader, you will want to highlight how your request will benefit him or her.

**DO IT TO IT: THE DIRECT PERSUASIVE APPROACH**

1. Present the request

2. Bring on the data! Use the levers, find your appeals

3. Conclude—move the reader to action

Using our cover letter example, you would want to highlight how you could transfer the skills you have learned in previous positions to enhance the new organization you want to work for. You would not want to include that you are interested in the position so that you can earn a higher salary and obtain a better job title.

## Conclusion

The conclusion of a direct persuasive message should call your audience to action. You should begin by restating your request. To ensure you obtain the desired results, make the action convenient and immediate for your audience with needed contact information and next steps. For example, in the conclusion of a cover letter, you would restate the position to which you are applying, provide your contact information, and encourage the reader to select you for the position.

# Indirect Approach: Persuade

The indirect approach to persuasive messaging requires a bit more skill and finesse. This type of a message usually requires some advance planning, so you truly align with your audience and position your reader to act. Use an indirect approach in persuasive messages when addressing a potentially resistant audience. This kind of message is often developed using the AIDA strategy.

Most audiences are very sensitive to a "sell" approach, and your tone can inadvertently cause the audience to resist your message or scrutinize it more closely. A flat out "sell" makes most of us suspicious. AIDA strategy helps you present content in a compelling, persuasive manner by sequencing your information strategically.

| AIDA (FOR INDIRECT PERSUASIVE MESSAGES) | |
| --- | --- |
| **ATTENTION & ALIGNMENT** | Build common ground with the audience by referencing common values. Pique interest with an engaging audience-centered appeal. |
| **INTEREST & INFORMATION** | Create a sense of interest by offering relevant information and details; set the stage by supporting your impending request. |
| **DEFLECT RESISTANCE & DISCUSS DIRECT BENEFITS** | Anticipate points of audience resistance, and counter with information. Identify and express how your request will benefit the audience directly. |
| **ACTION** | Make your request for audience action. Provide immediate opportunity for audience response. |

**Table 4** *AIDA*

## Introduction

### Alignment and Attention

In your first few sentences, get the audience's attention by building common ground. Refer to shared values and interests, mention a commonality, or compliment them on a recent achievement. Be sincere and balanced in your approach. If you seem excessively complimentary or overly familiar, your recipient may interpret your statement as inauthentic.

No: Our company is profitable and ecologically conscious. With the help of brilliant, motivated, amazing clients like you, our company will continue to grow and profit.

Yes: We share your interest in protecting the environment and appreciate your contributions to our company's green initiatives.

Remember, keep your message audience-centered, and write with the "you attitude." Notice the differences between the first and second examples above. The "no" statement focuses more on the sender than it does the receiver, and it employs a sequence of cliché, overstated compliments ("amazing," "motivated," and "brilliant") that lack sincerity and specificity. To effectively align with your audience, focus on them, and avoid trite, meaningless phrases. Most importantly, do not reveal your request—the indirect approach places the bottom line on the bottom. Before you make your "ask," you must build your case by discussing information and direct benefits.

## Interest and Information

In this section, present information about your product, service, or situation. Make it relevant for your reader or listener, and highlight details that will likely interest them. Remember, you haven't yet revealed your request; you are presenting data to help your audience understand your product, service, etc. In the next section, you will explain how your product, service, etc. directly benefits your audience members, so provide a basis on which you can make such claims.

No: Our "zero waste" policy includes guidelines for minimizing our environmental footprint.

Yes: The zero waste policy promotes the recycling, reuse, and reduction of paper products, and aims to replace older electronics with more energy-efficient models.

Be specific in your description and again, frame the information to the interests of your audience members. Minimizing one's environmental footprint is a worthy cause, but the statement itself is rather vague. The "yes" statement is much more descriptive and provides details that may pique the audience's interest. This section should support the next part of your message: direct benefits and resistance deflection.

## Direct Benefits and Deflection

Before you present your request, explain how your product or initiative will benefit your audience and do your best to pre-emptively quell their potential concerns. To do this successfully, describe what readers or listeners will gain by supporting or complying with your yet-to-be-revealed request. Think about it from your audience members' perspectives; explain what is in it for them, not you or your company.

No: By participating in the "zero waste" initiative, you will save the company a lot of money.

Yes: The "zero waste" policy preserves our planet and lowers overhead costs. Departments that comply with this policy will receive monetary credit for 75% of your total monthly savings. This credit can be distributed evenly among team members and applied to your paid time off account or yearly bonus.

Focus on how the information benefits audience members personally. What's in it for them? Indirect benefits like saving the company money rarely inspire action. In addition to discussing direct benefits, use this section to deflect points of resistance.

Once again, think from your audience members' perspectives. Are there potential points of resistance or areas of concern that could cause opposition? If there are points of resistance to anticipate (and deflect), you'll want to be careful not to make overstated assumptions. Nothing puts off a reader faster than an assumption you make about their thinking, and you can accidentally plant more points of resistance. For example, "You might think the price point is a little high…" In fact, the audience wasn't thinking that at all; after receiving your message, however, you can bet they are now. Frame deflection statements in a positive tone, and minimize the inconvenient or undesirable facets of your plan.

No: I know what you're thinking: "This sounds very inconvenient and time consuming." Perhaps this is true, but consider how your time and effort contributes to a greener workplace.

Yes: We are committed to making these adjustments easy to implement, and we're confident a few small changes will make a big difference for you and the environment.

Be strategic in your approaches to alignment, information, direct benefits, and deflection. These steps lead into the final element of your message: the request for audience action.

## Conclusion

### Action

Now that you've aligned, informed, deflected resistance, and identified direct benefits, you can finally make your request and call your audience to action.

Make the actions as easy to carry out as possible. Think about the strategy of the car dealership that sends out keys to everyone in the community with the message "Come on down on Saturday. This key starts one of the cars on our lot—if you find it, you'll win the car!" With a key in your hand, you might be more inclined to drive on over and give a car a test drive (which was probably the real intent of the message in the first place.) Be thinking about making the next step to "yes" as easy as possible for your audience.

You don't need a fancy giveaway or a fun prop to make your action easy and immediate. Present your request, then tell your audience how and when you'd like a response. It is critical that you make this step clear and provide all the necessary information and resources to facilitate your readers' next steps. Avoid uncertain, vague calls to action.

No: Thank you for taking the time to read this letter. Please register for this program, and contact me if you have questions or concerns.

Yes: Thank you for taking the time to learn more about this exciting opportunity.

Please click on the link below to register for your "zero waste" benefits before the June 5th deadline. Registration only takes a minute or two, and you can start earning your rewards today. www.company.com/zerowaste

In the last example, three key elements are present: the ask, a timeline/cutoff, and an easy, immediate opportunity to respond.

Now that you have the "secret handshake," put some of these strategies to the test. Regardless of your audience or the type of message, you'll find that these are easy strategies to memorize and put into practice. While you'll continue to develop and deepen your approach, you'll find that as you internalize these simple strategic moves, your own messages will become more targeted and polished. More and more, you'll find you reach the mark.

# Unit 1 References

Bates, D. (July 13, 2012). You've got (more) mail: The average office worker now spends over a quarter of their day dealing with email. *Daily Mail.*

Bolkan, J. (June 24, 2013). Report: Students taking online courses jumps 96 percent over 5 years. *Campus Technology*, March 2, 2015.

Dabbaugh, N. (2007). The online learner: Characteristics and pedagogical implications. *Contemporary Issues in Technology and Teacher Education, 7*(3), 217–226.

Gardner, H. (2006). *Changing minds: The art and science of changing our own and other people's minds.* Boston: Harvard Business School Press.

Gascoigne, C., & Parnell, J. (Winter 2014). Distance education readiness assessments. *Online Journal of Distance Learning Administration, XVII*(IV).

Globokar, J. (2010). *Introduction to online learning: A guide for students.* SAGE Publication, Inc.

Goudreau, J. (January 8, 2015). 17 tips for writing an excellent email subject line. *Business Insider.* Retrieved from http://www.businessinsider.com/how-to-write-an-email-subject-line-2015-1

Grice, H. P. (1975). Logic and conversation. In P. Cole & J. Morgan (Eds.), *Syntax and semantics: Speech acts* (Vol. 3) (pp. 45–47). New York, NY: Academic Press.

Groysberg, B., & Abrahams, R. (March 2014). Manage your work, manage your life. *Harvard Business Review.* Retrieved from https://hbr.org/2014/03/manage-your-work-manage-your-life

Hannay, M., & Newvine, T. (2006, March). Perceptions of distance learning: A comparison of online and traditional learning. *Journal of Online Learning and Teaching, 2 (1).* Retrieved from http://jolt.merlot. org/05011.htm

Hicher, R. (2014, August 30). International Business Communication Standards. http://www.ibcs-a.org/

Kallos, J. (2015). Business Email greetings matter. Retrieved from http://www.businessemailetiquette.com/greetings-matter/

Kolowich, S. (January 16, 2014). Exactly how many students take online courses? *The Chronicle of Higher Education: Wired Campus.* Retrieved March 1, 2015.

Matus, M. (April 21, 2014.). Online college success: Expert advice for preparing and prospering in a virtual space. *The Navy Times.*

*McVay online learning readiness* survey. In *A predictive validity study of the revised McVay readiness for online learning questionnaire.* In Hall M. (Ed.), Online Journal of Distance Learning Administration.

McVay, M. (2001). *How to be a successful distance student: Learning on the Internet.* New York: Prentice Hall.

NACE. (2014, August 3). National Association for Colleges and Employers: http://naceweb.org/s10242012/skills-abilities-qualities-new-hires/

Ohler, J. B. (2010). *Digital community, digital citizen.* Thousand Oaks, CA: Sage.

Otter, R. (2013). Comparing student and faculty perceptions of online and traditional courses. *The Internet and Higher Education, 19, 27–35.*

Peterson, B. (September 22, 2013). I [heart]the emoji revolution: A quirky character set revives the thrills of a visual language. *The Boston Globe.* Retrieved from http://www.bostonglobe.com/ ideas/2013/09/21/heart-emoji-revolution/2sQHETFxSE5GBppU2DbnDN/story.html

Prensky, M. (October 2001). Digital natives, digital immigrants. *On the Horizon, 9* (No. 5).

Quinton, S. (April 25, 2013). How online education saves everyone money. *NationalJournal.Com,* March 16, 2015.

Roper, A. (2007). How students develop online learning skills. *Educause Quarterly, 1, 62–65.* In Gascoigne & Parnell (2014).

Smith, P. J., & Murphy, K.L.: & Mahoney, S.E. (2003). Identifying factors underlying readiness for online learning: An exploratory study. *Distance Education, 24,* 57–68. In Gascoigne & Parnell (2014).

OEdb Staff Writers. (January 10, 2012). 10 advantages to taking online classes. Retrieved from http://oedb.org/ilibrarian/10-advantages-to-taking-online-classes/

Paul, R. a. (2002). In Elder, *Critical Thinking.* Upper Saddle River: Financial Times Prentice Hall Books.

The Radacati Group, I. (April 2014). *Email statistics report, 2014–2018.* (Statistics Report). Palo Alto, CA: The Radacati Group, Inc.

The Radacati Group, Inc. (2014). *Email market, 2014–2018.*

Wagner, T. (2008). *The global achievement gap.* New York: Basic Books.

Waldvogel, J. (1984). Greetings and closings in workplace email. *Journal of Computer-Mediated Communication, 12*(2), 456–477. Retrieved from http://onlinelibrary.wiley.com/doi/10.1111/ j.1083-6101.2007.00333.x/epdf

Walker, R. (2011). *Strategic management for leaders.* Stamford, CT: Cengage.

Wang, Q., Myers, M.D,; Sundaran, D. (December 2013). Digital natives and digital immigrants: Towards a model of digital fluency. *Business & Information Systems Engineering,* 5.6, 409–419.

Wong, W. (2009, March 3). *Chicago Tribune.* http://www.nbcnews.com/id/29796962/ns/technology_and_science-tech_and_gadgets/t/twitter-gets-you-fired-characters-or-less/#.VAs78MvjjIU

Worcester Polytechnic Institute. (August 13, 2007). Teaching with technology collaboratory: Characteristics of distance learning students. Retrieved from Retrieved from https://www.wpi.edu/Academics/ATC/Collaboratory/Teaching/students.html

Young, A., Norgard, C. (2006). Assessing the quality of online courses from the students' perspective. *The Internet and Higher Education, 9*(2), 107–11.

# UNIT 2:
# Professional Writing

# Planning Your Message

*"Easy reading is damned hard writing."* ~ *Nathaniel Hawthorne*

## Preparing to Write

Have you ever wondered why someone reacted the way they did to something you wrote? Did your email cause confusion or your text message elicit anger? Perhaps your boss returned your report to you for further editing, or your résumé, so thoughtfully crafted, landed with a dull "thud."

In today's screen-dependent, virtual world, we communicate in writing more than ever. While it is true that visual and auditory media comprise a larger share of communication (e.g., videos posted on the Internet, Apple FaceTime, Google Hangouts, Skype, VOIP, telephone, etc.), the sheer volume of communication has increased, and the written word remains one of the most powerful tools for expressing an idea. Unfortunately, as we have gotten better at producing visual and auditory media, our writing skills have suffered.

We designed this chapter to help you turn that tide and become a skillful business writer. In our highly connected business environment, you can take advantage of a quick video chat or phone call with anyone in the world. On the other hand, your written communication—be it an email, a memo, a report, or a letter—is the most lasting impression you can leave with someone. Easily forwarded and shared with others, it is an indelible record of your interaction, an encapsulation of your thought process, and a representation of who you are. What should your writing say about you? Take time to plan it, craft it, and polish it so it gets the reaction you intend.

### You Are What You Write

Your professional success depends upon how well you write. The first interaction you have with a potential employer, especially early in your career, will probably be through your written cover letter and résumé. Your opportunities for advancement will depend, in part, on how well you express your company's objectives in writing. When you seek new opportunities with other companies, the process will start all over again.

Communications professionals are not the only ones who know this to be true; a large and ever-growing body of evidence supports our claims about the importance of competent writing skills.

### ARE YOU READY FOR THE WORKPLACE?

In 2006, a consortium of four organizations, The Conference Board, Partnership for 21st Century Skills, Corporate Voices for Working Families, and the Society for Human Resource Management, released a report on a survey of more than 400 employers, entitled "Are They Really Ready for Work?"[1]

Among other findings, the report found that 27.8% of employers find that four-year college graduates are deficient in written communication skills, even though 89.7% of employers view these skills as "very important," more than any other desired skill for four-year college graduates.

One of those consortium members, Partnership for 21st Century Skills, surveyed registered voters a year later and found that 58% of voters ranked written communication as a 9 or 10 on a 10-point scale of importance; only 5% of those same voters ranked schools as a 9 or 10 on similar 10-point scale.[2]

In 2012, the American Management Association released the results of a survey it conducted of employers that found that communication skills were the highest priority, most measured, and most assessed during the hiring process.[3]

For as long as the National Association of Colleges and Employers (NACE, http://www.naceweb.org) have been conducting semi-annual surveys of employer needs, the ability to create and/or edit written reports has consistently been listed as a top-ten skill.

[1] http://www.p21.org/storage/documents/FINAL_REPORT_PDF09-29-06.pdf
[2] http://www.p21.org/storage/documents/P21_pollreport_singlepg.pdf
[3] http://www.amanet.org/uploaded/2012-Critical-Skills-Survey.pdf

## Employer Expectations

Employers generally commit to helping new employees acquire skills needed for their job functions, but they expect you to come into the organization with strong writing skills. While companies want employees with both written and verbal communication skills, it is your writing that will get your foot in their door. The statistics in the inset "Are You Ready for the Workplace?" clearly show the emphasis employers place on written communication skills. After all, a future employee will be representing the company in his or her everyday business correspondence. Your writing is literally a record of your communication competence; poor writing is hard to ignore, but effective writing is nearly impossible to forget.

Effective writing means more than just using correct spelling and proper grammar, though both are crucial. You must strategically construct your messages for maximum effectiveness. This chapter will help you put all of the pieces together.

## Business Writing Is Different

You have probably taken several writing courses and written numerous academic papers. You may wonder why you need to read yet another book on the topic of writing. You probably believe the writing you have done so well up to this point has prepared you for writing in the workforce.

That belief is wrong. Your skills in academic writing may be well established, but you will need to develop new skills to be an effective business writer. Business writing is different from other forms of writing in several ways. The following table highlights some of the differences between academic and business writing.

|  | ACADEMIC WRITING | BUSINESS WRITING |
|---|---|---|
| **PURPOSES FOR WRITING** | To explain knowledge or new ideas <br> To inform (positive or neutral) <br> To demonstrate author's understanding | To inform (positive, neutral, or negative) <br> To persuade |
| **TYPICAL AUDIENCES** | Academics or experts in their fields | Specifically targeted, depending on the unique purpose of each communication |
| **COMPLEXITY OF LANGUAGE** | Lengthy words and sentences <br> Repetition to emphasize points | Concise and precise, to be easily understood by as many stakeholders as possible |
| **SCOPE** | Specifically tailored for academics <br> Usually non-fiction | Specifically tailored to primary audience <br> Uses carefully chosen facts |
| **STRUCTURE** | Long paragraphs <br> Paragraphs indented | Short paragraphs <br> Paragraphs not indented |
| **LENGTH** | Usually longer | As short as possible |
| **SPECIFICITY** | Usually on a specific topic | Specific to meet the needs of primary Audience |

The primary difference between business and other forms of writing is that business writing is always tailored to a specific audience, depending on the situational context and purpose of the document. You must customize your business writing approach for your audience and purpose. Regardless of whether you are informing or persuading, consider what your audience already knows about your topic and what you want them to know.

It is common for a business writer to overshoot the "what the audience already knows" target. This overestimation is often due to the author's assumption that their audience has the same information he or she does. This happens so frequently there is a name for it: The Curse of Knowledge.

In their 2007 book, *Made to Stick*, an exploration of how to make your messages memorable, brothers Chip and Dan Heath coined the phrase "The Curse of Knowledge" to describe that sensation of forgetting a time when you did not know something. Perhaps you have sat through a business meeting in which colleagues are throwing around abbreviations and acronyms to describe processes, products, and competitors. As an intern or new employee, you may not know what these abbreviations and acronyms mean, and so you cannot tell a business process from a competitor. Your colleagues are so familiar with these shorthand terms that they do not even think about the fact that these phrases are totally foreign to you. Your colleagues suffer from The Curse of Knowledge.

The Heath brothers offer two ways to avoid The Curse of Knowledge. The first, offered facetiously, is to never learn anything. This, of course, is neither feasible nor practical. The second way and only true hope for overcoming The Curse of Knowledge is to be vigilant about remembering your audience and what they do or do not already know. Business writing is not about you; it should always be crafted with the audience and end purpose in mind.

To help you be effective business communicators, this unit and the next one will help you plan and compose messages using specific strategic approaches that you can tailor for your specific purposes and audiences. For your reference, we have also included a chapter of common workplace documents at the end of Unit 4.

## How to Begin

How do you know where to start when you write? How do you determine what is relevant and what is not? How do you make sure you write everything you want to write? How do you know what to keep and what to cut? How-to books on writing will tell you specific ways to create a document. But how do you generate content?

### TWO KINDS OF WRITERS

Writers fall somewhere on the continuum between free-writers and outliners.

**Free Writers** Some people write everything down on paper at once without editing; they simply let their pen flow and produce content. When they think they have all the information on the page, they go back and organize it by fitting the different parts into their structure or outline. This method works well when you are not exactly sure what you want to write because it helps you "think out loud." It also works well when you have very little content and need to allow your mind the open space to just write.

**Outliners** Other people are more structured in their approach. An outline allows you to start with the structure and generate content systematically into each content area as laid out in the outline. This method serves the logical thinker well since the process is step-by-step. It also works well when you know exactly what it is you want to convey and simply need to drop the content into the correct format or structure.

No matter your personal preference, you may find yourself trying out both methods to see what works best. If you are like most people, your personal style of writing will probably employ elements from both methods. It is not important how other people write; it is important to find what works best for you.

# Analyzing Your Audience

## Identifying and Analyzing Your Audience

Before writing a business message, you will need to determine who is going to read your message. In most cases, you will need to communicate with key players and decision makers in the situation at hand. For example, if you are proposing a new safety policy for your company, your audience might include the Chief Operations Officer, the Human Resources Director, and the Chief Financial Officer, since each of these parties will be involved in the decision. Once you have determined who your audience is, you can think about how to address their unique concerns so that you can persuade them to implement your proposal. You start by strategically analyzing your audience.

### *Primary and Secondary Audiences*

You will always have a primary audience to whom you are sending the message, but you will want to consider any secondary audiences too. A secondary audience is anyone who needs to see the message or someone who has requested that you write the message for a third party. Keeping all potential audiences in mind will help to ensure you deliver a message that reaches its target and engenders goodwill. For our purposes, we will focus on analyzing our primary audience.

### *Audience Analysis*

There are many aspects of the audience that you will need to consider. You will need to identify such things as your audience's demographics and lifestyle. By understanding your audience's interests and needs you can better determine their motivation for making decisions, which may help you to frame a message specifically for them. You should also consider how much your audience knows about the topic you are presenting so that you do not present unnecessary information or fail to include explanations your audience needs. Beware of The Curse of Knowledge!

The following list of questions can be a good place to begin your audience analysis:

- Who is the audience?
- What is their age, gender, educational background, etc.?
- What is the audience's previous knowledge of the subject?
- Why are they reading your document?
- What is your audience most interested in, and what are their most pressing needs?
- How will the information in your document be useful to your audience?
- What will your audience likely expect to learn from your document?

## Establishing Relevance

You now have a handful of questions to ask about your audience to help you understand them better. Understanding who your audience is and what they expect from you is critical to crafting a document that is relevant to them. The concept of relevance threads audience awareness and purpose together. You must convince your audience that what you have to say is relevant to them, meaning that:

1. It should advance their understanding of a topic they care about, and
2. It should provide the information they need to make the decision you want them to make.

The following is an example of an analysis of a specific audience group: new employees of ABC Wealth Management, Inc., welcoming them to the company and preparing them for their new hire orientation.

| WHO IS THE AUDIENCE? | New employees, beginning training next week. |
|---|---|
| WHAT IS THEIR AGE, GENDER, EDUCATIONAL BACKGROUND, ETC.? | Age and gender will vary, but they are highly educated. |
| WHAT IS THE AUDIENCE'S PREVIOUS KNOWLEDGE OF THE SUBJECT? | They researched the company and positions during the hiring process, but do not have any details about the upcoming orientation. |
| WHY ARE THEY READING YOUR DOCUMENT? | They are eager to begin work. |
| WHAT IS YOUR AUDIENCE MOST INTERESTED IN, AND WHAT ARE THEIR MOST PRESSING NEEDS? | They are interested in making a good impression, so they need to know what is expected. |
| HOW WILL THE INFORMATION IN YOUR DOCUMENT BE USEFUL TO YOUR AUDIENCE? | It will inform them about what they can expect and what is expected of them. The audience should walk away having their initial questions answered and explained. They should learn about a meeting they can attend, which will provide them answers to their questions. |
| WHAT WILL YOUR AUDIENCE LIKELY EXPECT TO LEARN FROM YOUR DOCUMENT? | They will expect to receive schedules, task descriptions, resources, etc. They will feel more at ease knowing the company plans to address their needs. |

Taking the time to analyze your audience positions you to write more compelling and effective messages. The next step is to think about your purpose and how it relates to your reader.

# Defining Your Purpose

Clearly defining and stating your purpose is essential to effectively communicating a message in any business context. If you define your purpose thoughtfully, you will connect with your audience and give yourself an anchor for the rest of your document.

Articulating your purpose can be difficult. It may help to look at some examples below. In the first example, the writer aligns with the reader and establishes relevance by stating the purpose and explaining how the information will help him.

> Dear Mr. Voss,
>
> We appreciate your desire for excellent customer service and increased profitability. Our corporate goal is to build and maintain customer satisfaction at all of our properties. With enhanced customer satisfaction, our company is able to thrive and increase profits. I am glad to inform you of new changes to our sustainability initiative, GREEN. These changes will increase our customer satisfaction and fuel your property's profitability.

In the next example, the author presents a common goal and gives the reader a reason to keep reading:

> Dear Mr. Kline,
>
> On behalf of the Organization X, we would like to congratulate you for being elected Mayor of Tucson. We appreciate your dedication to the growth, safety, infrastructure, and people of Tucson. Organization X also cares about the enrichment of Tucson.
>
> We are excited to provide accessibility and exposure to the arts to all Tucson residents. I am writing to introduce you to our new membership program catered to lower-income patrons.

## IDENTIFY YOUR PURPOSE

INFORM (POSITIVE OR NEUTRAL) You wish to convey positive or neutral information to your audience.

INFORM (NEGATIVE) You must deliver bad news or unpleasant information.

PERSUADE You want to influence your audience in some way.

To determine your purpose, you might begin by considering questions such as the following:

1. Why am I writing this message?

2. What has led up to this message?

3. What is the situation?

4. What is the desired outcome?

Once you determine the purpose of the message, you can plan the rest of your document accordingly. Every piece of information and analysis in your document should relate directly to your purpose. This will help you focus on the information you need to include, and discard that which you do not need.

For example, if you are the IT manager informing employees of a new system upgrade, you might first establish the need for the upgrade. Then, you might provide a comparison between the upgraded system and the current system being used. You will want to list the features and benefits of the new system for the specific work being performed. If there will be system downtime while you perform the upgrade, your audience would surely appreciate knowing about that. Finally, you will need to provide instructions for using the system, along with information on available support.

# Setting the Right Tone

Even if you have analyzed your audience and established a clear sense of purpose, it is possible to alienate your reader by using the wrong tone. Tone is critically important because your audience cannot physically see you or hear your voice; therefore, they do not have the benefit of your nonverbal cues to understand how you intend your message to be read. You may have limited experience in business writing, and you may not know how your writing comes across to another person. This section will help you put your best foot forward.

Your attitude toward your subject matter and your audience comes across in your tone. Your tone, for example, can be formal or informal, depending on the purpose of your message and its intended audience. If you sent an email to a friend and co-worker asking them to go to lunch, your tone would be more casual than if you were asking a supervisor. Your tone is also conveyed in your choice of words. You can sound angry, arrogant, or apologetic, depending on your vocabulary. You may describe someone as bossy rather than assertive, or you may ask for something immediately instead of at your earliest convenience; these choices add up to create the tone of your writing. Pro tip: read your writing out loud and put yourself in your reader's shoes. How would someone take this? Does it sound too pushy or impatient? Does it sound respectful without coming across as too passive? Did you exaggerate or say something over the top?

## The "You" Attitude

Setting the right tone involves putting your audience at the center of your document. To successfully get your message across to a specific audience, all information must be relevant to his or her situation, interests, and needs. The term "You Attitude" conveys the practical application of audience analysis. Several practical techniques will assist you in developing the appropriate tone, but the most important is to convey genuine empathy for the person or group to whom you are sending the message (Kamalani Hurley, 2007).

## Pronoun Consideration

When corresponding with a customer or client, you can use the second person pronoun ("you," "your," and "yours") to connect with and to put the focus on the reader rather than on you as the author or your company. In the examples below, you can see two different approaches to saying the same thing.

> **Instead of** "We have looked over your request for material on our services, and we will do our best to send out the material needed as soon as we can."
>
> **Write** "Thank you for your interest in our services. You will receive the material you requested within the week."

Read the two examples and consider which response makes you feel like the company values you.

There are times when the "you" pronoun is not preferable. On occasion, the second person pronoun can be offensive rather than inclusive. For example, if you need to tell a customer that he has made a mistake, it is best to avoid an accusatory tone in your language. In the following examples, fewer second person pronouns is the better choice for gaining the cooperation of the reader.

Consider which of these statements would elicit a more positive response, and which would make the customer rethink ordering from this company again. Nobody likes to be called a failure.

While using the second person pronoun "you" will help you connect with your readers and make them feel valued, in some cases, you may want to convey a more collaborative tone. For example, when writing to employees, consider using "we" to make them feel like they are part of the discussion, rather than like they are being spoken to or, even worse, about.

*Instead of* "You should read and follow all the safety rules imposed and posted by the company so that nobody gets hurt."

*Write* "In order to avoid accidents, we must all follow the safety rules posted in our break rooms and on our employee website."

By paying attention to the use of pronouns, you can successfully communicate with your audience and ensure a more positive response. While your readers may not even notice this technique, they will have a sense that they are being considered in every message.

Another practical technique to generate a "You Attitude" is to interpret information for the reader; that is, you must translate features into benefits. The following table demonstrates the evolution of moving the reader from "that's nice" to "that's for me."

| FEATURES (THAT'S NICE.) | BENEFITS (THAT'S FOR ME!) |
| --- | --- |
| We have the largest selection of coats in the city. | You can find the perfect coat for any situation or weather condition. |
| Our organization helps the homeless. | Your donation will help find a home for a homeless individual or family. |
| We can quickly print and bind reports. | Each of your 30-page reports can be professionally bound in 90 seconds. |

By showing how the features of a business are relevant to your audience, you can move them more quickly toward a decision. Of course, it is essential that your company's goals be aligned with the best interests of your audience, both for ethical and practical reasons.

Finally, the "You Attitude" conveys a positive and confident tone. As you work to achieve this, eliminate unnecessary fillers that weaken your delivery. As you read the two options below, ask yourself, "Which one would instill a greater level of confidence?"

*Instead of* "I will try my best to solve your problem with the resources I have."

*Write* "I will use every resource available to find a solution to your problem."

Your writing should be strong and confident. You do not want to sound wishy-washy, or worse, like you are making excuses. Keep these elements in mind as you plan your messages. The more careful thinking you do prior to composing, the better your message will be when you finally begin to write.

# Composing Your Message

This chapter offers strategies for composing common workplace documents. Whether you find yourself writing a report, emailing an update, or crafting a proposal, this chapter provides the framework for effective content development and organizational strategies that enable you to deliver a final written product that is effective, concise, and clear.

Before we begin, it is important to make a distinction between reports and correspondence messages. Correspondence messages are often used to convey or request information. They may sometimes contain report-like elements including some data and/or analysis, but in general, they provide a means of routine information exchange. Depending on the formality of your work environment, you might find some overlap in these approaches. For instance, if your manager sends you an email request for a summary of a news article, it may be perfectly appropriate to provide the summary in the body of your email response. However, some organizational cultures might encourage a more traditional report format for these types of exchanges. While correspondence messages tend to use more first and second person, reports favor the use of third person as it promotes a more objective and professional tone.

## Correspondence Messages

From emails to letters, correspondence in the workplace is the most common form of writing that takes place. Essentially, correspondence is any written or digital information that is exchanged between two or more parties. These exchanges could come in the form of postcards, notes, emails, or letters.

The content of these messages can vary greatly, and the examples below are but a few possibilities:

- making simple announcements
- describing protocol
- congratulating someone on a promotion or new job
- requesting something

- thanking someone
- letting a customer know that their order has shipped
- confirming an appointment or meeting time
- giving information that was requested

Obviously, some of these can be very short—one or two sentences—and others can be more lengthy. In general, business correspondence is predominantly under one page, as people are busy and want information quickly.

## Composing Business Correspondence

If you have experienced writer's block, you know how paralyzing it can be. The good news about business writing is that if you are clear in your purpose, you need never be stuck for what to say next. Ask yourself what the reader will need to know to enable them to take your desired action. In a business message, establish your purpose and audience. Then, make a list of all the necessary information and categorize it into sections that you can develop into paragraphs in the rest of the document. Consider the following scenario:

You are the marketing director for a local credit union. You and your six-person team are responsible for developing all of the credit union's advertisements. At a recent meeting with the company's top executives, you agreed to launch a new service. The credit union will start offering a series of three workshops to its current customers in January. You have been asked to coordinate a marketing campaign that will begin in November. To get started, you send an email to your team to arrange a meeting.

Here is your introduction:

| | |
|---|---|
| To: | marketingteam@creditunion.com |
| From: | ghaussmann@creditunion.com |
| Date: | September 8, 20XX |
| Re: | Marketing Team Meeting, September 12th |

Hello Team,

The company will be offering an exciting new service beginning next year, and our team has been tasked with creating the marketing campaign to be launched in November. We'll need to get started right away, so I'd like for us to meet this Friday, September 12th. Please look over the brief description of the service below and come with your most innovative ideas for this campaign.

Your purpose is clear and the audience has been established. So, what information should you include to ensure a productive first meeting? Put yourself into your readers' place and anticipate their questions. Some of these questions might include:

| DESCRIPTION OF SERVICE | MEETING LOGISTICS | TEAM RESPONSIBILITIES |
|---|---|---|
| What is the new service? | Who will be in attendance? | What level of preparation is required? |
| Who is the target market? | What is the format (discussion, etc)? | Are visual aids expected? |
| How will the target market benefit? | What time and how long will it be? | How much time will each individual have to present ideas? |

Once you have these questions written down, you should have no problem completing your message. You may need to do some legwork, such as arranging a meeting room or drafting an agenda, but you can use these questions as a checklist to ensure that your readers will arrive at the meeting fully prepared.

## Thank You Messages

Though most short correspondence does not need a full introductory paragraph as was described earlier, some semblance of the same structure should be present: beginning, middle, end. Some of these, like thank-you letters, have their own formulaic structure. Here is an example of a typical thank-you message:

Hello Mr. Cliff,

Thank you for taking the time to speak with me Friday about the internship opportunities at Colby and Whitlam.

It was nice to finally meet you after our phone calls and emails. I enjoyed learning about the roles that interns play in your company. I was heartened after our conversation as I realize that I have the qualifications and skills that this position requires. I am confident that my skills and abilities make me a great candidate for an internship.

I am excited by possibility of becoming a summer intern and would appreciate a follow-up as you comb through the candidates and get closer to making a decision. I am happy to provide any additional information you may need. I can be reached at (520) 555-1212 or at happyintern@bigjob.com

Thanks again, and I look forward to hearing from you soon.

Best regards,
Nicole Taylor

> Note the positive professional tone. Since this is a thank you letter, the BLOT is clear in the opening sentence.

> Note the body is only a few sentences, but It goes into more specific details.

> The polite close includes a summative purpose sentence, invites inquiry, and gives contact info.

## Meeting Invitation

Another common workplace message is a meeting invitation. Leaving out important pieces of information can lead to back and forth emails between multiple parties as the invitees try to get all of the facts that they need.

A surefire checklist for meeting invitations is below:

1. Succinct subject line with most important details: Team Meeting 3.14 @5:30 Rm 117
2. Meeting date start and end times
3. Location of the meeting
4. Purpose of the meeting
5. Expectations from attendees
6. Items attendees should bring
7. Agenda (if necessary)

Here is an example of a routine meeting invitation:

> This is to inform you that our monthly "Planning & Review" Meeting will be on Monday, March 10th at Conference Room #2 from 9-11 a.m.
>
> The following will be discussed during the meeting:
>
> - Staff review/requirements
>
> - Audit procedures
>
> - Sales review
>
> - Production review/requirements
>
> Please make sure that all team leaders are prepared to give updates regarding the status of ongoing projects. If you are unable to attend the meeting, please make sure that your assistant can deliver your report for you.
>
> Please feel free to add to this agenda by notifying us in advance prior to the day of the meeting.

This strategy can be used in composing email messages, memoranda, or business letters. It will also be useful when writing informal business reports; however, longer documents will require additional content development.

## Report Writing

Sharing information in a professional setting can come in different forms for different purposes. While the routine messages discussed above are the most common, you will also be required to compose longer and more formal messages throughout your career.

Sometime in the course of your career, you may be asked to write a report. It could be as simple as a one-page industry overview for a busy boss who wants to understand the lay of the land in an industry with which s/he is unfamiliar. Or, it could be a longer report on a crisis in an industry or within a particular company, i.e. Volkswagen, Nike, or Chipotle. Regardless of the length of the report, the general structure remains fixed: Introduction, Body, Conclusion.

That said, the only sections that change are the body, which could be forty or fifty pages long, and the inclusion of front (cover page, table of contents, and executive summary) and back matter (appendices).

The variations and degree to which you go in-depth in a report can be accommodated by proper formatting—everything from font size and style to placement and spacing of headings determines the organization of your information. Thus, writing a report is simply an expanded version of a short report that you may have to produce for a class. If you follow the rules governing headings, subheadings, etc., you will produce polished deliverables that underscore your competence and professionalism.

### How to Write a Report

As with any message—of any length—you will need to systematically work through the three-step writing process: planning, writing, revising. This three-part structure is tried and true, and taking short-cuts is not advised. Remember, your professional reputation is on the line whenever you write for an audience.

## Planning

It bears repeating that the key difference between business writing and academic writing is that business messages have a purpose and a specific audience. In academic writing, you are often writing to no one in particular, but you know that your instructor will be grading it, so you often skew your message to that audience of one.

In business writing, you must ask yourself a few key questions:

1. To whom am I writing?
2. Why am I writing it? (persuade, inform, deliver bad news)
3. What do they already know?
4. What do they need to know?
5. What is the proper tone I should use in this instance?
6. What do I ultimately want from them?

Next, you will need to *gather the information* you need to flesh out your message. If that includes research, then you will need to gather the facts and data that will support your claims and aims. Choose reputable publications from common business databases or peer-reviewed sources. Keep track of the citations for later referencing and to use in in-text citations and on the reference page.

Once you have the information you need, you need to take some time to organize your message. You will want to identify your main point/points, cluster supporting data around these points, choose your strategy (direct or indirect), determine the appropriate level of formality, and create an outline ordering the information in a logical construct.

## Writing

If you have successfully worked the planning process, the actual writing should take less time: You know what you want to say, you have done your research, and you know the structure and approach your message will follow.

Your introductory paragraph should have the standard information: Frame/Context, Purpose, WIIFY, and Forecast. Next, you will fill in the paragraphs under the headings that succinctly identify the main point of the paragraph/s. Each paragraph will follow the Claim, Evidence, Reasoning construction, and you will wrap it up with a standard conclusion that offers a brief, high-level summary (repeat the forecast), a WIIFY, an invitation for inquiry, and your contact information.

Remember to use strong verbs to drive the sentences and hold the readers' interest. As for tone, aim to sound even more formal than you might be inclined; it is better to error on the side of professionalism than to come off as too casual.

## Revising

Your work is not quite over! Revise your document carefully, checking for spelling and grammatical errors and making sure that it flows easily. Use transition words to maintain flow and clarify the relationship between sentences and between paragraphs and sections.

Once you are finished, you will have a professional business document that showcases your ability to plan, write, and polish a workplace message.

# Common Purposes of Business Reports

The type of content development outlined in the previous section is common for everyday workplace scenarios. However, more formal and comprehensive business reports will require more extensive research. You will also need to apply rigorous thought processes to extract meaning from the data you gather. You may do this by classifying information, analyzing data, and synthesizing data from more than one source.

You will also need to determine the type of reporting your audience is requesting from you to properly present the information you have gathered and analyzed. The three levels of reporting you will likely be asked to do are 1) reporting findings, 2) drawing conclusions, and 3) making recommendations. When researching information for a business report, you will always be asked to present your findings; however, often you will also be expected to show relevance and possibly make recommendations based on your findings. The next three sections will walk you through the three levels of reporting information for business purposes. Keep in mind that the purpose for all business research and reporting is to prompt and enable a company and/or its stakeholders to take action.

## Reporting Findings

When you are asked to report findings, you should present information completely and objectively. You may classify or summarize data using charts, graphs, or tables when appropriate to help your reader access information at a glance. As you discuss the graphics, you will need to interpret the data for the situation; that is, make the information meaningful and useful to the reader. You may even go as far as to offer factual explanations for the findings. You do not want to draw conclusions prematurely or offer opinions or recommendations if you have not been requested to do so.

Let's look at an example of reporting findings, using a survey conducted by Fresh-mart grocery store. Here are the results of a section of the survey in which customers were asked to rate the importance of service items. The chart is followed by a brief email message to the Fresh-mart CEO, Jeff Curtis, reporting and interpreting the results.

| FRESH-MART SURVEY: CUSTOMER SERVICE PROGRAMS | |
|---|---|
| SERVICE | AVERAGE RATING (OUT OF 5) |
| 2% discount on purchases of $20 or more | 4.50 |
| 5% senior discount on Wednesday | 4.10 |
| Free delivery of orders within a 10-mile radius of the store | 1.75 |
| Frequent shopper discount card | 3.97 |

Dear Mr. Curtis,

Average ratings of the section of the survey on customer service programs indicate strong customer interest in new services that enable them to save money.

Discounts on all purchases of $20 or more, a senior discount on Wednesday, and frequent shopper discount cards all received ratings above 3.95 out of 5.00, indicating that Fresh-mart customers consider those services to be important or very important. By contrast, removing fees from seldom-used services, such as free delivery, appears to be of little importance to Fresh-mart customers.

Let me know how I can help with Fresh-mart's decision on how we can use this data moving forward.

Best Regards,
Ted Neal

Notice that the explanation does not offer suggestions based on the data; it simply reports what was found and makes it relevant to the situation.

## Drawing Conclusions

When you are expected to take the report to the next level, you will need to draw a conclusion that suggests how the reader might respond to the findings. In this case, you do more than merely restate the findings, but you still remain objective. Your conclusion should flow naturally from the findings themselves and your clear analysis of them, and it should be justified by your findings. This demands that you consider the needs of your reader more thoroughly than you did when simply reporting the information. The following would be an appropriate conclusion to the previous email message, based on the Fresh-mart survey item.

**Conclusion:**

Since Fresh-mart customers are more interested in ways to save money on their grocery purchases than in saving money on peripheral services, we can increase customer satisfaction by offering a variety of discounts.

## Making Recommendations

A recommendation is a confident statement of a proposed action based on your findings and the conclusion you have drawn. As with your conclusion, a recommendation must flow from specific data and your analysis of it. In many cases, you will make more than one recommendation. In that case, you will need to organize your recommendations by some form of metric.

There are several criteria for organizing recommendations. These can include the following:

- **Time** How urgent is the problem? Should the recommendation be implemented in phases?
- **Priority** Which recommendations are the most critical? Organize your recommendations in descending order of priority.
- **Costs** How much will it cost to implement your recommendation(s)? What type of investment will be necessary?
- **Stakeholders** Who will your recommendations affect? What groups are critical to target first?

Be sure to state your metric (or metrics) clearly so your audience understands your logic and how to implement your recommendations. If your report includes an executive summary, echo this logic in the executive summary.

When making a recommendation, use imperative sentences and action verbs. State the recommendation specifically, including a plan for implementation. Ask yourself if this is an actionable recommendation. Could you implement it tomorrow if necessary?

By applying these strategies to your business writing, you can ensure the content of your documents is logical and is based on sound reasoning. You also ensure you are providing the reader with the precise, yet comprehensive, information required to act on your recommendations.

The following is an outline of what an initial recommendation might include in the Fresh-mart case. Note that the metric of organization is priority. Items are presented in order of importance to customers based on the rankings found on the previous survey. The following report presents an outline of your recommendation for the CEO of Fresh-mart.

## Recommendations for Increasing Customer Satisfaction

After analyzing the results of our recent customer satisfaction survey, it is clear that Fresh-mart shoppers want greater savings on groceries. To increase customer satisfaction and loyalty, Fresh-mart should initiate two new cost-saving services immediately. The outline below offers preliminary recommendations, listed in order of importance based on our customer-satisfaction survey. We should also conduct further research to determine the feasibility of a third service in the near future.

### Customer Savings Programs

The following recommendations will ensure our current customers stay loyal and will increase our customer base as we market these new services. Specifically, Fresh-mart should:

1. **Provide a 2% discount on orders totaling $20 or more.** We can implement this by:

   - Programming point-of-sale registers to compute a 2% discount on orders over $20

   - Training check-out associates to highlight savings on receipts and point them out to customers

   - Advertising this new service in store and on existing TV commercials

2. **Give an additional 3% discount to seniors on Wednesday.** We can do this by:

   - Programming point-of-sale registers with a key to compute a 3% discount

   - Training check-out associates on how to recognize customers who appear to be 60 years old or older and how to enter the discount code for such customers

   - Designing and publishing an attractive newspaper advertisement announcing the new policy

3. **Investigate the feasibility of issuing a "Frequent Shopper" discount card.** We should focus on determining the following:

   - Criteria to identify frequent shoppers

   - Type of discount card that we can offer

   - Costs of implementation, such as providing the card and maintaining records

### Conclusion and Next Steps

The cost for implementing the first two services is minimal. It will consist primarily of training current employees and will include the cost of advertising. However, by implementing these two new services, Fresh-mart will show its loyal customers that we are listening, and attract new customers who find these services appealing.

The IT department has received a copy of these findings and is prepared to program registers to compute discounts. Upon approval, Ms. Applegate's team will begin organizing a training program for our checkout associates. I welcome the opportunity to discuss these cost-saving, customer-requested services and to begin researching the feasibility of a Frequent Shopper card.

As you advance in your career, you will be called upon to deliver your research and analysis at each of the levels we have just discussed. At times, you will be expected to report research findings (just the facts). At other times, you will be asked to draw conclusions based on those findings. Eventually, you will be asked to provide recommendations to solve a problem or take advantage of an opportunity your organization is facing. In longer, more formal written reports, in which you are attempting to persuade your audience to take action, the organization may well be as important as the content itself. In order to hold your audience's interest and keep them reading, you'll need to tell a story that engages them from start to finish.

# Informal & Formal Reports

Reports come in many forms, and they vary in their levels of formality. Sometimes, report content is integrated into a correspondence message. For instance, a few pages ago, you read a sample email used to report findings. In that example, the document, in this case, an email, contained many features of general business correspondence. Elements like salutations and the use of first and second person may appear in some informal reporting; it really depends on your purpose, your audience, and the situation at hand. Think of formality as existing on a spectrum. The figure below illustrates where certain documents might fall on the continuum.

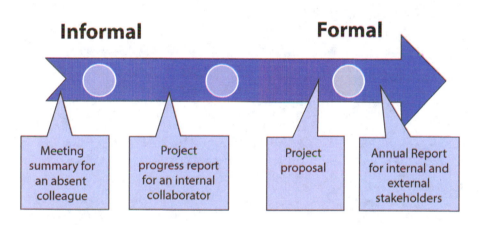

When selecting a report format, first, consider the audience. Are you reporting out to one or more readers? Then, determine how much information is needed to accomplish your objective. Generally, the longer and more detailed the content lends itself to a more formal approach. As indicated by the continuum above, reports can be informal, formal, or somewhere in between. Depending on your readers' needs, you may find yourself integrating some formal elements into a relatively informal report. For instance, you might find it appropriate to include a bibliography if you use sources or an appendix if you have supporting figures or information. In the following sections, we will explore the characteristics and applications of formal and informal reports.

# Informal Reports

Informal reports serve a variety of purposes and may be used to accomplish informative or persuasive purposes, and they are often designed as memos, letters, or modifications of these formats. Some common informal report types are listed below. As a delivery system for relatively brief and modestly-scoped content, the informal report can serve many purposes.

| | COMMON INFORMAL REPORT TYPES |
|---|---|
| Progress Report | Provides a project update to internal or external stakeholders |
| Periodic Report | Provides information or updates to supervisors on a regular basis |
| Trip or Meeting Report | Provides a detailed account of findings/outcomes following work travel or a meeting |
| Test Report | Describes findings from product experiments |
| Recommendation Report | Communicates support or opposition of a particular action or proposal |
| Summary Report | Details and distills information on a given topic |

The following memo was drafted by a student intern, in response to her supervisor's request for a summary of three shoe industry-related articles.

# Informal Report Sample Document: Research Summary

## INTEROFFICE MEMORANDUM

to:     Zack Wilson
from:   student
subject: Footwear Industry Research Summary
date:    March 22, 2019
cc:     N/A

Author uses a memo format

As you requested, I have evaluated three articles pertaining to athletic footwear products and produced relevant summaries for your use. This document will give you the information to adequately procure an appealing line of athletic footwear in university bookstores. To guide your focus, I have separated the analysis into three distinct topics: superior footwear brands, footwear ecommerce trends, and economic factors.

Frames for a particular recipient, & uses first and second person, a less formal approach

## Superior Footwear Brands

One of the foundations to maintaining revenue streams in retail is the proper brand selection. Low's (2016) article compares Under Armour and Nike as they compete for top market share in footwear. Nike's top lines are based off of basketball stars Michael Jordan and Lebron James. Under Armour has created its most recent shoe line based on current basketball prodigy, Stephen Curry. While the two companies leverage athletes as their primary foundation for footwear design the factor important to our business is overall sales trends. According to Low (2016), "a Slice Intelligence report that examined sales of the top four NBA-player shoes, Curry kicks are in vogue, but Nike is still king of the cash register" (p. 1). The information in the article shows that in regard to longevity and consistency of sales, Nike is the primary brand we should offer in broad capacity at our bookstores.

## Footwear E-Commerce Trends

University of Arizona bookstores currently offer online shoe retail, however, many challenges still remain in ensuring that our e-commerce sales portals are in adherence with modern retail trends. In her industry report on online shoe sales, Madeline Hurley demonstrates the growth of shoe retailers online and industry trends. According to Hurley (2016), online footwear retail has increased from 7.0% in 2011 to 14.2% in 2016. The reason for the growth of the industry online lies in consumer information trends. Over the past five years, online shopping has become increasingly consumer friendly. With a growing number of online operators, consumers can increasingly compare prices, read product reviews and browse merchandise with virtual ease (p. 6). Overall, the offering of consumer options and comparable product reviews increases online traffic.

Headings are used to clearly signal document sections

## Economic Factors

Economic factors that contribute to cyclical sales trends and retailer insolvency are crucial data points that our bookstores need to take into account. A Forbes article highlights data for the upcoming quarter in the shoe retail industry. He stated, "With 10 percent of the sporting goods retail space closing by Labor Day, the remaining market will be stronger and healthier" (Powell, 2016, p. 2). In our division, we can use this data to procure athletic shoes after Labor Day to minimize costs and stand out from the degrading competition in the retail space.

This summary analyzed three articles and their relevance in enhancing our footwear procurement division: superior footwear brands, footwear e-commerce trends, and economic factors. The outcomes of my analysis demonstrate that with a culmination of proper brand selection, e-commerce consumer accommodation, and seasonal sales focus our athletic shoe revenues can reach new highs. Thank you for letting me analyze these documents and formulate conclusions that can improve our footwear division. Feel free to contact me at student@gmail.com if you have questions.

## References

Hurley, M. (2016, September). IBIS world industry report OD5093. Retrieved March 19, 2017, from http://clients1.ibisworld.com/reports/us/industry/default.aspx?entid=5093

Low, E. (2016, June 02). Under Armour's golden boy vs. Nike's lifetime king: Whose shoes sell? *Investors Business Daily.* Retrieved March 19, 2017, from http://www.investors.com/news/under-armours-golden-boy-vs-nikes-lifetime-king-whose-shoes-sell/

Powell, M. (2016, June 06). Sneakernomics: What's really happening in the U.S. sneaker business? *Forbes.* Retrieved March 19, 2017, from https://www.forbes.com/sites/mattpowell/2016/06/06/sneakernomics-whats-really-happening-in-the-u-s-sneaker-business/#40a57f311dc3

References are listed at the end of the document

# Informal Report Sample Document: Strategy Summary

To: Marketing Team
From: Ben Marchos, Intern
Date: March 31, 2018
Subject: ZonaZoo's Marketing Strategies

The ZonaZoo is an award-winning student section and student-ticketing program for University of Arizona Athletics. This document provides a summary of the ZonaZoo's marketing strategies which center around member benefits and special events, both of which contribute to their success in student engagement.

## Member Benefits

*Attendance*

The Zoo markets itself to students by communicating the benefits enjoyed by members. Lower cost admittance is a very popular feature, so it is clearly highlighted on their website. Further, since many games sell out, they promise the first 9000 student members who swipe their CatCards a seat at each event (ZonaZoo, 2018). By having a large group of ZonaZoo members at each game, the club achieves its goal of supporting UA teams and benefits from a high-visibility factor, which has the potential to attract more students, media, and community members. Additionally, this kind of notoriety further enhances the club's reputation.

*T-Shirts*

Every ZonaZoo member receives a free branded t-shirt. This helps the club gain attention on game days and provides additional signage when worn by students. With over 9000 members, these shirts provide free advertising for the club and ensure name-recognition among fans and nonmembers.

*Newsletter*

The ZonaZoo markets to attract new members and retain those already in the club. All club members receive the ZonaZoo Gazette, an online newsletter that provides Zoo-related content to users, highlights club and member successes, and commemorates special game day moments. By maintaining a high level of member excitement and commitment, the club garners attention from others.

*Special Events*

The ZonaZoo hosts many pre-game events that invite community members to join in the game day excitement (ZonaZoo, 2018). All are invited to attend and enjoy learning UA cheers, hearing guest speakers from UA's athletic community, and sharing in a strong sense wildcat fever. Partnerships with local shops and restaurants add to the events, and these parties, rallies, and tailgating days attract attention from media outlets that broadcast footage of ZonaZoo and further promote the club on a state and countrywide level.

The ZonaZoo employs several key marketing initiatives. However, by communicating member benefits and hosting media-friendly special events, they continue to attract attention from sports enthusiasts on campus and all over the country.

# Transmittal Messages

When delivering a formal report, it may be appropriate to include a transmittal message. The transmittal message will serve as a cover letter or brief introduction to the business document. It provides context for the report and serves the purpose of a traditional introduction that offers context, a "what's in it for you?" (WIIFY), and purpose statements, and it provides a general overview of the report content. Many times, this type of targeted message is included in informal reports, but formal reports are often written for a wider audience, and they do not include the use of first or second person phrasing. So, the transmittal message alerts your contact or point person that the document is ready for them and their team. Depending on your receiver's channel preference, transmittal messages may be formatted as a letter or memo. If you send the report electronically, you may choose to write the transmittal in an email. The transmittal is essentially your introduction to a formal report. The message below illustrates the nature of a transmittal:

To: marin.a@company.com
From: liu.m@company.com
Date: March May 17, 2018
Subject: Under Armour Communication Plan

Hello Charles,

As planned, our team completed and attached the Under Armour communication strategy to assist the expansion team in their initiative to grow UA's reach in untapped markets. This plan explores our potential move into the Brazilian market and provides communications recommendations for the expansion. Through analyses of the current situation, past expansions, and opportunities in the Brazilian market, the enclosed document identifies critical stakeholders and details targeted messaging for each group. Executive management, manufacturers, retailers, and consumers emerged as most influential to the expansion's success. It is our hope that this plan will aid your team in bringing UA's quality products to new consumer audience. Please contact me with questions or requests for further information.

Regards,
Ava Marin

# Formal Reports

Formal reports are generally used to convey information on major findings, proposals, or extended research. Like informal reports, they are used for many purposes. Unlike informal reports, they often contain a great deal of content. So, the formal report format allows for effective, logical integration of content and supporting documents like figures and references. In addition, features like the table of contents make for easy navigation of materials.

This section will describe the parts of a formal report, the contents and organizational structure that create an effective final product. As the word implies, a formal report is written at a higher professional level than an informal report. Formal reports often include an external audience, thus the need for elevated language and clarity of purpose. Informal reports are often targeted at an internal audience and may use humor, idiomatic language, and other more casual elements. This is not true of a formal report. The writer might also consider that a formal report could be shared in a business environment outside of the United States. With differences in language and culture, a more formal and less idiomatic language style must be used to increase the probability that the document's message will not be lost on the audience.

Major projects such as the feasibility of a new service or product, a year-end review of an organization, or research into a specific field would all be appropriate topics for formal reports. Formal reports are often comprehensive and must address diverse and disparate audiences. The need for a clear organizational structure and relevant signposts is never stronger than when writing these documents. Depending on the topic covered, a formal report can be a few pages long to hundreds of pages. Again, these longer reports necessitate an organizational clarity that is easy to grasp from skimming the table of contents.

Generally, reports are divided into three main parts: front matter, body, and back matter. Brief descriptions of each are as follows:

## Front Matter

This section includes all of the elements that come before the actual body of the report. This important section lets the reader know the purpose and topic of the report and the structure and organization of what is to follow. It is here where the reader can determine whether the information they seek will be contained within this report. Save the audience time by clearly showing them what the report will include in detail.

**Title page:** Note that title pages may vary from organization to organization, but the title itself should reflect the purpose and scope of the report. The title should be neither too long nor too short, neither too vague nor too specific. Accurately capturing the high-level view of the content in the title itself is critical.

**Table of contents:** This offers an overview and a roadmap of the report itself. It should include a list of all the front and back matter with the exception of the title page. All the headings in the report will be listed in the order in which they appear in the document. A busy reader might look here to skim and find the section and the page number in which they are interested. The table of contents provides a useful way for readers to quickly find exactly what they are looking for. The table of contents also provides a clear progression for those writing or contributing to the report and helps keep the content on track.

**List of figures:** Immediately following the table of contents, a writer will include a list of figures if there are five or more included in the body of the report. This section will be separate from the table of contents beginning on its own page and will list them by title and will include their page number. Throughout the report itself, figures should be numbered consecutively throughout with Arabic numbers.

**List of tables, abbreviations, and symbols:** When these elements are numerous, they should be called out separately in their own section so that the audience can more readily comprehend the content of the report. This is especially true for technical reports and any content that might include many abbreviations and symbols.

## Body

The information that you have gathered during your research or investigation will be presented, analyzed, and synthesized in the body section of the report. If the document is persuasive, then a recommendations section must be included and the suggestions offered should clearly and logically follow from the careful analysis. The body of a formal report will include the executive summary, an introduction, the text itself, and any conclusions or recommendations.

**Executive summary:** This is a vital part of a formal report and is a high-level view of the entire report condensed to approximately one page of text. This will often be read by high-level executives who want to understand the gist of the report without getting into granular detail. Thus, this section is aptly named executive summary. This portion should clearly describe the purpose and scope of the project and provide conclusions that detail any recommendations made.

The executive summary is often written after the entire report so that key and relevant material is included and nothing critical is forgotten. Keep in mind the executive summary is meant as a stand-alone document and should not contain confusing jargon, acronyms, or symbols left unexplained. This document should be comprehensible and complete without any accompanying material yet should still allow the reader to understand the findings, conclusions, and recommendations—minus the detailed descriptions that generated said findings.

**Introduction:** As it has already been described in previous sections of this textbook, the introduction should let the reader know why the report was written (purpose/opportunity/problem), what the report contains (scope), and what specifically will follow, and in what order. The introduction should also articulate the value that the report will provide to its intended audience. Essentially, it is here that the report is framed and forecasted for the audience. This is another way of ensuring that the BLOT—Bottom Line on Top—has been successfully delivered.

**Body Content and Strategies:** The organization of this section will be determined by the purpose of the report, and generally this part will comprise the bulk of the report. A common organizational structure is SBAR.—Situation, Background, Analysis, and Results for an informative report and Recommendations for a persuasive document. But, again, a decision will have to be made as to the best way to structure the report for easy readability and the high skim factor. Headings and subheadings will be used to separate relevant sections. Be sure to use varying formatting conventions to designate differences between headings, subheadings, and sub-subheadings. The goal is always to make it easy on the reader to follow a logical and clear structure.

Tables, charts, and infographics can be used within the body to explain concepts, present data, or otherwise show complex material in a visual form. These visuals can also help to break up large bodies of text and provide much-needed white space for the eye.

Whatever organizational structure is chosen, the information should be clearly presented, analyzed, and synthesized with supporting reasons offered for the recommendations or conclusions. Again, if a recommendation is required, it should clearly be drawn from the analysis and the synthesis. Connections between the most important information should be concise and accurate, and all results should be drawn from cogent analysis.

**Conclusion/Recommendations:** Depending on the purpose of this report, this final section will summarize the key takeaways and main points of the message. If the report uses a direct approach and an informative strategy, this section will reiterate conclusions that were asserted in the introduction and proved in the body. The key points should be wrapped up here in the same order as they were presented in the body. Remember that no new evidence or facts will be presented in the conclusion; the careful groundwork will all have been completed in the body of the report. Keep in mind this is your last chance in the document to drive home the purpose of the report in a compelling and complete manner.

However, if the indirect approach is used, then the body, evidence and reasoning will lead to conclusions presented here in this section. If the strategy used is persuasive, the same goes for recommendations and suggestions. If the approach is direct, the conclusion will restate the recommendations from the introduction; if the approach is indirect, the conclusion will culminate in the recommendations for which a strong case has been built in the body. Finally, this is the place to direct the reader to take action and should clearly delineate next steps.

### Back Matter

Following the main body of the formal report are the references (or bibliography) and appendices. Each of these should begin on their own page.

**References:** In alphabetical order and using proper formatting (i.e. APA, MLA), cite all sources used to create the report. Keep in mind that you should also list sources that were consulted but not directly cited in the report. This also gives the reader more resources from which to do their own research.

**Appendices:** An appendix is an additional section where documents, tables, questionnaires, and/or any other supplementary material is saved. Housing the extra material here ensures that the flow of the report is not disturbed and concision is observed. Items in the appendix are organized as Appendix A, Appendix B, Appendix C, etc. Each appendix should be begun on a new page and appropriately labeled at the top.

The following sample document demonstrates how many of the above elements were integrated into a formal report. As you will see, the student authors elected not to list figures and abbreviations separately.

© Casimiro PT/Shutterstock.com

# UNDER ARMOUR
## FINAL COMMUNICATION PLAN
## Team 18

# Table of Contents

## Under Armour, Inc.

# Executive Summary

## Under Armour, Inc.

### Situation

While Under Armour, Inc. (UA) is extremely successful in North America, the brand has had difficulty increasing market share on a global scale. This communication plan addresses potential opportunities for UA to alleviate this issue.

Below is an assessment of expanding UA further into the Brazilian market. The UA brand is synonymous with innovation and quality, and that already-established perception will allow the company to flourish as it takes the first steps into global expansion.

### Background

Through extensive research of both the North American and Brazilian athletic apparel markets, the team has determined several key factors that will determine the success of this expansion initiative. Several crucial highlights are listed below:

- Brazil is the 7th largest rapidly-growing economy in the world
- 14% of manufacturing is locally sourced in Latin America
- Sport-centric culture creates a high demand for athletic apparel and footwear
- Competitors Nike and Adidas already have established presence in Brazil

With the positive forecasts for Brazilian market growth and the demand for athletic products high, our team has labeled Brazil as the top market for UA to consider while moving forward globally.

### Analysis

Ultimately, the Brazilian market is a low-risk, high-potential opportunity for companies looking to operate in foreign countries, making it the ideal option for UA's imminent expansion. To determine the success of the communication plan, the team leads must assess the achievement of two goals:

- 200% increase in UA's share of the Brazilian Apparel and Footwear market
- doubled number of retailers committed to selling the brand

While the Olympics will provide an initial platform to judge our success, UA's Brazilian campaign will continue indefinitely as the brand gains momentum in the market.

### Recommendation & Response

Research suggests the Brazilian market is an ideal place for UA's expansion, and the time to take advantage of this opportunity is now. The outline of the recommendations is as follows:

- Appropriate a budget of approximately $100 million
- Notify key stakeholders: Executive Management, Manufacturers, Retailers, Consumers
- Identify brand voice to unify UA across all markets, tailoring messages to stakeholders
- Assess plan success following 2016 Olympics before moving forward

Understanding Brazilian culture is crucial to the effectiveness of UA's communication plan. The UA Team is innovating, empowering, and rapidly expanding, and Brazil is the next step toward the company's further success.

# Communication Plan

## Under Armour, Inc.

The communications team compiled a series of recommendations based upon UA's mission to expand Under Armour (UA)'s presence in Brazil. This report includes an audit of the company's current issues, lack of global market presence, and concludes that the Brazilian market is a key step in creating a stronger brand presence worldwide.

The following recommendations will provide UA with the opportunity to understand our mission and determine the effectiveness of our research. The communication plan below reviews UA's past situation, current opportunities, and future potential, and explains internal and external stakeholders' needs for targeted messaging and effective channels. A budget and timeline are provided for each element of the communication plan.

### Assessing the Past

In 1995, University of Maryland football player Kevin Plank began his mission to find the perfect blend of materials for athletic wear that would not become quickly soaked through with sweat during his workouts. Plank engineered his first prototypes after touring New York's Garment District and proceeded to give them away to his former teammates, many of whom held current contracts with NFL teams (Under Armour, 2015). He only had one request of those who received his garments: "If you love it, call me." (Under Armour, 2015).

Utilizing the feedback from his former teammates, Plank refined his prototype, quickly emerging with a T-shirt built from microfibers that wicked moisture and kept athletes cool, dry, and light. Plank charged the limit on all of his credit cards and was working out of his grandmother's basement for twelve months before he made his first sale: outfitting all of Georgia Tech's athletes in the Under Armour brand.

Since that breakthrough, UA has grown exponentially in both profit and market share, launching it to the second-largest athletic apparel brand in the United States (Mirabella, 2014). UA's top competitors are Nike and Adidas, with approximately 30% and 6% of the North American market share respectively (Mirabella, 2014). While UA surpassed Adidas in both revenue and American market share in 2014, the brand's general lack of recognition in foreign markets where its competitors dominate is a major issue.

### Evaluating Opportunities

While UA's humble beginnings and the tale of CEO Kevin Plank's journey to success resonate well with North American consumers, the success story has yet to create a substantial impact on foreign markets (Gondo, 2015). However, our team recognizes an emerging market that caters to a variety of consumers with a similar appreciation for rags-to-riches stories: Brazil.

With an expanding middle class that accounts for 54% of the population, new brands looking to penetrate the market like UA will have no problem finding a consumer base (Gomes, 2015). Brazil is also ranked as the 7th largest economy in the world. Additionally, UA outsources 70% of its overall production, and 14% of the manufacturers can be found in Latin America (Sainte Croix, 2012).

One potential issue with the Brazilian market that may have scared UA off in the past is the country's high taxation on material goods. The Brazilian government charges a 35% tax on clothing sales, and payroll taxes consume approximately 42% of every employee's salary (Euromonitor, 2014). These levels of higher taxation will lead to increased price point on all UA products sold in Brazil. However, despite the 30–40% markup on merchandise, American companies such as The Gap have successfully maintained profitability while expanding into the Brazilian market (Euromonitor, 2014). Brazil's taxes may be high, but the economy is growing in comparison to growth around the rest of the world.

The Latin American Apparel and Footwear market grew 11% in 2013, while the market in the United States only grew 1.7% (Euromonitor, 2014). The country of Brazil is the largest apparel market in Latin America, accounting for 17.5% of total sales in the region (Euromonitor, 2014). Out of all Latin countries, Brazil places second in compound annual growth rate for sales at 4.3%, behind Chile at 8.7% (Euromonitor, 2014).

UA has already looked to China to expand. According to Forbes, the company has introduced an "experience store" into Shanghai (Forbes, 2014). This store is unique in that it allows the customers to see UA's story through videos. Plank wants to immerse the consumer in the story before they are marketed for the product. They currently have five stores with three more to come in China, although the overall market share remains relatively inconsequential.

As of now, UA has done little to publicize the possibility of expanding further on a global scale. Plank briefly discussed the immense potential in foreign markets and was quoted as saying, "Wherever we go around the globe, we will lead first with our story and bring the people into the best Under Armour experience possible" (Newswire, 2013). Despite this proclamation, UA's triumphant story is still unfolding, and Plank has yet to unveil plans for a foreign campaign. The communication team is prepared to provide UA with the next steps toward making the global "Under Armour experience" a reality, starting in Brazil.

## Moving Forward

Now that UA's presence has spread throughout North America, it is time for the company to prioritize international sales as a primary objective. Since 2008, North America has been UA's primary business, as the market is responsible for generating approximately 96% of the brand's total earnings (Passport, 2015).

Since 2013, UA has developed a moderate amount of market share in the Asia Pacific region, primarily in China. However, as reported by Passport's graph of UA's Share in 2013 (See Fig. 1), Brazil did not accumulate any shares (Passport, 2015). While the country has a smaller number of net retail sales than China, our team has chosen to focus expansion in Brazil due to the fact that it has a lower risk for operation and is therefore an ideal environment for further growth (Cunha, 2015) (See Fig. 2).

UA can remedy the current state of market myopia by focusing on expanding the brand's presence in Brazil as opposed to remaining in solely North America and, minimally, China. Should expansion prove to be successful, UA expects to collect at least $6 million from Brazil in 2018 (Passport, 2015). This value would add to the company's overall revenue dramatically, as the Chinese market is less volatile and there would be lower profits with a less-diverse market range.

According to the Economist, Brazil is forecasted to have a five-year high in demand for apparel with a staggering $25.2 billion in 2017. Footwear is also seeing an increase in demand reaching $19.7 billion in 2015 with forecasts projecting a demand come 2017 (See Fig. 3). If we were to ignore the bourgeoning opportunity of expanding into Brazil, our company would overlook the chance to dramatically grow our global market share and revenue. Expansion would also increase UA's competitive edge, as competitors such as Nike and Adidas have already gone global and are flourishing.

An effective communication plan will help to align us with future stakeholders in Brazil. Cultivating those relationships will allow us to run a more efficient and profitable business in Brazil, and therefore increase our overall market share while building the framework for further global expansion.

In order for UA to succeed internationally, especially within Brazil, the company needs to understand Brazil's traditions and culture. There are differences between all five cultural dimensions, but the largest difference is the individualism versus collectivism dimension (See Fig. 4). Brazil scored low on individualism, and is hence considered a collectivistic country. Therefore, doing business in Brazil means that is important to build up trustworthiness and to create long-lasting relationships with consumers and other businesses. Compared to the individualism of the United States, Under Armour will need to learn how to gain Brazil's trust in order to succeed.

### Communicating Effectively

Compared to its competitors, UA is a relative newcomer to the North American athletic apparel market. However, in the past decade, the company's market share has increased dramatically to 14%, which established it as the second-largest athletic apparel brand in the United States (Mirabella, 2014). This rapid growth has solidified UA as a household name domestically, but the opportunity to expand globally creates the need for a better understanding of other cultures in order to communicate successfully.

The key to communicating across cultures while maintaining a unified brand is to identify and implement a consistent brand voice. UA's most prevalent association in the North American market is that of the underdog: humble, innovative, and empowering. The company's mission is "to make all athletes better through passion, design, and the relentless pursuit of innovation," which is a goal that needs to be established in Brazil during expansion (Under Armour, 2015).

Each stakeholder requires a different pragmatic approach regarding these recommendations, the team intends on cultivating a universal brand voice and regulating message channels in order to promote the culture of unity for which UA is known. Below are descriptions of the four most crucial stakeholders for UA's expansion into Brazil and the tailored messages each will require as UA moves forward in this initiative.

#### *Executive Management*

The first step in this expansion plan is to notify UA's executive management at company headquarters in Baltimore. UA upper management consists of eight presidents, executive vice presidents, and officers who act as both the representatives and the decision-makers of the company (Under Armour, 2015).

In order to communicate with these executives most effectively, the communication team will schedule a formal announcement to be delivered by CEO Kevin Plank. The announcement will be in-house, but there will be a Skype link implemented should any of the executives be unable to attend.

The purpose of this meeting will be to maintain a feeling of common stake and ensure that each manager understands the next steps so as to better direct employees as the company moves forward. Additionally, by speaking in a more intimate environment, Plank will be able to continue cultivating the team-spirit mentality for which UA is known (Under Armour, 2015).

The message will focus on what is in it for the executives: specifically, how increasing the market share globally will positively impact UA's profits with minimal additional workload to the North American force, due to the implementation of a Brazilian communications team.

### Manufacturers

The majority of UA's merchandise are developed by nonaffiliated third-party manufacturers, whose fabrics and finished products are inspected by UA to gain approval. UA manufactures primarily overseas, utilizing short-term contracts with fabric mills and factories to produce approximately 70% of all branded apparel (Morgan, 2015). As of 2014, UA's products were primarily manufactured in Asia, Central and South America and Mexico.

Currently, UA's Chief Supply Chain Officer and his team meet with each of these manufacturers on a monthly basis to review market performance, projected sales, and adherence to the company's standards of quality and ethics (Morgan, 2015). These manufacturers are crucial to UA's success in expansion, as the movement toward a global initiative and increased market share will require a much higher volume of product to be manufactured.

To inform manufacturers that an increased supply will be required with the renewal of their contracts, UA will send memorandums to the contacts with whom monthly meetings are held (See Appendix B). Our team has determined that sending memorandums as opposed to formal letters will acknowledge the current relationships that UA has with their manufacturers, and therefore encourage a positive reception of the request.

The approach to take with manufacturers will be to focus on what the increase in volume will mean for workers: primarily, the opportunity for more jobs and larger profits. The manufacturers who choose to renew contracts under the new workload will be able to continue working as a part of the UA team, and will enjoy the benefits that UA provides for its affiliates (Under Armour, 2015). Our team is adamant that this approach will encourage manufacturers to continue producing with UA and strengthen their commitments to producing quality product for the expansion into Brazil.

### Retailers

In order to secure the potential sales of the UA brand to Brazilian consumers, we must first communicate our brand's value to several major retailers in Brazil. Without their full support, UA will be virtually unable to make strides in this new market. The three main retailers of interest are WalMart Brazil, Carrefour, and Casino Guichard, or, as it is known in Brazil, the "Extra Store."

The communication team will first send out a formal offer to all retailers in Brazil via letters to their corporate office (See Appendix C). After this initial step, the team will follow up with the most important companies by sending personalized representatives to engage protential partners.

The strategy throughout this contact with retailers will be to highlight what UA does better than competitors in ways specific to the Brazilian market. First, UA will communicate our lower price points in comparison to competitors such as Nike. This lower price point will appeal to retailers because the primary consumers of large department stores in Brazil earn between \$687.69 and \$1719.22 monthly yet have significantly growing purchasing power (Gomes, 2015).

To appeal to the retailers' internal business, we will reinforce the importance of our close-proximity manufacturing. Having factories within the area will make logistics easier and ensure full inventory of products, without the necessity of adding additional markups to compensate for tariffs. With this strategy, UA can grow the number of committed Brazilian retailers from 70 to 140 stores by the end of 2016.

### Consumers

Because of their influence regarding UA's revenue in this new market, Brazilian consumers need to be aware of new products available to them before they can make purchases. As a company, UA must ensure that the brand is well-represented and have reached every potential consumer in each target markets. Additionally, it is crucial that UA remains unified in vision and voice across all markets, so as to remain true to the integrity of the brand.

In reaching out to consumers, it is critical to establish a friendly connection between the North American and Brazilian markets in order to unify the brand and generate a positive image in our new venture. To establish the connection, UA will expand current spokesperson Gisele Bundchen's job description to act as a foreign liaison between both countries.

UA will also expand our social media platforms to connect most effectively with new consumers. Brazil is currently one of the largest users of social media in the world, with approximately 98% of the country using Facebook as of this year (Chao, 2015). Using a variety of platforms and reaching out through a respected figurehead, will initiate strong relationships with Brazilian consumers that will benefit UA in the future.

### Creating the Future

In order to successfully implement each approach to the stakeholders outlined above, UA must allocate a reasonable budget and abide by a strict timeline in order to make measures of success more accessible in the future.

### Budget

UA has allocated roughly \$100 million for our expansion into the Brazilian market (See Fig. 5). This money will be divided into four main parts: the Brazilian Communication Director, the Marketing Team, the Communication Plan, and the Ad Campaign. The communication director's salary will be \$2 million with an additional \$500,000 in benefits that will include health care, wellness and preventative, and life insurance.

The marketing team will be comprised of twenty people who will be paid \$200,000 apiece in salary, totaling to \$4 million. We also have provided our team with an additional million dollars to cover any materials needed in their research and development of our plan. For the Communication Plan, we have put aside \$7 million to pay for any materials we will need for the plan and transportation needed to travel to and from Brazil.

The most expensive component for our expansion into Brazil is our ad campaign, which totals approximately \$83 million. Projected cost for commercials in Brazil to be \$50 million, which is the most expensive part of the ad campaign. Another facet of the campaign is the sponsorships of athletes in Brazil, currently costing us \$30 million. Finally, \$3 million will cover social media and billboards.

*Timeline*

As UA's presence gradually grows in Brazil, the 2016 Olympic Games in Rio de Janiero will give the company another opportunity to expand their brand presence both in Brazil and around the world. To achieve a successful outcome, our team has created an initial one-year plan called the Road to Rio (See Fig. 6). While we will assess the plan's effectiveness following the Olympics, UA will continue implementing communicative measures and advertising in Brazil indefinitely.

Milestones along the Road to Rio include our initial announcement, the start of the Olympics, and the end of the Olympics, followed by the assessment of the plan's success to date. We will begin implementing the plan on August 5, 2015, a year from the 2016 Olympics.

On August 5, Plank will address executive management in a formal meeting, while the communication team will send out memorandums to all current manufacturers. The subsequent meetings, press conferences, and technical development with both groups will last until September 5, 2015.

Beginning September 6, 2015, the team will send formal letters to potential retailers in Brazil and will work with logistics and transitioning the UA brand into each desired store. This transition will require approximately three months, during which time UA sales representatives will be acting as liaisons for any future assistance to the new retailers.

After informing each key stakeholder, we will deploy our exploration team to research Brazil's culture and market to the country. This will last from September 6, 2015 until May 13, 2016, which is about 8 months. Guided by research, design for the Brazilian advertisement campaign will take about 3 months. It will be finialized and revealed to the public at the Olympics and through the use of primarily television and social media platforms.

Finally, for assessment, the team will evaluate the campaign's success following the end of the Olympics. For instance, the analysis will determine if and how much UA's revenues and market share have increased. To consider this initiative successful, UA should realize a 200% increase in market share from an estimated .5% to 1.5% total Apparel and Footwear market share (Euromonitor, 2015). As of now, UA has such a small market share of the Apparel and Footwear market that it is not even listed among the companies currently operating in Brazil.

This communication plan is tailored to the needs of UA as the company seeks to increase profits and recognition on a global scale. Through research of the Brazilian market, this report identified the most effective methods for reaching out to both current and potential stakeholders and maintaining a consistent brand voice and image while immersing the brand in one of the world's fastest-growing economies.

# References

Beekun, R., Stedham, Y., & Yamamura, J. (2003). Business ethics in Brazil and the US: A comparative investigation. *Journal of Business Ethics*, (42), 267–279. Retrieved March 2, 2018

Brazil In The Path Of A Sustainable Future. (2014). *Brazil in the Path of a Sustainable Future // Doing Business in Rio // 1.* Retrieved March 1, 2018, from http://www.ey.com/Publication/vwLUAssets/Estudo_Doing_Business_In_Rio_2014_EY_Brasil/$FILE/LR_doing_business_in_rio.pdf

Chao, L. (2018, February 4). Brazil: The Social Media Capital of the Universe. *The Wall Street Journal.* Retrieved March 3, 2018

Cunha, B., & Rodrigo, D. (n.d.). *Regulatory governance in Brazil: Inconsistent coordination, institutional fragmentation and halfway reforms.* Retrieved February 26, 2018, from http://regulation.upf.edu/exeter-12-papers/Paper.pdf

Export.gov—Welcome to Brazil! (n.d.). Retrieved from http://www.export.gov/brazil/index.asp Gomes, L. (2012, May 16). Brazil's business labyrinth of bureaucracy. Retrieved February 26, 2018, from http://www.bbc.com/news/business-18020623

Sainte Croix, S. (2012). *Middle Class Growth in Brazil.* The Rio Times: English. Retrieved March 2, 2018

Mirabella, L. (2014). Under Armour Launches Brand in Brazil. *The Baltimore Sun.* Retrieved March 2, 2018

# Appendix A: Figures
## Under Armour, Inc.

**Fig. 1**
Source: Passport

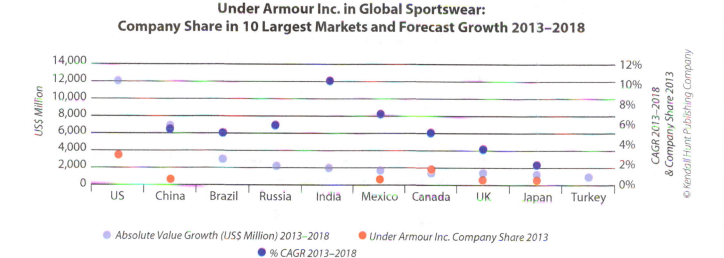

**Under Armour Inc. in Global Sportswear:**
**Company Share in 10 Largest Markets and Forecast Growth 2013–2018**

- Absolute Value Growth (US$ Million) 2013–2018
- Under Armour Inc. Company Share 2013
- % CAGR 2013–2018

**Fig. 2**
Source: Planet Retail

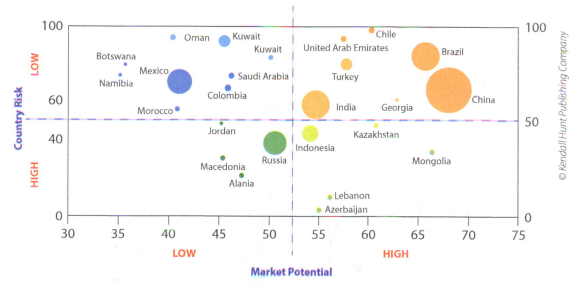

**Fig. 3**
Source: The Economist

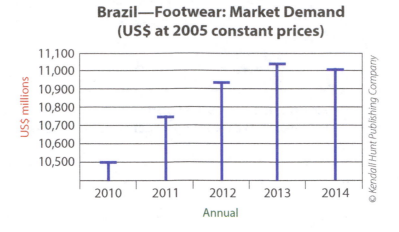

**Brazil—Footwear: Market Demand
(US$ at 2005 constant prices)**

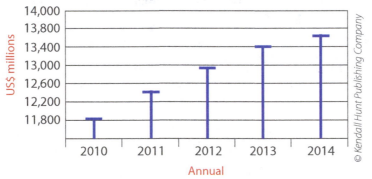

**Brazil—Clothing: Market Demand
(US$ at 2005 constant prices)**

**Fig. 4**
Source: Beekun

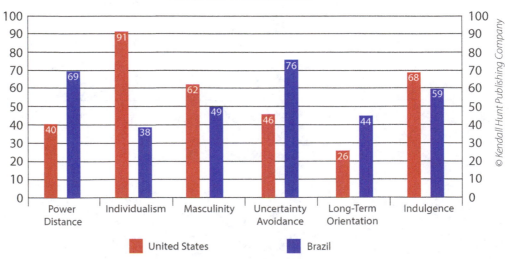

**Cultural Dimensions**

**Fig. 5**

**Brazilian Com. Director**

| | |
|---|---|
| Salary | 2M |
| Benefits | 500,000 |

**Marketing Team (20)**

| | |
|---|---|
| Salary | 4M |
| Other Resources | 1M |

**Communication Plan**

| | |
|---|---|
| Materials | 5M |
| Transportation | 2M |

**Ad Campaign**

| | |
|---|---|
| Commercials | 50M |
| Billboards | 1M |
| Social Media | 2M |
| Sponsorships | 30M |
| | **97.5M** |

**Fig. 6**

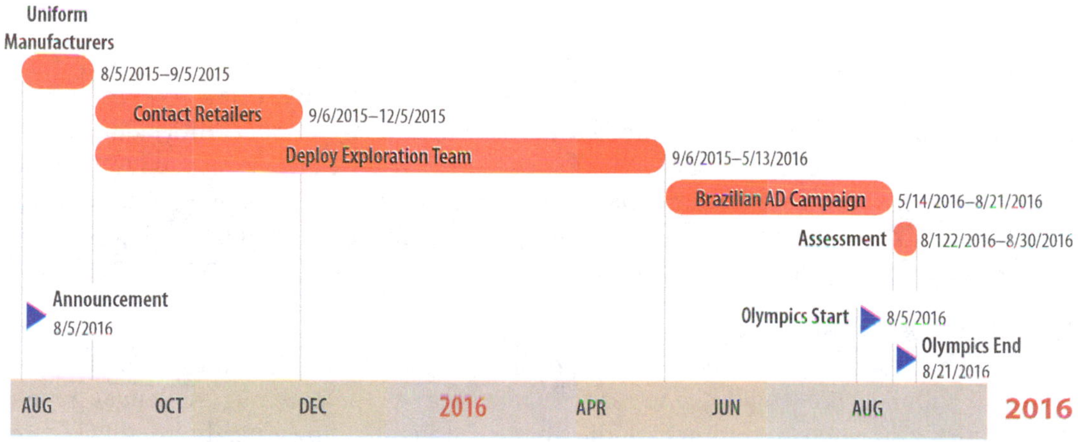

# Appendix B: Memo to Manufacturers

## MEMORANDUM

Date: August 4, 2018
Subject: Development Expansion
To: Under Armour Manufacturers
CC: Under Armour Executives
From: Under Armour, Inc.

In our ongoing pursuit to expand into new markets, we are happy to announce our plans to enter Brazil, the 7th largest market in the world. With our increased commitment to this plan, your manufacturing operation will have the opportunity to maximize production and increase profits. In the following, you will find the key components to our proposal to introduce Under Armour into Brazil. We have identified them as increased labor efforts, production capacity, and ability to secure raw materials.

### Labor

Our company requires that you seek out additional employees to keep up with this expansion. This could include temporary help, but employees who are dedicated in the long term are ideal. Ultimately, we would like to see you develop a strong labor force that will cut down costs in the long run. We see this expansion have a positive impact on your businesses. With increased demand for the products you provide, you will be able to employ others and improve the local economy.

### Production

Our quality assurance managers will need to be assured that you are able to keep up production with the levels that we are predicting. We will assess your capabilities during next month's manufacturing meeting and would like to see you have an increase in productivity by 20–30%. This may involve more than one manufacturer simultaneously producing the same product(s). These expansions in production will allow your manufacturing plants to grow and become a thriving business.

### Raw Materials

Along with labor and production, we will be looking at your relationships with your raw materials supplier. We would like to see the same effort as the previous challenges go into maintaining a strong relationship with the suppliers, thus allowing a steady stream of materials to the factory. We feel this is crucial to uphold the current demand as well as handling the influx of future orders.

Under Armour is excited to take on this new opportunity and are happy to have you with us. We will be staying in close contact with you over the next few weeks and make our final assessment on our next monthly meeting. Our company will continue to expect the same quality and service that it has received in the past. We see a lucrative future for everyone involved in this process, and we feel this is the beginning of an even brighter future for our collaborative efforts.

# Appendix C: Letter to Retailers

Communication Director Under Armour
123 Plank Ave.
Baltimore, Maryland 82001

September 5, 2015

Nathalie Lafont
Casino Guichard
1, Esplanade de France
Saint-Étienne, Rhône-Alpes 42008

Dear Nathalie,

Under Armour, an established American athletic apparel company, has recently decided to expand brand efforts into Latin America, primarily Brazil. Knowing that Casino Guichard is one of the most successful names in Brazilian retail, it is important for us to extend an offer to you first.

We believe that our products can be a great addition to what is offered in your Extra brand storefronts. Having a relatively new and exciting brand to Brazil will prove advantageous for Casino in an extremely competitive apparel retail market. The team at Under Armour has identified three advantages that will prove us to be an invaluable partnership:

- A lower price point than competitors
- Proximity of manufacturing
- A committed support staff

Considering the lower income and tax regulations of Brazil, we understand the need for a lower-priced product. Under Armour offers many products that are of a much lower price point than competitors such as Nike. For example, a pair of Under Armour Men's HIIT Woven Shorts sells for $39.99, while comparable woven training shorts from Nike cost at least $65 on the brand's web store.

One reason we can ensure such low prices is because of our close manufacturing. 40% of our manufacturing is completed in Latin America. With such close proximity to your stores in Brazil, we will be able to cut logistic costs and in turn lower our price points. This will also make it easier for the Extra stores to have the correct product on hand.

It is the employees themselves that set our brand apart. After recently installing a Director of Communication for Latin America, as well as a full marketing team, we are ready to meet the needs of the market and your company. The Director and their staff's sole purpose is to tend to the needs of our Brazilian partners and will be able to help during the transition.

The Under Armour team would like to thank you for your time and consideration. We hope to work with you soon. To reach us, you can contact the Latin America marketing team desk at any time by calling (520) 990-3188.

Sincerely,


Communication Director

This concludes the unit on planning and composing your message. Research, planning, organizing, and writing are key elements to producing a professional document. As with any writing, proofreading and polishing are the final steps to ensure that the finished product is distribution ready and professional. Document design, accurate information, and readily accessible infographics contribute to a high-quality final product tailored to your specific audience.

# Unit 2 References

Conciseness: Reducing wordiness in your writing. (February 2013). Purdue OWL— Online Writing Lab.

Purdue University. Retrieved from https://owl.english.purdue.edu/owl/resource/572/01/

Heath, C., & Heath, D. (2008). *Made to stick: Why some ideas survive and others die.* New York, NY: Random House.

Kamalani Hurley, P. (2007). *The you attitude and reader-centered writing.* Leeward Community College, University of Hawaii. Retrieved from: http://emedia.leeward.hawaii.edu/hurley/modules/mod2/2_docs/you_attitude.pdf

Oliu, W. E., Brusaw, C. T., & Alread, G. J. (2013). Writing that works: Communicating effectively on the job. Boston, MA: Bedford/St. Martin's.

# UNIT 3:
# **Writing Strategies**

# Informative Messages

Much business writing falls under the category of direct messages. Later chapters in this unit will explain persuasive and bad news messages, but this chapter will cover standard informative messaging in correspondence (email or letters) and in report writing.

It is important to note that informative messages do not make recommendations, suggestions, or otherwise offer the opinion of the writer. This is difficult for the novice writer, and some believe impossible for students. Notable grammarian and educator Jeffrey K. Pullum quipped, "No force on earth can prevent undergraduates from injecting opinion," (2009). As a wise master might say, resist you must!

## Overview

Informative messaging means just that: the message is meant to convey information. Common workplace informative messages range from reminding co-workers of a meeting to announcing a new addition to the building, detailing the plans for a merger, and so on.

| ADVANTAGES OF WRITTEN COMMUNICATION | |
| --- | --- |
| Accountability | Mass dissemination |
| Goodwill and image building | Permanent record |
| Legal document | Suitable for long messages |

© Kendall Hunt Publishing Company

Everyday emails are often informative. Most business professionals deal with email all day—both reading and writing them. These emails are often structurally similar. When a structure is understood, reading and writing becomes more effective. Letters have a standard salutation and closing; emails have a subject line and a greeting.

**Figure 1**

Written communication in business is vitally important. Think of the number of emails exchanged between co-workers, from management to staff, and from the C-Suite to the entire company. A company could not function without written communication. This is even truer in this technological age when virtual employees do not even go to a brick-and-mortar building. Face-to-face communication is not always possible, and written messages serve as efficient vehicles for coordinating, organizing, and disseminating information.

Some mistakenly operate on the principle that written messages are the same as verbal messages—only written down. The truth is that written language, often called "book language," is not the same as spoken language. People learn to speak before they learn to write, and this is true in every country and culture.

It takes many years for people to learn to write, and then another decade to learn complex grammatical and punctuation rules. In some countries, like Japan, approximately 2000 kanji (Japanese characters) need to be memorized in order to read a newspaper. Students in Japan have to learn 1000 kanji by sixth grade, so literacy is a much more daunting task in Japanese than it is in the English language.

Written speech differs from spoken language in many ways. One of the most important aspects of the written word is that it is permanent and serves as a record, a way to document exchanges. As such, these can be used in court or during a performance review in the workplace. Since written messages can be retained forever, what and how you write can help you—or hurt you.

Spoken language is full of incomplete thoughts, repetition, and interrupters. When writing, the language used is naturally more formal and correct. When speaking to someone, there are more contextual clues to help navigate the import of the message. You receive clues from tone and body language, and any ambiguity can be cleared up in real time. Not so with the written word. When composing, you have to carefully consider this lack of context and strive for clarity and lack of ambiguity.

Clearly, writing requires a lot of effort and thought, and that is why it is essential to learn the fundamentals of good business writing.

# Prewriting

First, the writer must ask him/herself questions:

1. Who is the audience?
2. What do they **already know** about what I'm writing?
3. What do they **not know**?
4. What do they **need to know**?
5. Would background information help the comprehension of my message?
6. Are next steps necessary to include?

Once you know to whom you are writing, why you are writing, and what the reader needs to know for your message to be fully understood, you need to determine the correct tone to use. Tone is often what identifies an inexperienced business writer: they either write too formally or casually. Determining the proper tone requires that you ask yourself some critical questions:

1. Am I writing up or down the chain of command?
2. Am I writing to peers?
3. Is my message going to upset people?
4. Am I on good terms with the person to whom I am writing?

Answering these questions honestly helps to determine the tone of your message; this is a critical step that should not be overlooked. In the workplace, a poorly worded message can damage your credibility and harm your chances for a promotion.

# Structure

Once you have concluded the prewriting critical thinking described above, it is time to draft your message. Written business messages have standard formats. First, all business writing is single spaced, left justified, and paragraphs are demarcated with a space between paragraphs, not by indenting. This is also called standard block format. Paragraphs should be kept to no more than seven lines—this means lines of text, not sentences. Longer messages will use headings and sub-headings, but more on that later in the section.

**Figure 2** *The internal structure of a written message is key to cohesion and flow.*

© VTT Studio/Shutterstock.com

The introduction and conclusion paragraphs of direct informative messages are fairly formulaic. When communicating across companies, states, countries, and cultures, adhering to a standard allows readers to know what to expect and where to expect it. Standardization is not evidence of a lack of creativity; rather, it increases the probability that your message will be efficient and effective.

By sticking to the structure, you reduce cognitive dissonance in your reader and increase the readability. How does this work? Stories, myths, and even jokes have three parts: a beginning, middle and end. Famous quotes often have three parts:

- *"Life, liberty, and the pursuit of happiness"*
- *"Government of the people, by the people, for the people"*
- *"Friends, Romans, Countrymen"*
- *"Blood, sweat, and tears"*
- *"Location, location, location"*
- *"Father, Son, and Holy Spirit"*
- *"Faith, hope, and charity"*
- *"Mind, body, spirit"*
- *"Stop, look, and listen"*
- *"Sex, lies, and videotape"*
- *"I came, I saw, I conquered"*

The human brain likes threes. Why? Neuroscientists studying Broca's region of the brain, the area responsible for language, have hypothesized that the area is responsible for language, action, and music as they share common syntactic-like structure (Fadiga, Craighero, & D'Ausilio, 2009).

In an article from *Psychology Today*, Dr. Norman Holland explains, "Broca's area may . . . organize putting one action in the middle of two others. Open the door; turn on the light; close the door. Broca's area may be what allows you to organize those three steps to go into a room."

When you write in concise sentences, short paragraphs, and use active verbs and direct, simple language, you are working with the brain's functioning and reducing the cognitive load. Since it recognizes patterns and the simplest pattern is three, business writing—at its simplest structure—is organized into three: introduction, body, and conclusion. Another way to describe it is by the old maxim: Tell me what you are going to tell me. Tell me. Then tell me what you told me.

# Common Organizational Patterns for Informative Messages

There are many ways to effectively structure an informative message. Some of the most common are in the following chart.

| CHRONOLOGICAL | SEQUENCE | COMPARISON | GEOGRAPHY/CATEGORY |
|---|---|---|---|
| Main points are sequenced in order of events to show the progression from start to finish of a series of events. | Main points are organized in the steps or sequence of a procedure or process. | Shows the advantages or disadvantages between two topics highlighting the similarities and/or differences. | Organized by grouping regions, states or countries or by topical categories like investments, sales, or profits. |

# Introductions

The introductory paragraph in a direct informative message tells the reader the point of the message. This is summarized by the acronym BLOT: Bottom Line On Top. This is achieved by incorporating four main points as described in the chart below.

The following is just one way to build an introduction with four simple sentences. Take it as a point of departure or, better yet, use it to break the dreaded "writer's block" by building your introduction one sentence at a time.

1. **CONTEXT/FRAME (FIRST SENTENCE)** Frame your document by describing the situation as best you can in one sentence. What led up to the writing of this document? What background information does the audience need to understand what you're about to discuss? How does the situation relate to the audience? Why should he or she care?

2. **PURPOSE/RELEVANCE (SECOND SENTENCE)** Now drop in your purpose statement. Why are you writing this document, and why are you sending it to this particular audience (rather than to someone else)? What is the most important thing you want your audience to know? This is a broad statement overviewing the content of the document.

3. **WIIFY (THIRD SENTENCE)** "What's In It For You," meaning the reader. Why should they read this? How is this going to help them? How can they use the information that you are giving them? Deliver the goods. Answer the question you raise in your purpose statement. What is the most important thing you want your audience to know? This can be the key takeaway from your research, a summary of your analysis, or it can be a recommendation.

4. **FORECAST (FOURTH SENTENCE)** Provide a road map. Specifically detail the topics that will be covered and in what order they will be presented. In a longer document, these topics can be used as section headings. The clearer the forecast, the easier to organize your document—and the easier it will be for the reader to find what s/he needs.

The goal of this paragraph is to tell the reader *about the document*, not to begin giving details from the body.

Think of it as a sticky note that you slap on a document, say a report, to let the recipient know what this particular document is. It answers these reader questions:

1. *Why is this on my desk/in my inbox? Remind me. Did I ask for it? (Frame/Context)*
2. *What is this about? (Purpose)*
3. *Why should I read this? How is it going to help me? (WIIFY)*
4. *What specifically is in this document? (Forecast)*

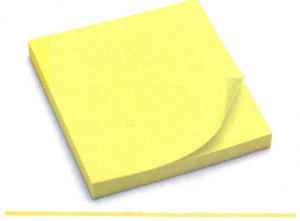

**Figure 3**  *The introduction of a direct informational message is like a sticky note that tells the recipient what the document is about.*

## Practice: Introductions

*Here is an example of a good introduction that includes all four necessary elements:*

*As we discussed in last week's meeting, our team will be producing a financial overview to assist in the introduction of our new fitness technology. This memo is primarily valuable for analyzing the financial impact that this technology could have on Under Armour by examining previous ventures into new markets. This document will provide financial information, highlight recent trends, and make predictions about new technologies.*

*Take a look at the following introductions and identify which of the four elements are missing:*

A. *I am glad that we all made the decision to choose Tesla Motors Inc. for our BCOM group project preferred company. Please take time to review the information below, as doing so will be crucial to the success of our team at this year's Case Competition. Specifically, this document will analyze Tesla Motors Inc. management by first looking at its history, recent changes in strategy, and trends in Tesla management that will influence the future of the corporation.*

B. *This document contains information regarding the recent health scare that Chipotle has experienced, and it will explain the severity and condition of the situation. Staying informed will dictate Chipotle's action in the coming months, actions that will impact stakeholders and profits. Included in this report will be a summary of Chipotle's health awareness, the E. Coli situation, and Chipotle's permanent and useful solutions moving forward.*

C. *As you requested, our team finished this report about analytical people. Analytics fit well on a team with Amiables because they look for specifics and details that the Amiable often miss. In general, this report will reduce turnover rate and create a better work environment by explaining how best to work with an Analytic. You will find a lot of important information on this report about Analytics.*

D. *At our last meeting, you asked for an introduction of one of the styles in the People Styles book. After you read this introduction, you will understand how to work with the Amiable style of people in your company. Then, this document will illustrate summary of Amiable style, two keys to understand analytical style, and how the Amiables deal with other styles.*

*Thus you can see the importance of a well-organized, to the point, clearly structured introduction. It sets up everything that is to follow, helps keep you on track as you write, and lets the reader know what to expect.*

# Conclusions

Because the structure of conclusions is so tightly tied to introductions, they are explained here before the body of the message.

The conclusion, like the introduction, should offer no new facts, data, or information on the topic covered in the body. It should summarize the highlights of the content. A conclusion also has a standard structure:

1. **RESTATE THE FORECAST (FIRST SENTENCE)** Take the last line—the forecast—from the introduction and repeat it here to remind the reader of the main topics that were just covered.

2. **REPEAT THE BLOT (SECOND SENTENCE)** Remind the reader of the gist of the content. Repeat the key takeaway. Keep this short and to the point. This is a broad statement highlighting the most salient information from the document.

3. **INVITE INQUIRY (THIRD SENTENCE)** It is always polite to let the reader know they can and should contact you if they have any questions or need anything further from you. You could also take the opportunity to remind them of next steps if that is relevant.

4. **PROVIDE CONTACT INFO (FOURTH SENTENCE)** Provide your contact information. Even if the reader already has this, it is considerate to include so that it is easy for them to either call or email without having to look up anything.

Here is an example of a well-constructed, concise conclusion that followed the example of the introductory paragraph in the previous section:

*This document provided UA's financial information and detailed recent industry trends. It also provided predictions for the impact that new fitness technology could have. Please email me at teamalpha@email.arizona.edu or call me at (520) 555-1212 if you have any questions or concerns.*

## Practice: Conclusions

*Read the following conclusion paragraphs written by actual students and identify the missing and/or unnecessary elements:*

A. *I hope that the previous sections provided a thorough overview of Chipotle's competitive environment in the food and service industry. Feel free to ask me any questions regarding my research, and share any other trends or opportunities for Chipotle that you have discovered.*

B. *Mattel is one of the strongest toy companies in the world, and have supplied fun for many generations. Though they may have had a down turn in Barbie revenue does not mean that were just going to stand by and let her get neglected. Mattel realized that the competitors were starting to develop an edge on them and if they wanted to get back in the game they were going to have to do some remodeling. After the renovation people have all different types of Barbie's to choose from. Will Barbie always be around? I would say at least for another 100 years. The reason for this is because Mattel's loyalty to their products. I believe this to be true because though there are fluctuations within the toy industry Barbie is a staple for Mattel and will continue to be.*

E. *Tesla's financial goal is to achieve long-term, sustained profitability. It is my opinion that Tesla Motors and its CEO Elon Musk have set themselves up to achieve these goals in the near future, and while their financial statistics are not promising in the short run, they show confidence in their company and promise of large amounts of growth in the long run. Feel free to contact me with any further inquiries you might have at teamtesla@email.arizona.edu.*

F. *Costco has seen tremendous success in Taiwan where it has little competition, a solid reputation, and solid profit numbers. Costco's success in Taiwan bodes well for expanding its operation into similar emerging markets like Brazil. I can be reached at goodemployee@costco.com or on my cell phone.*

## Body

Whether you are writing a short memo or composing a long report, the introduction and conclusion can be written before the body. When you break writing down into the three sections, it is much easier to stay organized. Organizing according to this simple structure makes writing less of an exercise in creativity because you know what you will be writing about and in what order.

Body paragraphs contain the following elements: Claims, Evidence, and Reasoning, or CER. The opening sentence should make a claim of some sort. You can think of it as an umbrella covering everything that comes underneath. Next, you support your claim with evidence that offers proof of its validity. This is where you use information and data from research. Finally, you may bolster your claim by giving specific examples. The last sentence should quickly sum the gist of the paragraph by reasoning your way through it. You must make sense of the information so that your readers can follow your logic without having to sort it out for themselves.

You can skip this final summative/reasoning sentence if the next paragraph is going to continue on the same topic. If that is the case, you will want to begin the next paragraph with a transitional word or phrase to signal the reader that the same topic is being continued.

| CLAIM | • Main point |
| | • Overview |
| EVIDENCE | • Research data |
| | • Examples |
| REASONING | • Make sense of data |
| | • Wrap it up or transition |

Here is a simple paragraph that clearly illustrates the structure:

*Many factors contribute to a lowering of the water tables in city aquifers. (claim) The removal of rock from mining operations, oil and gas extraction, and drainage of marshlands all lead to a problem called subsidence—the gradual sinking in of land. In Tucson, the fast removal of* groundwater causes the water lower in the aquifer to be extracted. This lower level of water has a higher salinity, tastes worse, and costs more to extract. (*evidence*) Overall, subsidence is caused by a complex combination of factors and adversely affect water tables across the United States. (*reasoning*).

## Practice: Proving It

*With each of the topic sentences below, list three pieces of evidence that provide proof of the claim.*

A. *Many factors contribute to maintaining a healthy weight.*

B. *Artificial Intelligence is used in many common technologies.*

C. *Military transport and the power grid are hardened against the threat of an Electromagnetic Pulse, or EMP.*

*After a topic sentence, choose a support sentence, then explain it with more detail, and then give an example. Essentially, these get more granular, as is shown in the example below*

Penguins come in many shapes and sizes.

   The Fairy penguin is the smallest on earth.

      Measuring only 16 inches tall, it lives in Australia.

         It comes out of the water at sunset to return to its burrow on Phillips Island outside of Melbourne.

Once you have crafted the introduction, body, and conclusion of your message, and you have edited and proofread it, go through the checklist below to make sure you have all the elements.

1. Framing statement
2. Purpose statement
3. WIIFY sentence
4. Detailed forecasting information
5. Claims at paragraph beginning
6. Information-filled paragraphs
7. Sufficient evidence, data, and examples in the paragraphs
8. Reasoning last sentence or transition to the next paragraph
9. Conclusion begins with a restatement of the forecast
10. Conclusion highlights the key takeaway
11. Message ends by inviting inquiry and giving contact information

Now that you are familiar with the structure of messages, it is time to describe some common types of workplace messages you might be asked to write.

# Communicating to Persuade

The art of persuasion is an ancient one. Dating back to Aristotle, the line of argument, or the act of persuasion, is familiar to most of us. Any time you take a position to convince someone to change their beliefs, feelings, or actions, you are engaging in the art of persuasion. Unlike the informational approach, where your primary objective is to shape and present data, when you enter into a persuasive strategy, you are actively trying to drive or advocate a particular outcome. This is where things start to get a little complicated and a lot more strategic in design. Perhaps this is why persuasion is often considered more art than science.

*Logos*, *Pathos*, and *Ethos* were Aristotle's words for specific persuasive appeals. In contemporary business contexts, these are still readily used, just under different names. Ethos refers to credibility, which depends on the degree to which your audience deems you trustworthy and competent. To influence others, you must impress them as someone who has a reasonable level of expertise or experience on the topic and has the audience members' best interests in mind. It is critical that both characteristics are present; having only one or the other does not work well in most situations. Imagine yourself as a salesperson when delivering a persuasive message.

**CLASSIC PERSUASIVE APPEALS**

**Ethos (credibility)**: Appeals to author's competence and character

**Pathos (emotion)**: Appeal to values and beliefs through emotional connection

**Logos (logic/facts)**: Appeal to reason through proven facts and logic

Most customers do not want to buy from those they perceive as lacking a sense of honesty and character, no matter how well informed that seller may appear. If a seller seems like a very good person, but demonstrates clear deficiencies in content mastery, this, too, proves problematic for the buyer. The most influential communicators are solid in subject matter and sincere in their motives. This is second nature to some people, but for others, it may entail self-reflection, ethical discernment, skill development in self-presentation strategies, social cognition (awareness of others), or a combination of some or all of the above. Be strategic in your self-presentation; the quality and tone of your written communication directly affects others' perceptions.

To build a convincing message, you'll need to leverage a credible set of evidence relevant to the audience and the case you are making. Your ability to use logic (Logos) and reasoning is critical to creating a persuasive case. Howard Gardner (2006) describes seven "levers" or logical elements used in effective persuasive appeals. Why pull your sled uphill when you can start at the top and zoom down? When you select data, think of the levers as available tactics to persuade your audience. Logical arguments usually feature a well-balanced integration of claims, evidence and reasoning. The claim presents the assertion or proposition, and the evidence offers examples or cases from which the assertion was generated. Reasoning ties the two together by explaining how or why that evidence soundly supports the claim.

**LEVERS**

Gardner (2006) identifies seven factors or levers that influence and persuade.

1. **Real world events**—similar "real life" examples
2. **Reason**—logical discourse
3. **Research**—fact-based evidence gathered from credible sources
4. **Resonance**—value or belief-based framing and evidence
5. **Re-description**—multiple and varied representations of similar evidence
6. **Resources/rewards**—audience benefit
7. **Resistance**—reframed rebuttal

With data in place and a sense of credibility, you're ready to appeal to your audience's emotions and values (Pathos). As a savvy consumer, you are probably highly aware when a marketing campaign appeals to your emotions. How does Apple produce all those "feels" around a product? Simple. They appeal to a consumer's emotions—loyalty, excitement, competition, etc. When you have a strong emotional attachment that drives you to purchase a product, you are succumbing to an emotional appeal. Emotions are a central feature of our existence, and they are influential in our decision-making processes. As a communicator, you must identify relevant emotional appeals and apply them in a balanced, ethical manner. Though powerful, emotional appeals are not adequate substitutes for credibility or logic.

When you put all the appeals together, you'll find that you have a substantial and powerful platform to convince an audience of your position. Your logical structure (another form of Logos) will support your ability to build and sustain your claims. In this instance, a strategic structural approach helps you to build a persuasive message. You can do this using a direct or indirect approach as illustrated in the sections below.

# Identifying Types of Persuasive Messages

Persuasive messages are ever-present in your personal and professional communications, and you most likely receive and send them every day. Aside from the ever-pervasive advertisements encountered through web, mobile, and print media, persuasive appeals play a key role in daily decision making. They may range anywhere from asking to borrow a colleague's pen to pitching a multi-million-dollar deliverable to a potential client. Some common applications are listed below:

- Application for employment or promotion
- Proposal for a project or service
- Request for a meeting
- Request for information, support, or special consideration
- Letter of recommendation
- Consumer-targeted sales or copy messaging
- Critique or evaluation
- Recommendations to address a particular challenge

This above list is a small sampling of the types of business messages you may employ as a working professional. It is important to note that communication needs are dynamic and nuanced. Your skill in persuasion is a critical competency that will aid you in crafting appropriate, effective business correspondence and composing formal or informal reports and proposals.

# Understanding Audience Responses to Persuasive Appeals

Based on your persuasive purpose, you will temper your message with politeness cues to demonstrate regard for your audience and, in turn, increase the likelihood of your desired outcome. Some requests, like one in which you ask to borrow a colleague's pen, do not call for high levels of persuasive finesse. Low-stakes requests—those that require little or no physical, mental, or emotional efforts from your audience—require little more than a brief and respectful line of text. However, the more complex and labor-intensive your ask, the greater care you must take in framing the message. Add to that factors such as whether the message is solicited or unexpected, consistent or inconsistent with audience values or preferences, and aligned with or contrary to your audience members' opinions, and you have a number of variables for which to account as you craft a correspondence or report.

## Receptive Audiences

Receptive audiences are generally supportive of your purpose or interests. From the outset, you can expect little resistance or reservation when delivering your message; however, you should not take anything for granted or come across as entitled or assumptive. Such missteps are often avoided through skillful use of tone, which we will address later in this section. Receptive audiences are more likely to grant your request or adopt recommended actions.

## Resistant Audiences

If your requested recommendations prove inconvenient or unimportant to your audience, your first challenge resides in motivating your recipients to first read your message. Unlike receptive audiences, resistant ones are less likely to take interest in your purpose. However, unlike receptive readers, resistant audiences are more likely to question your credibility.

## Matching Approach to Potential Audience Response

Should you be direct, and come right out and say what you want in the first paragraph? Or, should you be indirect, and build your case before making your request? The difference between the two is where you place your bottom line. In a persuasive document, the bottom line is your request or your recommendation (also called your "ask"). What are you asking your audience to consider or do? If you expect little resistance, you can come right out and make your request in the first paragraph. But if you expect more resistance, you need to move your bottom line down and make your case first.

# Using a Direct Persuasive Approach

Direct persuasive messages are most effective when addressing a receptive audience. You may also choose this approach if receivers are time-deprived or if you know they prefer direct communication.

**Frame and Forecast in the Introduction**

- Frame for your audience to provide context
- State your purpose—present the request
- Forecast information

**Position and Present Rationale (Body)**

- Provide evidence and reasoning for claims in well-tailored, logical sequence
- Anticipate reader's potential points of resistance and counter with credible facts that matter to them

**Restate Request and Call Audience to Action (Conclusion)**

- Make action or response convenient and immediate for reader with needed contact information and next steps

## Direct Persuasive Introduction

The introduction of a direct persuasive message should follow the same basic "bottom line on top" structure discussed earlier in this chapter. First, provide some context to frame the document. State your purpose (present your request) in the first few sentences of your introduction, and then, forecast the key points of your message. Simple, right? In many ways, yes. However, the tone in your delivery plays an important role in whether even receptive audiences respond—more on that in a bit.

## Direct Persuasive Body

The body of a direct persuasive message should explain or support your request. In the body, offer the audience supporting information, facts, details, or additional explanations to clarify your request or directive. This may include the reasons for your request or recommendation. Regardless of audience members' attitudes, you can create interest by highlighting how your proposed action will yield direct and indirect benefits for your audience. Additionally, you might counter potential points of resistance by emphasizing relevant facts to clarify key features of your proposal.

You will craft a great number of business messages throughout your career, and your ability to assess your audience and tailor your message accordingly is essential to building strong professional relationships and advancing your initiatives. Be strategic in the way you structure the body content. Like any other direct message, it should reflect a clear, logical, and accessible design; however, you must choose the appropriate sequence of information, level of detail, degree of formality, and integration of levers for each situation and audience. The table below notes some common organizational patterns associated with persuasive messages. These patterns may be adjusted or combined based on situational needs.

### *Common Organizational Patterns for Direct Persuasive Messages*

There are many ways to effectively structure a persuasive message. Some of the most common are in the following chart.

| PROBLEM/SOLUTION | SBAR | COMPARATIVE ADVANTAGES | TOPICAL |
|---|---|---|---|
| Main points are sequenced to first illustrate a problem or need, then offer a proposed solution to address expressed needs. | Main points are sequenced to present Situation, Background, Analysis, and Recommendations. | Main points demonstrate value of proposed action by comparing and eliminating alternative options. | Main points each address a key persuasive argument and are sequenced by author to highlight strongest claims. |

## Direct Persuasive Conclusions

The conclusion of a direct persuasive message should call your audience to action. You should begin by restating your request and you may briefly reiterate key benefits to your audience. To ensure you obtain the desired results, make the action convenient and immediate for your audience, with needed contact information or next steps. Depending on the urgency of your message and relationship with the recipient, you may provide a deadline by which he or she should respond.

# Direct Persuasive Examples

The following examples illustrate how some of these strategies are applied in correspondence and informal reports.

Direct Persuasive Example 1: Response to Interdepartmental request for vendor recommendation.

To: Operations Management Team
From: Communication Strategy Team
Subject: Shipping Partner Recommendation
Date: February 3, 2018

Thank you for inviting the Strategic Communications team's recommendation regarding Fistbump's preferred shipping partner. In light of their shipping failures during last year's holiday season, we propose management discontinue service with Company X and have all orders fulfilled through a different logistics company. We share in your interest in providing customers with efficient, dependable service, and we are confident this transition will help us avoid future issues and improve the Fistbump experience for our customers.

> Introduction frames the message, states the ask, and forecasts the problem/solution sequence

> Highlights senders' and audience's shared values.

Last holiday season, Company X failed to meet delivery deadlines for over one third of all orders placed in December and January. Our credibility suffered as retailers resorted to using their own funds to issue shipping discounts, and many disappointed customers expressed their frustration through popular social media platforms. Unfortunate events like the holiday shipping breakdown require a quick recovery, and by taking active steps to prevent future incidents, we communicate our dedication to total customer satisfaction.

> Explains problem, demonstrates need

Selecting a new shipping partner will

- Reduce costs associated with shipping refunds and product returns
- Demonstrate Fistbump's commitment to convenience and consistency
- Improve Fistbump's reputation on social media and company review sites
- Maintain Fistbump's loyal customer and retail partner bases

> Presents solution and related benefits

> Applies bulleted list design to draw attention to benefits

These benefits are meaningful and they may outweigh some or all of the costs related to securing a new shipping contract.

In the interest of our continued growth, the Communication Strategy team advises management to designate a new preferred shipping partner to underscore Fistbump's credibility and commitment to customer satisfaction. Please contact us at stratcomm@fistbump.com with questions or concerns, and keep our team informed of your decision.

> Restates the ask and appropriately calls audience to action

To: Have Mina
From: Intern
Subject: WebStore's Holacratic Shift
Date: February 3, 2018

Thank you for providing me with the readings on Holacracy and for requesting my perspective on Web-Store's choice to adopt this unconventional organizational style. This analysis is intended to assist you in communicating this concept to clients. Though WebStore's move to Holacratic management caused some confusion, it was ultimately a good choice for the company. The new management style fits the WebStore. com vision, aligns with most of their already successful practices, and serves to create a more cohesive employee base.

**Holacracy Fits the WebStore Culture**

WebStore is known for its corporate counter-culture. According to the *Atlantic*, the company has a reputation for unconventional work practices. For instance, they offer each new hire four thousand dollars to reject the job offer. This is one of many quirky yet strategic moves designed to hire and retain dedicated, like-minded employees and create buy-in from its members. Given WebStore's already unique approach to business, it may be the perfect environment in which to test new management designs.

**Holacracy is Not Radically Different from WebStore's Former Management Policies**

According to Steve Denning of *Forbes* magazine, Holacracy is not a dramatic shift in organizational hierarchy; rather, it is simply a new approach to managing those hierarchies. Denning argues that despite role shifts, like the elimination of the word "manager" from job titles, people still operate in managerial capacities. The shift from more inclusive language may serve to encourage a culture of openness and accessibility more than it serves to change leadership roles. The new approach does not radically alter WebStore's business model, but it does introduce a new frame for how work is described.

**Holacracy May Increase Employee Commitment**

When WebStore's CEO, Carrie Ma, announced the shift to Holacrocy, she asked employees to adopt the practice or take advantage of a three-moth severance and healthcare package to find a job about which they could be passionate. *Business Insider* magazine reported that a large number, thirty percent, opted to leave the company. Though this caused widespread skepticism among investors and analysts, it is too early to assert the exodus was a negative consequence. It is very possible that this process eliminated unen-thused, under-committed, or uninterested employees and maintained a core of high-performing workers better suited to help WebStore grow.

Though controversial, WebStore's decision to adopt Holacracy was a bold choice that will likely benefit the company in the long run. WebStore is a great testing ground for new practices, and the shift is not as profound as it seems. This transition caused some concern, but it helped them retain a solid core of dedicated employees. This case demonstrates that WebStore's shift to Holacracy was the right choice. Thank you for the opportunity to share my thoughts on this interesting case study. Please contact me if I can provide any additional information.

---

Introduction frames message, states position, and forecasts main points which are arranged topically.

Author integrates a WIIFY (what's in it for you) statement to bolster purpose.

Author uses headings to highlight key claims.

Author attributes information to sources.

Conclusion restates claim, summarizes main points, and includes an appropriate call to action for the nature of the message.

# Using an Indirect Persuasive Approach

If any of the following are true, consider using an indirect strategy:

1. Your audience has not asked you to prepare this document for them;
2. Your request requires audience members' time, energy, or resources;
3. You are not sure whether they will agree with you;
4. You have reason to believe that they will disagree with you;
5. You want to play it safe and build your case before you make your request.

If your document is unsolicited and you are not sure that your audience will agree with you, then take the indirect approach and build your case before making your request. When in doubt, use the indirect approach. The next two parts of this section will help you organize your document successfully and sequence the information you need to present.

The indirect approach to persuasive messaging requires a bit more skill and finesse. This type of a message usually requires some advance planning to truly align with your audience and position your reader to act. Use an indirect approach in persuasive messages when addressing a potentially resistant audience. This kind of message is often developed using the AIDA strategy.

| AIDA (A STRATEGY FOR INDIRECT PERSUASIVE MESSAGES) | |
| --- | --- |
| **ATTENTION & ALIGNMENT** | Build common ground with the audience by referencing common values. Pique interest with an engaging audience-centered appeal. |
| **INTEREST & INFORMATION** | Create a sense of interest by offering relevant information and details; set the stage by supporting your impending request. |
| **DEFLECT RESISTANCE & DISCUSS DIRECT BENEFITS** | Anticipate points of audience resistance, and counter with information. Identify and express how your request will benefit the audience directly. |
| **ACTION** | Make your request for audience action. Provide immediate opportunity for audience response. |

Most audiences are very sensitive to a "sales" approach, and your tone can inadvertently cause the audience to resist your message or question your credibility. A flat out "sell" makes most of us suspicious. AIDA strategy helps you present content in a compelling, persuasive manner by sequencing your information strategically.

# Introduction

## Alignment and Attention

In your first few sentences, get the audience's attention by building common ground. Refer to shared values and interests, mention a commonality, or compliment them on a recent achievement. Be sincere and balanced in your approach. If you seem excessively complimentary or overly familiar, your recipient may interpret your statement as inauthentic. To effectively align with your audience, focus on them and avoid trite, meaningless clichés. Most importantly, do not reveal your request—the indirect approach places the bottom line on bottom, i.e., toward the end of the message. Before you make your "ask," you must build your case by presenting information and direct benefits.

# Body

## Interest and Information

In this section, present information about your product, service, or situation. Make it relevant for your reader or listener, and highlight details that will likely interest them. Remember, you haven't yet revealed your request; you are presenting data to help your audience understand your product, service, etc. In the next section, you will explain how your product, service, etc., directly benefits your audience members, so provide a basis on which you can make such claims.

Be specific in your description and again, frame the information to the interests of your audience members. Use descriptive language and provide details that may pique the audience's interest. This section should support the next part of your message: direct benefits and resistance deflection.

## Direct Benefits and Deflection

Before you present your request, explain how your product or initiative will benefit your audience, and do your best to pre-emptively quell their potential concerns. To do this successfully, describe what readers or listeners will gain by supporting or complying with your yet-to-be-revealed request. Think about it from your audience members' perspectives; explain what is in it for them, not what's in it for you or your company.

Focus on how the information benefits audience members personally. What's in it for them? Indirect benefits like saving the company money rarely inspire action. In addition to discussing direct benefits, use this section to deflect points of resistance.

Once again, think from your audience members' perspectives. Are there potential points of resistance or areas of concern that could cause opposition? If there are points of resistance to anticipate (and deflect), you'll want to be careful not to make over-stated assumptions. Nothing puts off a reader faster than an assumption you make about their thinking, and you can accidentally plant more points of resistance. For example, "You might think the price point is a little high . . ." When in fact the audience wasn't thinking that at all; after receiving your message, however, you can bet they are now. Frame deflection statements in a positive tone, and minimize the inconvenient or undesirable facets of your plan.

Be strategic in your approaches to alignment, information, direct benefits and deflection. These steps lead into the final element of your message: the request for audience action.

# Conclusion

## Action

Now that you've aligned, informed, deflected resistance and identified direct benefits, you can finally make your request and call your audience to action. The bottom line—your "ask"—should appear for the first time here.

Make the actions as easy to carry out as possible. Think about the strategy of the car dealership that sends out keys to everyone in the community with the message "Come on down on

Saturday. This key starts one of the cars on our lot—if you find it, you'll win the car!" With a key in your hand, you might be more inclined to drive on over and give a car a test drive (which was probably the real intent of the message in the first place). Be thinking about making the next step to "yes" as easy as possible for your audience.

You don't need a fancy giveaway or a fun prop to make your action easy and immediate. Present your request, then tell your audience how and when you'd like a response. It is critical that you make this step clear and provide all the necessary information and resources to facilitate your readers' next steps. Avoid uncertain, vague calls to action.

**Indirect Persuasive Example 1: Request for financial support**

Tina Van Smith
66 Big Train St
Tucson, AZ 85721

February 2, 2014

Mayor Colin Kline
1 City Hall Square
Tucson, AZ 85701

Dear Mr. Kline,

On behalf of orgnaization X, we congratulate you as the new Mayor of Tucson. We appreciate your dedication to the growth, safety, infrastructure, and people of Tucson. Organization X also cares about the enrichment of Tucson residents. I am writing to introduce you to our new membership program catered to lover-income patrons.

This lower-income patron membership program aims to reduce crime rates in Tucson, but enriching the lives of Tucson residents through exposure to the arts. Research has shown that poverty is directly related to crime. Tucson has a high poverty rate of over 20%; this program is an opportunity to reduce the poverty and crime rates in the city. This initiative will allow lower-income patrons to have the opportunity to be better involved in the Tucson community.

Enriching the lives of Tucson residents will also lead to positive publicity for you. In turn, more people will be educated about your initiatives and will want to support you. Your support of these efforts will allow you to become a more proactive figure in Tucson. Most importantly, through this venture, Tucson will become a better city.

We would like to partner with you on this new program. In order to make this iniative a success, we need funds to subsidize discounted membership rates for lower income patrons. We ask for your assistance to help underwrite this program. Please email me at director@artsong.com for more information. I look forward to hearing from you soon.

Sincerely,

*This students uses a letter to send an indirect persuasive message to an individua outside the writer's organization.*

*Alignment – presents a common goal and gives the reader a reason to keep reading.*

*Information – provides key information based on the audience's needs and wants.*

*Direct Benefit – shows reader what they can gain.*

*Call to Action – makes ask and provides next steps.*

## Indirect Persuasive Example 2: Wellness program participation encouragement message

28 December 2017

BeWell, Inc. Employees
90 E First Ave
Rahway, New Jersey, 07165
(908) 423-1000

Dear BeWell Team Members,

Builds common ground by expressing shared values

As a company, we constantly strive for a healthier future. Every day, we take part in improving the health and well-being of people around the world. Just as we enhance our customers' lives, we support your family's healthy lifestyle habits. A healthier body and mind has been proven to create higher levels of happiness and satisfaction in and outside of work. As we aspire to be the best healthcare company in the world, we want to provide you with the healthy work-life balance you deserve.

Demonstrates regard for reader and readers' families

Recognizes reader's needs and entitlements

Provides information relevant to upcoming "ask," and highlights points of interests for audience

Every year, more and more people incorporate physical activity into their daily schedules. Since 2013, physical fitness has increased among adults in America. This comes as no surprise; people who live healthier are happier, longer living, and suffer from fewer health-related issues (Hyber, 2017). The Employee Wellness Program (EWP) at BeWell offers you and your family completely free memberships to a select group of fitness centers. Membership to these centers includes access to gym equipment, exercise classes, and nutrition consultations with on-site dieticians.

Presents direct benefits

Not only does BeWell's EWP better your health, it provides a return on your investment. Apex Health, company similar to our own, saved $120 million on healthcare costs in ten years as a result of their EWP. The money we save from our EWP can be allocated to employee reward programs. For instance, savings can be applied to increase base vacation time or enhance other incentive programs. Earning another vacation day is much better than taking a sick day.

Call to action is clear, easy, and immediate

More than anything, BeWell cares about the improved well-being of each and every one of our employees. Our Employee Wellness Program benefits your family and our BeWell family as a whole. We want you to be happy with yourself, your health, and your work-life balance. Start the new year out with a free gym membership and commitment to regular exercise. Please visit BeWellemploywellness.com before January 15th to register for the EWP. It's time to start living right—we are all in this together.

Be Well,

Human Resources Department
BeWell & Company, Inc.

# Tailoring Your Tone for Persuasive Messages

In this text, we often refer to framing as a means of contextualizing your document; however, framing—the perspective from which you tell a story—carries through your entire message and quietly informs your reader about you as an author. It provides key data points for readers as they assess your credibility: your competence and your character. Attend to both what you say and how you say it; consider what your message implies about your intentions and priorities. Frame your message and mind your manners; poorly executed tone will undercut quality content.

## Avoid Implied Entitlement

It is very off-putting when communicators make assumptions. In the example below, the author requests, or in the pre-revised message, demands an informational interview with a relative stranger.

### Before Revision

Hello Freda,

I asked Jeff to connect us because I am very interested in consulting. I am a second-year MBA student, and I am looking for a position with an established firm. Given your career path, I'm sure you have valuable tips and insights I can use in interviews. I would like to set up a quick, fifteen-minute call so I can ask you some questions about your experience in the field. My first interview is in a week, so I need to talk before next Thursday. Thanks so much. I look forward to hearing from you soon.

Warm Regards

| Lacks "you" attitude |
| Self-centered perspective |
| Ineffective attempt to lessen inconvenience as sender already assumes reader will comply |
| Presumes reader will agree |
| Insincere |
| Undeserved expectation of prompt response |

### After Revision

Hello Freda,

Thank you for accepting my LinkedIn invitation. I am a friend of Jeff Carol's, and he speaks very highly of you and your work in project management. As a second year MBA student, I am focused on furthering my knowledge of the field and developing an industry-relevant skillset. Having read and enjoyed your white paper on best practices, I am exceedingly interested in your approach. Your system for team reporting exemplifies a shrewd combination of convention and creativity. If you are willing and your schedule permits, I would greatly appreciate an opportunity to learn more about your experience as a successful project manager. Please let me know if you are open to a fifteen-minute phone or Skype meeting in the near or distant future. I realize your time is valuable and imagine it's very limited, so I appreciate your consideration either way.

Warm Regards,

| Intro demonstrates appreciation, builds common ground and rapport |
| Sender implies genuine interest and demonstrates author's intellectual curiosity |
| Thoughtful recognition of reader's work |
| Request is framed as a request, not a demand |
| Recognizes importance of reader's time and energy |

# Respect Readers' Autonomy

Few people enjoy being told how to think, and fewer appreciate having their decision-making power reduced to someone else's orders. Do not lead your audience with a heavy hand. Instead, recognize their agency as free thinkers. Compose a quality argument, and let the reader draw his or her own conclusion. Also, avoid implicit messages that assume your readers' thoughts, preferences, or values.

## Before Revision

Arrogantly assumes sender will dictate audience response

Unnecessarily presumptive and self flattering

Reject's readers' right to draw their own conclusions

This proposal is submitted in response to the Development Team's call for suggestions, and it will convince you to choose a cloud-based service for our data storage. I have conducted ample research to help you decide this is the best choice for our company's needs.

## After Revision

Demonstrates due diligence on the author's part

Objective tone boost's author's credibility

Acknowledges recipient's key concerns

After a survey of relevant materials and consideration of available options, I composed the following recommendation to address our data storage needs. All potential solutions present benefits and drawbacks; however, my research suggests cloud-based storage is our company's best option for logging data, ensuring security, and providing employees a user-friendly interface.

## Before Revision

Gross generalization

Unfounded assumption

Another gross generalization and hasty assumption

We all love smartphones. In fact, you use yours so often you probably can't remember what life was like before you had one. Everyone knows that an investment this important should be protected, and that is why we created Prosurance—the most comprehensive insurance available for smart phone owners.

## After Revision

Statement is more reasonable in its reach: It does not speak for all people or readers

Dramatic generalization more acceptable given the attribution to some, not all people

Invites audience to identify with this group and may spark interest in info to follow

Some people love their smartphones so much that they don't want to think about living in a world where phone, camera, game, email, text, video, and web browsing capabilities require access to more than one device. We created Prosurance for those people. It's the most comprehensive insurance available for mobile device owners, and it assures users they'll never go a day without their smartphone.

# Maintain an Objective Tone

Your message is only as effective as your audiences' perceptions of your credibility. Even when addressing a receptive audience, it's important to maintain an objective tone. Readers may question an author's authenticity, trustworthiness, and even intelligence if the message lacks a sense of balance or poise.

## *Before Revision*

Clearly, Maya thinks she shouldn't have to do her fair share of the work. She prefers to skate by on her likable personality and let her teammates pick up the slack. Our organization should not reward this kind of thinking, as it contributes to lowered morale among our high performers.

> Presumes to know and proceeds to judge Maya's internal thoughts and motivations

> Personal attack based on assumption

> Again, claims to understand Maya's thoughts and motivations

## *After Revision*

Based on her peer evaluation results, it appears Maya's teammates enjoy her personality but perceive her contributions to the team as inadequate. Evaluators reported feeling inconvenienced by her lack of follow-through and frustrated by her inconsistency. My analysis indicates Maya is not ready for a leadership role at this time.

> Cites data and does not draw conclusions about Maya as a person

> Provides basis for claim

> Avoids personal attacks and relies on data, not personal opinion, to drive recommendation.

# Make the Ask

If you are going to ask for something, make it count. Whether you choose a direct or indirect approach, make sure your audience has a sense of what you'd like them to do. If you are drafting a persuasive message, you've decided to make a request or a recommendation, and you have done so after analyzing your audience and confirming the appropriateness of your appeal. Sometimes, writers strategize a fantastic persuasive message, but let the air out of its effectiveness by closing with a weak or ambiguous request.

## *Before Revision*

Thank you for supporting our effort to provide quality educational materials to children in our community. Your contributions ensure every elementary school student has the resources needed to recognize their dreams and build a brighter future for us all. We hope you will make a donation this year.

> Good sentiment and appreciative tone

> Vague, ineffective ask

## After Revision

Good sentiment and appreciative tone

Specific, immediate, convenient ask and call to action

Thank you for supporting our effort to provide quality educational materials to children in our community. Your contributions ensure every elementary school student has the resources needed to recognize their dreams and build a brighter future for us all. Please renew your annual gift of $100 today by visiting www.donate.com/donate. With your help, we can meet our fundraising goal of $15,000 before June 11th.

Whether composing routine correspondence or reports, this chapter offered you strategies and organizational schemas for structuring your messages. By choosing the correct approach, your written deliverables will be on the mark and will showcase the professional level of your writing.

# Chapter *3-3*

# Delivering Negative News

## Conveying an Unwelcome Message

The world of business is full of ventures, triumphs, and failures. Though we try our best to avoid the latter, delivering negative news is a skill critical to competent professional communication. If it is done poorly, the consequences can be significant, rippling out beyond the original recipient to other stakeholder groups and destroying trust and loyalty. However, if a writer prepares his reader for impact and demonstrates empathy, the business relationship may even be strengthened in spite of the unwelcome news. The old saying "what goes around, comes around" is not something a company can take lightly, so it is important to remember that how news is delivered is often just as important as the news itself.

First and foremost, a company should consider how decisions made will impact everyone involved. Conducting a stakeholder analysis specific to a new policy or corporate decision can help a business anticipate resistance or negative fallout and move forward accordingly. If a company is to operate ethically and maintain credibility, it must ensure it is meeting the needs and expectations of all stakeholders involved.

A stakeholder analysis includes the following aspects: identifying specific individuals and groups who might be affected, understanding how they are affected, anticipating how their reaction may impact the company, making decisions, and determining a communication plan based on this analysis. The following table shows one way to organize this analysis. The list might be limited to one or two groups, or it may include a dozen or more depending on the situation, but a smart business considers ripple effects as well as immediate and obvious responses. For a more detailed approach to advanced strategic communication with stakeholders, please refer to Unit 7.

| STAKEHOLDER GROUP | IMPACT ON THEM | THEIR IMPACT ON US | COMMUNICATION PLAN |
|---|---|---|---|
| 1. | | | |
| 2. | | | |

Consider the following example of a company that learned this lesson the hard way.

### NETFLIX

On September 19, 2011, Reed Hastings, CEO of Netflix, made a decision without considering his stakeholders. In a blog post on the company's website, he announced that the combined DVD and Streaming service the company had been offering would be split into two separate companies. Netflix would provide streaming services and Quickster would provide mail-out DVD service. (Quickster, 2011)

This, of course, meant two separate accounts as well as an increase in cost if a customer wanted to maintain his/her current level of service. While this seemed like natural evolution for the company, it didn't sit well with some previously loyal customers.

The company lost over a million subscribers over the next few days and stocks plummeted.

Three weeks later, on October 10th, the decision was reversed. In fact, the tone with which Mr. Hastings communicated to the public was quite different. He acknowledged his rashness and overconfidence based on previous success, opening with the simple statement, "I messed up . . ." His message went on to basically acknowledge that they had moved too fast and should have listened better to their customers. In an unusually swift reversal, Netflix announced its decision to keep its DVD-by-mail and online streaming services together under one name and one website. "We underestimated the appeal of the single website and a single service," Steve Swasey, a Netflix spokesman, said in an interview, adding: "We greatly underestimated it." (Stetler, 2011)

How could Netflix have handled the situation better? In this unit, we will discuss the importance of analyzing your audience, both primary and secondary, before delivering negative news. We will also look at ways to convey unwanted news in a more appropriate manner. It's all about taking the time to understand the impact on your reader(s) and demonstrate genuine empathy. Delivering bad news does not have to produce poor results.

Let's first identify other situations in business where negative news must be conveyed. As you skim through the list of examples, think about how you might react to each one. In some cases, you might feel mildly agitated at the news, but not necessarily upset. Other situations may elicit stronger reactions of fear and/or anger. We'll talk more about these natural reactions in the next section.

The following list contains types of bad news messages that are common in business. While these are necessary events, it is important to look beyond the decision you have made and to establish what your desired best outcome would be.

## Types of Bad News Messages

Negative information can take many forms, including:

- Rescheduling an appointment
- Saying "no" to a request
- Rejecting a proposal or an application
- Demoting or terminating an employee
- Denying a claim
- Announcing a recall
- Declaring a crisis

You can certainly think of situations in the news or in your own experience where a company had to deliver negative news like the examples in the list. In some cases, the audience or recipient of the news may simply make a change to his/her calendar and move on with little hesitation. If this is the case, the one delivering the bad news can simply deliver the news directly. However, if the news is likely to create resistance or worse, an indirect approach is in order. Here, we'll focus on the second and third columns of our stakeholder analysis. We will also delve into the world of psychology. After all, business is all about people, and the most successful will have a good understanding of human nature. There are two types of reactions that will help determine how a message should be communicated.

## Understanding Audience Reaction to Bad News

As discussed in the previous chapter on persuasive messages, there are generally two types of audiences for bad news messages too.

- **Receptive**—news is inconvenient but acceptable
  May feel annoyed and respond disapprovingly, but will likely comply without incident.

- **Resistant**—news is damaging or disruptive
  May experience fear and panic and exhibit either a fight or flight response.

## Identifying Resistant Audiences

In this section, you will learn how to identify when an audience may be resistant to what you are writing.

First, it is necessary to understand a little about what people most value and are most afraid of losing. Looking at the triangle depicting Maslow's Hierarchy of Needs (Maslow, 1943), we can see 5 levels of human needs and why each is important to our existence. The most basic needs are those we cannot live without, such as air, water, food, etc. Even these most basic needs can be threatened by employment status or other professional situations.

Employment is specifically mentioned in the second level, along with personal and community well-being. In order to feel "safe," people must have adequate resources for themselves and their families and be in relatively good health. An employer is instrumental in helping individuals achieve these goals. Salary ensures the ability to purchase basic necessities, and company health insurance provides a means for maintaining good health and treating illnesses.

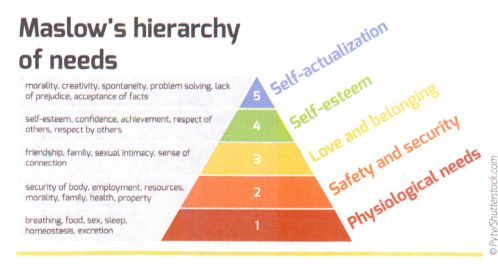

**Figure 1**   *The things people need are also the things they are most afraid of losing.*

In the fourth level, we see the need for both self-esteem and respect from others. These are closely related to an individual's financial situation. Having gainful employment gives a person a sense of pride and security. What happens when a person feels his or her needs and values are being threatened, and what might that mean in the workplace? What about a customer applying for a loan from his/her bank or someone applying for a job? If the answer they receive is positive, they'll experience a sense of relief or contentment. However, if they receive a negative answer and it is perceived as a threat to their needs and values, their emotions may range from depression to resentment.

### The Two Most Common Responses to a Threat Are Fight or Flight

If an employee feels his or her safety or self-esteem are being threatened, the first response might be to fight back. This may result in arguments between co-workers and mistreatment of customers. This anxiety will most likely be evident in a significantly reduced job performance and may affect employee morale throughout the workplace. It may also result in lawsuits and negative publicity.

The second type of response to a perceived threat involves "flight" or avoidance. Some people do not like to confront a problem directly; instead they complain to co-workers or argue over unimportant matters while avoiding the real issue. This response, like the fight response, can cause anxiety in those around the person, resulting in a negative work environment and may lead to a negative corporate image.

In business, there are many situations that can cause people to feel their self-worth or livelihood is being threatened. In most cases, a person is informed of the situation in some type of written message. Since negative news messages may elicit a fight or flight reaction, it is essential to anticipate how a reader will respond in various situations and adapt our communication regarding the issue.

# Writing the Bad News Message

Now that you can more easily identify and understand the responses your readers may demonstrate, we will look at how delivering written news either directly or indirectly can help create messages that will be more easily accepted. First we'll look at delivering this type of news with a direct approach; then, we'll take a close look at communicating negative news with an indirect approach. Of course, the approach you take should match potential audience reaction.

# Direct Approach: Delivering Negative News

If your audience will likely be accepting of the news or if the news is urgent and requires an immediate response, follow a direct approach. Sometimes, a situation calls for a direct, immediate message. Imagine a car company needing to inform the public about a critical product recall, or a food chain needing to warn consumers of contaminated ingredients: time is of the essence, and clarity is essential. In this instance, the audience needs the information delivered directly.

Here is the pattern for a direct bad news message:

# Introduction

## Establish Rapport

Begin your message with a cordial introductory sentence or greeting. Use the "You" Attitude, but keep the lead-in brief, and get down to business. This helps win the audience to your side, even a little, before you drop your bombshell.

## Present Negative News

The introduction of a direct negative informational message must present the bad news. This might be seen as pulling off the Band-Aid™, as the goal is to make it as quick and painless as possible. So, state the reason for your communication. In this case, present the bad news.

# Body

## State the Reasons or Causes

Explain the reasons for the negative news. Offer your audience an account explaining the reason or cause for the negative news. Avoid making disparaging remarks or denying responsibility. It is usually best to be as dispassionate as possible here. Think of the old Dragnet tagline: "Just the facts."

## Explain Details

It may be appropriate to explain some details of the negative event or message. If you have information that might benefit the audience, you can share this in the body of your message. Show the audience that you recognize their needs, and appreciate the impact your negative news has on their lives. It is crucial that you do this with sincerity.

# Conclusion

## Close with Goodwill

Conclude a direct bad news message with a message of goodwill. This should include an invitation for future interaction.

## Sample Direct Bad News Message

The following email is a negative response to an invitation to attend a charity golf tournament. The two men are friends and several other golfers are being invited. Thus, the direct approach is appropriate. Notice that direct does not mean blunt or uncaring.

Hi Don,

I appreciate your invitation to attend the charity golf tournament at the Sheraton on March 3rd. As much as I'd like to be there, I won't be able to make it this year.

I am attending a conference that week on the latest trends in home security. Our company is updating products and services, and I'll be making purchasing recommendations based on what I see there. While I'd rather be on the golf course, it's imperative that I attend this conference.

I know your fund-raiser will be a success. I'll send a contribution for the charity even though I can't attend the event, and I'll call you when I get back to see how it went.

Best Regards,
Steve

How would you feel about this bad news if you were Don? As you can see, if handled correctly, bad news can actually enrich the relationship and leave a positive impression on the recipient. Notice that empathy is not just conveyed by empty words. Actions speak louder than words, so put your money where your mouth is when possible.

Now let's turn our attention to the resistant audience or the urgent negative news.

# Indirect Approach: Delivering Negative News

When dealing with unfortunate, but non-life-threatening news, communicators may benefit from taking an indirect approach. This eases your audience into the message, preparing them emotionally and logically for the bottom line. Though an audience might expect an immediate and direct notification of danger, indirect messages are often more effective for conveying bad news, especially when that audience may be resistant or hostile.

In the direct approach, remember, the purpose or **Bottom Line** is on top. This is what is meant by the acronym BLOT. You tell your readers exactly why you are writing, and how it relates to them, in the first paragraph. The body paragraphs of the message; then, provide more details on the situation and inform the reader of reasons for and consequences of the decision. Action may be required by the reader, and this will be stated in the final paragraph.

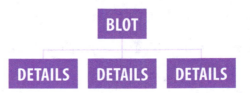

In an indirect message, the structure is reversed. Details are presented first, and the Bottom Line (the bad news and how it affects the reader) is presented near the end of the message.

So how is a negative message like this organized? How does it begin and when is the bad news presented? Consider the approach below. Then we'll walk you through each of the four elements and provide a sample document to make it easier to understand.

## INDIRECT BAD NEWS

**BUFFER**

Prepare the reader and soften the blow.

**EXPLAIN YOUR REASONS**

Help the reader understand what led to the decision.

**BLOB**

The BLOB is the bad news. You can deemphasize it by placement and wording.

**CLOSE WITH GOODWILL**

Close your message with a sincere recognition of how the news will affect them and offer an alternative if appropriate

## Introduction

### Start with a Buffer

Think about the buffer like the airbag of an automobile. In the photo, it is clear that this man is about to experience a negative event. Is he calm about the inevitable crash? No, he's fearful and resistant. If he could change the outcome, he certainly would; however, he cannot. The results may be softened if his automobile is properly equipped with an air bag. The airbag will inflate when the crash occurs and it will protect the man from more serious injuries. In addition, his vehicle may offer online services which will be activated by the crash. These services may include an automatic 911 call and even instructions on what the driver should do.

© Dean Drobot/Snutterstock.com

**Figure 2** *The buffer of an indirect message is like a car's airbag: it softens the blow of an otherwise unpleasant experience.*

When delivering negative news, a buffer can soften the blow, and the rest of the message can provide support to the reader.

A buffer is a statement that establishes common ground with your audience and may communicate appreciation, understanding, or praise for your audience. It should be relevant and sincere in nature. Don't become effusive in a buffer; indicate the topic at hand while you align yourself with your reader. For example, if you have to close down a franchise but want your customer base to continue to frequent your other franchises that are further away, you might say, "Like you, we've always been committed to going the extra mile to make sure we get it right at Happy Burger." You've now aligned yourself with your audience and appealed to their sense of "going the distance" to get what they want. With alignment, you are ready to move forward with your message, and your reader is more likely to read on.

## Body

### Offer Reasons

In an indirect negative news message, present the reasons or causes before you reveal the unpleasant bottom line. If you do this well, your reader sees how this bad news naturally follows the reasoning, and it brings them into your thought process, conveying respect. In effect, priming the reader for the bad news to come can lessen its shock or disappointing effects. In fact, when done effectively, the reader may reach the same conclusion you have and understand the need for the negative outcome. He/she may still not like the outcome, but he/she will accept it more readily.

### State the Negative News

Once you have created some common ground and prepared the audience for the unfortunate news, you must reveal the news itself. Be clear, but don't dwell on this news or offer unnecessary details. Consider how you phrase the bad news, and attempt to sandwich it between the reason and the goodwill. If possible, minimize the bad news with a silver lining. For example, you may point out that the inconvenience of a franchise closure means larger dining space at the newer, bigger Happy Burger. Other ways to deemphasize the bad news are presented in the table below.

| STRATEGY | INEFFECTIVE | EFFECTIVE |
| --- | --- | --- |
| Use passive voice | You did not buy a warranty. | A warranty was not purchased. |
| Subordinate it | Your credit is bad. We cannot approve your loan. | While we cannot approve your loan at this time, we will gladly consider it once your credit has improved. |
| Use positive language | Employees must not park in the customer lot. | Employees may park in the designated lot on the east side of the building. |
| Imply it | You did not get the position. | The position has been awarded to an external candidate. |

## Conclusion

### Close with Goodwill

Once you have prepared your audience and delivered the bad news, close your message with goodwill. You may reference the silver lining, and if you are willing, offer an alternative that meets an immediate need:

*"Please accept the attached coupon to use at your nearest Happy Burger. You can easily find a location near you by going to our website: www.happyburger.com/locations."*

You may also invite future communication, but not about the negative news itself:

*"Thank you for supporting Happy Burger, your family-friendly neighborhood restaurant. We appreciate your understanding and look forward to serving you our award-winning burgers for years to come."*

The conclusion is brief, positive, and respectful in tone. The bad news message, especially when indirect, demonstrates a unique challenge for communicators. It requires a sincere understanding of the situation and audience, and the ability to honestly address the matter at hand in way that maintains a positive sender/receiver relationship.

In some cases, well-wishes will suffice. However, remember that actions speak louder than words, and avoid empty words of consolation. If there is something you can do to help readers with a necessary transition, do so, and put them into action to receive your assistance. This will help them to move past the problem and into the solution, winning you favor as someone who cares.

# Sample Scenario and Indirect Bad News Message

The following example of a negative news message involves a rejection of a job application. Since the company wants to maintain a good image and might consider this applicant at a later date, it is important that the message helps the reader to accept the message. She may not like it, but she will better understand the reasons behind the decision and will feel valued by the company.

The introduction, or buffer, establishes a connection with the reader. In some cases, the writer may express appreciation or compliment the reader for something he or she has done. Sometimes a buffer simply reviews the facts of a situation so that the reader is more prepared for the upcoming news. In any case, if the writer establishes common ground first, the reader will be less defensive and more open to hearing an explanation. As you read this letter to Ms. Beltran, analyze its effectiveness:

> Dear Ms. Beltran,
>
> Thank you for your interest in the Inventory Management position at Ace Hardware. My staff and I enjoyed meeting with you, and we all agreed that you possessed several of the skills and qualifications we were looking for.

Notice that the writer shows appreciation and compliments the reader on her skills and qualifications. However, to avoid sounding overly positive, a single word provides a neutral "hint" at the rest of the message. That single word is "several" instead of "all" skills and qualifications needed. So, while the reader feels respected, she is beginning to think there's more to the upcoming message she needs to understand. So she reads on . . .

The next paragraph presents an explanation for the decision before announcing that Ms. Beltran did not get the job. The writer discusses the requirements and the previous knowledge necessary for someone to fill the position. The reader will see that she does not possess all the qualifications the company requires, and may even come to the same conclusion the writer has on her own.

> The Inventory Management position requires an individual with a unique combination of skills and experience. Since we work with various independent and government contractors, we need someone with extensive knowledge of the hardware industry and specific experience in responding to RFPs. Through the interviewing process, we found someone who met all our criteria and have offered the position to her.

When and how does the reader learn that she has not been selected? An indirect bad news message attempts to avoid negative terms, so in this case the news is implied, ". . . we . . . have offered the position to . . ." (someone else). At this point, the reader understands the company's decision.

An indirect bad news message does not stop there, however. To demonstrate to the reader that he or she is valued, the writer offers encouragement and the option of reapplying for another position at a later date.

> With your exceptional skills and credentials, you will, no doubt, add value to the retail company fortunate enough to hire you. In the meantime, we would like to keep your resume on file for six months, and if a general store manager position opens up, you will be the first to be considered.

This "goodwill" gesture will ensure that the reader understands and accepts the decision and will help her to focus on what is possible, not what isn't. The indirect approach is useful whenever you anticipate a negative response to the news you are presenting and when you want to maintain a positive relationship with the reader as well as a positive public image.

## Sample Scenario and Indirect Bad News Message

In this chapter, we have walked you through the strategy behind delivering bad news. In this section, we will review the approach and look at another example that uses the indirect structure.

In the following situation, Sean Harrison, the Director of HR, must deliver bad news about a sensitive topic. The situation is as follows:

On Friday, a laptop was stolen from a representative in the human resources department of your company. The stolen laptop contained Social Security numbers and contact information for 3,600 current and former employees. You have been asked to draft a letter to be sent by Mr. Sean Harrison, the Director of HR, to each of the employees affected by the computer theft. Mr. Harrison realizes this is a serious matter, which puts each of these employees at a potential risk for identity theft.

Your company is concerned about its employees and also wants to preempt any negative publicity, lawsuits or other claims. Mr. Harrison knows he must show genuine concern for employees' personal and financial safety, while assuring them that the company is doing everything possible to locate the laptop computer and secure this sensitive information.

Mr. Harrison crafts a letter that provides a buffer and explains the situation before delivering the bad news. He closes the letter by focusing on specific next steps that should be taken to reduce any potential risk and by offering to keep the employee updated on any developments. As you read through, ask yourself if you would feel valued by the company.

September 22, 2014

Ms. Rebecca Albright

7390 E. Kimble Avenue

Tucson, Arizona 85710

Dear Ms. Albright,

All of us at Nordstrom value our past employees as much as our current ones, and thank you for your years of service within our company. Our company always has our employees' best interest in mind when dealing with sensitive information. The human resources department, in particular, strives to keep personal employee information private when issuing checks and sending out other important documents.

Recent technology advancements have made completing this task much more efficient, but have also challenged the company with additional risks. HR has numerous security checks and safeguards that protect personal employee information from being compromised. However, large companies such as ours can still fall victim to theft. It is for this reason that we are contacting you. A laptop from our human resources department containing Social Security and contact information of several past and present employees, including yourself, was stolen yesterday. We have no proof that this information has been accessed or is being used in a fraudulent manner. Nonetheless, our security department, along with local law enforcement, is working to locate the laptop and retrieve the compromised information as quickly as possible in an attempt to keep all employee information safe.

In the meantime, our company is offering free credit monitoring for one year for every employee whose information may have been affected. To claim your free credit report from TransUnion credit bureau, call 1 (877) 322-8228 or visit their website through this link at http://www.annualcreditreport.com. If you provide them with your name, we have already set up a fund for your credit report to be paid for in full. In addition, we urge you to be proactive and check regularly with your bank(s) to see if any fraudulent activities have occurred.

We are committed to ensuring your information stays secure and hope you will utilize the services provided. We will have more information about this situation soon and will be contacting you with updates through email. In the meantime, you can also check our website's recent news for further updates.

Best Regards,


Sean Harrison

Director of HR

# Tone—Indifference or Empathy; What Do Your Words Convey?

You have probably gathered that tone plays an important role in delivering bad news successfully. Applying the "You" Attitude in the buffer helps to establish common ground. Using passive voice and avoiding the "you" pronoun when it denotes blame helps to explain the reason behind a decision in an acceptable manner. Presenting the bad news in more positive terms or implying it reduces the impact it has on the reader. Finally, closing the message with a sincere goodwill effort establishes your concern and willingness to assist.

# So, What Do You (the Writer) Have to Gain?

All of these strategies work together to create a message that will allow your reader to move forward into the solution instead of staying stuck in the problem. This, in turn, will help you (and your company) maintain a positive image with all stakeholder groups involved.

Now that you understand the "code book" for how to write direct informative, persuasive, and bad news messages in the workplace, put some of these strategies to the test. Regardless of your audience or the type of message, you'll find that these are easy strategies to memorize and put into practice. While you continue to develop and deepen your approach, you will find that your own messages will become more targeted and polished. More and more, you'll find you reach the mark. There is now only one strategic area left for you to master in business writing: it is time to learn about document design.

# Document Design

## Maximum Effectiveness, Minimum Effort

It does not matter how solid your strategy or how thorough your content: if you deliver information in ugly, inaccessible, or incomprehensible ways, your message will be confusing or worse, ignored. Consider all of the reading you are doing for this and other classes. Your authors (and the army of designers employed by our publisher) dedicated considerable effort to making this textbook as visually appealing as possible. We did this not just because we like pretty things, but because we know the truth about communication: how we organize and present information is just as important as the information itself. Effective information design helps achieve two goals: that your intended audience will actually read your documents, and that they will best understand what they read.

Information design is integral to what is commonly known as readability, or the ability of readers to understand information presented. Most common readability scores, such as Flesch Reading Ease and Flesch-Kincaid Grade Level, rely on calculations using the average sentence length and average number of syllables per word. Though this is a rich field of research, it is only important right now that you know that most Americans can read at the eighth or ninth grade level, for a Reading Ease score of roughly 60 to 70.

Documents with longer sentences and longer words will lower a document's Reading Ease score while increasing its Grade Level score. If one of your goals as a business communicator is to ensure your writing is both read and understood by as large an audience as possible, it behooves you to find the right balance between too long and too short. If your writing is too short, you run the risk of more sophisticated readers—often those in positions of authority—not reading what you've written. If your writing is too long, you damage the ability of everyone to understand your meaning.

As key components of readability scores, word, sentence, and paragraph length directly affect the amount of space taken by text on a page. Therefore, if you want to improve readability—and you absolutely should want to do that—you must consider how much space on the page your content takes and how it is arranged. The amount of space not taken up by text or other content is called white space. You can set yourself up for white space success by configuring your document's layout before you type a word. Start with the page margins, which are the spaces between the four edges of a page and the content on the page.

## Margins

If your margins are too small, your readers might feel overwhelmed by how much text is on the page. If your margins are too large, your readers might think that you have not been as thorough as you could have been in generating your content. A good rule of thumb is to set your margins between ½ inch and 1 inch on all four sides; we advise against setting margins less than ½ inch or more than 1 inch. You may find that you need to occasionally make small adjustments to margins to accommodate a headline or a footnote, or to move the last word of a paragraph off a second page that is otherwise blank. Use this tactic sparingly. If the last few words of a paragraph have gone onto the next page, try to cut something from the rest of the paragraph first before adjusting margins.

## Paragraphs

At this point, you have read a sizable portion of this textbook. You have certainly read other textbooks before this one. You also likely read websites, magazines, perhaps newspapers. Think about all of your reading experience to date. What is your initial reaction whenever you come to a page and see a very long paragraph? If you are anything like your authors, one of your first impulses might be to stop reading right there. Perhaps you get grumpy that the author of that wall of text was very inconsiderate for not making the paragraph easier to read. You might even be less inclined to believe the author of that big block or to follow a request they make.

Here's some cold, hard truth for you: those negative reactions are exactly what you will elicit with giant monoliths of solid text. As a drafting technique, it is perfectly acceptable for you to get as many thoughts as you can onto paper or a computer screen; just make sure you break it up and revise before you package your document for its intended audience. A good rule of thumb is that your business paragraphs should be between five and seven lines long. Any paragraph shorter than five lines makes you look like you have not fully developed your ideas, while any paragraph longer than seven lines will make your audience tune out. The longer the paragraph, the faster they tune out.

With all of these rules for structuring paragraphs, you might start feeling like writing takes too much effort. Quality writing does take hard work, but we have one way to make it a little easier for you. One common convention of business writing is that we do not indent paragraphs. This is a quick and easy shortcut to help you save time as you write your business documents. Instead of taking the time to indent every paragraph, you can just happily type away, secure in the knowledge that you are contributing to a world full of sleek and elegant business documents.

There is, of course, an argument to be made for indenting paragraphs. Before the days of word processors and computers, it was common practice for one paragraph to start on the line immediately following the previous paragraph. When the paragraphs were grouped so closely together, indenting made sense as a visual signal to the reader that a new paragraph was starting. Now with the advent of electronic means for producing standardized layouts with consistent space between paragraphs—something old school typewriters could not guarantee—you can add an extra line break between them. This has the added benefit of adding a little more white space to every page.

With that mention of an extra line break between paragraphs, you might be thinking that it would be a good idea to add extra spacing between the lines within a paragraph. This is commonly known as double-spacing and is a staple of academic writing. If you did think that, you would be wrong. Remember one of the key differences between academic and business writing: the former asks you to fill a minimum number of pages, while the latter asks you to limit yourself to a maximum number of pages.

You cannot cover everything you need to cover when working within maximum page constraints when you double space your writing. To put it another way, your boss probably would not be happy if you were using twice as much paper as necessary (and spending twice as much on office supplies) to convey the same information. If you look at your single-spaced document and judge that the lines are just too close together, you can increase the line spacing to as much as 1.15 lines. Having a small amount of white space between lines does help with readability, but don't go overboard.

## Words

Now that we have looked at the page and the paragraphs, we turn our attention to the words that make up those paragraphs on the page. We cover the crucial mechanics of grammar elsewhere in this text; here we will focus on the physical mechanics of the written word. Words are composed of letters, and those letters are represented in typefaces. Typefaces prescribe a set of common style rules for letters, numbers, and other characters. Variations on those styles can be grouped together into typeface families. When you apply a specific size to a typeface, it becomes a font.

The font you choose for your business writing does make a difference in the readability of your documents. Some typefaces are better suited to paragraph text, while others have more impact when used sparingly in headlines. There are two major varieties of typefaces: serif and sans-serif. The word *serif* has Germanic origins and roughly translates to "dash" or "line." A typeface with serifs is recognizable by the little hooks and tails that hang off of its letters. The most commonly recognized serif typeface is Times New Roman. In fact, serif typefaces are sometimes referred to as "Roman."

**Figure 1** *Sans Serif (Century Gothic, left) vs Serif (Times New Roman, right) typefaces*

Conversely, sans-serif typefaces lack any of that additional ornamentation. These typefaces are also sometimes referred to as "Grotesque" or "Gothic." A recognizable example of a sans-serif typeface is Arial. Both serif and sans-serif typefaces are often styled in different weights or line thicknesses. Those weights can range from narrow or thin, through normal or regular, to semibold, thick, heavy, and bold. The typeface itself and the typeface weight you choose in any given business communication situation will depend on what you use the text for. Just like any other tool in your business communication toolkit, use the right one for the task at hand. Heavier weights work best when used sparingly, for emphasis; thinner weights may be difficult to read.

Merriam Webster's *Manual for Writers and Editors* reports that the people who study typeface readability have found that serif fonts are easier to quickly read and understand. For this reason, use serif fonts for paragraph text. Sans-serif typefaces are better suited for short bursts: headlines, titles, and anything that allows for a larger size or shorter length. Do be careful about mixing typefaces. We recommend using no more than one serif and one sans-serif typeface per document. The more typefaces you use, the more cluttered and unprofessional your document appears.

## Not Words

You've likely heard that old bromide, "a picture is worth a thousand words." Though trite, it does hold some truth in business communication. Sometimes, our words just are not enough to inform or persuade our audiences. We might use a picture to illustrate a key point, a table to organize statistical data, or a graph to convey complex financial information. When using any of these elements, you must be just as strategic with them as you are with your words.

Interpreting visual elements can place a heavy cognitive load on your reader. This means that it may take more effort for a reader to switch from words to visuals, then interpret the visual material into understandable concepts. You can help alleviate this cognitive load by helping your audience pre-process the visual information. Never just drop a graph, chart, image, or other visual element into your document without first introducing it with text. Visual elements need context in order for the audience to understand how they support the bottom line of the document. Remember, it is your job as a business communicator to make your information as easy as possible for your audience to understand or follow.

Just as you need an introduction to visual material to provide context and ease your reader into this new form of content, you also should write a summative statement after the visual material to transition the reader back to the body text. See Figure 2 on the next page for an example of the context and summative statements used to bookend a visual element.

While visual elements like charts, graphs, pictures, and tables can help break up a document into easier to read and understand pieces, there are other document layout tools you can pull from your business communication bag of tricks to further this goal.

## All Right, Break It Up

The two most common layout tools at your disposal are headlines and lists. Lists can come in two forms: bullets and outlines. Both of these tools serve two purposes: giving the reader a break from the cognitive stress of straight text and organizing information into discrete units. By creating these distinct sections and placing relevant information accordingly, you help your audience more quickly process the information.

## Section Headings/Subheadings

One effective way of structuring the information you want to present is through "chunking," or breaking similar pieces of information into discrete sections. This organizational strategy helps your reader keep track of related information and helps you ensure that you control the flow of that information to maximize reader comprehension.

The easiest way for you to use this approach is to think about the major topics you want to cover. For example, let's say you are composing an industry report that seeks to provide your audience with relevant information about the size of the industry, recent trends, barriers to entry, and major players. These are all major topics that give you the opportunity to structure your information in an accessible way. To make the most of this strategy, you might start planning your message by creating a basic outline. Each outline level could then become a separate section, complete with its own heading.

The following chart shows the sales of widgets, doodads, and gadgets by region of the country.

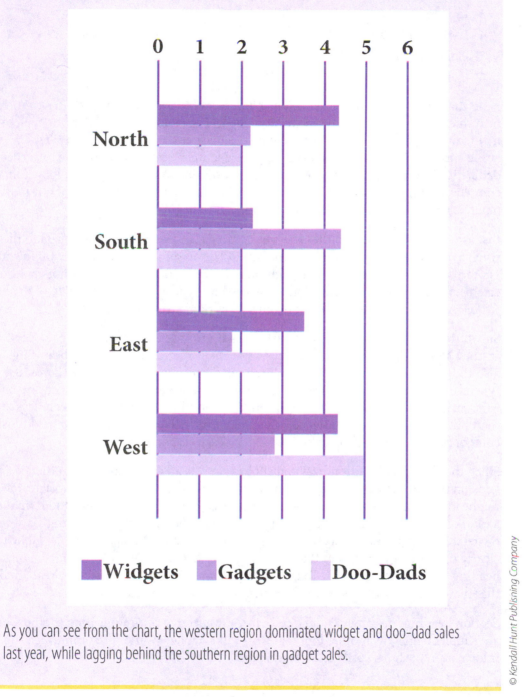

As you can see from the chart, the western region dominated widget and doo-dad sales last year, while lagging behind the southern region in gadget sales.

**Figure 2** *Context and summative statements bookending a visual element.*

For the hypothetical industry report above, you might create an outline as follows:

1. Introduction
2. Industry Size
3. Industry Trends
4. Barriers to Entry
5. Competitors
6. Conclusion

Note that in addition to the main topics to be covered, you also make sure to include an introduction and a conclusion to the document. Regardless of the length or type of document, always provide a frame for the message itself at the beginning and tie it all together at the end. If this was to be a short, one-page document, you might be able to succeed with dedicating one paragraph to each topic in your outline. As documents get longer and more complex, it helps to break up different sections. This is especially true when it may not be obvious where one topic is to end and the next is to begin.

Just as with newspaper headlines, section headings (and subheadings) indicate to the reader when a new topic begins. Your headlines should be on separate lines and set off in some way via formatting. For example, you might make the typeface of your headings bold or italicized, cast them in a different color, use a different typeface, change the size of the heading words. As with any other element of your formatting, just be consistent.

Subsections—and their corresponding subheadings—are considered part of larger sections, so they should be formatted similarly to the main section headings. Subheadings should also indicate their subordinate status to the main heading. For example, if you use a bold typeface for a main section heading, you might choose to italicize that section's subheadings. Since bold typefaces indicate prominence and italic typefaces indicate less strength than bold typefaces, your audience will automatically interpret the relative relationships of content falling under headings formatted with each respective style.

Since the use of section headings and subheadings is all about boosting audience comprehension through structural elements, make sure your line spacing is appropriate, too. Floating headings, in which there is equal white space both before and after them, make them look like orphans: neither the paragraph before nor the paragraph following want to claim ownership. Instead, eliminate the extra line break directly after a heading or subheading to clearly indicate to your reader that the paragraph that starts on the next line belongs to the heading immediately above it. To make the document as easy as possible to read, make sure that there *is* an extra break on the line immediately before each heading.

Section headings are an essential device in your effective communication toolbox, but they are supplemented by another tool that works like a magic wand for communicating lists of information in short, easily understood bursts.

# Bullets and Outline Lists

You are probably used to creating outlines as a method for organizing your thoughts or preparing to write important documents. You probably also use lists in one form or another for helping you remember important items or tasks. Where would any of us be without our grocery and to-do lists?

One of the reasons that outlines and lists are so useful is because they provide the reader with a way to quickly visualize important information instead of having to read complete sentences or full paragraphs. Outlines and lists are the shortcuts on the path to audience comprehension. When used correctly, they save an audience time and make the information presented more accessible. It is possible to overdo the use of bulleted or multilevel outlines; neither can adequately substitute for genuine and thorough analysis and synthesis that can only be effectively conveyed through complete sentences and paragraphs.

Lists and outlines are shortcuts and should be treated accordingly. There is no point in sticking a bullet point in front of a paragraph that consists of two or more complete sentences. If you're writing a paragraph, let it be a paragraph. Bullet lists are best used for short thoughts: single words, succinct phrases, or brief clauses. If you find that you have written a bulleted list that consists of complete sentences at each level, you might as well just make that list a paragraph.

Sometimes, the information you seek to present consists of complex internal relationships. Not every piece of information is directly or equally related to every other piece of information. In these circumstances, you might choose to use a multilevel list or outline. Just as there are relationships between headings and subheadings, there are relationships between levels in a list or outline. All items in the top level of a list or outline should have equal relationship to the items on that same level.

There may be sublevels under those top-level items, and each of those sublevel items under each top-level item should have equal relationship to the other sublevel items under the same top-level item (though not to the sublevel items under other top-level items). That is a mildly confusing way of telling you to keep like information together. Sublevels must be related to each other and the top-level item under which they fall.

There is one more important point about bullet and multilevel outline lists. Items on any level can never exist in isolation. Avoid lonely bullets, the phenomenon of having only one bulleted item at a particular level of a list. You should not use bullet points or outline numbers if there is only one item on that level. In the case of outlines, that means that every 1 has a 2 and every a has a b.

> **AVOID LONELY BULLETS.**
> Every 1 has a 2 and every a has a b.

Since bullet lists and outlines are intended to help organize more than one piece of information, it does not make sense to use these formatting tools when you are only presenting one piece of information. If you have additional information you would like to use to elaborate on a bullet point, but there is not enough additional information to split into two sublevels, just include that information on the next line below the main point. Just do not use a bullet or letter/number; the additional information is part of the top-level item, not sufficient enough to justify its own sublevel.

This chapter helped you think through document formatting to make your writing both visually appealing and easier to understand. Part of any effective written strategy must include attention to document design. This is an element of writing strategy that is often overlooked, at the peril of the author or her causes.

# Unit 3 References

Clark, B. (2015) How to Use the 'Rule of Three' to Create Engaging Content. Retrieved from http://www.copyblogger.com/rule-of-three/

Fadiga, L., Craighero, L. and D'Ausilio, A. (2009), Broca's Area in Language, Action, and Music Annals of the New York Academy of Sciences, 1169: 448–458

Holland, N. (2010). 3 Simple Rules for Writing That Match the Human Brain. Retrieved from https://www.psychologytoday.com/blog/is-your-brain-culture/201006/3-simple-rules-writing-match-the-human-brain

Maslow, A. H. (1943). A Theory of Human Motivation. *Psychological Review.*

Kincaid, J.P., Fishburne, R.P. Jr., Rogers, R.L., & Chissom, B.S. (February 1975). "Derivation of new readability formulas (Automated Readability Index, Fog Count and Flesch Reading Ease Formula) for Navy enlisted personnel." Research Branch Report 8-75, Millington, TN: Naval Technical Training, U. S. Naval Air Station, Memphis, TN.

Merriam-Webster. (1998). *Merriam-Webster's Manual for Writers and Editors* (Rev Sub ed.). Merriam-Webster.

Paiz, J., Angeli, E., Wagner, J., Lawrick, E., Moore, K., Anderson, M., Soderlund, L., & Brizee, A. (2016, May 13). *APA headings and seriation.* Retrieved from https://owl.english.purdue.edu

Pullam, G. (2009). 50 Years of Stupid Grammar Advice. Retrieved from http://chronicle.com

Quickster: Netflix to Split DVD Service into New Business (September 19, 2011). HuffingtonPost. Retrieved from: http://www.huffingtonpost.com/2011/09/19/qwikster-netflix-streaming-dvds_n_969135.html

Stelter, B. (October 10, 2011). Netflix, in Reversal, Will keep its Services Together. New YorkTimes. Retrieved from: http://mediadecoder.blogs.nytimes.com/2011/10/10/netflix-abandons-plan-to-rent-dvds-on-qwikster/?_r=0

# UNIT 4:
## Grammar

# Understanding Grammar

Communicating in the workplace includes producing written documents for a variety of audiences. As future business leaders, the level of proficiency that you demonstrate in your writing represents you and your brand. Your writing should evidence high standards and showcase your ability to think critically, to organize and reason logically, and to design documents effectively. In addition, your writing should be free of grammatical and punctuation errors.

Punctuating improperly or using sloppy grammar is like wearing lousy tennis shoes with a suit: you get ridiculed by those who know better—like bosses, like the people doing the hiring, like the manager in charge of your next promotion.

Writing well is a standard to which you should hold yourself, regardless of your native language. Many students in the United States are never explicitly taught grammar, so many have never learned the correct way to punctuate a sentence. It is never too late to learn; in fact, now is the optimum time to learn, since employers are actively seeking candidates with strong written communication skills.

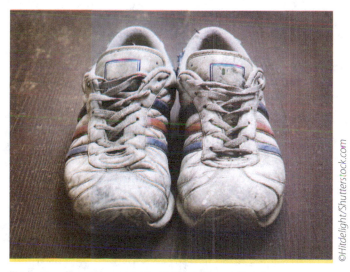

©Hitdelight/Shutterstock.com

**Figure 1**   *Sloppy Grammar is Like Old Tennis Shoes: It Stinks!*

You will project confidence when you know that your sentences and paragraphs are correctly punctuated. Nothing compares to knowing that you are right. Good writers are few and far between, but it is a learnable skill and not a genetic gift. You have to learn the rules, and use them to revise your work.

Earlier in this book, you read about the types of errors most often made by those new to business writing: disruptive, credibility, etiquette, and accent. This unit will focus on the first two, disruptive and credibility errors, and give examples of the most common errors made. This unit also boils down the basics of punctuation and effective sentence structures. By targeting key problem areas in student writing and describing standards that make writing effective and professional, this chapter will help you become a stronger writer. You will learn about writing concisely, choosing strong verbs, and properly punctuating different sentence constructions—areas of weakness in much student writing.

# A Word about Concision

Above all else, be brief and to-the-point. Business writing has a specific purpose and audience. Both of these variables determine what you will write. How you write it will never change: get to the point clearly, quickly, and correctly. Your sentences should be fairly short, and your paragraphs should not be more than eight lines long. White space is important in helping the eye travel across the words and the brain process the incoming visual input.

Writing concisely is easier said than done. Similar to design concepts discussed earlier, removing distractors and keeping the lines clean and simple are good rules. With the exception of long reports, the majority of daily workplace writing is less than a page long. Like a sales pitch or an elevator pitch, you only have so much time and space to get your point across, so you need to distill your sentences to the fewest and best word choices. Business writing requires that you consider your **audience** and your **purpose**, and serve those two masters exclusively.

How do you write concisely? By rewriting. Most first drafts are wordy and wandering as you seek the best way to convey your message. It takes a lot of experience to knock out a clean first draft, even in a short email. Accept the fact that you will need to rewrite messages many times before they are audience-ready.

In the next section, you will learn the "Six Principles" to effective writing. Once you master these, you will write professionally and correctly.

# Grammar

## The Basics: Nouns and Verbs

When writing, you have few choices to make about the nouns you use, because the subject of the sentence is what it is. You can choose synonyms for the nouns, i.e. the manager, the girl, etc., or use pronouns like he/she/they/it, but you typically have to work with what you have. Not so with the verbs you use.

Verbs are the engine of the sentence, driving it toward meaning. You can speed, steer, career, insist, detail, manage—all strong active verbs that allow the doer of the sentence to actually *do something*. The magic happens when you choose strong verbs.

*Elena gave the report to her manager.*

Elena, the subject of the sentence, is a noun and cannot be replaced by anything other than the pronoun *she* or maybe her title, "the sales manager." Nouns are people, places, or things and often act as the subject of a sentence. The verb is the action of the sentence. The verb tells the reader what happened and who did it.

# Principle #1: Use Active Verbs

So, what is a strong verb? Active verbs are stronger and more impactful than passive verbs because they are doing something, not being done unto. The subject does the action of the verb in the sequence doer-action or doer-action-receiver of the action. Below are some examples of both types of sentence. Some of these sentences have a direct object, a phrase or noun that denotes the receiver of the action.

*Subject + Verb + Who or What? = Direct Object*

| ACTIVE | PASSIVE |
|---|---|
| Sanjay threw the quarterly report. | The quarterly report was thrown by Sanjay. |
| Sanjay threw the quarterly report on his desk. | The quarterly report was thrown on his desk by Sanjay. |
| BP released the accident report. | The accident report was released by BP. |
| BP released the accident report to the press. | The accident report was released to the press by BP. |
| The manager ran the full-page ad. | The full-page ad was run by the manager. |
| The CEO quoted Mark Twain on a daily basis. | Mark Twain is quoted on a daily basis by the CEO. |
| Jeni wrote the most concise email to her boss. | The most concise email to the boss was written by Jeni. |

The passive construction is not wrong; it's simply not as direct and does not link the action closely with the doer. Passive voice is used in science writing to maintain a sense of objectivity, and to keep the writer out of the conclusions drawn.

**Incorrect:** *We found that genetically modified corn causes tumors in mice.*
**Correct:** *The data suggest that genetically modified corn causes tumors in mice.*

**Incorrect:** *My research suggests a correlation between hours slept and
weight gain.*
**Correct:** *Evidence suggests a correlation between hours slept and weight gain.*

Writers correctly use passive constructs when the doer or subject is unknown.

**Unknown subject:** *The laptop was stolen.*
*A bomb went off in the courthouse.*

A final suitable use of passive voice is to deflect attention from the doer or performer of an action. Examples of these include deflecting blame, avoiding responsibility, or delivering bad news. You often hear passive voice in press releases and in courtrooms where companies and/or people do not want to take responsibility for actions. Consider this from an oil company after a spill: "A few gallons might have been spilled." Or this from a serial speeder, "Posted speed limits were not always followed." By not having a subject or a doer, the focus is taken off of the actor of the sentence.

**Deflecting blame:** *The window was shattered.*
*The alibi was not corroborated.*

**Avoiding responsibility:** *Mistakes were made.*
*Shots were fired.*

**Delivering bad news:** *Water will be shut off if payment isn't made.*
*Ten points will be taken off for late submissions.*

A final reason business writing relies on active voice is for concision; the passive constructs are often longer than their active counterparts—and concision is the goal.

Thus, you can see that avoiding the passive voice and finding active verbs makes your sentences more immediate and less evasive. Likewise, avoid "to be" verbs as they, too, lack muscle and punch. Note: Using *to be* verbs is not wrong, but using too many makes for writing that lacks impact. The following chart shows the different tenses of the *to be* verbs.

| | PRESENT | PAST | PERFECT | PROGRESSIVE |
|---|---|---|---|---|
| I | am | was | have been/had been | am/was being |
| he/she/it | is | was | has been/had been | is/was being |
| you/we/they | are | were | have been/had been | are/were being |

Now, let's look at *to be* verbs used in sentences and compare them to the revised versions that use active verbs.

| WEAK | STRONG |
|---|---|
| Those women **are** strong leaders. | Those women **emerged** as strong leaders. |
| The sales team **was recognized** as top performing. | Management **recognized** the sales team as top performing. |
| I **am** the supervisor of 15 full-time employees. | I **supervise** 15 full-time employees. |
| The owner **was being responsible** when she changed the locks. | The responsible owner **changed** the locks. |

*To be* verbs are handy and familiar, so watch for them sneaking into your writing. Part of revising requires reviewing verb choices and working to make sentences stronger. This partial list provides some strong verbs you can use when feeling stuck:

| | | | | |
|---|---|---|---|---|
| save | eliminate | coach | implement | present |
| inquire | accomplish | represent | express | base |
| resemble | recruit | influence | regard | track |
| staff | consider | contradict | facilitate | educate |
| launch | process | transform | analyze | undergo |
| streamline | discuss | preserve | verify | negotiate |
| personify | challenge | eradicate | advise | embody |
| convey | exhibit | demand | produce | believe |

When you consistently use strong, active verbs and revise to eliminate many *to be* verbs, your writing will improve significantly. Again, this takes practice and repetition, so keep revising and learning to spot the offending verb constructions when they arise. The process of revising deserves the effort.

## Practice #1: Verbs

A. Replace the *to be* verbs in the following sentences with one of the active verbs in the chart above.

1. Senator Robbins was loud in his request for more iced tea.
2. She was able to exert enough pressure to change public opinions.
3. Mr. Biocce is all about keeping tradition alive and well.
4. Benny is always fighting with his dad.
5. Meg was trying to help her students find a solution to the problem.

B. Change one of the nouns to a verb and move it to the front of the sentence.

1. Roger was exhibiting signs of agreeing to the merger.
2. The editor was eradicating the weak verbs from the manuscript.
3. He is always contradicting me.
4. Wembly is careful when he drives the bus.
5. Jorge is the star of the daytime drama.

C. Combine choppy sentences to eliminate to be verbs and provide flow.

1. Dumping toxic waste in the river would be in violation of environmental laws and officials are in acknowledgment of this.
2. The only responsibility that they were given by their professor was to turn their work in on time and not to plagiarize.
3. Kanye West was the musical artist who influenced my son the most and is the source of his inspiration.
4. There were shouting mobs in the streets, and they were breaking windows and looting stores.
5. Our department is managed by Dr. Begay, and she is the one who makes all of the big decisions.

D. Front-load sentences by moving the doer to the beginning of the sentence and choosing a strong verb.

1. The toxicology report was finished on Thursday by Dr. Gupta.
2. Results of the final exam were posted on the course site by Dr. Michaels early Friday morning.
3. Damning evidence in the case against the CEO were brought to light by the SEC.
4. The current economic crisis was explained to us by our uncle who is a financial advisor.
5. I want the quarterly report brought to me by you by 3 p.m.

# Principle #2: Use Concrete Nouns

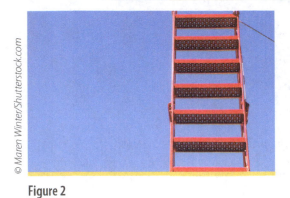

**Figure 2**

Now that the importance of using active verbs has been established, it is equally important to use concrete nouns. Concrete rather than vague language is another consideration to writing with clarity.

S.I. Hayakawa, a linguist and semanticist concerned with inflammatory rhetoric and propaganda during World War II, studied the level of abstraction evidenced in some of Adolf Hitler's speeches. Hayakawa created a "ladder of abstraction" to categorize words from their most concrete and identifiable, to the highest levels of abstraction. Business writing aims for specificity and clarity; thus, choosing words from the lowest rung of the ladder is often the goal.

| LEVEL OF ABSTRACTION | EXAMPLES |
| --- | --- |
| 4 most | wealth, happiness, love, success, health, power, beauty, life form, vehicle |
| 3 | men, women, people, they, we, car, managers, directors, professionals, dogs |
| 2 | Lower class, pre-teens, married couples, romantic comedies, HR director, golden retrievers, German car |
| 1 least | Knock Out roses, 12-year-old, Lydia, Ron and Rebecca Gardner, TV show *Friends*, my golden retriever, Benji, her father's BMW |

With specificity, clear images come to the mind of the reader. If you write that a man drove a vehicle to his favorite store, the reader may imagine this in unintended ways. Perhaps they picture a thin old man driving a beat-up truck to the hardware store, when the writer meant her boss, the CEO of Whole Foods, driving a Prius to the Native Seeds store. Likewise, if you write that the company's sales were up from last quarter, giving specific numbers in context increases the chance that your reader will get the exact message you attempted to convey.

## Practice #2: Concrete Nouns

*Replace the abstract nouns in the following sentences with specific, concrete nouns that leave little room for ambiguity.*

1. *Some people were watching sports on a TV in a bar.*
2. *Pre-teens like to shop at the mall for various cheap items.*
3. *Happiness is achieved through harmonious activities.*
4. *True health comes from staying busy.*
5. *Our company exceeded its wildest dreams last year.*
6. *If we keep up with trends, we can take our start-up to the next level.*
7. *With a serious investment of capital, our company can reach its full potential.*
8. *I am seeking a job where I can move up quickly and have a generous benefits package.*
9. *My skills are many, and I am a good communicator and leader.*
10. *She became wealthy by investing and diversifying.*

## Principle #3: Avoid There Is/There Are & It Is/It Was

Though these are passive constructs, they deserve their own section because of their overuse by inexperienced writers. They are easy. It is true. The simplest solution is to look for these beginnings—and revise them. Again, revision is key to writing well. Sometimes, quick writing provides good content and ideas, but revision polishes them and makes them shine. Take the time to rid your writing of most of these constructs. How is this done? Again, by finding a strong, active verb.

### Practice #3 There is/There are

1. There is little point to driving all the way to San Francisco when you can take BART.
2. It was the sales force that needed to be re-trained.
3. It is inevitable that attrition rates increase when student services are cut.
4. There are many positions at the company that require advanced degrees.
5. It was no one's fault that the copier finally broke.
6. There are a number of companies in China that do business with the United States.
7. It is best to let employees go on a Friday.
8. There were screaming kids running down the pier.
9. It was Connor who told his boss about the social media abuse in the office.
10. There is one explanation for the inconsistencies in the ledger sheets.

## Principle #4: Avoid Why/How, the Reason for, Due to the Fact That

Using phrases like *the reason for, how, why, due to the fact that* to explain something is a common pitfall of the novice writer. Eliminate these from your writing by cutting straight to the point. Think of these words as little red flags signaling the necessity of revising the sentence.

### Practice #4: How/Why

1. She couldn't explain the reason for its disappearance.
2. This document will provide information on how Costco can expand into Brazil and the reasons behind why this is a good decision.
3. As you requested, here is a report about management's proposal as to why India is the place to expand to.
4. I have outlined why I believe Costco is currently performing as one of the best in its sector of business, but I believe slight changes to our business plan is how we become bigger and better.
5. This analysis will inform you on the current successes of Nike, and why Nike through the years has always won globally where many others falter.
6. The reasons the corporate takeover failed are because no one anticipated the public backlash.

6. *The reason why employees resort to taking sick days is because they aren't given enough personal leave days.*

7. *Due to the fact that interviewees are nervous, interviewers should begin with a few easy questions.*

8. *She was fired due to the fact that she lied on her resume.*

9. *In light of the fact that he wrote the entire proposal, he should get the promotion.*

## Principle #5: Watch Out for Misplaced and Dangling Modifiers

### Misplaced Modifiers

Modifiers are words or phrases that, well, modify or change and amend something else. The placement of modifiers is critical: put them in the wrong place, and the meaning of the sentence is altered entirely. Perhaps the most common and familiar are limiting modifiers:

Just, only, nearly, hardly, almost, merely—or by the acronym, JON HAM.

An easy way to illustrate the importance of word order with limiting modifiers is with the word only.

1. *Ricardo only gave Izzy flowers.*
2. *Ricardo gave only Izzy flowers.*
3. *Ricardo gave Izzy only flowers.*

© Featureflash Photo Agency/Shutterstock.com

**Figure 3** *An easy way to remember the most common and familiar modifiers is to misspell actor Jon Hamm's name: JON HAM.*

The first sentence means that the only thing Ricardo did with the flowers was give them to Izzy. He didn't throw them at her, nor did he eat them.

The second sentence means that the only person to whom Ricardo gave flowers was Izzy, not Izzy and Nola.

The third sentence means that Ricardo didn't give Izzy flowers and chocolate—flowers were the only thing he gave her.

Sometimes modifiers sit between two words and could modify either, thus causing confusion in the reader.

**Incorrect:** *Running quickly freaks out guard dogs.*

The ambiguity here is the reader doesn't know if someone who is running fast freaks out guard dogs, or if guard dogs freak out quickly when someone runs. A third possibility is that taking guard dogs for a fast run freaks them out. Depending on what was intended, these revisions are correct:

**Correct:** *When you run quickly, it freaks out the guard dogs.*

**Correct:** *When you run, the guard dogs quickly freak out.*

**Correct:** *When you take the guard dogs out for a quick run, they freak out.*

An easy way to use modifiers correctly is to place them next to the word they are modifying—not between two words they could possibly modify.

## Dangling Modifiers

Modifiers need correct placement for correct meaning. Single words can be used as modifiers, but often mistakes are made with phrases that fail to modify what was intended, resulting in a dangling modifier, or, colloquially, a dangler. They are called danglers because they seem to be modifying a subject that isn't there; thus, they are just dangling in the sentence. The key to getting these constructs right is to name the person/doer immediately after the modifying phrase. Often, these phrases begin the sentence, so that is a good place to look when revising.

> **Incorrect:** *After finishing dinner, the dog was eager for the scraps.*

In this sentence, the dog finished dinner, not one who presumably was going to give him scraps.

> **Correct:** *After finishing dinner, Chad gave his eager dog the scraps.*

Remembering to follow an introductory phrase or clause with the noun or subject corrects most errors.

> **Incorrect:** *Driving down the street, spilled oranges were everywhere causing Carlos to swerve.*

Written thusly, the oranges were the ones driving down the street.

> **Correct:** *Driving down the street, Carlos had to swerve to avoid spilled oranges.*

# Principle #6: Keep Structures Parallel

We have looked at a few ways that credibility errors can undermine your ability to write effective business messages. Next, we will look at disruptive errors. When disruptive errors are made, the reader is not able to read the message straight through. Disruptive errors cause a stop or pause followed by a rereading by the audience, literally interrupting the flow of reading. The danger with these types of errors is that the reader will not comprehend your message.

Credibility errors bring your competence into question, but disruptive errors bring the content into question because they can cause the message to be misinterpreted.

One common disruptive error concerns parallelism. What is parallel structure? We know parallel parking and have a passing familiarity with parallel lines from math, but what is parallelism in a sentence or bullets?

Like parallel lines, parallel items in a sentence line up evenly with one another. It also works a little bit like math–but that's a little later. First, let's look at non-parallel structures:

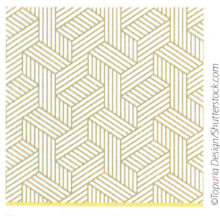

1. *Ahmed enjoys computer science, communications, and doing math.*
2. *Roger redecorated his office with a new desk, chairs, and he painted the walls gray.*
3. *Lindy gets a panicked feeling when her homework is due, her room is a mess, and playing chess against her brother.*

These are wrong because they do not use parallel phrases or words. It's a rhythm issue too: "studying, testing, and memorizing" is parallel. All three use the gerund (ing) form of the verb.

**Figure 4**   *Keep It Parallel.*

©Topuria Design/Shutterstock.com

Let's look at some of the same sentences when they are rhythmic and, therefore, parallel:

1. *Ahmed enjoys computer science, communications, and math.*
2. *Roger redecorated his office with a new desk, chairs, and gray walls.*
3. *Lindy gets a panicked feeling when her homework is due, her room is a mess, and her brother beats her at chess.*

Notice how the forms of the word are the same. As always, keep your eye on the verb. This is where the math comes into play. Do you remember how you solve this equation? 3(**a**+**b**+**c**) You have to distribute the 3 to the **a** and the **b** and the **c**.

You have to do the same thing with a verb that precedes a parallel list. In the following sentence the verb is acting like the 3 in the math example.

- *Our art teacher told us to draw a flower, a vase, and an apple. (draw a flower, draw a vase, draw an apple)*
- *When hitting a golf ball, you need to keep your head down, your eye on the ball, and your knees bent. (keep your head down, keep your eye on the ball, keep your knees bent)*
- *I like to draw, write, and cook. (to draw, to write, to cook)*

## Keeping Bullets Parallel

Keeping bullet points parallel is a rule that is routinely broken. Elevate your game and hold yourself to the standards of proper grammar: Bullets must be parallel.

**You can start them all with a verb.**

Growing a garden is easy:

- choose quality soil
- find a shady spot
- buy heirloom seeds
- water sparingly

By following these simple instructions, you can easily grow your own garden.

**You can start them all with a noun.**

When choosing a career path, keep the most important considerations in mind:

- Opportunities for advancement
- Salary range
- Benefits
- Working conditions
- Corporate culture and climates

By keeping these considerations in mind, choosing the best job will be easier.

Parallel structures are just another way of staying consistent in your writing. Like most other grammatical points, the idea is to stick to a structure and a rhythm to make comprehension easy for your reader.

In sum, keep your writing right and tight and use strong verbs and parallel constructs to elevate the level of your messages. Writing correctly is a skill that will serve you well in the workplace.

## Practice #6: Parallelism

*Make these sentences parallel:*

1. It is harder to maintain a diet than starting one.
2. In the Army, you are told what to eat and to do so in the mess hall.
3. Olivia told her castmates that she bought new tap shoes and of her dream of being a dancer.
4. Robin liked dancing, talking, and the organization of big parties.
5. Delivering the cakes in a rain storm, the caterers thought it smarter to cover the cakes than walking with them in the rain.
6. Mr. Carlson begins every day by perusing the stock markets of foreign countries and then he checks the Nasdaq exchange.
7. Harvard Business School is selective about its candidates, and it is admitting only 4.5% of applicants.
8. I have a long to-do list: I have to skim the pool, to clean out my closet, and to pay the cable bill.
9. Once her check is deposited, Dolores puts money into her savings account, 401K, and credit card balance.
10. Andy hoped to get an extension on his paper, skip class, and to spend the morning kayaking.

*Create parallel bullets with the following non-parallel list:*

- Make sure you finish the assignment
- Proofreading is important
- Carefully edit your message
- D2L: Upload it here
- Don't forget to click "Confirm submission"

# Chapter 4-2

# Understanding Punctuation

## Punctuation

### Credibility Errors

While earlier sections describe best practices and broad suggestions for stronger, more impactful writing, this next section describes credibility errors. Faulty subject/verb agreement and some punctuation and spelling errors, while they do not typically disrupt communication, do create doubt in the mind of the reader about the competence of the writer. Too many of these types of errors will cause the reader to lose confidence in the writer's basic credibility. Once lost, one's professional credibility is difficult to regain.

## Sentence Structure

The English language uses four basic types of sentences. Here they are, in order of complexity:

| SIMPLE SENTENCE | The dog ran. |
|---|---|
| COMPLEX SENTENCE | Whenever he had the chance, the dog ran. |
| COMPOUND SENTENCE | The dog ran around the park, and he sniffed every bush. |
| COMPOUND-COMPLEX SENTENCE | Whenever he had the chance, the dog ran around the park and sniffed every bush. |

### Four Ways of Combining Sentences

Not only does business writing consist mainly of these four types of sentences, but there are also four easy ways to combine sentences. Once you have mastered these four ways and the proper punctuation, command of the written word will be yours forever.

## Way #1: Use Simple Sentences

This is self-explanatory. A simple sentence includes a subject and a verb and requires no punctuation. Beware of adding two simple sentences together with just a comma. This is called a comma-splice, and they are quite common in first drafts.

> **Incorrect:** *Buffered Vitamin C wards off colds in the winter, it has immune building properties.*
> **Correct:** *Buffered Vitamin C wards off colds in the winter. It has immune building properties.*

Though the second sentence is correct, you can see that stringing a bunch of simple sentences together sounds a lot like beginning reading books: See Spot run. Run, Spot run! Jane sees Spot run. Young children learn simple sentences first and gradually add more complexity as their brain's capacity increases. While they may understand complex structures, they do not begin actually using them until about age four. Since the goal of business professionals is to sound credible, be sure to vary your sentence structures and avoid placing too many simple sentences one after another.

## Way #2: Commas after Introductory Phrases and Clauses

Sometimes, on a Sunday, people like to start their sentences with introductory phrases. The purpose of this little lead-in is to set the stage for the main part of the sentence. It usually tells **how**, **what**, **where**, **when**, or **why**.

> Introductory words and phrases set the stage for the rest of the sentence: What happened? Where and when did it happen? How did it happen and why?

They are perfectly correct and acceptable…except when you look back at your paper and see that every sentence begins with one.

Too many sentences structured the same way does not allow for variation that keeps the reader interested. In English, we have dependent and independent clauses. As the name implies, one can stand alone and doesn't need any support—the independent clause. It is a complete sentence. The dependent clause, on the other hand, cannot stand alone and needs to attach itself to an independent clause. Alone, the dependent clause is a fragment.

If you have an entire paragraph consisting of sentences that read—**dependent clause, independent clause**—it becomes distracting because of the repetitive tone. It would be nearly as distracting as ending all of the sentences with a question mark? Wouldn't it be? Don't you think it's annoying? Though few of us read out loud, we still "hear" the words in our head as we read, and we do note repetitive patterns that constitute the author's voice. Varying your sentence structures increases visual and auditory appeal.

Sentences that begin with an introductory word or phrase require a comma after that word or phrase and are called **complex sentences**. You know you have an introductory phrase or clause that requires a comma after it when you can remove it and the rest of the sentence can stand alone. Some examples of introductory words and phrases are presented here:

| Although | That said | First | After… | Case in point |
|----------|-----------|-------|--------|---------------|
| Besides | Last week | Yes | Before… | Until… |
| In addition | Consequently | Generally | Suddenly | Because |

One way to spot introductory phrases is to look for the signal of any time phrase.

- *A couple of weeks ago,*
- *Last semester,*
- *Before World War II,*
- *During the blizzard,*
- *A week from Tuesday,*

Another way is to spot them is to watch for prepositions starting the phrase. Remember, prepositions are anywhere a cat can go: under, on, in, behind, next to, etc.

- *Under the shade of the striped umbrella,*
- *On any given Sunday,*
- *On the sandy beach under a towel,*

A final type of introductory phrase is a conditional phrase that begins with *If*.

- *If you would like to go,*
- *If I were the president,*
- *If we wanted to get in shape quickly,*
- *If you think about it long enough,*

## Examples of Complex Sentences

The following sentences are complex sentences, as evidenced by the introductory phrase or clause followed by a comma.

1. *After leaving the office, Leila discovered she had forgotten her laptop charger.*
2. *When he heard a ding in the middle of the meeting, Matt ducked his head and realized that he had forgotten to put his cell phone on silent.*
3. *Last Friday, Sam was standing in front of the corporate offices in the pouring rain.*

> **Remember:** Moving a phrase to the end of the sentence is an easy way to check if you need to use a comma.

Another way to determine if you need a comma is by taking that beginning clause or phrase and moving it to the end of the sentence:

1. *Leila discovered she had forgotten her laptop charger after leaving the office.*
2. *Matt ducked his head and realized that he forgotten to put his phone on silent when he heard it ding in the middle of a meeting.*
3. *Sam was standing in front of the corporate offices in the pouring rain last Friday.*

If you can move the word or phrase from the beginning to the end of the sentence and it still makes sense there, then it is identified as an introductory phrase or clause. As such, it will need a comma *after* it when it begins a sentence. When in doubt, or if you become comma-shy, just move the word or phrase to the end of the sentence and leave it there—you will not need a comma. This slide to the end of the sentence is an easy comma test and a quick way to change your sentences should you become stuck with repetitive constructs.

*Supply the necessary comma after the introductory words or phrases in the following sentences.*

1. *Whenever it starts raining John starts singing.*
2. *In the past few months stock prices have fallen 4%.*
3. *After the most recent election the country is more polarized than ever.*
4. *Under the spreading branches of Africa's umbrella thorn tree a lioness dozed with her cubs.*
5. *On the sand nearest the cliffs clumps of wild flowers were blooming in a proliferation of reds and yellows.*
6. *During the hurricane families huddled together in interior rooms of their homes to avoid breaking windows and flying debris.*
7. *To raise enough money to go to Buenos Aires Brandon increased the percentage of his wages that were going to savings.*
8. *In order to better understand the behavior of the tsetse fly scientist hatch millions of larva each year in order to study them.*
9. *Without the help of stem cells spinal cord regrowth research would not have come as far as it has.*
10. *If you really feel like helping grab a shovel instead of just standing there.*

# Way #3: Use Coordinating Conjunctions and Commas in Compound Sentences

Coordinating conjunctions are For, And, Nor, But, Or, Yet, and So; they can be remembered by the acronym FANBOYS.

Coordinating conjunctions are used to combine two complete sentences or independent clauses, thereby making **compound sentences**. You use compound sentences to lend more flow to your writing and to combine sentences that would otherwise sound choppy.

Here is the rule: Use a comma before a FANBOYS if both sides of the sentence can stand alone.

> I like coffee and very sweet tea.

The best way to check your own writing when deciding whether to use a comma, try the "pinkie test" by covering over the FANBOYS "and." Can the part on the left and right of your finger stand alone as their own sentences? No? Then do not use a comma. That sentence is correct as it is written without a comma because "very sweet tea" is not a complete sentence and cannot stand alone.

> I like coffee and I like really hot tea.

Now try it: I like coffee (pinkie finger here). I like really hot tea. Yes, they can both stand alone, so the FANBOYS needs a comma before it.

> I like coffee, and I like really hot tea.

The tip-off is if you have a subject after the FANBOYS, you are going to need a comma.

> I called the office looking for Steve and left a message for him.
>
> I called the office looking for Steve, and I left a message for him.
>
> April hates to write but loves presenting, peer tutoring, and working in groups.
>
> April hates to write, but she loves presenting, peer tutoring, and working in groups.

Don't expect to get it right the first time. Always go back over your work, look for the telltale FANBOYS, and then use the **pinkie test** to see if you need a comma–or not. When sentences are thusly combined, they are called **compound sentences**.

The English language is infamous for having many exceptions to every rule. Fortunately, the FANBOYS rule has only one exception: Do not use a comma before so when it means *so that*—whether the word *that* is written or not.

> **Correct:** *She always carried her cell phone charger so she can keep her phone charged after a long day at the office.*

Even though the pinkie test would dictate that a comma before so was necessary since both sides can stand alone, because so in this sentence means *so that*, no comma is used.

## Practice #2: FANBOYS Commas

*Some of these sentences need a comma added or deleted, and some of them are correct. Edit them for correctness.*

1. Sam appeared to wander around aimlessly but he knew exactly where he was going and why.

2. The files from the Castor Co. lawsuit were on Indira's desk, but she had no idea who had put them there.

3. Captain Ramsey piloted the ship through the tempest, and barked orders as the frightened crew slid around the slick deck.

4. I have found that female hermit crabs will come out of the shells when given a bath, but not all of them.

5. You can call the doctor or you can see to the wound yourself.

6. The professor appeared shy and somewhat aloof in meetings yet his student evaluations of his approachability were the highest in the department.

7. Ibrahim, the art gallery's curator, turned the stained glass lamp shade toward the light, so he could more easily study the subtle patterns and variations of color.

8. The thief never looked back for he knew the police were chasing him.

9. Crocodiles are meat eaters and it doesn't matter if the meat is fresh, or if it is rotten.

10. Reyk turned in his college applications minutes before the deadline, and nearly gave his parents a collective heart attack.

*Combine these choppy sentences for flow using one of the FANBOYS. Add commas as necessary.*

1. He isn't honest. He isn't ethical.

2. Boston University is a beautiful school. BU has an excellent reputation.

3. New Year's resolutions are ineffective. They also put unnecessary pressure on people to be perfect.

4. Drinking too much coffee can upset your stomach. It can also help you stay up late to finish a paper.

5. Deandra recognized the handwriting immediately. She had been married to the man who wrote it for years.

6. North Korea has been testing rocket engines and heat-shields for an ICBM. North Korea has also been developing the technology to guide a missile after re-entry into the atmosphere.

7. Opera started in Italy at the end of the 16th century. Opera is part of the Western classical music tradition.

8. Cambodia is a large country in Southeast Asia with a population of almost 14 million. Tokyo, a city in a small country, has the same population.

9. She did not deny that she had seen the will. She did not confirm it, either.

10. Spiral notebooks are sturdy. Spiral notebooks come in regular and college ruled spacing.

## Choosing Compound or Complex Sentence Structures

In addition to knowing how to punctuate them properly, you also need to know when to use these two types of sentences. In business writing, you want the most important information to go in the independent clause. Compound sentences are more emphatic; complex sentences less emphatic. If you have bad news to give, you would be wise to deliver it in a complex sentence. If you have good news you want to stress, either put it in a simple sentence or a compound sentence. The complex sentence is indirect and lulls the reader by slowly getting to the point.

| GOOD NEWS | BAD NEWS |
|---|---|
| Simple Sentence: You have won the lottery! | Simple Sentence: You did not win the lottery! |
| Compound Sentence: You have won the lottery, and you will be rich forever! | Complex Sentence: Although you play your last $20 every single week, this week the lottery was won by a grandfather in Michigan. |
| Complex Sentence: Since you have the right numbers on your lottery ticket, you have won the lottery! | Compound Sentence: You did not win the lottery, but a lucky grandfather in Michigan did! |

In the bad news examples, using a complex sentence and leading with disarming information can soften the blow for the bad news that follows. Many times bad news messages start out with a buffering sentence or paragraph. Just as in the movies when the police knock on someone's door in the middle of the night, they don't yell, "There's been a horrible accident!" at the bewildered homeowners. They lead with a buffer like confirming the homeowners' names, asking if they own a White Honda Accord, requesting permission to come in . . . they take their time and deliver the bad news after a respectful lead-in. Keep this in mind when you consider the purpose of your message or sentence and your reader's reaction to it.

So remember: Use a comma after an introductory phrase or clause. Use a compound or simple sentence to deliver good news fast using FANBOYS and a comma to combine them. Use a complex sentence structure with an introductory word or phrase and a comma to soften and delay the delivery of bad news.

## Way #4: Using Semicolons: Comma's Snobby Cousin

Once you have learned to properly use the introductory comma and FANBOYS comma properly, you can move on to another way to combine sentences for flow and variety. Knowing how to properly use a semicolon will also help you avoid credibility errors in your writing. First, actually *look* at the semicolon.

A semicolon is a pause longer than a comma but shorter than a period or colon.

The semicolon asks you to wait for the ending of the point you are making, but it's not as exciting as a colon. A semicolon says, "Wait, there's more . . ." A key consideration is that you have to stay on the same topic. You cannot use it with two unrelated sentences.

> Ronnie is worried about punctuating longer sentences; however, he just needs to grasp the use of the semicolon.
>
> Or . . .
>
> Ronnie has trouble figuring out how to punctuate longer sentences; he has yet to meet the semicolon.

You can use it with a transitional word like **however, therefore, moreover,** as long as you put a semicolon before the word and a comma after it. The most common transitional words and phrases used with semicolons are listed below.

| | | | |
|---|---|---|---|
| accordingly | eventually | in any case | on the contrary |
| afterwards | evidently | in any event | on the other hand |
| again | finally | in fact | otherwise |
| anyhow | for example | in like manner | perhaps |
| as a result | for instance | in short | possibly |
| at last | for this reason | likewise | still |
| at the same time | furthermore | meanwhile | that is |
| besides | hence | moreover | then |
| consequently | however | namely | therefore |
| doubtless | indeed | nevertheless | thus |
| due to this | in addition | next | coincidentally |

**Incorrect:** *Andrea neglected to let her bank know that she would be traveling in China, consequently the ATMs in Shanghai rejected her card.*

**Incorrect:** *Andrea neglected to let her bank know that she would be traveling in China; consequently the ATMs in Shanghai rejected her card.*

**Correct:** *Andrea neglected to let her bank know that she would be traveling in China; consequently, the ATMs in Shanghai rejected her card.*

You can combine closely-related complete sentences with a semicolon and no transition word:

- *Some bosses are hot-headed; anyone in their path risks drawing their wrath.*
- *Tamara did not return the internship leader's phone call; she was playing hard to get.*
- *That PowerPoint was good; I've seen better*

Remember, like the use of the comma before a FANBOY, both sides of semicolon have to be independent clauses able to stand alone. This means they also have to pass the "pinkie test." Cover the middle with your pinkie. If both sides can stand alone, use a semicolon.

**Correct punctuation with FANBOYS:** We are planning a catered feast for the company picnic, and we have hired a talented mariachi group to perform.

If you are going to use a semicolon and a transition word, it has to be a big beefy word like *moreover, therefore,* or *however.* A fun way to remember this is, if you feel like you should use a British accent when saying the transition word, you probably need a semicolon.

**Correct punctuation with a transitional word:** We are planning a catered feast for the company picnic; moreover, we have hired a talented mariachi group to perform.

Don't be afraid to use semicolons; however, as with a (phony) British accent, don't overdo it.

## Practice #3: Semicolons

*Combine the following sentences by using a semicolon and a transitional word:*

1. *The chef's specialty is seared swordfish. It is not available on the lunch menu.*
2. *The man pleaded not guilty. He claimed to know the identity of the mastermind behind the jewel heist.*
3. *You need to clean the leather with a soft damp cloth. You need to let the cowboy boots dry completely before you apply the polish.*
4. *Brandon was calling his boss. His boss was emailing him telling him that they needed to talk about the system outage.*
5. *The fishermen caught their limit of sockeye salmon. They roasted the biggest one over the open fire on a spit.*
6. *The caterer bought twenty pounds of lean hamburger meat. She bought 30 hamburger buns.*
7. *Tickets to Iceland are cheap in the winter. You could have a honeymoon that doesn't go over your budget.*
8. *Mountain climbers know the dangers of changing weather conditions on Mt. Everest. That doesn't stop them from attempting to summit the mighty mountain year after year.*
9. *You may not be a good ball striker when you first learn to play golf. With enough practice and time at the range, you will improve.*
10. *I can never remember how to use lay and lie. I have problems with my lefts and rights.*

# Colons: The Real Story

We have covered commas and semicolons; let's now look at the colon and its uses. The key takeaway to remember about the colon is that it has to follow a complete sentence. Again, misusing colons also brings your credibility into question.

**Incorrect:** *The things I want are: money, fame, and a closetful of shoes.*
**Correct:** *I want the following: money, fame, and a closet full of shoes.*

**Incorrect:** *You may want to bring: sunscreen, music, water, and something to eat.*
**Correct:** *You may want to bring a few essentials to the beach: sunscreen, music, water, and something to eat.*

Also note, you do not capitalize the first letter of the first word in a list following a colon. However, if what follows the colon is a complete sentence, you must punctuate it as such and capitalize the first letter of the first word.

*My colleague always cautioned against excessive worry with a standard warning: Don't borrow trouble.*

*The professor reminded the students of the plagiarism rule at least five times: Do not use your roommate's paper!*

Finally, you can use a colon to introduce a list that is either bulleted or numbered. It is a judgment call whether you will capitalize or punctuate. The important takeaway is that you must be consistent.

---

I want an assistant who can do the following:

1. screen phone calls
2. compose memos quickly
3. deal with difficult clients
4. keep me on schedule

I will only consider an assistant who can handle all four of these things at once.

---

Use colons after complete sentences when introducing a list or bullets, and punctuate consistently. Following that simple rule will allow you to use colons sparingly but with confidence.

# Putting It All Together

Though it seems a daunting task to produce professional documents in the workplace, this chapter enumerated the finer points of making certain your writing is taken seriously. Errors of any kind bring into question your abilities and, ultimately, your credibility. You should review this chapter anytime you are ready to deliver a piece of writing and want to ensure that you have polished and revised down to the smallest of punctuation marks.

## Practice #4: Putting It All Together

*Putting together all that you have learned about punctuation, grammar, and concision, revise the following paragraphs until they are concise and correct:*

*Nike, Inc. is struggling in one of the most important markets in the world, Greater China. Nike is failing to target and accommodate to the athletic Chinese consumer. China's population stands at 1.3 billion people which is why the Chinese market has an immense influence on the world's economy. Not properly marketing and adapting to the wants Chinese consumers have creates a huge loss of potential sales for Nike, Inc. In 2012, Nike, Inc. predicted China sales to reach $4 billion by 2016 (Forbes). This issue is now recognized as a priority for Nike since competitors like Adidas and Under Armour are gaining ground on Nike in a crucial market for the corporation's success.*

*Google's goal is to have produced the first completely autonomous car to a public market. In reaching this goal it is critical that Google progresses the product on a strict timeline. The first stage of their timeline is the completion of their cars current research and development. Google can not release a vehicle that is subpar, meaning that their car must be completed before presenting it to potential partners. Forging a partnership is the next step, as once they have teamed up with a major car manufacturer they can begin the final two steps in the collaboration of both design and safety.*

*At the core of our issue is the relationship Aetna has with the government, specifically, the Affordable Care Act. While this piece of legislation has made business difficult for us, we realize the position that we are in. We know for the future of our company we must work with local and federal governments in order to have long-term success in any market. Our recommendation is to create a group within our company that solely maintains a positive relationship with the United States Department of Health. This benefits our company in many ways including knowledge of current and upcoming legislation, constructive meetings, and having productive dialogue between our entities.*

*This recommendation report follows our previous SBA report, where we covered issues regarding Aetna's collaboration with the Affordable Car Act and the affects of these dilemmas. Our team has researched and reported the dilemmas Aetna faces and now, below, provided recommendations and costs pertaining to our plan for fixing these issues. Topics below consist of reduction of labor hours, cost cutting for shareholders, Aetna and the government (ACA), and, lastly, bettering public relations. The overall cost of our team's implemented plan is approximately $31,060,000. This total cost is broken down and dispersed under each section below, for a better understanding on how our team reached this totaled cost.*

Finally, if you are ready to put all you have learned to use, revise, edit, and proofread the following cover letter. Use all of your skills to hone it to a concise message. Do not worry about changing the content—do so as needed.

*Dear MS ...*

*I have been waiting for an opportunity like this to write to you. My name is Rick Wagner. Please take into consideration my application for the position of Goldman Sachs financial analysis. I have dual degrees in finance and accounting. I am good at analyzing financial markets and I can identify the relationship between market trends and current events.*

*I am an excellent student and a hard worker. I always read the money market news in the Wall street Journal. And some time buy some equity and financial derivative in the stock track. In the CME challenger competition, our team got a 8% holding period return during the 2 week's future trading. I try my best to conquer my human emotion bias. And I really want to be a financial analysis in the Goldman Sachs. I believe I can write some high qualified researches in this perfect company.*

*In that regard, I would appreciate the opportunity to meet with you to discuss my qualification and the possibility of joining your organization. Please find enclosed my resume for your review. I look forward to hearing from you.*

*Sincerely,*

*Good Student/Bad Writer*

---

For additional grammar help, these sites provide excellent advice.

| GRAMMAR GIRL | http://www.quickanddirtytips.com/grammar-girl |
|---|---|
| GRAMMAR MONSTER | http://www.grammar-monster.com/ |
| GRAMMAR BOOK | http://www.grammarbook.com/ |

# Sample Messages

Now that you have learned the planning, writing, documentation, formatting, and editing of your own writing, this chapter offers sample documents of all the strategies covered in the previous chapters. The samples in this chapter can serve as models that you can use to organize and format your own deliverables.

## Email

Email is an important type of message that is used frequently in the workplace. Your communication through email in the workplace requires more formality than posting on social media. Emails can be sent internally within your organization or externally to individuals in another organization. Email may be used as follows:

- To deliver direct or indirect messages
- To deliver positive, neutral, or negative information
- To persuade

To: managingdirector@companya.com
From: corporatevp@companya.com
Date: September 1, 2014
Subject: New Company Initiative

Dear Mr. Voss,

We appreciate your desire for excellent customer service and increased profitability. Our corporate goal is to build and maintain customer satisfaction at all of our properties. With enhanced customer satisfaction, our company is able to thrive and increase profits. I am glad to inform you of new changes to our sustainability initiative, GREEN. These changes will increase our customer satisfaction and fuel your property's profitability.

**Benefits of GREEN**

According to source 1, our company is currently ranked number one in the industry in terms of market share. However, we are ranked third in terms of sustainability measures. Both Company B and Company D lead the industry in sustainability initiatives. Therefore, they enjoy the benefits of increased public relations and profitability for their properties.

With our new initiative, your property will also have the opportunity to increase public engagement, customer loyalty, and overall profitability. Recently, we have found that customers care about an organization's sustainability, and almost 75% of people consider the company's sustainability efforts when making a booking.

Research shows that initiatives such as GREEN increase employee morale. Our employees are passionate about the program, resulting in higher efficiency and decreased turnover. Initiatives such as GREEN have also been shown to increase operation efficiency and enhance brand recognition. These benefits will enhance your public relations and increase profitability for your property.

Managing directors at our other properties have found GREEN is easy to initiate and sustain. They also save resources through the initiative. For instance, water is one of the easiest resources to save. We can reduce water usage at our properties in a variety of ways, from watering property landscapes with reclaimed water, to allowing guests to reuse towels and linens during their stay. There are various techniques to implement GREEN on your property.

The new standard for Company A includes linking 10% of your base salary and 100% of your annual bonuses to your progress toward a 5% reduction of water usage by the end of 2015. This is an attainable goal that can increase your salary and bonus. With this new change, we can be more profitable as a company. In addition, you can be more efficient as a property manager, keeping both employees and customers satisfied.

**Action Item**

Please choose a representative to send to our corporate-wide training about the best way to reach these goals and meet the key GREEN performance measures. Please email me at corporatevp@companya.com or call me at 999-888-7777, to sign up your representative. I look forward to hearing from you.

Sincerely,

Student A

# Letter

A letter is a formal workplace message. Letters can be sent internally within your organization when the communication needs to be official, such as with HR notifications. However, letters are typically used for external communication. Letters may be used as follows:

- To deliver direct or indirect messages
- To deliver positive, neutral, or negative information
- To persuade

Tina Van Smith
66 Big Train St
Tucson, AZ 85721

February 2, 2014

Mayor Colin Kline
1 City Hall Square
Tucson, AZ 85701

Dear Mr. Kline,

On behalf of the Organization X, we congratulate you as the new Mayor of Tucson. We appreciate your dedication to the growth, safety, infrastructure, and people of Tucson. Organization X also cares about the enrichment of Tucson. We are excited to provide accessibility and exposure to the arts to all Tucson residents. I am writing to introduce you to our new membership program catered to lower-income patrons.

This lower-income patron membership program aims to reduce crime rates in Tucson, by enriching the lives of Tucson residents through exposure to the arts. Research has shown that poverty is directly related to crime. Tucson has a high poverty rate of over 20%; this program is an opportunity to reduce the poverty and crime rates in the city. This initiative will allow lower-income patrons to have the opportunity to be better involved in the Tucson community.

Enriching the lives of Tucson residents will also lead to positive publicity for you. In turn, more people will be educated about your initiatives and will want to support you. Your support of these efforts will allow you to become a more proactive figure in Tucson. Most importantly, through this venture, Tucson will become a better city.

We would like to partner with you on this new program. In order to make this initiative a success, we need funds to subsidize discounted membership rates for lower income patrons. We ask for your assistance to help underwrite this program. Please email me at director@artsorg.com for more information. I look forward to hearing from you soon.

Sincerely,

Jane Smith
ArtsOrg Executive Director

This student uses a letter to send an indirect persuasive message to an individual outside the writer's organization.

**A**lignment—presents a common goal and gives the reader a reason to keep reading.

**I**nformation—provides key information based on the audience's needs and wants.

**D**irect Benefit—shows reader what they can gain.

Call to **A**ction—makes ask and provides next steps.

# Memo

With the popularity and efficiency of email, memos are not used as often in today's workplace as they were in the past. Memos are generally used internally, though on rare occasions can be sent externally to individuals in another organization. Memos may be used as follows:

- To deliver direct or indirect messages
- To deliver positive, neutral, or negative information
- To persuade

**MEMORANDUM**

To: Fred Jones
From: Kali Corner
Subject: Project Overview
Date: 8/4/14

This memorandum will summarize the problem that Company XYZ currently faces, the key stakeholders involved, and the unique situational variables. I will inform you of relevant information and explain key concerns of the project. This information will allow you to evaluate my progress throughout the project.

Company XYZ's new product is an excellent concept which needs to be brought to market. However, the company is attempting to launch with limited funds. In order to increase the startup funds, my team will develop a marketing strategy that will allow the company to pitch its concept to prospective venture capitalists. In addition, we have the added challenge of developing an actionable marketing plan that will appeal to the end users of the new product. It is our goal to create the necessary framework for Company XYZ to use to obtain funding and bring the product to market.

**Stakeholders**

The major stakeholders in this project are the founders of Company XYZ, venture capitalists who decide to invest in the company, and end users.

**Venture Capitalists**

Venture capitalists will want a strong, comprehensive marketing initiative to make the product sell. They are concerned with receiving a return on investment.

**End Users**

The end users include school districts, administration, teachers, students, and parents. End users will want to know how the new product can augment their needs. If successful, we could change the direction of technology in the classroom and enhance learning and teaching in modern education.

**Situational Variables**

Company XYZ anticipates that the product will be at the beta stages in December 2014. The product is designed to be the first of its kind on the market. Therefore, we will not have direct competitors. Our team must conduct research to better understand the industry Company XYZ competes in and the target markets that the new products will appeal to.

It will be our responsibility to develop a strong marketing strategy based on best practices and extensive industry research, giving the company a solid base for product launch. Company XYZ is developing a revolutionary product. Our team is ready to conduct the research to bring this new concept to market through a strategic approach. You should now have a sense of my current status and intended direction on the project. Please contact me at kali@companyxyz.com if you have any questions.

---

This student example uses a memo to send a direct informational message to an internal recipient within the sender's organization.

The introduction includes the message purpose, frames the information for the audience, and forecasts key information.

All information is analyzed for the audience in the body of the message.

The writer concludes the message with a summary, repeating her bottom line, and an invitation to inquire.

Note: Do not use a salutation, closing, or signature in a memo.

# Industry Report

The following two documents are student examples of industry reports. These are informative reports written for larger audiences and designed to provide readers with a concise but comprehensive overview of a particular industry. Therefore, they feature a more formal layout than routine correspondence messages, and the introductions and conclusions are not addressed to a particular receiver. In addition, the authors avoid using the first and second person voicing more common in shorter, exchange-driven communication.

**CORRECTIONAL FACILITIES
INDUSTRY REPORT**

Course Number

Date

## Introduction

The largest in the world, the United States Correctional Facilities Industry has shown a positive increase in population prior to the 2000s. Recently, the Correctional Facilities industry has been showing more consistent trends, especially in the last three to five years. Topics that will be covered are segments, products and services, target markets, market drivers, major players, financial performances in domestic markets, presence in international markets, industry trends, and industry opportunities.

**BREAKDOWN OF PRODUCTS AND SERVICES**

- Community Correctional Facility
- Minimum Security Prisons
- Medium Security Prisons
- Maximum Security Prisons

0.061  0.026

0.277

0.636

*Source: IBIS World Database*

## Products and Services

There are a total of 4 main services the industry offers. The first are Community Correctional Facilities that make up 27.7% of total revenues (O'Hollaren, 2016, p. 5). Community Correctional Facilities have very few restrictions and do not have correction officers. Facility workers are not allowed to use force or anything physical to restrain inmates. Inmates in these facilities, inmates can leave for job related opportunities but must return to the prison later in the evening ("U.S prison populations: Trends and implications," 2013, para 12).

Minimum Security Prisons represent 6.1% of total revenue of the entire Prison industry. These facilities have dorm-like living, and the staff to inmate ratio is comparably low to the other prison facilities. In addition, many inmates in minimum security prisons can be released early with transitional programs ("U.S prison populations: Trends and implications," 2013, para 12).

Medium Security Prisons represent the largest proportion of the revenue of the Correctional Facility Industry, making up 63.6% of total revenues. Housing in these facilities are mostly cell-type, but with the overcrowding problems with these facilities some cells are dorm style. These facilities have higher staff to inmate ratios than minimum security prisons ("U.S prison populations: Trends and implications," 2013, para. 12). Maximum Security Prisons represents the smallest proportion compared to the other services making up 2.6% of total revenues. These facility house either one or two inmates per cell, and most are unable to leave their cell for longer than one hour a day. These facilities have the highest staff to inmate ratio, but provide the least amount of trainings for their staff.

## Major Markets

There are a total of four major markets that are a part of the Correctional Facilities Industry, and below is a pie chart representing each market and how much revenue they contribute in the industry.

The Federal Bureau of Prisons makes up the smallest proportion of the Correctional Facilities Industry with only 13% of total revenue from the industry. The Federal Bureau of Prisons was founded in 1930, and their mission is to have more humane prisons. The BOP over sees 170,000 inmates and almost 40,000 employees.

The US Marshals Services was founded in 1789, and is the enforcement arm in our federal courts. The USMS's main responsibilities include protecting the federal judiciary, selling assets from criminal activities, and housing detainees before they are sentenced to jail.

The United States Immigration and Customs Enforcement was the outcome of a merger in 2003 between the United States Customs Services and the Immigration and Naturalization Service. The ICE is in charge of protecting the US with border controls, immigration, and other related activities.

State and Local Governments, on the other hand, are in charge of local criminal activities. States with a large number of prisoners with tight budgets expand their market right after the recession. Since tax receipts increase with the growing and improving economy, the correctional facilities are under less pressure to budget and spend less money.

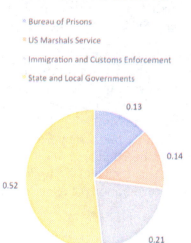

## BREAKDOWN OF MAJOR MARKETS

- Bureau of Prisons
- US Marshals Service
- Immigration and Customs Enforcement
- State and Local Governments

0.13
0.14
0.52
0.21

*Source: IBIS World Database*

### Market Drivers

An Incarceration Rate represents the amount people in prisons. As this incarceration rate increases, prisons start to become more overcrowded, and becomes more likely to higher people at these correctional facilities. The incarceration rate is expected to increase in 2016, according to IBIS World Data base (O'Hollaren, 2016, p.3).

Since privately owned correctional facilities gain revenue from federal and state government contracts, so changes in Government Consumption and Investment will change demand for correctional facility industry services. An increase in government consumption and investments will increase demand for services. The government consumption is expected to increase in 2016 and that will present more opportunities for the Correctional Facilities Industry (O'Hollaren, 2016, p.3).

Increases in Crime Rate will intuitively increase the arrest and prison occupancy rate, and inevitably will raise demand for these industry services. The crime rate is expected to decrease in 2016, which will result in a threat for the industry growth (O'Hollaren, 2016, p.3).

### Major Players

The first major player in the Correctional Facilities industry are the Corrections Corporations of America, founded in 1983 in Nashville Tennessee. CCA currently holds a market share of 34.9%, they are the largest owner in private correctional facility industry. The second major player in this industry is The GEO Group with a total market share of 27.1%. Their headquarters is in Boca Raton, Florida. As of the end of 2015, The GEO Group currently control 64 correctional facilities in 19 states and the Dominican Republic. Some other companies in this industry include the Management & Training Corporation, and their estimated market share is less than 5%. This company is privately held, and was first established in 1981. Their headquarters are located Centerville, Utah, and they operate a total of five main business segments: job corps, corrections, international workforce development, MTC works, and MTC medical (O'Hollaren, 2016, p. 7).

### Financial Performance in Domestic Markets

There has been a steady growth in revenues for the GEO Group, Inc. throughout the past five years. The Correctional Corporation of America, has stayed stagnant for the past five years, but still generates more revenue than the GEO Group. According to Marketline (2016), the GEO Group, Inc. has not only been working domestically, but also internationally with Australia. They are planning large-scale projects soon that are projected to increase revenue. Given this information, I predict that the GEO Group will reach, if not surpass, the revenues of the Correctional Corporations of America within the next five to ten years.

*Source: Annual Report and IBIS World*

### Presence in International Markets

While the United States Prison Industry is the largest in the world, Russia and South Africa are closely following behind. Since the Correctional Facility Industry is mostly service based, international trade is limited.

*This section is weak as it offers very little information.*

### Industry Threats

*Use of color adds to skim-friendliness.*

**Falling profit:** Since most costs for the Correctional Facility Industry are fixed, there really isn't much room for growth in revenue for this industry for the next five years. As the incarceration rates begin to fall slowly, the costs for each prisoner continue to rise and revenue also decreases. This inevitably causes profits to decrease leaving little room for new employees and growth in the industry (O'Hollaren, 2016, p. 4).

**Public Image:** In early 2015, prison inmates in Willacy County Correctional Center in Texas went on strike to protest a poor Medicare plan for prisoners. According to former inmates and guards responded to this protest by shooting prisoners with rubber bullets and other weapons. This peaceful protest soon turned into a riot (Tyx, 2015, para. 3). Events like these start to create a negative image of these privately owned correctional facilities and people start to question where the line is drawn between humanity and being a correctional facility in these prisons.

**Prison Overcrowding:** As the prison population continues to grow, these facilities are starting to become overcrowded and impossible to live in. Prison overcrowding is becoming a very large and concerning problem in the United States. The cause of this overcrowding is because of harsher sentences for unlawful activities, and changes in the law causing more people to be put in these correctional institutes. Overcrowding can cause problems such as more than one person per cell, misconduct of prisoners from having less personal space, and other psychological problems from having too many people in one jail facility ("Prison overcrowding is a growing concern in the U.S.," para. 3–5).

**Attitudes toward Psychiatry Trainings:** A study was conducted to discuss the attitude toward psychological problems within the prisons across the United States. The published paper states, "There is a critical need for psychiatrists in the correctional system, and the correctional system in many states is the largest mental health provider," (Furhrlein, Jha, Brenner, & North, 2014, p. 294). If the Correctional Facilities Industry continues to ignore mental illness as a serious problem, it will only cause more negative effects for the industry in its entirety.

## Industry Opportunity

**Special Cell Designs:** A large problem mentioned earlier in Industry Threats gave insight into the prison overcrowding problem in the United States. While a standard prisoner is required by the American Correctional Association to have 80 square feet in their cell. This often creates many problems (see Prison Overcrowding). Richard E. Vehlow writes in his article that there is room for improvement, and gives specific ways to fix this overcrowding problem. As he states in his article, "For optimum performance of a duct network in an institutional environment, especially with regards to inmate cells, good register balancing is paramount" (2011). By following the plan that Vehlow has laid out, we can improve on the overcrowding problem which would also improve the industry public image as well.

## Conclusion

The Correctional Facilities Industry is the owner, manager, and leaser of prisons, community correctional facilities, and juvenile detention facilities. With an annual revenue looking to increase by .06% in the next five years, the industry seems to have a positive outlook. As crime rates and incarceration rates start to decrease, there is less prison overcrowding. This creates less pressure for the industry to grow rapidly. As the United States Department of Justice start to move toward less privatize prison facilities, governments will hopefully follow.

## References

Corrections Corporation of America MarketLine company profile. (2016, October). *Business Source Complete*. Retreived April 21, 2017, from EBSCO Host.

Fuehrlein, B. S., Jha, M. K., Brenner, M. A., North, C. A. (2014 April). Availability and attitudes toward correctional psychiatry training: Results of a national survey training directors. *The Journal of Behavioral Health Services & Research*. Retrieved April 15, 2017, from ABI/INFORM Collection.

O'Hollaren, K. (2016, November). IBIS World Industry Report 56121. Correctional Facilities in the US. Retrieved April 15, 2017, from IBISWorld database.

Prison overcrowding is a growing concern in the U.S. *Portland State University* Retrieved April 22, 2017, from http://online.ccj.pdx.edu/news-resources/articles/prison-overcrowding-is-a-growing-concern-in-the-u-s.html.

The GEO Group Inc. MarketLine company profile. (2016, December). *Business Source Complete*. Retrieved April 15, 2017, from EBSCO Host.

Tyx, D. B. (2015 March). Goodbye to Tent City. *Texas Observer*. Retrieved April 22, 2017, from https://www.texasobserver.org/south-texas-prison-riot-willacy-county-economic-future/

U.S prison populations: Trends and implications. (2003 May). *The Sentencing Project*. Retrieved April 22, 2017, from https://www.prisonpolicy.org/scans/sp/1044.pdf

Vehlow, R. E. (2011). Special design considerations for institutional and correctional facilities. *ASHRAE Transactions*. Retrieved April 15, 2017, from Business Insights: Essentials.

# INDUSTRY REPORT: CORRECTIONAL FACILITIES

Student

Date

## Introduction

The correctional facility industry is a mature and slow growing industry. Outsourcing prison operations and the incarceration rate are key demand determinants that drive sales and revenue. This document provides a detailed overview of various aspects and drivers of the correctional facilities industry. The key points highlighted in this memo are market segments/target markets, products/services, prevalent companies, presence in international markets, market drivers, industry challenges/threats, financial performance in domestic markets, and industry opportunities.

## Overview

The correctional facilities industry is comprised of operators that own and or manage correctional facilities and halfway houses and generates $5.3 billion in revenue annually. The industry is expected to grow at a yearly rate of 0.6% from 2016 to 2021. Two key external drivers of the correctional facility industry are the incarceration rate and crime rate, both of which were projected to fall at 0.5% and 0.1% respectively. This, in combination with the public scrutiny surrounding the treatment of inmates has caused the overall profit margin to fall over the last five years (2011–2016). In the coming years until 2021, revenue is expected to reach $5.4 billion. However, with the continued fall in crime rates, the correctional facility industry remains exposed to downside risk, which ultimately complicates revenue growth (O'Hollaren, 2016, Industry Outlook).

## Market Segments/Target Markets

According to the Ibisworld database's 2016 industry report, the correctional facilities industry receives all of its revenue from federal and state contracts. The four major customer segments for this industry are state and local governments, Immigration and Customs Enforcement, the US Marshals Service, and the Bureau of Prisons.

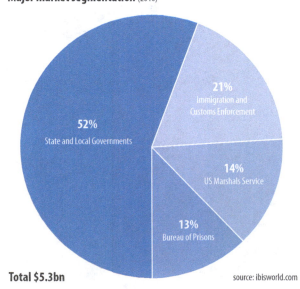

**Major market segmentation** (2016)

52% State and Local Governments

21% Immigration and Customs Enforcement

14% US Marshals Service

13% Bureau of Prisons

Total $5.3bn

source: ibisworld.com

## State and Local Governments

State and local governments account for 52% of the overall industry revenue, which hire industry operators to house inmates and manage facilities. According to the Bureau of Justice, as of 2014, 30 states housed a portion of their inmates in private facilities, and seven states held at least 20% of their prisoners in private institutions (O'Hollaren, 2016, Major Markets). However, market research indicates that states are slowly eliminating the use of private prisons, and as the economy improves, state correctional departments feel less pressure to cut back on their budgets.

## US Immigration and Customs Enforcement

21% of the total industry revenue is generated by US Immigration and Customs Enforcement (ICE), who is responsible for enforcing laws regarding border control, customs, trade, and immigration. Since the number of migrants (mainly from Mexico, Guatemala, Honduras, and El Salvador) increased by nearly 25% in the last ten years, major companies within the industry are considering expanding the capacity for housing illegal immigrants (ICE, 2016). Since ICE does not operate under the Department of Justice, the DOJ's recent policy change to slowly eliminate private federal prisons does not affect its use of private facilities.

## US Marshals Service

The US Marshals Service (USMS) makes up 14% of the industry revenue. The USMS is primarily responsible for housing and transporting federal prisoners before they are sentenced or acquitted. Since the US Marshals Service does not own or operate any of its own correctional facilities, it relies completely on state, federal, and private prisons to house prisoners under its supervision and care. In 2014, 5.5% of inmates received by the USMS were kept in private institutions (O'Hollaren, 2016, Major Markets).

## Federal Bureau of Prison

The smallest market segment, the Federal Bureau of Prisons (BOP), accounts for 13% of the industry revenue. The Federal Bureau of Prisons strives to provide "progressive and humane" rehabilitation to federal prisoners, and oversees the care of over 170,000 inmates (O'Hollaren, 2016, Major Markets). Though the BOP was reluctant to turn over entire facilities to private sectors at first, severe overcrowding led them to partner with private operators, such as The Geo Group. Revenue from the BOP is expected to fall in the coming years as the DOJ has elected to eliminate private federal prisons, and the total federal inmate population is declining.

## Products/Services

The correctional facilities industry operates under different security levels depending on the type and number of inmates they house. The services offered by this industry are segmented into community correctional facilities, minimum, medium, and maximum security prisons, and halfway houses.

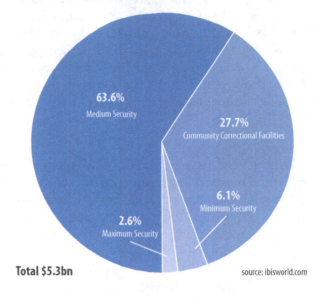

**Products and services segmentation** (2016)

63.6%
Medium Security

27.7%
Community Correctional Facilities

6.1%
Minimum Security

2.6%
Maximum Security

Total $5.3bn

source: ibisworld.com

### Community Correctional Facilities

Twenty-seven percent of total industry revenue is estimated to come from community correctional facilities. These facilities are much more lax than typical correctional facilities, and staff are not permitted to use force to restrain inmates. Inmates in this type of facility are often allowed to leave the grounds during the day for work, but must return to the facility at night (O'Hollaren, 2016, Products and Markets). As the use of private federal prisons is eliminated, community correctional facilities are expected to generate a larger share of total revenue.

### Minimum Security Facilities

Minimum security facilities make up 6.1% of the total industry revenue. Minimum security institutions usually have dormitory style inmate housing, and have a low staff-to-inmate ratio. These facilities emphasize rehabilitation and are work and program oriented. However, with the new policy implemented by the Department of Justice to eliminate federal private prisons, the future of minimum security institutions is unstable (Business Insights, 2016).

### Medium Security Facilities

Sixty-three point three percent of the correctional facility industry revenue comes from medium security facilities. This type of facility is characterized by high fences with detection systems or concrete walls, and cell-type housing. However, medium security facilities face challenges such as prisoner misconduct and violence, along with psychological damage to inmates due to prison overcrowding (Haney, 2006). Like minimum security prisons, medium security institutions also offer work and treatment programs, but the revenue is projected to remain relatively the same, as it is unaffected by the DOJ policy.

### Maximum Security Facilities

Maximum security facilities account for about 2.6% of the overall industry revenue. Inmates in this type of institution are housed in single occupant cells, and are seldom let out during the day. Maximum security prisons have the highest staff-to-inmate ratio, and focus less than the other facilities on rehabilitation. Revenue for this segment is also expected to remain steady and relatively unaffected by the DOJ policy (Business Insights, 2016).

## Prevalent Companies

The correctional facilities industry is divided into three segments, the Corrections Corporation of America making up 34.9% of the market share, The Geo Group making up 27.1%, and other smaller companies accounting for 38%.

This section overview is redundant; the same information is in the chart below.

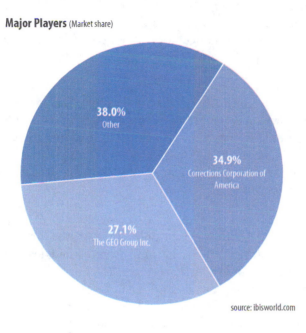

**Major Players** (Market share)

38.0% Other

34.9% Corrections Corporation of America

27.1% The GEO Group Inc.

source: ibisworld.com

## Corrections Corporation of America

The Corrections Corporation of America (CCA) is the largest owner and operator of private correctional facilities in the nation. As of 2016, the CCA managed 42% of all beds under contract with private operators and had more than 14,000 employees (MarketLine, 2016). In 2015, the CCA accounted for $1.7 billion of total industry revenue, and is expected to grow at an annual rate for 1.8% in the years following 2016. In response to the DOJ's effort to eliminate private federal prisons, the CCA is shifting their focus to partnering with state and local markets and expanding into the inmate rehabilitation market to bolster revenue and profits.

## The Geo Group

The Geo Group (GEO) is a real estate investment trust that specializes in the ownership, leasing, and management of private correctional facilities and halfway houses. GEO is headquartered in Boca Raton, Florida, but operates internationally in the UK, Canada, Australia, and South Africa. In 2015, GEO reported total revenue of $1.8 billion, and controlled 64 correctional facilities. Since GEO's main customers are federal agencies, its revenue has steadily increased since 2011 due to higher demands for private facility operators and budgetary restrictions for federal and state governments (MarketLine, 2016).

## Presence in International Markets

Given the nature of the correctional facilities industry, there is no international trade, and therefore low globalization rates. The only major presence in international markets comes from The Geo Group, the second largest industry player (MarketLine, 2016). As mentioned above, GEO currently operates in the US, UK, Canada, Australia, and South Africa. In 2012, 14% of GEO's total revenue came from international services (Mason, 2013). However, even though the United States currently maintains the highest number of privately detained prisoners, at least 11 countries including Australia, Scotland, England, and Wales are engaged in some level of prison privatization.

This section overview is more effective as it frames the content to come.

### Australia

Australia's first private prison was owned and operated by Correctional Corporation of Australia, in international venture of the Corrections Corporation of America. As of 2011, five out of eight Australian states implemented some form of prison privatization (Mason, 2013). Like in the US and UK, Australian private prisons focus more on the detention of immigrants than on prison management. However, Australia's immigrant detention system is different because it is completely operated by for-profit companies.

### South Africa

Prison privatization in South Africa is condensed into two main facilities, the Kutama-Sinthumule Correctional Centre, operated by The Geo Group, and the Mangaung Maximum Security Correctional Centre, managed by G4S, a UK based company. As of 2011, about 4% of South Africa's prison population was being detained by private facilities, in comparison to 19% in Australia, and 8% in the United States (Mason, 2013).

## Market Drivers

The correctional facilities industry is heavily driven by the incarceration rate. As the incarceration rate grows, prisons become overcrowded, leading federal and state governments to expand industry services. The incarceration rate is projected to grow in the years following 2016. The rate of relapses back to crime from inmates also influence the correctional facilities industry, as prisons remain filled and industry demand grows. Another key external driver is the crime rate. Intuitively, as the crime rate rises, so should the incarceration rate. However, crime rate is expected to decrease in the years following 2016.

### Incarceration Rate

According to Harris (2017), US penal authorities house "more than 2.3 million people in 1,719 state prisons, 102 federal prisons, 942 juvenile correctional facilities, 3,283 local jails, and 79 Indian Country jails as well as in military prisons, immigration detention facilities, civil commitment centers, and prisons in the US territories" (p. 119). The United States has the highest rate of incarceration among industrialized nations, due to "tough on crime" legislations that followed the logic of reducing crime by imprisoning as many perpetrators as possible. This approach has led to overcrowding in prisons and low recidivism rates.

### Crime Rate

Supporters of the "tough on crime" approach argue that in locking up offenders, crime rate has been decreased. However, the rise in incarceration is only responsible for 25% of the decrease in crime, and that the overall crime rate is decreasing significantly. Harris (2017) maintains that in the years since 1991, the FBI reported that the number of violent crimes per year have decreased by more than 50% (p. 120). Dropping crime rates with increasing mass incarceration are just one of several reasons for public outcry and scrutiny against the correctional facilities industry.

## Industry Challenges/Threats

Recent controversies involving prison riots over poor sanitation and treatment of inmates has challenged the stance of private prisons. In light of the policy implemented by the Department of Justice to curb and eventually eliminate federal private prisons, states are encouraged to reduce the number of inmates kept in private facilities to combat public opposition. In response to public outcry against mass incarceration due to the traditional "tough on crime" approach, federal and state governments are expected to use more progressive criminal justice policies in an attempt to reduce the prison population. However, in appeasing the public by implementing these changes, industry profit is threatened, and is expected to fall in the years following 2016, as there will be fewer prisoners and less revenue generated by private prisons (O'Hollaren, 2016, Industry Outlook).

## Mental Health of Inmates

Mental health disorders in inmates have consistently been a prevalent issue in the correctional facilities industry. Despite court orders for access to adequate health care in prisons and public criticism, inmates' access to health care and mental health care have been extremely inconsistent (Gonzalez & Connell, 2014). Research done by Gonzalez and Connell indicated that inmates with untreated mental health conditions were at higher risk for rehabilitation treatment failure and were more likely to commit crime upon release from prison. While higher incarceration rates drive the correctional facility industry, research studies such as this one only fuel public outrage and drive the industry to make changes regarding treatment of inmates.

## Mass Incarceration

The "tough on crime" approach implies that the more offenders are imprisoned, the lower the crime rate will be. However, research has indicated being incarcerated can have detrimental effects rather than restorative, rehabilitative ones. Compared with the non-incarcerated populations, incarcerated individuals were much more likely to catch infectious diseases, have chronic health conditions (such as hypertension, diabetes, etc.), problems with addiction, and mental health disorders (Wildeman & Wang, 2017). Since there is strong evidence linking mass incarceration with detrimental effects to inmates' wellbeing, there is high pressure on the correctional facility industry to reduce the number of inmates, which in turn threatens revenue and industry growth.

## Financial Performance in Domestic Markets

As of 2016, the correctional facilities industry is considered to be a $5.3 billion industry. In the years preceding 2016, the industry was growing at a rate of 1.5% yearly, but is projected to have an annual growth of 0.6% annually in the five years following 2016. The correctional facilities industry generates an average annual profit of $591.7 million as of 2016 (O'Hollaren, 2016, Industry at a Glance). Due to strong demand for private institutions and services, this industry is expected to experience slow but continual growth over the next five years. Government contracts have also grown in size, promoting the growth of the major companies within the industry (Chatham, 2014). In particular, The Geo Group has grown significantly in the years since 2011 when they acquired Cornell Companies and expanded the number of facilities operated and managed by GEO. GEO's revenue grew at a rate of 8.1% annually from 2011 to 2016 (MarketLine, 2016).

## Industry Opportunities

Since the correctional facilities industry is heavily regulated federally and by the state, it has high barriers to entry. New companies looking to enter the market not only face strict regulations, but also large capital costs and must receive accreditation from a national program, such as the American Correctional Association (O'Hollaren, 2016, Competitive Landscape). However, there is much more opportunity with lower barriers to entry for new entrants that supply supportive services to correctional facilities (i.e. doctors, educational services, psychologists, social workers), and do not own their own facilities. In 2015, McGraw-Hill Education addressed the need for accessible and high-quality testing materials for adults in correctional facilities. Research done by McGraw-Hill indicated that allowing individuals in corrections to obtain a high school equivalency degree can smooth the transition from prison to community life, as well as offer skills for future employment, and college prep (McGraw-Hill, 2015).

## Summary

The correctional facilities industry is a mature, multi-billion dollar industry. Of the $5.3 billion generated in revenue, more than two thirds comes from two major companies in the industry, Corrections Corporation of America, and The Geo Group. These companies own and manage correctional facilities, and provide community facilities, and minimum, medium, and maximum security prisons to state and federal government customers. Faced with public backlash concerning the treatment of inmates and the fast growing number of incarcerated individuals, overall industry growth is projected to slow down in the next five years. While there are high barriers to entry within this industry, new entrants to the market can find their way in through supportive services.

Conclusion is written for a wide audience and does not include an invitation for inquiry as it would in a correspondence message.

## References

Business Insights: Essentials. (2016). Correctional facilities. *Encyclopedia of American Industries*, 1, 1. Retrieved from http://bi.galegroup.com.ezproxy4. library.arizona.edu/essentials/article/GALE%7CRN2501400984/ aed4ac157fa9272d6bcbb2b1a8da6d13?u=uarizona_main

Chatham: Newstex. (2014). United States correctional facilities market: Demand for private facilities will grow as prisons remain overcrowded. *Newstex Trade & Industry Blogs*. Retrieved from http://ezproxy.library. arizona.edu/login?url=http://search.proquest.com.ezproxy2.library.arizona. edu/docview/1634882424?accountid=8360

Gonzalez, J. M. R., & Connell, N. M. (2014). Mental health of prisoners: Identifying barriers to mental health treatment and medication continuity. *American Journal of Public Health*, 104(12), 2328-33. Retrieved from http:// ezproxy.library.arizona.edu/login?url=http://search.proquest.com.ezproxy4. library.arizona.edu/docview/1628902908?accountid=8360

Haney, C. (2006). The wages of prison overcrowding: Harmful psychological consequences and dysfunctional correctional reactions. *Washington University Journal of Law & Policy, 22*, 265–293. Retrieved from http:// openscholarship.wustl.edu/cgi/viewcontent.cgi?article=1360&context= law_journal_law_policy

Harris, H. (2017). The prisoner dilemma. *Foreign Affairs*, 96(2), 118–129. Retrieved from http://ezproxy.library.arizona.edu/login?url=http://search. ebscohost.com/login.aspx?direct=true&db=bth&AN=121177806&site= ehost-live

MarketLine. (2016). Corrections Corporation of America. *MarketLine Company Profile*, 1–20. Retrieved from http://eds.a.ebscohost.com. ezproxy2.library.arizona.edu/ehost/pdfviewer/pdfviewer?sid=c1f49fdb- 8297-4470-bf81-26ed7a5ed86f%40sessionmgr4007&vid=4& hid=4113

MarketLine. (2016). The GEO Group, Inc. *MarketLine Company Profile*, 1–20. Retrieved from http://eds.b.ebscohost.com.ezproxy4.library.arizona.edu/ ehost/pdfviewer/pdfviewer?sid=c2dce433-4894-4a5a-aa2c-b9d1f55ab5f2%4 0sessionmgr102&vid=6&hid=117

Mason, C. (2013). International growth trends in prison privatization. *The Sentencing Project*, 1–12. Retrieved from http://www.sentencingproject.org/ publications/international-growth-trends-in-prison-privatization/

McGraw-Hill Education. (2015). McGraw-Hill Education expands accessibility for adult ed test preparation tools with new offline and Spanish offerings: Need for test prep accessibility for native Spanish speakers, rural students and adults in correctional facilities drives two new adult education solutions. PR Newswire. Retrieved from http://ezproxy.library.arizona.edu/ login?url=http://search.proquest.com.ezproxy2.library.arizona.edu/docview /1675009056?accountid=8360

O'Hollaren, K. (2016, November). IBISWorld Industry Report 56121. Correctional Facilities in the US. Retrieved from *IBISWorld database*.

US Immigration and Customs Enforcement. (2016). FY 2016 ICE immigration removals. Retrieved from https://www.ice.gov/removal-statistics/2016

Wildeman, C., & Wang, E.A. (2016). Mass incarceration, public health, and widening inequality in the USA. *The Lancet, 389,* 1464–1474. http://doi.org. ezproxy2.library.arizona.edu/10.1016/S0140-6736(17)30259-3

# Direct Informational Memos with APA Citations

For the samples on the following pages, students were asked to summarize three articles in a brief, informative memo, and use APA format to cite sources. In each memo, students demonstrate their abilities to properly cite sources using APA format for in-text citations and a reference page. When citing in text, students used paraphrased and quoted material and integrated these elements with and without signal phrases.

## MEMORANDUM

**To**: Zack Wilson
**From**: Student
**Date**: March 27, 2019
**Subject**: Footwear Information

In response to your request for information regarding the footwear industry, I have compiled the following document outlining important aspects of the market. This information will assist you in deciding whether to expand the University of Arizona Bookstore's presence in the shoe industry. I have included relevant data from IBISWorld, Investor's Business Daily, and Forbes.

### IBISWorld

According to an IBISWorld Industry Report, the online shoe industry is profitable, but growth is slowing. The industry earns an annual $12 billion in revenue, of which $590.2 million is converted into profit (Hurley, 2016, Industry Performance). Online shoe sales have experienced rapid growth in the past few years, however, Hurley (2016) asserts that "growth will continue, albeit at a slower rate as the industry's markets become saturated" (Industry Performance). Amazon claims a large portion of this industry, but smaller online boutique shoe retailers are also increasing in popularity, and therefore, the online shoe business is highly competitive. Overall, Hurley predicts positive growth and continued interest in the online shoe industry.

### Investor's Business Daily

A June, 2016 article from Investor's Business Daily analyzes the differences in footwear lines from Nike and Under Armour, based on which celebrities represent which shoes. Overall, a celebrity endorsement is an excellent way to boost sales of shoes, especially when that celebrity is a highly talked-about athlete. Nike partnered with Michael Jordan to create Air Jordans, which capture a 75% market share when compared to three other popular celebrity-branded shoes (Low, 2016). Different professional basketball players endorse multiple brands of popular shoes, and both Under Armour and Nike are profiting from these celebrities' increasing popularity.

### Forbes

Forbes contributor Powell explored the footwear market in a June 2016 article. He found that while performance running shoes are losing popularity and lifestyle running shoes are gaining popularity, "total running sales are up in the low-singles" (Powell, 2016, para. 5). As of the June 2016, walking and outdoor sandals were experiencing low sales due to a wet spring (Powell, 2016). The market for these types of shoes is reactive to weather, which can be risky to manufacturers and investors. Overall, Forbes predicts slow but steady returns for those in the footwear industry.

As shown in the above information from IBISWorld, Investor's Business Daily, and Forbes, the footwear industry is diverse and profitable, if approached in the correct way. Online retailing, celebrity endorsements, and producing lifestyle running shoes are all viable options for the UA Bookstore. Thank you for the opportunity to compile this document. If you have any further questions, please contact me at student@email.com

## References

Hurley, M. (2016, September). IBISWorld Industry Report OD5093. Online shoe sales. Retrieved from IBISWorld database.

Low, E. (2016, June). Under Armour's golden boy vs. Nike's lifetime king: Whose shoes sell? *Investor's Business Daily*. Retrieved from EBSCOhost database.

Powell, M. (2016, June). Sneakernomics: What's really happening in the U.S. sneaker business? *Forbes*. Retrieved from https://www.forbes.com/sites/mattpowell/2016/06/06/sneakernomics-whats-really-happening-in-the-u-s-sneaker-business/2/#448d7c5a75e6

## INTEROFFICE MEMORANDUM

| | |
|---|---|
| to: | Zack Wilson |
| from: | student |
| subject: | Footwear Industry Research Summary |
| date: | March 22, 2019 |
| cc: | N/A |

As you requested, I have evaluated three articles pertaining to athletic footwear products and produced relevant summaries for your use. This document will give you the information to adequately procure an appealing line of athletic footwear in university bookstores. To guide your focus, I have separated the analysis into three distinct topics: superior footwear brands, footwear ecommerce trends, and economic factors.

### Superior Footwear Brands

One of the foundations to maintaining revenue streams in retail is the proper brand selection. Low's (2016) article compares Under Armour and Nike as they compete for top market share in footwear. Nike's top lines are based off of basketball stars Michael Jordan and Lebron James. Under Armour has created its most recent shoe line based on current basketball prodigy, Stephen Curry. While the two companies leverage athletes as their primary foundation for footwear design the factor important to our business is overall sales trends. According to Low (2016), "a Slice Intelligence report that examined sales of the top four NBA-player shoes, Curry kicks are in vogue, but Nike is still king of the cash register" (p. 1). The information in the article shows that in regard to longevity and consistency of sales, Nike is the primary brand we should offer in broad capacity at our bookstores.

### Footwear E-Commerce Trends

University of Arizona bookstores currently offer online shoe retail, however, many challenges still remain in ensuring that our e-commerce sales portals are in adherence with modern retail trends. In her industry report on online shoe sales, Madeline Hurley demonstrates the growth of shoe retailers online and industry trends. According to Hurley (2016), online footwear retail has increased from 7.0% in 2011 to 14.2% in 2016. The reason for the growth of the industry online lies in consumer information trends. Over the past five years, online shopping has become increasingly consumer friendly. With a growing number of online operators, consumers can increasingly compare prices, read product reviews and browse merchandise with virtual ease (p. 6). Overall, the offering of consumer options and comparable product reviews increases online traffic.

### Economic Factors

Economic factors that contribute to cyclical sales trends and retailer insolvency are crucial data points that our bookstores need to take into account. A Forbes article highlights data for the upcoming quarter in the shoe retail industry. He stated, "With 10 percent of the sporting goods retail space closing by Labor Day, the remaining market will be stronger and healthier" (Powell, 2016, p. 2). In our division, we can use this data to procure athletic shoes after Labor Day to minimize costs and stand out from the degrading competition in the retail space.

*Introduction frames and forecasts.*

*Effective heading that accurately describes content.*

*Effective citation using a signal phrase.*

*Well-integrated quote with a signal phrase.*

*Content is clearly organized and logically grouped.*

*Effective quote without signal phrase.*

This summary analyzed three articles and their relevance in enhancing our footwear procurement division: superior footwear brands, footwear e-commerce trends, and economic factors. The outcomes of my analysis demonstrate that with a culmination of proper brand selection, e-commerce consumer accommodation, and seasonal sales focus our athletic shoe revenues can reach new highs. Thank you for letting me analyze these documents and formulate conclusions that can improve our footwear division. Feel free to contact me at student@gmail.com if you have questions.

Conclusion clearly summarizes and invites inquiry.

## References

Hurley, M. (2016, September). IBIS world industry report OD5093. Retrieved March 19, 2017, from http://clients1.ibisworld.com/reports/us/industry/default.aspx?entid=5093

Low, E. (2016, June 02). Under Armour's golden boy vs. Nike's lifetime king: Whose shoes sell? *Investors Business Daily*. Retrieved March 19, 2017, from http://www.investors.com/news/under-armours-golden-boy-vs-nikes-lifetime-king-whose-shoes-sell/

Powell, M. (2016, June 06). Sneakernomics: What's really happening in the U.S. sneaker business? *Forbes*. Retrieved March 19, 2017, from https://www.forbes.com/sites/mattpowell/2016/06/06/sneakernomics-whats-really-happening-in-the-u-s-sneaker-business/#40a57f311dc3

# Annotated Bibliography

An annotated bibliography is a list of citations to books, articles, and documents. Each citation is followed by a descriptive and evaluative paragraph (the annotation). The purpose of the annotation is to summarize the content of the source and to inform the reader of the relevance, accuracy, and quality of each of the sources cited.

Cook, D. (2012). OtterBox profits in providing protection. Northern Colorado Business Report, 17(17), 5B—14B.

Summary
This article describes more of the history of OtterBox and their strategies that led to the success of the company. The founder and CEO, Curt Richardson, had built $350 million in revenue and even after the recession, he managed 106% in revenue growth from 2010 to 2011. He also increased the number of employees that work for him, which now ranges near about 500 employees. This article describes how the company targets emerging markets like Apple, Nokia, and Blackberry to maintain their position in the front of other manufacturers of cases. It describes in the article how Otter-Box has gained the reputation as "worth the money."

Quality and Accuracy
The source is reliable because it is a widely-cited, respected publication.

Relevance
This article will provide the background of OtterBox our team needs to effectively build on previous success. We can analyze the various strategies used to increase revenue and to maintain a competitive advantage. This will ensure that we maintain corporate integrity and add value to the company in our upcoming report.

Graziano, D. (2012, June 22). Smartphone accessory revenues valued at $20 billion in 2012. BGR. Retrieved September 10, 2014 from http://bgr.com/2012/06/22/mo-bile-accessories-revenues-Increase-smartphones/

Summary
This is the article where the information about the smartphone industry as a whole was accessed. The smartphone accessory industry was expected to earn about $20 billion in 2012 making it a very profitable industry to get into. There was a study done that showed per device, each consumer spent about $56.

Quality and Accuracy
The source is a noted leader in technology journalism.

Relevance
This article will provide the evidence we need to persuade current and potential investors that this industry is strong and will continue to grow.

Professional Photo & Video Tripods, Heads, Lighting, & Bags. Manfrotto. (n.d). Professional Photo & Video Tripods, Heads, Lighting, & Bags. Manfrotto. Retrieved September 10, 2014, from http://www.manfrotto.us/

Summary
This is the main website for Manfrotto, from which I received information about their product that was competing against the lightstrap. Their product is the KYLP+ and is the first all-in-one photographic set for the iPhone 5/5s. It discusses the features of this product with its ability to shoot in low light scenarios and includes three interchangeable lenses allowing the

customer to shoot in fisheye, landscape, and portrait. It also describes the parts that it comes with which include a tripod and small kickstand to help with stability in the photo.

### Quality and Accuracy
The source is likely highly accurate but does demonstrate obvious bias toward Manfrotto products because the source is the Manfrotto website.

### Relevance
This article will enable us to post detailed product descriptions as we build our company's new Facebook page.

Stern, J. (2014, March 12). The only way to double your phone's battery life. Wall Street Journal (Online). p. 1.

### Summary
This article compares products that all increase battery life. Mophie is not the only product anymore that expands battery life. The way the article describes it, Morphie also may not be the best anymore as far as recharge speed and quality goes. The article describes how it is hard to stand out against competitors, so Mophie constantly tries to stay ahead. It talks about providing a one-year warranty and that there are products under Mophie for both Androids and iPhones.

### Quality and Accuracy
The source is reliable because it is a widely-cited, respected news publication. It was accessed through Business Source Complete, a popular academic database at the University of Arizona.

### Relevance
This article provides an objective view of Mophie and its potential risks moving forward. This will allow us to research and propose new ways to stay ahead of the competition.

Strauss, K. (2013). From a barn to a $200 million enterprise: Mophie. Forbes Com, 7.

### Summary
This article describes how Mophie became a competitor in the high-value phone accessory industry from its start in a barn. The co-founders, Daniel Huang and Shawn Dougherty, started this business in 2006 by making speakers and cases for iPods and other types of mp3 players. This company had made about $200 million in 2013, which really solidified its success. Mophie makes builds not only for Apple, but for Samsung, HTC, and other smartphone companies. This article discusses their transition from simply making speakers to making intelligent cases.

### Quality and Accuracy
Accessed through the University of Arizona library website from Business Source Complete, a notable online database.

### Relevance
This article shows the various distribution channels Mophie utilizes to reach its target market. This will be useful as we anticipate next quarter's sales.

Vuong, A. (n.d.). Case logic, otterbox top competitors in tough case business. –The Denver Post. Retrieved September 10, 2014, from http://www.denverpost.com/ci_20553796/case-logic-otterbox-top-competitors-tough-case-business

### Summary
This article describes the top competitors in the smartphone accessory industry with OtterBox being one of them. It contains information about the industry as a whole as well, which is where the statistics about the revenue growth came from. In 2010, the mobile accessory revenue grew 18% and close to half of mobile phone buyers also get an accessory at the same time of purchase. It assesses the business and says that manufacturing cases for iPhones and other phones are continuing to boom, but the market is so competitive that it requires companies to stay on their toes or else they will drown in the competition. This article also references OtterBox being the market leader in terms of revenue and describes how they even have a new division in their company that specifically deals with forecasting what products will be popular and what their design might look like.

### Quality and Accuracy
The Denver Post is an award-winning and well-respected daily newspaper, so it likely that this article is accurate and reliable.

### Relevance
This article shows the strength of the smart phone industry and the market position of OtterBox. This will add evidence to the claims that the company is worth the investment.

Wolf, A. (2013). Manfrotto broadens U.S. business, outsources distribution. TWICE: This Week In Consumer Electronics, 28(9), 33.

### Summary
This article describes Manfrotto's decision to target the pro-digital imaging and video production accessories in order to appeal to a wider range of consumers in the mainstream consumer market. The rise of social media is what inspired the company to join the competitive race to be on top among other accessory manufacturers. Manfrotto has its products in retail stores such as Target, Best Buy, and Walmart. This article also talks about how their company likes to let the staff focus on new products and emerging markets that the company can break into.

### Quality and Accuracy
The article was accessed from Business Source Complete, a database on the University of Arizona's library website.

### Relevance
This information will be useful in selecting the most profitable distribution centers and in developing a marketing campaign that reaches a wider demographic.

Griffin unveils new pattern cases for iPhones. (2009, October 26). Retrieved September 9, 2014, from http://eds.a.ebscohost.com.

### Summary

This source was used to get a better understanding of Speck's competitive advantage and strengths. It was published in 2009, which shows that this company has been making cases since the iPhone 3 was on the market. The article was concise, yet informative, as it promoted and informed the reader on the company's durable mobile phone cases.

### Quality and Accuracy

EBSCO Host is a respected and reputable database offered through the University of Arizona library.

### Relevance

This article will be useful in determining which iPhone accessories have been most popular so that we can recommend development of our current line.

Moldvay, C. (2013). IBISWorld Industry Report 81331. Conservation & Human Rights Organizations in the US. Retrieved September 21, 2013 from IBIS-World database.

### Summary

This on-line article sheds light on Belkin's competitive advantage in the smartphone industry. It was interesting to find that the company provides not only a wide variety of smartphone accessories, but promotes other smart appliances as well.

### Quality and Accuracy

IBISWorld is another University of Arizona-offered database, so I have high confidence in this source's reliability, accuracy, and quality.

### Relevance

This information will be useful when contracting new distributers for our Belkin products.

In this unit, you learned about audience and tone, professionalism and editing, formatting and polishing. Revisit this unit when you either need a refresher explanation or an exemplary sample. By following the processes outlined, you can ensure that your writing is targeted at the right audience, hits the proper tone, uses the appropriate strategy, and is error free. Using the information in this unit, you will be well on your way to writing professional documents reliably, time after time—an ability that will serve you well in the classroom and in the workplace.

# Unit 4 References

Conciseness: Reducing wordiness in your writing. (February 2013). Purdue OWL—Online Writing Lab.

Heath, C., & Heath, D. (2008). *Made to stick: Why some ideas survive and others die.* New York, NY: Random House.

Kamalani Hurley, P. (2007). *The you attitude and reader-centered writing.* Leeward Community College, University of Hawaii. Retrieved from: http://emedia.leeward.hawaii.edu/hurley/modules/mod2/2_docs/you_attitude.pdf

Purdue University Online Writing Lab (1995–2017). *Conciseness.* Retrieved from https://owl.english.purdue.edu/owl/resource/572/01/

University of Wisconsin Madison Writing Center (2009). *3a. The best misplaced and dangling modifiers of all time.* Retrieved from http://writing.wisc.edu/Handbook/CommonErrors_BestMod.html

# UNIT 5:
# Team and Interpersonal Communication

# Understanding the Power of a Professional Persona

## Why Does This Matter?

The technological revolution has permanently changed the way we conduct business, live our daily lives, and construct reality. As technology shrinks the world, and digital mediums grow our reach, the ways we communicate with one another have been accelerated, altered, and adapted into different forms. More than ever, the ability to connect, collaborate, and engage with one another through communication tools and practices shape how we emerge as professionals and leaders in the workplace.

When you consider the enormous amount of time we spend communicating in the workplace, it is no surprise that this is a critical area to master. A study published in 2009 by *Business Outlook*, based on responses from more than 1,000 employees at Fortune 1000 companies, found workers send and receive an average of 1,798 messages each day via telephone, email, faxes, papers, and face-to-face exchanges. Consistently, employers recognize the value of an employee who can communicate effectively in both the written and spoken word. Essentially, the value you bring to the workplace is how effectively you connect, collaborate, and engage with those around you.

## What Does Warren Buffet Know?

Warren Buffet told the 2009 graduating students from Columbia's Business School that he would give any one of them $100,000 on the spot if they would only give him 10% of their earnings for life. This was heartening for those in the class, but it was what he said next that surprised many: he went on to say that if he discovered one of those students was also articulate and had presence and good speaking skills, he would immediately increase his offer by adding $50,000 to the original offer. This begs the question: What does Warren Buffet know about the value of skillful communication? What does he know that would be worth a 50% increase in his offer?

Buffet told each one of those students that their ability to communicate successfully would be the factor that would distinguish them in their career, and if they had those skills now, he would stand to gain even more over the long run. After all, what is $100,000 when compared to 10% of someone's lifetime earnings? Then again, he is Warren Buffet, widely considered to be the most successful investor and one of the wealthiest people in the world. He got that way for a reason.

## How Will This Help Me at Work?

Your ability to connect with others—to communicate fluently both individually and collectively in groups, will largely determine your success. Whether you are managing others, disseminating information, building teams, or leading an organization, your ability to connect and engage with those around you is how you distinguish yourself. Every interaction that takes place within the workplace involves communication in one way or another. If you accept that the ultimate goal of successful communication is to develop mutual understanding, then you can begin to see how important oral communication is in the daily fabric of our lives—both in and out of the workplace.

Regardless of the occupation you choose, you rely on communication to get your job done. How do we know if we have successfully communicated? How do we know if the arrow has hit its mark? There are several ways to tell we have communicated effectively; however, here we will only look at one of the most discussed: social construction of reality and its effects. In their book, *The Social Construction of Reality,* Peter L. Berger and Thomas Luckmann introduced a different view of reality. They argued that all knowledge, including the most basic common sense knowledge of everyday reality, is actually derived from and created and maintained by social interactions (Berger, 1967).

This process of creating a social reality is also the process of making meaning; it takes more than one individual to communicate and construct meaning for communication to take place. This is probably one of the most basic of human efforts. We know the oral tradition of humans predates any kind of written communication by thousands of years. Spoken language must have been used to communicate the most basic of needs: where to go for water, where to gather food, where danger lurked. Those first words were spoken, and communicating effectively often determined whether one survived.

If we take a social constructivist's view, the evolution of the human race (all of its historical events and cultural development) is the end result of communication. Perhaps you have heard the old saying, "history is recounted by the victor." In the making of history, the story behind the events, the "frame" for the event, is often recounted from a particular viewpoint. This is the power of the victor's position: the story remains yours to tell. Such is the power of language in action. When you think about it, you have a lot of power in co-constructing reality for your co-workers, your family, and your community. As a leader in the workplace, your ability to frame and communicate a message largely determines how successful you are at getting buy-in for any of your ideas.

How do we get this buy-in? How do we determine what to say and how to say it? As we evaluate and examine successful strategies for workplace communication, we will start our focus by looking first at individual attributes and strategies for communication. Second, we will turn our focus to the nature of communicating in teams. One way to think about this is to realize that you are where the message originates, and with whom you communicate determines how far your message will travel. In this chapter, we will start with you. By taking a high-level look at becoming more self-aware through a discussion of interpersonal communication concepts and strategies, this chapter will equip you with a deeper understanding of why you communicate and how to do it most successfully. Next, we will focus on communication within teams: strategies for success, team dynamics, pitfalls, and best practices. Together, these sections should provide you with the right information to successfully connect, collaborate, and engage.

# How Can I Apply New Strategies?

## Intrapersonal and Interpersonal Communication

How your audience perceives your communication is more important than how you intend it. Before you effectively communicate with anyone else, you must first have a solid sense of self: who you are, what you value, what your goals are, and how you want others to see you. How you see yourself is not necessarily the same as how others see you. Though it is possible to succeed in business by misrepresenting who you are, that is neither ethical nor sustainable. Successful business communicators are honest and transparent about who they are and what they represent.

Let's look more closely at this concept of self. Before venturing into the business world, think about the following elements that make you who you are.

> "This above all else: to thine own self be true. And it must follow, as the night the day, thou canst not then be false to any man."
>
> - William Shakespeare, *Hamlet*

### Who are you?

Your answers to these questions (among others) make you a unique individual with inherent worth.

Where are you from and where do you live now?

What languages do you speak?

Who is in your family?

Who are your friends?

What are your hobbies?

What kind of clothing do you like to wear?

What are your favorite foods?

What makes you laugh?

What makes you cry?

### What are your values?

Your answers to these questions help to determine how you are likely to interact with others.

What do you consider right or wrong?

What is important to you?

Do you derive these values from religion or another moral or ethical code?

Did you learn these values from your culture or develop them on your own?

How important are these values in your everyday life?

Are your values changeable based on new evidence?

Are you set in your ways and convinced that your values are the only right values?

## What are your goals?

Your answers to these questions look into the future and help you move forward.

What do you want to do with your life?

What is important for you to do within the next year? Within the next five years? Ten years? Twenty?

How high of a priority is each goal?

Do you have a plan for achieving your goals?

Do you need help achieving your goals?

Who will help you achieve your goals?

What will get in the way of achieving your goals? How will you overcome those obstacles?

What strengths do you have that will help you achieve your goals?

Honest self-reflection as you explore these questions will help you to understand your own values, goals, strengths, and social tendencies so that you can maneuver through life with more confidence in who you are and what you are able to contribute. Socrates understood this and went as far as to say, "an unexamined life is not worth living." This may sound extreme, but it is true that the better you understand yourself, the more meaning you will find in everything you do. You will also have greater success conveying your ideas to others since you will have a better sense of how they see you.

## How do you want others to see you?

Do you want people to think of you as reliable? Smart? Athletic? Hard working? Funny? Adventurous? Attractive? You cannot be all things to all people, but you can decide which adjectives best describe you and work to ensure that others agree with those descriptions.

**Figure 1**    *It Helps to Know How Others Perceive You*

How we view ourselves is often in direct conflict with how other people see us—never more so than when we are young. We may think of ourselves as passionate and fearless, while others see our actions as reckless and hear our words as naïve. It is not enough to simply be self-aware, but you must also try to engage others with a sense of how they see you. This can be one of the most challenging and frightening aspects of communication practice: discovering that others see you very differently from the way you see yourself.

The good news is that you can use the following tips to help you manage your professional persona in ways that are both authentic and support how you want to be seen at work.

## How Do We Communicate?
## Elements of the Transactional Model of Communication

Unless talking to oneself, every communication event involves a sender and receiver. A sender creates or encodes a message, which is then decoded, i.e., interpreted, by a conversation partner, the receiver. The transactional model holds that partners send and receive

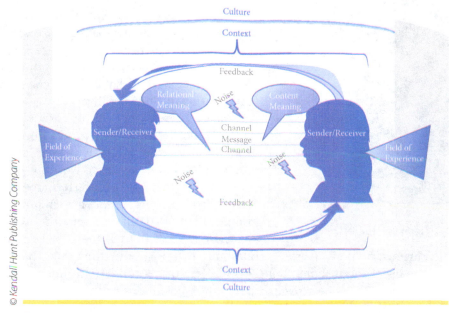

**Figure 2**  *Communication Process*

messages simultaneously whereas older, more mechanistic models assumed these actions could only be done one at a time. A special feature of the communication process demonstrates the melding of these roles, and we will discuss that in a moment. For now, consider the basic design: a sender, who sends a message to a receiver. A message is sent through a channel, which may be verbal, nonverbal, mediated, or a mixture of all three. Verbal communication refers to spoken language, and nonverbal messages are those expressed through body language and facial expression.

Face-to-face conversations allow for the exchange of both nonverbal and verbal messages; they provide important information about our interactions. In many cases, we communicate through mediated channels like email, phone calls, texts, letters, and third party involvement (e.g., "give Anna my regards"). Any channel that does not allow for the real-time exchange of verbal and nonverbal messages is characterized as mediated. Every communication event has the potential for interference. Interference, or noise, refers to distractions in our communication environment.

Though we can't eliminate distractions, we can do our best to reduce physical, psychological, physiological, and semantic noises. For instance, a speaker may reduce incidents of semantic interference by avoiding complex, specialized, or unfamiliar vocabulary. Semantic interference could fall under the category of disruptive errors that we discussed in the standards section.

One can certainly benefit from understanding roles of sender/receiver, noise, message, fields of experience and channels; after all, these are basic elements of the communication process. However, competent communicators appreciate the intangible, more abstract features that make the communication process challenging, rewarding, and endlessly fascinating. Take, for instance, concepts of feedback, interpretation, and meaning. This is where it gets interesting.

Early models depicted communication as a turn-taking event. I would encode/send a message, and you would receive/decode it. Then, you would encode/send a message to me, which I would receive/decode before encoding another message back. In this model, senders and receivers can only do one thing at a time: send or receive. Feedback, however, demonstrates our ability to both send and receive messages at the same time.

**Figure 3**    *Jaime's Thinking Face*

Feedback refers to the intentional or unintentional (mostly) nonverbal cues displayed by conversation partners in the process of meaning creation. You give, receive, and interpret feedback regularly. Chances are, you even do it unintentionally at times. Everything we do, from our facial expression, clothing choice, body posture and positioning to the production of sounds and words is communicative. Take for instance the case of Jaime, a writer working for a local politician in a large Midwestern town. In the past, when in conversation, a friend or colleague would often ask Jaime if something was wrong. Surprised, he would tell them that nothing was wrong and, curious, would then ask his colleague why they would think that. "Because, you look like you're upset about something," was the general response to his query. This seems like no big deal, but Jaime's peer reviews were not as positive as he thought they should be, so he decided to look into it.

It took a few of these instances of people expressing concern for his mood for him to understand the problem: He furrowed his brow when he was concentrating. Apparently, others thought he had an unpleasant "thinking face," because many people interpret this expression as one of disappointment or displeasure. Jaime never felt, nor meant to communicate, any discontentment. This demonstrates the nature of feedback; we broadcast information about ourselves and our attitudes, regardless of our intentions or perceived role as sender versus receiver.

Therefore, feedback makes the roles of sender and receiver simultaneous. We both send and receive messages at the same time, and with this knowledge, we can try to avoid sending confusing or negative messages by monitoring our feedback. For example, knowing what he now knows, Jaime can make an effort to display friendlier facial expressions, even when he is deep in thought. Ultimately, however, we can't always control how others perceive our messages. An individual interprets information based on his or her own field of experience.

Your field of experience is the culmination of everything you have seen and done until this point in your life, and all of the life experiences that shape who you are and how you see the world. Some people refer to this as your perception, perspective, or point of view. Regardless of what you call it, your field of experience acts as the filter through which you interpret information, and no two filters are exactly the same. There are people with whom our fields of experience overlap and we have a good deal in common, but every perspective is unique to the person to whom it belongs. Think of how critical this is to the communication process, and how you, as a communicator, can benefit by appreciating others' fields of experience.

Your understanding of listeners' feelings, values, and experience should inform your communication strategy because meaning rests in the interpretation of a message. Further, messages can be more complex than they appear. Every message has the potential to convey two levels of meaning. Waltzwick, et al. (1967) describes these as content and relational meanings.

Content meaning simply refers to the denotative, or literal meaning of a word or phrase. The statement, "Please pass the salt," in its content meaning, stands as a request for a particular item. On its own, "please pass the salt" is a relatively simple phrase. Perhaps you make dinner for a good friend, and this request is made at the table. When asked for the salt, the content meaning is clear; your friend wants the salt. However, messages often carry a second, sometimes more powerful level of meaning. Relational, or connotative meaning refers to what the message implies, or means in the context of our relationship.

What, if any, underlying statement is made about power, equity, respect, or attitudes between communicators? Depending on your field of experience, you might interpret this request in different ways. If you feel confident about your cooking skills, you may simply pass the salt and think nothing of it. Conversely, if you are insecure about your culinary aptitude, or if you sense your friend doesn't care for the meal, you may perceive the request as an insult to your effort, or an indication that your guest truly dislikes the food. The example above demonstrates the interconnectedness of message design, field of experience, and interpretation. As communicators, we should consider others' fields of experience and consider the intended and possibly unintended meanings connected to our messages.

This awareness enables a competent speaker to craft statements less likely to carry negative or inadvertent meanings. Remember, meaning is made in the interpretation of a message, so both senders and receivers are responsible for the co-creation of understanding. If your dinner guest

**Figure 4**  *Please Pass the Salt!*

**Figure 5**  *Please Pass the Salt!*

knew about your insecurity, they may have said, "This is delicious…I'd love a touch of salt for my rice." However, communicators cannot always know, nor sense, exactly how someone sees the world. So, as you interpreted the request for salt, you should have considered your own perceptual bias and how it may have altered the intention of the comment. Interpretations are also dependent on the situations, or contexts in which we communicate.

Contexts carry expectations of appropriate behaviors. Take the following statement: "I'm bored. Let's go to a movie," and consider how its meaning is affected by context. The meaning changes if you say this to a friend as you're sitting in your living room instead of saying the same thing, to the same friend, as you're sitting at a funeral or a work event. Situation matters. Of course it does—situation matters.

Though people communicate daily and seemingly effortlessly, this process is a complicated amalgamation of interdependent, variable factors. These factors are relatively simple when taken one at a time, but the interplay of these variables make communication a complex, sometimes unpredictable process. The more you consider the elements of the transactional model, the better you can attend to the needs of the listener and contribute to a meaningful exchange.

As a sender and receiver, you can

- monitor your own feedback and adapt to others' feedback,
- craft messages in light of others' fields of experience,
- choose the most appropriate channels through which to send messages,
- reduce noise by anticipating and limiting potentially distracting behaviors,

- identify levels of meaning and limit unintended relational messages, and
- choose the appropriate messages for the contexts and cultures in which you communicate.

In other words, you can build communication competence and apply these concepts to your interactions in and out of the workplace. The more you understand each of these concepts, the better able you will be to use them to your advantage. Imagine working with a colleague who does not monitor any feedback, takes everything literally, and never seems to be sensitive to his or her listeners' fields of experience. You can imagine that this person would not have a lot of admirers, nor would she or he be wanted on many work teams or committees.

Communication competence is important to getting ahead in your chosen field. Further, your industry and/or organization has its own culture replete with traditions, values, beliefs, and expectations. Your knowledge of this culture and attention to the communication process will help you tailor messages for professional success. Best of all, your attention to communication will most likely extend beyond professional relations to your personal interactions. Spend some time reflecting on the transactional model, and try to identify its elements in your daily interactions.

The more you consciously attend to the different concepts and variables of communication, the better you will be at navigating your way through the complexities of this most human of interactions. As stated earlier, the transactional model is a continuous process in which individuals send and receive messages simultaneously. Sometimes, as with mediated communication, we lack the opportunity to give and receive immediate feedback. Of course, this changes the nature of the exchange, but we can still apply concepts of noise, fields of experience, levels of meaning, context, and culture.

It is most important to remember that communication is a shared event; we co-create meaning and strive for understanding together. Therefore, our communication approach should be guided by consideration for the audience and your desired impression.

## Understanding Self-Presentation

An organization is a complex system of relationships, many of which are interpersonal, one on one. The better you manage your professional persona, the more effectively you cultivate the emotionally, professionally, and politically rewarding relationships that position you for success. In their book, *Interpersonal Communication: A Goals Based Approach*, Cody, Canary, and Manusov (2008) neatly fold decades of research into a single three-part approach. We communicate to accomplish one or more of three interdependent goals: instrumental, relational, and self-presentational (Clark & Delia, 1979; Dillard, Sergin, & Harden 1989; Dillard 1990; Hect, 1984; Wilson 1990).

Instrumental objectives are those that aim to influence others' thoughts or actions. Relational goals are characterized by a desire to increase or decrease intimacy in a relationship. When we communicate to project a particular image or to make a desired impression, we operate in the art of self-presentation. Though there are many paradigms for framing interpersonal communication concepts, the goals-based approach is a particularly valuable asset in your business repertoire because it highlights three distinct yet interrelated skill sets central to your effectiveness as a communicator.

We discuss self-presentational, relational, and instrumental goals throughout this chapter and the book as a whole. Most business communication strategies aim to satisfy one or more of these interpersonal goals, so it behooves you to sharpen these skills if you wish to wheel, deal, go-get, open doors, close sales, or any combination of the five. Let's start with your brand.

## Creating Your Brand

If you have not thought about your professional persona, it is time to start. At this point in your academic and professional career, you should have a brand, your own special set of professionally desirable characteristics. This goes beyond telling colleagues and prospective employers you are a "people person" or "detail-oriented self-starter." This is where it gets real. If you haven't yet done so, reflect what you bring to an organizational or team effort. What is your area of excellence? What makes you so special? You might begin by answering some of the questions about yourself listed a few pages ago.

Your professional persona is a work in progress that appropriately requires a great deal of
work. Identifying your strong suits is the relatively easy part; integrating them into your daily
actions (even when you think no one is looking)
is the more challenging and important endeavor.
The time to start these activities is not your first
day on the job. It was yesterday. Your classmates,
instructors, and employers are all members of
your professional network, and the impressions
you make now will follow you for years to come.

It's time for you to dress, act, and deliver for the
job you want. You must demonstrate your value,
and do so in a way that is understated yet unmis-

**Figure 6**    *Creating Your Brand*

takable, with fearsome stealth, in a stylish way that is rooted in a genuine self-regard and respect for other people. Your professional identity is a factor in and product of the quality of your relationships and your ability to influence those around you.

## Using Self-Presentation Strategies

Actions do speak louder than words. Much of your professional identity is legitimized by your behaviors. You can say whatever you want, but if you neither perform nor carry your-self accordingly, you will not make a stellar lasting impression. People use a variety of self-presentation strategies to project a particular image, and you have likely seen both successful and unsuccessful efforts. In fact, you have probably used one or more of these strategies yourself. A selection of common self-presentation strategies follows. Depending on how and when each strategy is used, attempts can range from highly effective to counter-productive.

### Ingratiation

Ingratiation strategies aim to create a sense of liking and goodwill. Communicators ingrati-ate themselves by demonstrating interest in and similarity to others (Jones & Pittman, 1982; Vonk, 2002). These behaviors often include:

- Agreement
- Compliments
- Favors

Of course, one's success is dependent on the audience's perceptions of authenticity. Ingratia-tion is generally viewed as **authentic**—rooted in genuine interest and affirmation, or **illicit**—insincere and motivated by self-serving purposes.

## Exemplification

Exemplification is the act of demonstrating qualities desirable to people with whom you want to be associated. Communicators employ this strategy to project an image of integrity, or model behavior. Exemplification messages convey the communicator's adherence to a strong ethical or moral code (Gilbert & Jones, 1986). This strategy is enacted through behaviors that reflect:

- Altruism and selflessness
- Accordance with rules or standards
- Commitment to integrity

Exemplification can benefit a communicator by highlighting his or her devotion to work or relationships (Jones & Pittman, 1982). However, as with any self-presentation strategy, it can backfire if it's overused or perceived as insincere.

## Power Displays

These displays draw on one's legitimate position of power to appear strong, competent, and worthy of respect. It is sometimes necessary to assert your position of power, especially if doing so (re-) establishes the order needed to complete a task. For example, a team leader might say, "That's enough discussion; let's take a vote and move on." Here, the leader uses a power display to keep the group on task.

If skillfully and sparingly employed, power displays are effective means of self-presentation and situational control (Schutz, 1998). Conversely, some power-related displays, like intimidation and supplication, yield short-term results but incur long-term costs.

## Intimidation

The ability to inspire fear in others is not a particularly favorable trait, and intimidators are often seen as bullies. Intimidation may include:

- An absence of ingratiation, exemplification, and friendly relations
- Challenges or threats to resources

This strategy does little to advance one's social or professional standing. The same is true for the contrasting counter approach, supplication.

## Supplication

Supplicants present themselves as weak. This strategy exploits others' tendency to help those in need. By communicating their inability to perform, people using this strategy assert power because their behaviors usually prompt others to do their work for them. This passive-aggressive behavior may include:

- Claims of confusion (genuine or feigned)
- Requests for assistance
- A willingness to forfeit responsibilities

Whether or not you have used ingratiation or supplication strategies, it is likely you've seen them in action.

## Self-Promotion

Self-promotional strategies are used by individuals who want others to view them as competent and effective. Though some situations like a job interview require successful self-promotion tactics, they remain a challenging feat. Earlier, we touted stealth as a valuable characteristic in self-presentation. This is particularly important when self-promoting. In fact, communicators rarely succeed in self-promotional efforts. The self-promoter's paradox posits that, even when effective in creating perceptions of competence and ability, this approach does little for one's likeability (Gardner & Cleavenger, 1998). There's a take-home message here: don't boast or brag.

Self-promoters may use two popular tactics in attempts to more indirectly achieve their ends:

### Sandbagging

Sandbaggers often misrepresent their abilities (Gibson & Sachau, 2000). Think of the classic pool shark. He or she claims to have little experience or knowledge of the game, yet he or she manages to take you, and the dollars for which you're competing, every time. By downplaying or completely omitting information about experience or ability, the sandbagger hopes to impress others as a naturally gifted performer.

### Self-handicapping

According to Sheppard and Arkin (1989), communicators may manage their reputation or self-esteem by identifying an external factor to which they can attribute their failure. This is often done prior to the act in question. For example, a teammate might say, "I stayed up all night studying for the finance exam, and I didn't have a chance to rehearse my part of today's presentation. I doubt I'll do well." This tactic, though somewhat transparent to the trained eye, may benefit your teammate in one of two ways. If he or she presents poorly, there is a pre-furnished explanation to account for the failure. If he or she happens to perform well, others will likely be impressed by his or her ability to perform despite unfavorable circumstances. This is also sometimes incorrectly recognized as managing expectations.

The strategies above represent a sampling of items that belong to an ever-expanding typology of self-presentation behaviors. All are informative and fascinating additions to your arsenal of communication competence tools. Self-presentation strategies, if properly employed, help you build relationships and garner others' support.

## Understanding Politeness Theory

Erving Goffman (1967) coined the term *face* to describe the aspect of our identity created by our interactions with others, whether in public or private. Much of our self-concept arises from communication with others, and in general, people communicate with the intention of creating a desired impression. Competent communicators attend to their conversation partners' face needs. Goffman argues that we protect one another's face out of "self-respect" and "consideration for others." In order to do so, we avoid posing face (identity) threats to ourselves and others by acting in accordance with communication rules and expectations. In other words, we follow the rules because we understand that it helps preserve our own self-identity and helps others do the same.

Building on Goffman's (1959, 1967) works, Brown and Levinson (1987) developed Politeness Theory, which is grounded in the protection of face. They hold that individuals have both positive and negative face needs. Positive face needs are those that apply to an individual's desire to be well liked and respected, while negative face needs appeal to a person's desire to be free from inconvenience or obligation.

As social creatures, it is assumed we will tend to others' face needs so that they might do the same for us. If I ask my colleague to drive me to the airport, my request may threaten his or her negative face, or desire to be free from inconvenience. Knowing this, I can appeal to his or her negative face needs when asking for his or her help. For example, I might say, "I know this is an inconvenient request, and that your time is valuable, but is there any way you can give me a ride to the airport?" Communicators want to have their face needs recognized, even if those needs are not necessarily met. If I ask, or worse, assume my colleague will give me a ride without recognizing his or her face needs, I disregard his or her identity needs and risk threatening my own positive face, or my desire to be well liked. For this reason, "Hey, you need to give me a ride to the airport" is considered an impolite statement.

If you act in a way that recognizes your colleague's face needs, you are more likely to preserve your own positive face needs. There are many ways to do this. You could present the request with a negative face appeal, "I know this is an inconvenient favor, and that your time is valuable, but is there any way you can give me a ride to the airport?" then provide your colleague with a thank you note and gift certificate to his or her favorite lunch spot when they drop you off. In this case, you appealed to his or her need to be free from imposition **and** his or her need to be well liked. Further, you've maintained your own positive face by demonstrating your appreciation for your colleague's kindness.

When forming messages, consider the face needs of all communicators involved. Attending to your face needs and those of your conversation partners will further develop your competence and success as a communicator.

## Putting Theory into Practice

Consider this scenario: it is Friday afternoon, and Jill has been working hard all week to complete a big project for a major client. Though she is due to leave promptly at 5:00 p.m. because she has dinner plans with a friend who is in town visiting, her boss comes to her office at 4:30 p.m. to tell Jill that the client has requested some major changes. The entire team will have to work late into the night and probably through the weekend to make those changes. If you were Jill, how would you reply to your supervisor?

This kind of situation is fairly common in the business world. You are asked to balance competing personal and professional obligations between various stakeholders. Surely the content of your response would be based on very individual factors. Suppose Jill does not like her job and is looking for a way out; she might reply to her boss that she has plans and cannot stay late, hoping that this response will lead to her being fired.

Most of us, however, like our jobs or at least want to do well in them. Jill had other plans, and canceling them would mean that she would not get to see a friend she had not seen for years. She must balance this desire to control her own schedule with her competing desire to excel in her job. Jill might decide to try to reschedule her plans with her long-lost friend so she can stay late with the rest of her team. Doing this would demonstrate to her boss—and to her peers—that she is willing to make sacrifices for the team. But how would she communicate that?

Jill considers herself a funny and competent person who values her relationships above all else. As a relationship-oriented person, Jill finds it very difficult to choose between seeing a long-lost friend and staying late to work on a project with her work team. Jill values hard work and a job well done, but she also values nurturing the relationships in her life, particularly those that she has had for a long time. No matter what Jill decides to do, she is going to upset someone. How she communicates her decision can minimize the damage—or make it worse.

Assume that Jill decides to leave work and go see her friend. How should she inform her supervisor of her decision? Jill considers herself competent and values relationships, so she wants to communicate in a way that demonstrates both of these things to her supervisor. She might tell the supervisor that she will come into work early the next morning to complete her part of the project. If the supervisor also values relationships as much as Jill does, Jill might want to talk about the friend she has not seen in years. If the supervisor is more career-focused, Jill might not want to dwell on the old friend part.

Jill will have to consider a number of other factors in deciding how she will respond to her supervisor's request.

## Factoring Relationships into Communication

How we communicate is just as important as what we communicate. Many factors influence the how of communication, but one of the most significant factors is your relationship with the person with whom you are trying to communicate. Relationships, both personal and professional, can be complicated. Here are some relationship attributes to consider when formulating a communication strategy.

### Power

This is the ability of one person to influence the life of the other person. You might have more power in a relationship if you are the supervisor because you can make compensation and work environment decisions about the people you supervise. Therefore, your supervisors have power over you. Customers can also be powerful while peers often wield equal power. You must always consider how the other person in the relationship might exert his or her power (for better or worse) in response to your communication. In our scenario above, Jill's supervisor has more power. The supervisor could choose to punish or fire Jill if she decides to go out with her friend instead of staying late. Jill does have some power in this situation though: her decision will affect her supervisor and her team in terms of workload and stress levels.

**Figure 7**   *Power: Don't Abuse It*

©Yuriy Rudyy/Shutterstock.com

### Familiarity

This is how well the two people in the relationship know each other. If you have been working with your supervisor for a very long time and have many shared experiences, you could probably get away with using a more conversational tone. On the other hand, you might have to contact a stakeholder who has never met you. In that case, more formality is advised, at least initially. How well your audience knows you can influence how they perceive your communication.

Jill and her supervisor have known each other for five years. They started out as co-workers before the supervisor was promoted over Jill. They have a high level of familiarity, which also helped them develop a sense of mutual trust and respect. Jill can probably feel a little more comfortable being honest and up front with the supervisor than she would if they did not know each other very well.

Just like personal relationships, professional relationships are not static; they grow and evolve over time. As with all relationships, workplace relationships require time and effort. The more experience you have with relationships, the better you become at identifying how much time and effort each relationship is worth in the long run. It is likely that you will want to maintain professional relationships for extended periods of time; after all, you never know from where your next job opportunity will come. A good rule of thumb is to try never to burn bridges professionally. You should consider the potential value of the relationship over the long term and how your communication might increase or decrease that value.

Jill and her supervisor know each other well and have a positive working relationship. Jill considers her supervisor an ally in the workplace. Jill sees a strong possibility for long-term value in her professional relationship with her supervisor, based largely on shared experiences and successful interactions.

## Shared values

Relationships are often based on more than just circumstances. Just because you work with someone does not in itself mean that you have a relationship with that person. Co-workers often forge relationships because they share certain values. Values are our personal systems of beliefs, the things that we hold dear. These can be arcane, like religious beliefs, or practical, like wanting your company to be successful. Identifying the values you share with others can be an excellent first step in developing your communication strategy.

Jill and her supervisor both want to please their client and see the company succeed. They also have similar tastes in music and food. Jill values individuality and creativity more than her supervisor, who prefers following known rules and protocols. The values that Jill and her supervisor share may make their relationship stronger than the values that set them apart from each other.

Effective communication requires that you balance all of these relationship elements and many other contextual factors. One contextual factor, for example, is the timing of your communication. In our scenario above, if Jill decided she would rather go see her friend than work late, she would need to decide when to tell her boss. If she responded to her supervisor's request immediately, and let him or her know that she would not stay, her supervisor might think that Jill does not care about her job at all. On the other hand, if she waits too long to let her supervisor know that she will not stay late, her boss and co-workers may think she is a flake who left them hanging at the last minute. Neither of these options is strategically wise, and neither takes into consideration how the recipients could interpret Jill's message. More importantly, neither option considers how Jill's decision would impact those around her.

# Communication Accommodation Theory

Social scientist Howard Giles developed Communication Accommodation Theory to evaluate how communication styles reflect and influence the nature of relationships, attitudes, assumptions, and belonging. We create a sense of closeness or distance based on how we relate to others. Namely, we do so in our choice to converge or diverge our speaking style with others.

When we converge our speech and behaviors with another person, we match his or her style of interaction through tone, semantics, and even phonology. One of your authors once had a roommate from Atlanta, Georgia. Having lived in California for several years, she had lost her southern accent. However, it would reappear when phoning her parents, or when in the company of fellow southerners. Another of your authors tends to pick up local accents when he travels to different places, often without even realizing that he is speaking in a new dialect. People tend to converge their speech habits with those to whom they feel—and wish to feel—connected.

You may share a special language with your friends, like terms, nicknames, or phrases that you rarely use with others. Perhaps you have even developed a specialized vocabulary only the two of you understand. In sharing this type of communicative similarity, you also share a relational connection. People can converge language after years of friendship or upon their first meeting. If you appropriately match your conversation partner's style, you send a relational message of acceptance and respect; a sign of mutual understanding. It is often an identity-confirming experience that conveys a sense of similarity between speakers.

Divergence, on the other hand, does just the opposite; it communicates a sense of distance. If we choose to diverge our language, we tend to communicate dissimilarity or reinforce power and relationship roles. Take a look at the convergent and divergent response example below. In this case, a manager is addressed in a very informal tone. In rare cases, this type of address may be appropriate to a unique organizational culture or professional relationship. If so, the manager demonstrates convergence through an equally informal response. It is more probable that this employee's phrasing falls outside the realm of preferred professional conduct. To communicate this, her manager replies with a divergent message. This response sends a rather clear relational message to the employee: "This is inappropriate, and I will not engage through informal conversation." Depending on Ms. Lee's interpretation of her manager's response, she may also view the divergent response as a warning, and/or as an indication of her manager's dislike for her personally. There are many possible interpretations of the divergent response, but few lend themselves to favorable appraisals.

| EMPLOYEE: "HEY, BOSS! DID YOU HAVE A CRAZY MAD RELAXING WEEKEND?" | |
|---|---|
| Manager's Convergent Response | "Oh yeah, I did. Just cold chillin' in my baby crib—you know how I do." |
| Manager's Divergent Response | "Thank you for inquiring, Ms. Lee. My weekend was quite restful." |

In general, speakers seek to converge with others as a means of connection and ingratiation. It is very important, however, that a speaker's convergent style is perceived as genuine. When speaking with others whose language is markedly different, it is most beneficial to mind the rules of polite engagement and avoid contrived attempts to demonstrate similarity. People dislike inauthentic gestures of commonality more than they appreciate shared behaviors. Further, Communication Accommodation Theory suggests that we accommodate, to the appropriate extent, the preferences of our communication partners. Be yourself, with an intention to attend to your listeners and the situation at hand.

## Don't Be a Jerk: Practice Empathy

Nobody wants to be "that guy," the co-worker who never seems to take his or her colleagues into consideration. You cannot control how others think or feel, but you can make choices that make their thoughts and feelings more predictable. Being able to accurately anticipate audience reactions to your communication is a powerful business skill. A highly effective way of learning to anticipate audience reactions is using a concept called *empathy*.

Empathy involves trying to understand someone else's perspective, to see the world as another person sees it. Empathy is often discussed in the social sciences and in medicine because it helps us understand the human condition in order to provide better care. According to nursing researcher Teresa Wiseman, empathy has four elements (Wiseman, 1996).

**Figure 8**   *Empathy Makes Everything Easier*

1. **Perspective-taking**

In the United States, we might describe this as "wearing someone else's shoes." When we take somebody else's perspective, we think more critically about the other person's experiences, values, biases, and everything else they bring to the moment that we are communicating with them.

In Jill's situation, she should try to think about her supervisor's perspective. If Jill put herself in her supervisor's shoes, how would she react if a subordinate came to her and said that she could not work late? What additional challenges would this create for the supervisor? Would this be fair to the rest of the team?

2. **Non-judgment**

Just as we must consider the other person's biases and values, it is important that we try not to judge those values and biases. At our core, all humans want to be accepted and understood on our own terms. An audience is likely to be more receptive if they do not feel judged.

Jill's decision to meet her friend might upset her supervisor. Jill could get defensive and tell her supervisor that he or she is overreacting, but that is probably just going to make the situation worse. Jill should try to understand why her supervisor might be upset without judging the reaction.

3. **Recognizing emotion**

Though it is not always obvious in a business setting, people do experience genuine emotions regarding just about everything. A truly empathic—and effective—communicator can "read" another person's emotional state and adapt accordingly. If the person with whom you are speaking is upset, it is important to try to understand why. Emotion can be a powerful element in persuasion, which is an important tool in the business communication toolbox. Recognizing and helping to harness emotion can serve you well.

Jill should look closely for cues about her supervisor's emotional state after delivering her decision to leave on time. Jill's communication strategy and response going forward must depend, at least in part, on the emotional impact that her declaration has on her supervisor. If the supervisor seems disappointed or sad, even unintentionally (we all show emotion even when we try not to), Jill might need to say something that will soften the blow, like that she will have her smartphone with her at all times and can be contacted in case of an emergency.

4. **Communicating understanding**

It is not enough for you to simply hear what the other person is trying to communicate; you must demonstrate to them that you understand it. Remember that all humans want to be understood; even if you don't agree with someone, they will be more receptive to you if you let them know that you understand them. Disagreement after mutual understanding is demonstrated is also less likely to become contentious.

Jill cannot expect to just go into her supervisor's office, deliver her decision about leaving early, and then expect to leave. They will necessarily have a conversation, and Jill, if she wants to keep her job, will likely have to demonstrate that she hears and understands her supervisor's response. We provide some helpful tools for doing this in the next section.

Most companies thrive on practicing empathy with their customers. It should be noted, however, that some very large companies, such as Apple and Walmart, do not practice empathy and instead dictate to their customers what they think the customers should want. These companies can succeed with this strategy because they are so large and have devoted customer bases. For most businesses, however, empathizing with customers, suppliers, and other stakeholders is vitally important to success.

## Harnessing Active Listening Skills

Now that you understand the concept of empathy and why it is important to business success, you may still be wondering how you can demonstrate that you are empathetic to the people with whom you communicate. One effective tool, which we also borrow from social and medical science, is active listening.

Active listening involves hearing and understanding not just the words that the other person says, but also all of the underlying meaning as communicated through nonverbal cues and context and then communicating that understanding back. Active listening helps in a few key ways:

- Builds trust between two parties
- Improves understanding of what is really being communicated
- Validates the speaker's thoughts and feelings
- Creates more mutually beneficial [business] outcomes (Davidhizer, 2004)

With these benefits associated with active listening, it is surprising that more people do not practice this key skill! Here are some of the most common and effective tactics involved in active listening:

- **Parroting:** Repeat back to the person the last few words or phrases that he or she said to demonstrate that you are indeed listening.
- **Reflecting back:** Mirror the other person's tone and mood. If the other person is very excited, respond quickly and emphatically; if he or she is quiet or upset, respond more softly.
- **Asking questions:** Seek to understand his or her perspective more completely. This is more effective when confined to the immediate topic at hand.
- **Paraphrasing:** Try to restate what the other person has said in your own words. This can be easily done by asking a question: "I think what you said is...is that correct?" or "Did I hear you say...?"
- **Maintaining eye contact:** Look directly at the other person while they are speaking. Important: not all cultures see this as a sign of respect. In the United States, this is a physical cue that demonstrates that you are paying attention, but in some cultures, this could be interpreted as a sign of disrespect. Please use your best judgment when applying this form of active listening in your own culture.
- **Nodding and using vocal sounds:** As you listen, occasionally nod your head and use positive vocal acknowledgments (such as "uh huh" and "I see") to demonstrate that you both hear and understand. The danger here is that you can use this tactic reflexively without actually actively paying attention. Don't nod and use vocal acknowledgments unless you are actually listening to and understand the speaker!

These tactics show you how to listen, but we must also consider why we listen. Here are a few examples and reasons why we listen to others in a business setting (Solomon & Theiss, 2012):

- **Discriminatory listening** is when we listen to differentiate meaning. We might listen to our vendors to try and determine what day of the week they will be delivering materials. From our example above, Jill might listen to her boss's response to her unwillingness to stay late to determine if the response was sarcastic or sincere.
- **Appreciative listening** is when we listen for the sake of enjoying what we will hear. We engage in appreciative listening when we listen to music or watch television or movies. We want to appreciate the sound.
- **Comprehensive listening** is when we listen in order to understand <u>meaning</u>. While discriminatory listening can be very simple—differentiating between two possible interpretations of sound—comprehensive listening can be much more complex. In comprehensive listening, we try to understand and retain deeper meaning. Jill might use comprehensive listening to try to understand why her supervisor wants her to stay late despite her previous plans.
- **Evaluative listening** is when we take comprehensive listening one step further. Beyond just understanding deep meaning, we make judgments based on it. Evaluative listening can be used to examine the strength, character, or content of either the speaker or the message. Jill might use evaluative listening to find subtext (underlying, unspoken meaning) in her supervisor's response.
- **Empathic listening** is when we listen to help others meet their needs. This is the most powerful form of listening because it enables the listener to connect with the speaker on a deeper, more personal level. Jill should use empathic listening with her supervisor because it will demonstrate that she truly understands her boss' needs, and that she has weighed all options thoroughly.

It is important to note that these types of listening are not mutually exclusive; we use them all simultaneously and in rotation throughout each day, often without thinking. One key to becoming a truly effective business communicator is to become more mindful about what type of listening to employ in any given circumstance and then using your active listening skills to do so.

Throughout this chapter, we have discussed the importance of developing a professional persona, and, obviously, that persona is only useful when it is shared. As you move into your chosen career field, you will have daily interactions with co-workers, supervisors, partners, and clients. Business communication, however, is much more than a series of individual interactions. In virtually every job you have, you will work as part of a team. Your ability to apply the previously discussed business communication skills to a team setting will be a key to your future success. To help enhance your work with others, the focus of the next chapter is effective team communication.

# Connect, Collaborate, and Engage

In the previous chapter, you learned about managing your own professional persona and about communicating effectively with others. These skills will help to ensure your success in a variety of career situations. You will need them to interact with academic advisors as you complete your business degrees. You will also need them to secure an internship and to land and advance in your dream job. At every step, one thing will be true: you cannot go it alone. You will soon discover the value of working in teams to complete projects in university courses, during internships, and in the workplace. In this section, you will learn to apply several of the communication strategies you have already learned to team settings. You will also discover some valuable insights into team dynamics.

## Managing Team Meetings and Group Communication

### Mastering Small Group Communication

Like it or not, productively working in small groups is a key to success in the workplace. Your ability to successfully work on teams is commonly assessed in the application process for most organizations. Interview questions often screen for your ability to work effectively in teams; job shadowing measures your ability to work with others; and often mini-competitions with other applicants, panel interview questions, or "think on your feet" moments measure your ability to effectively work with a group of other individuals. Teams are one of the essential basic building blocks of any organization.

©g-stockstudio/Shutterstock.com

**Figure 1**  *Teams Take Work*

*Benefit of team* (handwritten, left margin)

Most of the work completed in organizations is interdependent (Daft, 2011). When they are effective, teams can provide benefits for both organizations and employees through higher productivity, quality improvements, greater flexibility and speed, a more horizontal management structure, increased employee involvement and satisfaction, and lower turnover (Glassop, 2002). Working on a great team can be exhilarating; working on a low performing team is like being condemned to one of Dante's circles of hell. No two ways about it, working on a successful team takes skill and effort. Your personal success relies on your ability to lead or follow in a group setting in order to successfully communicate and navigate the challenging political trade winds that can knock a team off course. While you will experience many workplace configurations, one way to ensure your success is to learn some of the best ways to manage your participation in some common group activities. Having face-to-face conversations, participating in meetings, and managing high stakes discussions are fundamental to your success.

This section will examine common team dynamics, best team practices, common group communication pitfalls, and finally, the role and nature of conflict, and how to keep it in check on your teams.

## Making Meetings More Effective

Meetings can be the bane of teamwork, but they also provide the opportunity for group alignment, discussion, debate, and decision making. Meetings are so common in the work world, they are often abused and can be a waste of everyone's time. Lisa Belkin, writing in the *New York Times*, describes a collaborative study by Microsoft, America Online, and Salary.com regarding the actual amount of time workers worked in an average day and week. The study concluded that the average worker actually worked only three days per week or about 1.5 hours per day. The study identified that the rest of the working time was "wasted," with unproductive meetings heading the list (Williams, 2012). Many organizations provide training for their employees on conducting effective meetings in order to minimize the potential for wasting time and lowering productivity.

Organizations spend a good deal of time and effort trying to resolve the issue of unproductive meetings. One landmark study completed in 1999 advocated for altering the format of meetings so that all participants had to stand throughout. Sit-down meetings were 34% longer than stand-up meetings, but they produced no better decisions. There were also significant differences in satisfaction with the meeting and task information use during the meeting (Bluedorn, Turban, & Love, 1999). A working commitment by everyone to make meetings productive and timely seemed to contribute to an overall environment of collaboration and goodwill.

Despite the dangers they pose, meetings confirm one of the principles of oral communication: people prefer to meet because face-to-face communication "feels" good. It is a rich medium that reinforces our fundamental human need to connect and have in-the-moment communication.

*Effective Teams* (handwritten, left margin)

Additionally, meetings encourage social interaction, keep everyone in the loop, and reaffirm status. People feel they are important when they can voice their opinion or be involved in the decision-making process (Ashkenas, 2010). In fact, meetings can feel so good, they can be a gateway drug for groupthink and lowered productivity. For example, several years ago in GlaxoSmithKline's research organization, there was a realization that, as a result of multiple project meetings and the inclusion of all functions on drug development teams, many people were spending as much time in meetings as they were on actual drug development work (Ashkenas, 2010). One way to combat the negative effects of meetings is to be aware of best practices and be sure to observe them in meetings.

## Articulating Your Meeting Purpose

As with any effective message, the purpose of a meeting should be clear, and it should be conveyed to your audience. Your first decision should be if the meeting actually has to happen. If coordination costs are high, then you need to be sure that assembling everyone has a distinct purpose, and that all participants are informed and prepared when they attend.

> "If you are not careful, a meeting moves at the speed of the slowest mind in the room . . . all but one participant will be bored, all but one mind under-used."
>
> – Dale Dauten

Typically, there are four common types of meetings. **Decision-making meetings** gather consensus, entertain divergent viewpoints, and make decisions among group members. **Project kickoff meetings** make sure all roles and tasks are understood. **Working meetings** can assist in solving problems or finalizing deliverables. Finally, **staff meetings** keep everyone informed of new policies, organizational updates, and information sharing. Meetings should not be confused with individuals who like to work in tandem or together, or simply "hanging out." To keep your meetings on track, they should be planned in advance and participants should be notified of any expectations so they can arrive prepared and ready to devote their time and resources to tasks at hand.

## Have an Agenda

A meeting agenda is an organizational strategy and time management tool that helps inform meeting participants of the content of the meeting and the sequencing of conversations. For a meeting to be effective, it requires a clear agenda and timetable. An effective meeting is planned to determine how much time each item will require and then telegraphing that information to participants. The meeting facilitator can easily keep a meeting effectively managed by driving discussions within allotted time frames. Managing a meeting is similar to crafting a careful message: you want to be sure that you get to all the information you wish to share with your audience. In a face-to-face encounter, managing time effectively is key to your success.

Effective meeting agendas list anticipated attendees and note which attendees will facilitate different agenda items. To keep your agenda on track, assign a rough estimate of the time that you will spend addressing each item at the meeting. For teams with more social members, you may find it helpful to include some brief time either at the beginning or end of the meeting to catch up or check in.

## Making Decisions as a Team

Driving decisions can be difficult in a real time environment. Varying opinions, depths of knowledge, and communication styles can pose challenges to effective decision making. For an effective meeting, a facilitator needs to present the decision, capture pros and cons, and ask the team to formalize the decision. Identifying the process that will be used to make the decision can be as important as the decision that gets made.

If there is conflict among the group, an effective strategy is to ask each individual for his or her viewpoint, effectively giving everyone time to consider multiple points of view. A wise communicator carefully considers all viewpoints. If the decision can be made democratically by vote, this is one way to proceed. If there are external factors that the facilitator must consider, then sometimes you must solicit information from the group, and then make an informed decision. Decision making can be a complex process, but in a meeting situation, it is important to manage time, confirm viewpoints, and listen carefully.

### Learn How to Align Yourself: Paraphrasing

When driving consensus or agreement, it helps to confirm understanding for everyone by taking the time to paraphrase what has been said. As an active listening tool described in the previous chapter, paraphrasing can be a powerful tool for bringing members of a team together around a common concept or goal. In the same way that you might conclude a message or tie together multiple points, paraphrasing provides you with the opportunity to re-state a common theme, agreement, or discussion point so everyone is clear as to what has been said. Paraphrasing also provides your audience with an opportunity to correct any misperceptions or miscommunication.

### COMMON SIGN POST LANGUAGE PHRASES:

1. Identify a key or main idea (What we need to talk about today. . .)

2. Signal importance (The most important thing I want to talk about today. . .)

3. Emphasize a key take away (If there is one thing I want you to remember from today's meeting. . .)

4. Use numbers (There are three points I want to make: one. . .)

5. Introduce a new topic (So, this moves us to the next point of discussion. . .)

6. Conclude (So, in summary, we have decided. . .)

### Wake Them Up: Use Sign Post Language

To provide punch and clarity to your point, using sign post language helps direct your audience to key points and important information while alerting them to the direction the conversation is headed. Sign post language includes emphasizing importance or signaling transitions.

### Using Active Listening for More Than One-on-One Conversations

As much as meetings provide a time for the team to have a fair and frank exchange of views, it is equally important that participants enter into an active listening mode. Since meetings are an opportunity to deepen bonds and build credibility among team members, listening to others share divergent viewpoints strengthens team bonds while deepening the understanding of the information required to drive more effective decisions. Listening should provide you with the additional opportunity to track your team's decisions, the reasons behind these decisions, and the undercurrents on the team. Nothing is more annoying than a team member who doesn't track evolving conversations, decisions as they are being made, or action items. Don't be "that guy"!

### Using the Video Conference/Teleconference

Often, one or more team members need to attend meetings remotely. In these instances, video conferencing or teleconferencing is commonly used. When a team member isn't physically present in a meeting, special care must be made to include the absent member in the conversation, decision making, and information exchange. Take the time to invite the remote member in and solicit opinions, viewpoints, or additional information to keep the person involved in the conversation. If the remote team member cannot see the other meeting participants, likely because they are conferencing in via telephone, it is important for the other members to identify themselves when they speak.

If you are the person who is on the other end of the phone or webcam, remember to pay active attention and seek clarification for moments you might be missing. Ask individuals to describe or re-state points that might not be clear to you since you are missing the

©Rawpixel.com/Shutterstock.com

**Figure 2**    *Teleconferencing Requires Practice*

nonverbal cues. If you are on a webcam, be sure to minimize any distractions and maintain eye contact with the camera. Even small gestures will be amplified. Keep in mind that gestures or expressions that indicate you are not tracking or closely engaged will likewise be maximized.

### Hold One Another Accountable: Remember When We Said…

Finally, once a meeting has concluded, it is common to distribute minutes to summarize and capture the key information discussed on the agenda. Included in the minutes should be the date of the meeting, participants, and any key decisions or pending action items. To keep team members engaged, accountability measures help make sure the decisions that were made and/or action items distributed keep moving forward. Dashboards, work exchanges, or group documents that track progress of work, deadlines, and completed items help teams stay on task and complete the work on time and within agreed parameters. Your agenda is often a useful starting place for crafting your minutes.

Each team makes its own magic. What works for one group won't necessarily be effective for another group. However, meetings are where your communication competencies are put to the test. Mastering these will help develop your credibility and build your reputation. This is particularly true in high stakes conversations.

# Having High Stakes Conversations

Inevitably in the give and take of teamwork, you will enter into situations where difficult or sensitive conversations will take place. Understanding when and where these types of conversations should take place can go a long way toward making sure your message is understood. These types of conversations are called "high stakes" conversations because they demonstrate your ability to manage the moment, understand how your audience is feeling, and know if you need to speed up or slow down the exchange.

Whether you need to confront a coworker, a team member, or even a supervisor, there are moments when your reputation rests on your ability to address a sensitive topic and maintain a good working relationship. When someone needs to receive sensitive news—perhaps feedback regarding poor performance or bad news involving an organizational restructuring—you need to determine the best channel and method for delivering this type of information. Often these types of exchanges involve both written and verbal communication; this allows for control of the message and generates a record of the event. Understanding the information that needs to be conveyed

**Figure 3**   *Seek First to Understand*

and the recipient's overall receptivity to the message are keys to your success. Let's take a look at some of the high stakes conversations that typically function best in a face-to-face situation.

### Giving Feedback

While performance evaluations are a formal way to provide an employee with his or her overall strengths and areas for improvement, why wait until the end of a project to report back out? Regular feedback helps keep everyone engaged and productive. Frequently, for a

**Figure 4**   *We Remember How We Feel More Than What Was Said*

team to break through to the next level of productivity, honest feedback is needed. The best way to address misunderstandings, varying expectations, or competing goals and interests is through feedback. Feedback is frequently given in a face-to-face situation so that each person has the opportunity to self-correct in the moment or to change a situation before it becomes more detrimental. When your team enters the performance zone, and it is time to deliver a complex and coordinated deliverable, having strong enough relationships allowing for frank and fair feedback can keep your team on track and performing at a high level.

Feedback can sometimes be difficult to handle, but it should always be regarded as a gift. Too often in the workplace, individuals do not receive feedback soon enough to be able to alter a course of action, resulting in poor work performance. It is considered a best practice to give co-workers, team members, and peers feedback so as to build relationships, sustain networks, and enhance performance.

So why do we avoid giving honest feedback? Why is it easier to avoid the situation, take on extra work, or build a mini-coalition inside the team? One reason is that it makes us uncomfortable to enter into a conversation where someone might be embarrassed or feel confronted. We don't want to jeopardize a working relationship, or we might not feel comfortable enough with others on the team to enter into this type of discussion. We may not have confidence in our own leadership position or relationship with the feedback recipient. This is one instance where knowing how to deliver a challenging message can make a real difference in being heard, and ultimately, improving your team's performance.

## MAKE IT A DELICIOUS FEEDBACK SANDWICH, PLEASE

1. Align with the individual. (That's the bread)

2. Approach the topic. (That's the filler. . .. lettuce, tomato, cheese)

3. Give the news. (That's the meat)

4. Go back to alignment. (The bottom bread)

5. Add flair. (That's any special sauce or condiments, which are up to you)

## *Delivering Sensitive Information: It Really is How You Say It…*

Similar to managing conflict, bad news will surface on your team. Tough messages have to be delivered all the time in the workplace. Sometimes bad news is delivered to clients or customers; other times you must deliver bad news to co-workers, employees, or even your boss.

How you manage your delivery goes a long way towards what your audience will remember and retain. It is important to establish a clear connection with the person receiving the bad news so they can leave the situation with a clear understanding of what has been said. Depending on the relationship of the individuals, and the nature of the bad news, typically these types of conversations are held privately or with a witness.

No one really likes to receive a negative message, no matter how confident they are. Unless the circumstances are extreme, it is usually wise to revert to the "sandwich." In this instance, you will want to allude to the context of the situation and state the purpose of the conversation, but you want to take the time to find common ground and align with the individual prior to heading into the bad news.

Provide some time for each person to orient to the conversation. You will need to raise the topic or purpose of the meeting and wait until the other individual is listening before you move forward with the bad news. After you've delivered the difficult message, you want to return to how you are aligned with the individual. This type of "sandwiching"—aligning, delivering the bad news, then realigning—helps the individual understand the bad news while also retaining his or her sense of connection with you. This is framing at its best, and it should be used with compassion, so the recipient feels respected, listened to, and regarded. There is no way out of delivering bad news; we all have to do it at some point. But you can deliver it with a sense of empathy, support, and in such a manner to keep your working relationships intact.

## Navigating Team Dynamics

Working with others as part of a team represents the truly collaborative nature of being human. Businesses have realized the power of teams and the positive dynamics that team synergy produces for an organization. In its simplest form, team synergy is achieved when a group attains more than the sum of its parts. The positive aspects of team synergy have led to an overwhelming majority of organizations employing teams to accomplish key business functions of the company. It is likely you will be working in one or more teams in the workplace.

Therefore, it is important to understand how and why to communicate effectively with your team to harness the true power your team possesses.

## Accommodating Team Member Differences

It should be no surprise that you are not the same as everyone else in the world. We are all different, and this is a good thing. Workplace teams are no exception to this rule. Teams are made up of individuals with differences in work pace, communication preferences, workplace motivations, and ideas of success. These differences in individual team members are beneficial in challenging teams to be innovative and not to conform to groupthink, which will be discussed in the upcoming chapter on Team Pitfalls. In building a strong and well-balanced team, it is best to have a team made up of diverse backgrounds and styles. However, sometimes these differences can cause challenges in communicating to and understanding each team member.

### HOW CAN YOU BE A BETTER TEAM MEMBER?

1. Help socialize new members onto the team. If you are all new team members, know it takes a bit of time for the group to settle into place.
2. Become aware of your own communication and personality styles.
3. Be sensitive to diversity on a team— demographic, cultural, cognitive, and social.
4. Understand your role.
5. Be open to feedback.
6. Improve your verbal and nonverbal messaging.
7. Develop your listening skills.

## Synchronize Your Watches!

Generally, cultures regard time in different ways. Mono- and polychronemic time associations reflect a culture's temporal attitudes. Monochronemic cultures, like those in America, tend to have a very strict orientation toward time. When operating in a monochronemic culture, one regards time as a precise, and rather strictly enforced concept. In this case, an appointment at two o'clock means exactly two o'clock. Arriving at two thirty for a two o'clock job interview would likely rule you out as a candidate.

There are exceptions to this rule, and these exceptions are usually afforded to those with higher power or status. Though you might ruin your chances of employment by arriving late to your interview, the hiring manager would probably think very little of your waiting in the reception area, for a rather long duration, until he or she is available to see you.

Polychronemic cultures have a more relaxed, abstract orientation toward time. In this case, two o'clock might be more of an approximation than a precise point of time. This does not mean that polychronemic cultures are less productive or reliable. It simply reflects a difference in perceptual anchors and their social contracts regarding time and space. As with other communication rules, communicators demonstrate competence through the recognition of, and adherence to, the preferences of the culture in which they are communicating. Check with your teammates and clearly establish your expectations around timing; you will save a lot of, well, time, and avoid unnecessary frustration.

## Understanding Your Team Members Is Necessary to Communicating Effectively

We communicate with others through our words, actions, and inactions. However, as we explained earlier, our field of experience typically governs our communication. When working on a team, you are working with a distinct field of experience from every team member you encounter. Your understanding of team members' feelings, values, and perspectives should inform your communication with them. It is important that we are able to identify and understand these differences in order to communicate more effectively and avoid misunderstandings. Therefore, it is vital to make a genuine effort to understand each member of your team and how his or her frame of reference impacts the situation, and work to be adaptable to the unique needs of your team members. No one field of experience is better than the other. In fact, different fields of experience provide more diverse viewpoints and create more positive team dynamics. Teams with positive dynamics understand each other and the importance of capitalizing on each member's strengths to allow the team to function successfully.

One would think, that after acquiring all this knowledge and understanding how to apply these insights, teamwork would be the utopia of the business world. However, let us not forget one fact: your team members all have minds of their own! This basic truth can lead to a variety of conflicts that can hinder, or even derail, the progress of a team. In the next section, you will learn how to recognize trouble before it begins and how to handle conflict constructively.

# Addressing Team Pitfalls and Conflicts

**F**ew people seek out conflict. In fact, our natural reactions to a threat are either to ignore it or to stomp it into the ground. Both of these responses to a conflict on a team will result in problems, either in the long run or in the moment. In order to prepare you for the various types of conflict that can arise on a team, this section will present insight into what causes conflict and clear strategies for managing it. You can develop the ability to recognize and address conflict before it turns ugly.

## Avoiding Group Communication Pitfalls

In his book, The *Five Dysfunctions of Teams*, Patrick M. Lencioni presents the issues that most frequently keep teams from success. As a team's structure begins to falter and fail, group communication pitfalls surface. He lists the five dysfunctions and explains how they affect team functionality.

1. **Absence of trust**—Trust is the currency of the 21st-century workplace. Without it, your team won't be able to be nearly as productive. Trust takes time and is based on a number of relationship factors, but at the core are credibility, integrity, results, and competence. Before you ask people to trust you, you need to demonstrate you are trustworthy.
2. **Fear of conflict**—Without the psychological safety to be able to have a healthy debate, your team won't be able to address issues that keep it from thriving.
3. **Lack of commitment**—A team needs a clear sense of task and must buy into goals before they are able to function optimally.
4. **Avoidance of accountability**—Without keeping one another accountable for the quality of work, results, and output, your team will start to falter.
5. **Inattention to results**—If there is no accountability, team members begin to place their own needs ahead of the team (Leoni, 2002).

Avoid these common pitfalls by working through communication-based issues that are well within your reach. As your team moves forward through the stages of forming a healthy team, be sure to recognize dysfunctions as they surface, and be ready to mitigate them through your own actions, consistency, and accountability.

## Addressing Social Loafing

Have you ever had someone on your team who decided just to sit back and let the rest of the team do all the heavy lifting? Why is that person always the same individual who strides forward and joins everyone else in taking credit for the team's final results? Social loafing is a common enough occurrence on teams and is annoying for those who find themselves doing the legwork. Social loafing is also sometimes called free riding; no matter what you call it, it is an irritant to have an individual like this on your team.

If you have a free-rider on your team, the group is responsible for holding this individual accountable. If you are enabling this individual, you should check in with group processes (as well as your own need to "cover" this person) and step up the structure in terms of team processes to provide clear expectations, timelines, and accountability. If these processes are documented and still result in free-riding, solicit outside input, preferably with someone who exercises more authority, to identify the root cause of the problem.

**Figure 1**   *The Loafer*

Don't be surprised if you discover deeper issues on the team once you address a free rider. Perhaps this individual feels marginalized. You may discover cognitive differences or a lack of skill. You may find out that the way the team is being led, or the processes you have in place are not providing a way for this individual to contribute. In many instances, finding a reasonable or alternate way for the individual to contribute helps improve processes for the entire team. Regardless of the reason, your group should agree early on that one of its norms will be to confront social loafers immediately and address the issue at hand.

## Preventing Groupthink

One common area where groups can begin to falter is settling into *groupthink*.

When groups do not have the mechanisms in place to manage conflict or feel pressure to conform, the danger of groupthink surfaces. Many examples exist of corporations or agencies that experienced large and public failures due to a talented group of individuals who acted so cohesively they failed to consider obvious and critical information. The Cuban Missile Crisis, Bay of Pigs, Watergate, and the explosion of the Challenger Space Shuttle are classic examples of groupthink (Myers & Anderson, 2008).

How is it that whole teams of highly trained professionals can overlook data or information that should alert them to impending disaster? Groupthink is a powerful phenomenon. Essentially, a highly cohesive group's ability to make an effective decision is hampered by the pressure to maintain group cohesion (Myers & Anderson, 2008). A highly cohesive team is usually a desirable state—both for those on the team and individuals managing the team. When a team can no longer entertain outside information due to group norms and conformity, the quality of decision-making drops swiftly.

Be sure your team has an appointed mechanism to challenge the information being discussed so you can entertain multiple viewpoints. Host a healthy debate. Make sure your team takes the time to check its own pulse and keep a sense of unity, but be wary of feelings of invulnerability. That's when you enter into the danger zone for groupthink. By putting into practice the steps outlined to avoid groupthink, you should be able to steer your team clear of any disasters.

## Recognizing the Roles People Play

Typically, once a team forms, individuals begin to assume roles on the team. Depending on the individual's role and how deeply invested he or she is in it directly affects group communication. There are three types of roles that surface on teams: task roles, socio-emotional roles (maintenance roles), or individualistic roles (Walker, 2011). Team members may play one, two, or all three types of roles at any given time.

Task roles tend to be familiar to most team members: the initiator, the information seeker, the information giver, the coordinator, the critic, and the recorder. Depending on the environment in which you are working, leaders can be assigned or emerge. Leaders can even be situational with a team responding and assigning an individual to lead a task based on expertise, availability, or desire. Task roles, if clearly defined, usually assist in improving team processes.

Some roles are related to team maintenance, the roles that keep a team functioning smoothly by participating in the emotional health of the group. These roles range from the encourager, the compromiser, the gatekeeper, the standard setter, the commentator, and the follower (Walker, 2011). Each of these roles serves a function to help keep the team operating smoothly and satisfying the emotional needs of team members.

However, the third set of roles, individualistic, can cause the most damage (Walker, 2011). Typically, these types of individuals do not contribute much more than drama and conflict. Learning to recognize these types of individuals and find ways to work productively with them will save the team from unnecessarily high levels of conflict or lowered productivity.

# Managing Conflict

Conflict is highly probable once realities set in on working teams. Usually, competing interests, conflicting needs, and additional pressures of performance and time restraints surface in the life cycle of any team. Your ability to understand the different types of conflict will go a long way toward making life more bearable on your team.

---

### HOW TO AVOID GROUPTHINK

- Encourage group members to voice objections and critically evaluate ideas.

- Detach from your ego and seek an objective view of problems or decisions.

- Divide the group and see if you can come up with different solutions or approaches.

- Deliberately discuss group processes or results with others outside the group to solicit feedback.

- Appoint a devil's advocate and rotate that role on the team.

*(Gibson & Hodgetts, 1986)*

---

### FOLKS TO WATCH OUT FOR (INDIVIDUALISTIC ROLES)

Aggressor—Expresses disapproval of ideas, feelings of others; attacks group

Blocker—Resists the group's influence; opposes the team unnecessarily

Dominator—Asserts authority or superiority; is manipulative

Evader/self-confessor—Expresses personal interests, feelings or opinions unrelated to group goals

Help Seeker—Expresses insecurity, confusion, self-deprecation, constantly needs help

Recognition Seeker—Calls attention to self; self-aggrandizing

Playboy/girl—Uninvolved with the group; often cynical or nonchalant.

Special-interest pleader—Remains apart from the group by trying to represent another social group

*(Walker, 2011)*

Some conflict can actually enhance overall team productivity and results. A robust discussion around the different ideas or opinions, or appointing a devil's advocate to challenge divergent viewpoints, helps minimize disruptive conflict. When individuals work harder to make themselves heard, or spend more time gathering evidence to prove their position, the outcomes can be richer and more varied. In other words, a team can get better results. When conflict creeps up to higher levels, the team's ability to function can be put into jeopardy.

Learn to recognize deviant behaviors that violate group norms or place unnecessary "drag" on the team. Examples include not participating in group discussions, missing group meetings, fighting for leadership, constantly challenging other team members' opinions, or forming coalitions (Pendell, 1990). If you have a team member who leaves early or chronically shows up late, he or she is violating group norms. If two team members consistently battle for leadership by manipulating, undermining, or ostracizing other group members, the team cannot function to its full capacity. Establishing team norms that are acceptable, then holding one another accountable can go a long way toward improving group climate and productivity.

## Are Your Teammates Buying What You're Selling?

A rule sometimes applied to the retail industry is the 20/20/60 rule. This rule gives sales representatives a little perspective on how customers view them and how individual customers are most likely to respond to their sales pitch. The rule states that 20% of your prospects will love you and immediately want to do business with you; 20% will hate you and never buy from you unless you're the only supplier left on earth; the remaining 60% will form no immediate opinion of you. This last group may be interested but remain skeptical until they have had more time to size you up and make a more informed decision. This rule can also help in team settings as you begin to size up the other members and try to find meaningful ways to collaborate with each other. How does this rule suggest we behave in new situations? First, don't worry so much about the 40% who have already made up their minds. Enjoy the camaraderie of those who love you, and do your best not to annoy those who hate you. Focus the majority of your attention on the remaining 60% because your actions and words will sway them one way or the other. Do your best to understand them and to flex your normal style of interaction and labor to collaborate more effectively with these team members. By focusing your attention on making the team as productive as possible, you may even win over the 20% who were initially not that fond of you.

But what do we do when real conflicts arise? In business, it is unrealistic to think that a company can avoid crises altogether. However, the company's image will not ultimately be determined by whether or not a crisis occurs, but by how it is handled. It is vital to have a plan for managing conflicts in place before they occur. Learning to manage conflicts on your own work teams is an important place to begin to learn how to manage major workplace crises.

## Achieving Conflict Resolution

In a healthy work environment, conflict must arise so that multiple viewpoints and alternatives can be considered. On your team, how well you can manage conflict and find resolution largely determines the overall levels of productivity and innovation in the workplace. While the field of conflict resolution is large, there are some common practices to consider.

First, seek to understand. Based on an earlier theory by Chris Argyris, Peter Senge created the "ladder of inference," a framework for understanding how we develop our beliefs and translate them into actions. The lowest rung of the ladder is all of the observable data and facts available to us. The next rung up is our selected reality, or those facts and data that we choose to pay most attention to. Climbing the ladder to the next rung, we interpret and assign meaning to our selected facts and data. It's not a large step up from there to the next rung, assumptions. Our assumptions lead to conclusions, and our conclusions lead to our beliefs. Once we have solidified our beliefs, action is not far off (Senge, 1990). It is exceptionally easy to jump to conclusions about a teammate's intentions based on his or her observable actions. When confronting conflict on a team, it is best to climb back down your ladder of inference. Remember: what you observe may not be the whole story or you could be misinterpreting the situation. Assume goodwill until you can re-evaluate the facts you selected and the meaning you assigned to them.

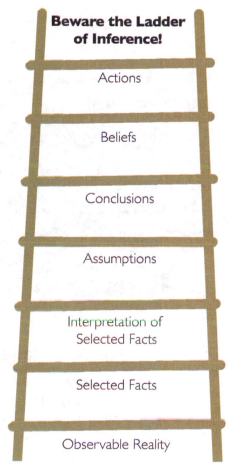

Unfortunately, sometimes our assumptions are validated. When tempers flare, or we find ourselves embroiled in a conflict, it is easy to fall into an "us vs. them" mentality. In these circumstances, a face-to-face meeting can help facilitate and work toward resolution more quickly than if other communication channels are used. Regardless of how you are involved in the conflict, the same basic principles of verbal communication will assist you as you move forward with finding common understanding.

In the table below, you can quickly assess an appropriate response style based on the situation. Being able to understand the final required outcome can help you to identify the most effective strategy to use when addressing a problematic team issue.

| STYLE | APPROPRIATE SITUATION |
|---|---|
| Avoiding | 1. The issue is trivial. <br> 2. Group members need to take a break. <br> 3. Confronting group members is unnecessary. |
| Dominating | 4. The issue is trivial. <br> 5. A timely decision is needed. <br> 6. The group members lack expertise. |
| Compromising | 7. The group members can't reach consensus. <br> 8. The dominating style has no effect. <br> 9. A temporary solution is needed. |
| Obliging | 10. The issue is more important to group members than you. <br> 11. The relationship among group members is worth preserving. <br> 12. You lack expertise. |
| Integrating | 13. The issue is complex. <br> 14. The group has the necessary resources. <br> 15. The issue requires group member collaboration. |

(Rahim, 2002)

## Analytical Conflicts

Let's consider the various types of conflicts that arise in a small group setting. Understanding the most common basis for conflicts on teams will help you develop strategies for effectively resolving those conflicts. There are four general categories of conflict: analytical, task-related, interpersonal, and the power struggle (Barrett, 2006).

Analytical conflicts emerge around disagreements about the basic approach to handling an issue or about the proposed answers to major questions. This type of conflict can be very constructive as long as individual members do not take personally any disagreement expressed about their ideas. The team leader should facilitate a discussion that is respectful to make it easier for members to be flexible and willing to select the most efficient approach for the team's objectives rather than guarding their own suggestion or idea at all costs.

**Figure 2**  *Conflicts Can Be Resolved!*

## Task-Related Conflicts

Task-related conflicts are usually associated with deadlines placed on various stages of the project. It is important that all members have been part of developing the initial work plan and have agreed on specific deadlines. Each member must be honest about the amount of time he or she needs to complete a task and build that into the work plan. This way, every member is responsible for delivering quality work on time. It is also important, however, for the team to be flexible and willing to extend deadlines or offer assistance, without blame, when one member has a legitimate reason for failing to meet a deadline.

## Power Struggle Conflicts

Power struggle or role conflicts occur when leadership is not established early on, or when a member perceives inefficiency in the existing leader. Clarity and agreement on roles can go a long way in preventing this type of conflict. However, shared ownership is also an effective way to maintain a respectful working environment. Since most projects have various components, an individual can take the lead on the sections he or she is most interested in and qualified for. This horizontal leadership style can help to reduce power struggle conflicts, and this is essential if the team is to be productive. You will want to be careful that ownership over individual pieces of a project is not misinterpreted as the leader ceding all of his or her power to other team members as this may result in problems down the line.

## Interpersonal Conflicts

Interpersonal conflicts may be the most disruptive to a team's dynamics. Personality and cultural differences can create subtle cracks in the make-up of the group. One member may offend another without even being aware of it, and once offended, the other member may be extremely difficult to win back. Much of this can be avoided by understanding one another's values and styles as discussed in previous sections of this text. However, some situations will need a more systematic approach if the team is to become a unified whole.

# Work Your A's to Resolve Conflict

While there are many theories on how to best resolve conflicts within teams, the Chevron Chart of Five A's, developed by Deborah Borisoff and David Victor, presents a practical approach that has been successfully adopted by many U.S. companies (Borisoff & Victor, 1998). The following is an overview of the process of the Five A's, followed by a description of what is involved in each stage.

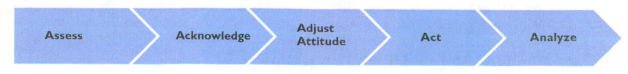

| Assess | Acknowledge | Adjust Attitude | Act | Analyze |

## Assess

When a conflict comes to light, the first thing to do is allow time for everyone to calm down. Use this time to gather the appropriate facts and to identify areas of possible compromise. Talk to those involved to assess what each party wants from the situation and make a preliminary determination on the best way to approach the conflict.

## Acknowledge

When you bring the individuals or the team together, listen to everyone's concerns. Climb down your ladder of inference and encourage members to try to see each other's viewpoint. This step, in itself, often leads to resolution as team members will gain a better understanding of one another's viewpoints and be less likely to take the disagreement personally. This change in perception is the goal of the next stage.

## Adjust Attitude

As you discuss the differing opinions, avoid stereotyping or making judgments based on bias of any type. Remain objective and encourage the rest of the team to do the same. Remain flexible and be open to any number of possible resolutions, keeping "respect" at the forefront of the discussion. Create a tolerant atmosphere in which others may adjust their own attitudes to move the project forward.

## Act

Once you perceive that others are ready to move on, stick to the issue at hand as you suggest a course of action. Avoid making promises that are unrealistic or presenting the issue in a win-lose context. Demonstrate sincerity in your suggestions. Then listen, repeat and clarify information until you are satisfied that everyone is in agreement. Put team members into action, as this will nullify the "hangover" effect and allow members to focus on the task at hand, rather than on the recent conflict.

## Analyze

Continue to monitor the situation. Review the progress with individuals and from a distance, and implement any changes necessary to keep the team on track.

By following this process, a team leader can bring members together and create a stronger working unit. While many conflicts can be prevented by preliminary team development strategies and by agreeing on objectives, some situations will require attention so that they do not disrupt the team project or grow into irreparable interpersonal conflicts. Resolving conflicts effectively can improve the emotional intelligence of the group, resulting in a more positive and productive work environment.

## Resolving Conflict in the Moment

Sometimes a conflict needs a swift resolution to prevent derailing the entire project. You may not have time to follow a formal process for conflict resolution. In those instances, the following tips are useful to remember.

## Don't Get Hot Under the Collar: Reframe!

Framing is always a skillful strategy to employ, and in a conflict situation, it can help both parties seek out common ground. You may need to reframe your opening statements to accommodate opposing or divergent viewpoints. This can help all parties focus on what they can agree upon instead of what is driving them apart. Be sure to include what you hope to achieve from the resolution and that you are seeking a win for all parties involved. Finding common ground within your frame statement is just as important as establishing common ground in a difficult conversation.

©shipfactory/Shutterstock.com

**Figure 3**  *Body Language Speaks Volumes*

## Nonverbal Body Language: What Are You Really Saying?

Be sure to assume open body language that indicates you are respectful, receptive, and aligned with your audience. Avoid body language that indicates you are defensive or closed off. This includes crossed arms and rigid posture. Be very careful to avoid accusatory body language (pointing, gesticulating, and flailing). Face the individual as he or she is speaking in an open and relaxed position. Mirror his or her understanding with gestures of agreement.

## Listen. No, Seriously…

Listening and being attentive can be one of the most important factors toward defusing a hostile exchange. If you provide your opponent with a sense of calm understanding, you will move more quickly toward resolution. Be sure to listen for buried patterns or concerns that are trying to surface. Use paraphrasing language to confirm you understand the opposing parties' issues and concerns, avoiding any language that might be misconstrued as negative.

As you navigate your way toward a resolution that all parties can buy into, remember to monitor them for any signs of withdrawal. Being able to finesse the situation means addressing the concerns and issues of all parties in a way that everyone feels is a fair and just compromise. Using your oral communication strategies will assist you greatly as you handle this type of high-stakes conversation.

Asking clarifying questions and making confirmation statements will help guarantee your audience successfully understood your intended message. No matter how clear you think you are, if your listener isn't getting it, you need to change what you are doing, or the communication is not effective. You don't need to be right; you need to be understood.

# Best Practices for Teams

In this unit, we have covered a number of strategies for ensuring effective communication in the workplace. In this section, we will apply these to professional team settings. In addition, we'll present several best practices to ensure high-functioning teams, with positive dynamics, that communicate and collaborate well. Establishing sound team foundations at the onset of the project is essential. These team foundations include sharing a common goal, collective competencies and contribution, developing and using a work plan, establishing a team leader, and employing communication that works for all team members. In addition to these team foundations, your team should strive to incorporate successful ongoing strategies for collaboration throughout your project.

## Sharing a Common Goal

Each team member should be committed to the success of the team and the goal for which the team strives. It is important that each individual on the team sees value in the team's common goal. Sharing a common goal encourages team members to be mutually accountable in achieving it. Although each team member's motivation behind the desire to accomplish the goal might be different, a common team goal is necessary.

In order to establish a common goal, your team should spend some time getting to know each other. The work of getting to know your team members starts before you actually start working on the project. Each team member should discuss his or her individual goals for the project, in addition to what aspects of the project he or she is passionate about. All team members should work to understand each other's goals, drivers, and perceptions. Based on the goals of every individual, the team can establish a common shared goal for which everyone strives. It is important for the team to consistently reference the goal throughout the project to remind all team members of its value.

## Cultivating Collective Competencies and Contribution

An effective team is made up of individuals who collectively bring the competencies necessary to fulfill a task. It is important to know and understand your strengths and weaknesses, and those of your teammates, in order to have a high-functioning team. Likewise, it is essential that all team members contribute equally to the best of their abilities. In a perfect world, every team would have the ideal balance of skills and every member would strive to contribute fully and equally.

In the real world, we need to understand the skill sets and motivations of our team members, so we are able to leverage collective strengths and overcome collective weaknesses. Shared contribution and shared benefits are important so that each member can reap the rewards of his or her time and energy. At the beginning of your project, team members should discuss their individual skill sets, strengths, and weaknesses. It is important to be honest and let your team members know if you are particularly good at creating PowerPoint presentations, but not as capable as a public speaker. This knowledge will allow teams to divide tasks based on skill sets and areas of interest. It will also allow the team to help one another improve in areas that are challenging to them.

## Developing and Using a Work Plan

At the onset of each new task or project, a team should develop a work plan. The work plan should incorporate a timeline that allows all members of the team to be aware of key deadlines, deliverables, and milestones. A work plan enables each individual to plan schedules and responsibilities accordingly; it addresses the process and sets clear expectations. The following chart is an example of a work plan that takes into account the following information: driving research questions, plan to conduct the necessary research, a timeline, and responsible team members.

| DRIVING RESEARCH QUESTIONS | PLAN TO CONDUCT RESEARCH | TIMELINE | TEAM MEMBERS RESPONSIBLE |
|---|---|---|---|
| What information and tools do University of Arizona alumni feel they did not receive to best prepare them for workplace transition? | Survey to Alumni distributed through Alumni network | Sept. 23rd: Survey Finalized<br>Sept. 24th: Internal Review<br>Sept. 29th: External Review<br>October 1st: Distribute Survey | Casey<br>Lisa |
| What information are University of Arizona students currently receiving about transitioning into the work place? | Interviews with career coaches & advisors | Sept. 24th: Schedule Interviews<br>October 1st: Conduct Interviews | John<br>Stephanie |
| According to society and secondary research, what are the most prevalent issues facing new graduates today? | Database research Personal experience Personal network | Completed by October 14th | Tom |
| What is the major message that will be delivered to graduating seniors? | Analyze Survey answers<br>Bring all three research groups together<br>Make Charts/Graphs<br>Develop Major Topics | October 10th: Survey closes<br>October 11th–16th: Analyze survey data<br>October 19th: Major topics/message developed | Group |
| What are the most effective mediums and modes used to deliver information to busy students? | Secondary research<br>Brainstorm creative ways to present unique major topics | Oct.20th: Choose finalized deliverables<br>Oct.21st–22nd: Plan Deliverables<br>Oct.23rd–Nov.3rd: Make and practice deliverables<br>Nov. 4th: Present Results | Group |

**Table 1**   *Work Plan*

By establishing a team work plan, all team members know what is expected of them as well as the corresponding deadlines for completing each task.

## Select a Team Leader

In the workplace, it is common for team members to not directly report to the team leader. This is also typically true for teams working on class projects. However, establishing a team leader is essential. The team leader has many responsibilities, including ensuring organization of tasks, facilitating discussion, and encouraging team member participation. It is important that all members of the team understand that the team leader is not responsible for completing all of the work. The leader is responsible for ensuring the team is on track and functioning well in order for everyone to complete the work together.

## Communicate Inclusively

It is important to communicate through channels that work for all team members. While face-to-face communication is desirable, it may not always be a feasible option. At the time a team is formed, team members should take time to express preferred communication channels and protocols. Being open and honest about how you prefer to send and receive information from your team members will allow for clear communication. In addition, using document sharing services like Google Drive allows all team members to contribute and view the contributions others have made.

## Produce Deliverables Ahead of Schedule

We all have many priorities to balance, and often unforeseen challenges arise that keep us from completing quality team deliverables on time. Through years of experience in working with student teams, one of the best pieces of advice we can offer is to complete deliverables early and build in time for unforeseen challenges. Creating quality team deliverables that are cohesive takes time. You want to ensure your deliverables flow and are written in one unified voice. A common error in team writing and presentations is to throw together distinctly different deliverables with multiple voices and try to present them as a team product. These attempts are easy to spot. The audience then perceives your team as disconnected, confused, and unable to work well together. In order to produce cohesive team deliverables, every member needs to produce quality work by the team's internal deadline. This will allow for a unified team deliverable.

## Take Notes at Every Meeting and Conclude with Action Items

When time is tight and you are meeting with your group to divide tasks for the numerous looming deadlines, it is important that a team member is responsible for taking notes. This allows the team to capture agreed-upon tasks and deadlines. Making these notes accessible to everyone on a shared document will increase the probability that the tasks are completed correctly and on time. Concluding meetings with action items will ensure all team members know next steps and what is expected of them. A review of action items should conclude both face-to-face and virtual meetings.

## Practice Presentations as a Team

Presentations take hours to complete. Every member of the team spends time crafting the content on slides and perfecting his or her verbal and nonverbal delivery. There is nothing worse for an audience than viewing a final presentation that is being run through for the first time. It is always evident when a team has not rehearsed together because they are not behaving as a cohesive unit that knows how to transition seamlessly from member to member throughout the presentation. In order to have a streamlined and successful presentation, you must practice together as a team prior to your final presentation.

## Conduct Team 360° Evaluations After Each Major Deliverable

It is important to evaluate yourself and your team members at several stages throughout a project. Providing feedback on each member's performance, contribution, and openness to ideas will assist in keeping the team cohesive and productive. The following are example criteria by which to rate each other:

- Shows up to team meetings on time and prepared
- Actively participates during team meetings
- Listens attentively to teammates

- Produces accurate and quality deliverables that require little to no further editing on or before agreed upon team deadlines
- Is respectful of outside ideas and opinions, even when those ideas conflict with his or her own
- Holds team members accountable for poor quality work or lack of effort

Honestly answering these questions about each other as a team will help you and your fellow team members improve your teamwork skills throughout the project.

Adhering to the foundational and ongoing best practice strategies listed above will help create teams that are dependable, deliver quality tasks on time, actively participate, and work well together. This not only guarantees higher quality deliverables, but it also ensures a more enjoyable work experience for all team members.

This chapter has presented several strategies for connecting with and engaging others in the workplace. Most of the strategies have involved verbal communication and nonverbal cues. As important as these skills are, the most common method of communication in today's virtual and global marketplace is still writing. Although we send email messages and texts in our daily lives, we need to understand how vital an effectively written message might be to getting that first interview. The first contact you have with a potential employer will likely be an email message or cover letter, and you know how important first impressions can be. To help you with this, Unit 7 is entirely devoted to ensuring you are an effective communicator by thoroughly understanding your stakeholders.

# Unit 5 References

Ashkenas, R. (2010). Why we secretly love meetings. *Harvard Business Review*, 55–59.

Barrett, D. (2006). *Leadership communication*. Burr Ridge, IL: McGraw Hill Publishers.

Berger, P. &. (1967). *The social construction of reality: A treatise in the sociology of knowledge*. Harpswell, ME: Anchor.

Bluedorn, A. C., Turban, D. B., & Love, M. S. (1999). The effects of stand-up and sit-down meeting formats on meeting outcomes. *Journal of Applied Psychology*, 277–285.

Borisoff, D., & Victor, D. (1998). *Conflict management: A communication skills approach* (2nd ed.). Boston: Allyn and Bacon.

Brown, P., & Levinson, S. (1987). *Politeness: Some universals in language usage*. Cambridge, United Kingdom: Cambridge University Press.

Brugoon, J. B. (2008). Cognitive biases and nonverbal cue availability in detecting deception. *Human Communication Research*, 572–599.

Bull, P. (1987). *Posture and gesture*. Oxford: Pergamon Press.

Canary, D. J., Cody, M. J., & Manusov, V. L. (2008). *Interpersonal communication: A goals-based approach* (4th ed.). New York, NY: Bedford/St. Martin.

Clark, R. A., & Delia, J. G. (1979). Topoi and rhetorical competence. *The Quarterly Journal of Speech*, 65, 187–206.

Daft, R. (2011). *The leadership experience*. Stamford, CT: Cengage.

Davidhizer, R. (2004). Listening—A nursing strategy to transcend culture. *Journal of Practical Nursing*, 22–24.

Dillard, J. P. (1990). A goal-driven model of interpersonal influence. In J. Dillard (Ed.), *Seeking compliance: The production of interpersonal influence messages* (pp. 41–56). Scottsdale, AZ: Gorsuch Scarisbrick.

Dillard, J. P., Segrin, C., & Hardin, J. M. (1989). Primary and secondary goals in the production of interpersonal influence messages. *Communication Monographs, 56,* 19–38.

Ekman, P. (2003). *Emotions revealed: Recognizing faces and feelings to improve communication and improve lives.* New York: New York Times Books.

Gardner, W. L., & Cleavenger, D. (1998). The impression management strategies associated with transformational leadership at the world-class level: A psychological assessment. *Management Communication Quarterly, 12,* 3–41.

Gibson, B., & Sachau, D. (2000). Sandbagging as a self-presentational style: Claiming to be less than you are. *Personality and Social Psychology Bulletin, 26,* 56–70.

Gibson, J., & Hodgetts, R. (1986). *Organizational Communication: A managerial approach.* New York: Academic Press.

Gilbert, D. T., & Jones, E. E. (1986). Exemplification: The self-presentation of moral character. *Journal of Personality, 54,* 591–615.

Giles, H. (1980). Accommodation theory: Some new directions. In N. S. de Silve (Ed.), *Aspects of linguistic behavior* (pp. 105–136). York, England: York University Press.

Glassop, L. (2002). The organizational benefit of teams. *Human Relations 55, no.2,* 225–249.

Goffman, E. (1959). *The presentation of self in everyday life.* New York, NY: Doubleday.

Goffman, E. (1967). On face work. In *Interaction ritual: Essays on face-to-face interaction* (pp. 5–47). Great Britain: Cox & Wyman Ltd.

Hecht, M. L. (1984). Satisfying communication and relationship labels: Intimacy and length of relationship as perceptual frames of naturalistic conversations. *Western Journal of Communication, 48,* 201–216.

Hogan, K. S. (2003). *Can't get through 8 barriers to communication.* LA: Pelican Press.

Jones, E. E., & Pittman, T. S. (1982). Toward a general theory of strategic self-presentation. In J. M. Suls (Ed.), *Psychological perspectives on the self* (pp. 231–262). Hillsdale, NJ: Erlbaum.

Lencioni, P. (2002). *The five dysfunctions of teams.* NYC: Jossey Bass.

Motley, M., & Candsen, C. (1988). Facial expression of emotion: A comparison of posed expressions versus spontaneous expressions in an interpersonal communication setting. *Western Journal of Communication,* 1–22.

Myers, S., & Anderson, C. (2008). *The fundamentals of small group communication.* London: Sage.

Pease, B. P. (2004). *The definitive book of body language.* NYC: Bantam.

Pendell, S. D. (1990). Deviance and conflict in small group decision making: An exploratory study. *Small Group Research*, 393–403.

Rahim, M. (2002). Toward a theory of managing organizational conflict. *International Journal of Conflict Management*, 206–235.

Schab, F. (2014, May 27). *Learning the language of non-verbal communication*. Retrieved from Six Degrees: http://www.six-degrees.com/pdf/sensory-branding-and-communications-sensoryQ.pdf

Schutz, A. (1998). Assertive, offensive, protective, and defensive styles of self-presentation: A taxonomy. *Journal of Psychology, 132*, 611–628.

Senge, P. (1990). *The Fifth Discipline: The art and practice of the learning organization*. New York: Doubleday.

Sheppard, J. A., & Arkin, R. M. (1989). Determinants of self-handicapping: Task importance and the importance of preexisting handicaps on self-generated handicaps. *Personality and Social Psychological Bulletin, 15*, 101–112.

Solomon, D., & Theiss, J. (2012). *Interpersonal communication as art and science*. New York: Routledge.

Vonk, R. (2002). Self-serving interpretations of flattery: Why ingratiation works. *Journal of Personality and Social Psychology, 82*, 515–526.

Walker, R. (2011). *Strategic management communication*. Stamford: Cengage.

Watzlawick, P., Beavin-Bavelas, J., & Jackson, D. (1967). Some tentative axioms of communication. *Pragmatics of human communication: A study of interactional patterns, pathologies and paradoxes* (pp. 48–71). New York, NY: W. W. Norton.

Williams, R. B. (2012, April 15). *Wired for success. Retrieved from Psychology Today*: http://www. psychologytoday.com/blog/wired-success/201204/why-meetings-kill-productivity

Wilson, S. R. (1990). Development and test of a cognitive rules model of interaction goals. *Communications Monographs, 57*(2), 81–103.

Wiseman, T. (1996). A concept analysis of empathy. *Journal of Advanced Nursing, 23*, 1162–1167.

# UNIT 6:
# Professional Presentations

# The Power of Presentations

Recently, a young group of student consultants gave a presentation to a group of client executives. They were asked to present their semester-long research on a project funded by the executives' company. Ten minutes into the presentation, one of the executive's phones started to buzz. He casually flicked the screen on and started to scroll. Something caught his interest because he picked up the phone, held up his hand to the students and said, "Wait, do you have something really important I need to know?"

The students gaped at him. Yes, they had a full semester's worth of work that had been carefully researched, analyzed, and painstakingly pressed into the service of a presentation.

The executive stepped in: "Can you just tell me *right now*, should we invest more into this product or not?"

One of the students stepped forward, and said, "Well, we don't think so." "Great," the executive said, his phone already half way to his ear. "Just send me the deck, I can read it later." He gathered up his belongings, started to talk loudly on his phone, and left the room.

The students continued on with their presentation, but the rest of the client group was clearly bored. They checked email on their phones, declined to enter into any discussion around recommendations, and left as soon as the presentation was over. The students were crushed. They had worked so hard. What went wrong?

Sadly, these scenarios take place every day in the workplace. Presentations are a common, and perhaps overly used, mechanism for delivering information. Routinely, we use presentations in one form or another to deliver a wide variety of messages from sharing information, training, driving discussion, and reporting results. Yet, if we rely so heavily on the format, why did Amazon recently ban the use of Power Point file format (PPT) at its meetings? Jeff Bezos insists PowerPoint "makes it easy for the presenter and difficult for the audience" (Williams, 2013). He insists that a meeting driven by PPT results in the reduction of quality thinking and encourages rapid (and poor) decision making.

Currently, Amazon's meetings revolve around the six-page narrative memo. With memos distributed 24 hours in advance, the first 20 minutes of every meeting is devoted to reading high-level summaries of key issues. According to Bezos, the quality of conversation is higher because there are no slide decks. LinkedIn CEO, Jeff Weiner, has also eliminated slide-driven presentations from meetings, relying instead on skillful speakers and written content to drive decision making. (Williams, 2013) What do these CEOs know? In the boardroom, the conference room, the staff room, and at trainings, presenters make messages miserable, not memorable. Does this mean the death of PPT? Probably not. Is this an indicator that the quality of your next critical presentation should be audience centric, engaging, and not overly reliant on bullets? Most definitely.

"A presentation is an opportunity to listen to your audience."

-Nick Morgan

Why have presentations become such an over-used medium? Many people prefer the rich medium of meeting face-to-face with an audience so they can know how to tailor information in the moment. In other instances, trying to build a coalition or consensus for decision making requires everyone present in the same moment to hear information, ask questions, and entertain multiple viewpoints. Our ability to connect with one another, to get to the essence of what others think, need, or want makes presentations "feel" like a rich and valuable means of communicating.

Since presentations are a preferred mechanism, you should be doubly aware of the potency of this medium and select it when you are absolutely sure you know your audience and their needs. Sadly, we have watched more than one ambitious group of young consultants put forward data that offer no new insight, no treatment of the data, no "aha!" moment. In our professional careers, we witnessed more than one executive stop a presentation and say, "Just send me the deck. If you aren't going to add value to the material, I know how to read. You are wasting my time." They then get up and leave the room. No one can afford that kind of hit on his or her professional credibility. So your first rule is audience-centric: know your audience. Understand their needs. Question if a presentation is going to truly address the situation and is the best means for distributing this information. If it is, then follow the 3Bs:

1. Be Brief.
2. Be Bright.
3. Be Gone.

**YOU DO THE MATH…**

People can read or listen: they cannot do both. So your audience can either listen to you or read your slides. If it takes the audience an average of 25 seconds to read a wordy slide. Since your audience cannot listen at the same time, if you have 40 slides, they will be reading for 16 minutes of your presentation instead of listening to you. (Duarte, 2010)

In this unit, you will find useful information on everything from planning the presentation to finessing the audience. Along the way, we will answer questions on how to move your audience to action, preferably along the lines of your recommendations. We provide some concrete methods for structuring your presentation to meet your audience's needs. Equally important, you will learn new ways to identify and harness your presentation style to become a more effective speaker.

If you ever struggled with team presentations, you will discover some sound, practical tips to make your next presentation a success. Once you understand the art of the question, and how to advance your presentation during the discussion segment, your presentation skills will leap up a level. Finally, understanding the power of visual design will put the finishing touches on your next successful presentation.

# What to Know Before You Go

One key component to planning your presentation is to fully understand both the nature of the presentation and the expectations of the audience. As Tony Jeary likes to say, "Life is a Series of Presentations." And truly, it is. You are evaluated on how well you can gather your thoughts and engage your audience, whether you are in the proverbial "elevator ride" with an important guest or you are called upon to expand a viewpoint at a meeting. You need to have the skills to formulate and drive your message regardless of where you are.

One important factor to understand is the nature of the presentation. Ask yourself: is it formal or informal? Does the audience expect to interact with you throughout the presentation or only during a discussion segment? Are you going to entertain any questions from the press, or are you simply delivering a statement?

An informal presentation usually occurs in an internal setting within an organization. This type of presentation is frequently held among team members in the form of an update, exchange of information, or to drive decision making. While the general structure and approach adhere to guidelines for any structured messaging, the style is more casual. Typically, presenters sit with the audience around a table and handouts are used to capture notes and collect feedback. Presenters often encourage ongoing dialogue throughout the presentation to gather both feedback and make alterations in the moment. The informal presentation is typically used to engage in-house team members as they conduct daily work and meet milestones.

**Figure 1** *Informal Presentation*

©Monkey Business Images/Shutterstock.com

## Formal Presentation

Formal presentations are used for both internal and external stakeholders. The nature of a formal presentation is more structured and provides the audience with a clearly-defined sense of purpose and approach. Typically, discussion segments are reserved for the end of the presentation. A formal presentation is polished, professional, and tightly composed to provide the audience with an optimal experience in the flow of information, structural coherence, and visual design strategies. Formal presentations are used with audiences of many different sizes and for a variety of purposes. The key distinction between a formal presentation vs. an informal presentation is the level of preparation, polish, and formality of the performance.

## Consultative Presentation

A consultative presentation is an interactive presentation. The audience joins in the presentation and directs the presenter by a series of questions about content. This style of presentation can be run as a high-level

**Figure 2** *Formal Presentation*

©Dean Drobot/Shutterstock.com

**Figure 3**   *Speak with Your Audience*

summary in as few as 10 minutes or expanded into a much longer and more comprehensive presentation, based on the ability to tailor the information to the audience's specific needs. It is not unusual for a consultant or "interactive" presenter to know how to zero in on a specific data set, set of recommendations, or content area that an audience member needs to know. This might be a very high-level view or a very in-depth discussion of a specific recommendation.

While this is a challenging type of presentation to master, a skillful presenter can manage digressions and keep the conversation unfolding towards a target message. This type of presentation, when done well, can be very persuasive, as the entire message is tailored to audience concerns. This format allows the presenter to fluidly move through visual materials (typically with hyperlinks or embedded slides) without a preconceived order or structure. The ability to intuitively "read" an audience, build skillful transitions, and display deep mastery of content largely determines the success of this type of presentation.

# Setting the Stage

Each type of presentation you make, regardless of the level of formality, sets up audience expectations on how to engage with you. Sometimes you get to set the stage; other times, you have to roll with what is prepared for you. Whether you give a tabletop briefing or deliver a keynote address, how you engage and connect with your audience is key to your success.

## Table Talk Discussion/Briefing

This type of briefing is frequently used when you need to provide an update to drive decision making within your organization. This type of exchange is driven by the presenter with an agenda and usually some interactive visual materials, to provide a summative view of either a decision, or an update of completed work. The format for such an exchange is a high-stakes conversation formulated as an ongoing question and answer session. It is the presenter's responsibility to answer questions, then bridge the answer to the next key point.

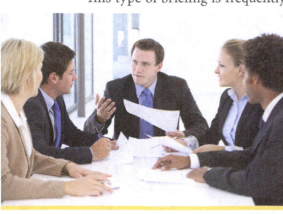

**Figure 4**   *Table Discussions*

This is a masterful form of presentation driven exclusively by the audience members' needs, and it requires a fairly skillful presenter to make sure the recipients (executive or decision makers) receive all the requisite information according to their specific needs.

Generally, a persuasive strategy is used. The presenter identifies the problem, then outlines the opportunity or solution via data and examples. Recommendations usually drive the conversation. A skillful presenter delivers information in a cascading structure, so each answer builds upon necessary information to drive a targeted decision.

## Speech

Occasionally in the workplace, you might be called upon to give a speech or a "talk" about a particular topic. Typically, this type of an event is often used to honor or commemorate. Speeches are often composed word-for-word and delivered in a formal setting. The best speech-givers engage and speak directly to their audience in a conversational tone; the poorest read from their notes or use a teleprompter, providing a more "rehearsed" and canned message. The delivery of this type of message usually determines how successful it is. A speech usually proceeds unchallenged by the audience. In terms of engagement, this has a low interaction rate with the audience; however, for a formal occasion, this type of speaking is considered to be acceptable, even respectful if honoring a specific individual or event.

**Figure 5** *Formal Speech*

## Press Conference

Press conferences are typically used to provide an organization with the opportunity to deliver a specific message to the media. The occasion of a press conference can be the announcement of a new product or service, clarification of a disruption in organizational procedure, or to provide critical information in the event of a crisis.

**Figure 6** *Face the Press*

A press conference is always interactive. The press and other concerned stakeholders often ask pointed and direct questions. Since media is involved, the company spokesperson is usually highly coached on what can and cannot be said. For legal reasons, in light of a crisis, usually a strategic message is vetted by both a communications and legal team. This is a high-stakes scenario in which the wrong answer or incorrect wording can be disastrous for the individual or the company's reputation. To keep messaging aligned, a SOCO, or Single Overriding Communication Objective, is used to deliver a central unified position and message for the issue at hand. Given the 24-hour news cycle and the widespread influence the media carries, communication in these scenarios is usually carefully scripted and coached.

## Town Hall

Similar to the press conference, a Town Hall is an internal stakeholder event that provides a forum for any member of an organization to ask questions of the leadership team. Similar to the Press Conference, the audience dictates the type of questions asked. It is up to the skill of the facilitator or leadership team to provide timely and tailored information, to spark conversation, and to drive consensus so that the event is viewed favorably by those in attendance. Designed to foster engagement with internal stakeholders, town halls are often held to share sensitive information or

**Figure 7** *Town Hall Debate*

announcements requiring active discussion with the audience. Some corporate cultures host town halls on an ongoing basis to engage specific groups; other organizations host this on an "as-needed" basis. Some organizations televise events of this nature or even host an "online" town hall to provide audience members with access and/or footage to a globalized leadership team.

Regardless of the type of presentation, you need to follow the same guidance as any other verbal communication in that presentations require a frame statement, clear language, and an opportunity to engage with the audience in the moment. As with any verbal communication, the power that comes from meeting your audience in the moment and being able to manage concerns determines your level of success. The key to a winning presentation rests in your ability to plan and prepare.

# What's the Plan?

As with any message, a presentation takes considerable planning. Have you ever worked on a team presentation, and had your team members say, "Oh, I know what I'm going to say. I'll just talk about X. Don't worry, I got it"? Everyone nods, spends some time building slides and talking about sequencing. The team adjourns. When the presentation happens, things fall apart. One person talks for far too long, another person forgets several key points, and one person is embarrassingly short on knowledge and relies upon reading the slides word for word. In the academic world, the grades are poor. In the work world, however, jobs are lost. Or executives get up and walk out of the room.

How do you get everyone on the same page to join you on the journey you wish to make? The best presentations are the ones that sound like compelling conversations. They look effortless because they unfold like a well-crafted story. They feel effortless because they put you—the viewer—in a central role of discovery. They sound effortless because the presenter is so confident and artful in the telling you become a part of the conversation. All of these elements can only come together with a lot of planning, and that requires a game plan and a road map.

How can you make sure that your presentation rocks your boss's socks? How can you avoid the moment of being asked to submit a deck and have your audience walk out of the room? With some strategic planning, understanding the rules of the game, and knowing how to work a room, you too can become a master at this game. It is more than theatre, more than performance, more than excellent research: a good presentation is about genuine human connection. If you are going to change hearts and minds, you must fully understand the rules of engagement. To fully engage, you have to plan how to grab your audience and move them to action.

# What Does Your Audience Need? Moving from Thinking to Doing

The single biggest mistake most presenters make is driving the presentation from their own viewpoint out of the sheer enjoyment of being "the sage on the stage." This is a critical error that results in disconnected and misaligned audiences. The first thing you must do is shift your thinking from the presentation being centered on you to centering firmly on the audience. The fastest way to do this is to determine what you want your audience to DO.

Most presentations move their audience from WHY (what is the problem and why it exists)—to HOW, or what the audience needs to DO to move forward and implement a solution. For your message to be successful, you need to map out clearly what your audience currently thinks and what they do. The image below illustrates moving the audience through a series of actions from "the state of now" to the "new state of bliss." Moving your audience to act is to get your audience to believe in your message.

While this sounds simple, when put into practice the results can be dramatic in helping frame and organize a presentation. To see this practice in action, consider the fictional case of a company called Company Slow to Learn, Inc. (CSL) in the caselet below. Use the data in this caselet to help you understand how to move through the critical nature of identifying a frame statement, shaping a presentation, and thinking of how best to convince the senior management team to buy into your ideas.

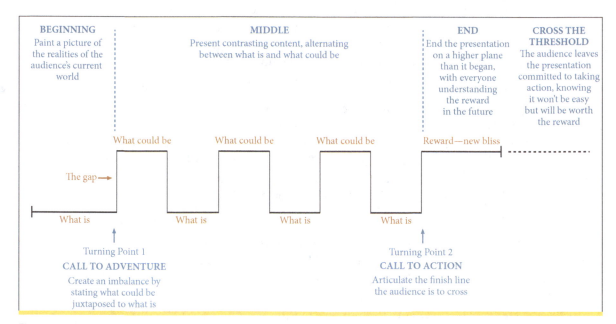

**Figure 1** *Presentation expert Nancy Duarte offers an approach to move your audience from think to do*

# Working Case: The Company Slow to Learn, Inc. (CSL)

Imagine you are on a team hired to assist CSL, a company in the educational software industry plagued with slower and slower release of products. CSL's senior management team assembled your team because they cannot figure out why, despite an aggressive merger and acquisition of three new software companies, they are failing to meet their production goals. These are the same production goals projected to double or triple within six months of their merger, based on market growth and the past performance of their three key acquisitions.

The management team shared with you the process of acquisitions and financial goals laid out for the organization. Currently, the company's revenue targets for the year (with no acquisition) were $950M. Conservative estimates put the newly-acquired companies at bringing additional revenues up to $1.5B within 6 months, and up to $1.7B upon the completion of the next fiscal year with products in the pipeline and current releases staying on schedule. Currently, the company is behind the $950M normal projections, with a projected hit of 10% for the upcoming quarter at current product release rates. They predict that, at the current rate, it will cost the company $350M every six months that the problem goes uncorrected.

Senior management was surprised by these results, particularly as they were in active growth mode. In the past year, CSL acquired three companies, each producing their own software applications in discrete industry sectors. CSL's merger and acquisition rolled these companies into the larger organization but left them largely intact to minimize any production disruptions. Recovering from the upfront costs of the acquisition meant that production from all divisions needed to stay consistent, if not accelerate.

During your meetings, senior management informed you they kept each division distinct to minimize operational disruptions and as a sign of good faith toward the newly acquired existing management teams. Each new division was assured they needed to operate as a distinct entity; when a division was ready to launch a new product, they were asked to work closely with CSL's centralized units for distribution. CSL's centralized team of software engineers managed all quality control (testing for bugs) and clearance for final product release. Additionally, a centralized marketing service coordinated research, launch, and marketing for all new product lines the company offers. Sales, in this instance, were a subsidiary of the marketing group, so all communication and customer service flowed through that centralized unit.

Despite their attempt to maintain integrity to each unit, CSL has fallen behind on product release and missed critical moments in the educational software industry lifecycles. Rather than hitting their targets projected for the newly acquired product lines, all product releases across the organization suffered. Fiscal performance for the past quarter was sorely off its projections. Senior management appeared unable to find the right solution to the problem. Before the mergers were completed, management offset any forecasted increase in workload for centralized divisions. Appropriate staffing was added well in advance of the mergers. Further, senior management let the three newly acquired companies retain their own internal quality control and marketing teams. Despite these measures, these two centralized departments have been accused of inefficiencies and the inability to serve all eight divisions. Backlogs, conflicting release dates, competition for resources, and pronounced decline in productivity has the company missing financial goals and performing poorly in a rapidly moving market.

In this instance, a logical place for your team to begin to plan your presentation would be to think clearly through what CSL thinks and does, and what you believe they need to Think and Do to address this issue.

| | FROM | TO |
|---|---|---|
| **WHAT THEY THINK** | **What is the common mindset?**<br><br>With recent rapid growth, management thinks divisions must be kept distinct to minimize disruption and keep productivity locked in on where it has always been. | **What do you want this audience to think?**<br><br>Evidence shows they can improve their communication processes by creating more streamlined communication channels between internal divisions (marketing and engineering) to increase process efficiencies. |
| **WHAT THEY DO** | **What are the current actions?**<br><br>Each individual unit has its own system of communication until products are ready for release. All units are required to streamline products to a centralized QC unit for bug check. Then to a centralized marketing unit to assist in product launch and release. | **What is your call to action? What do you want them to do?**<br><br>Examine their organizational communication systems to identify obstacles, duplications, roadblocks, and information flow. You want them to streamline their process by adopting more coordinated, transparent, and timely internal communication strategies. |

**Table 1** *Think and Do*

# What REALLY Is the Problem? Find the 5<sup>th</sup> Why

One of the most important aspects of building your presentation is verifying the problem or issue at hand. While this sounds obvious, it is often overlooked by those creating a presentation. Or, as Henry Boettinger wrote, "Rule 1: The only reason for the existence of a presentation of an idea is that it be an answer to a problem..." (Boettinger, 1969).

If you ask for your audience's attention, then you are using up their valuable time to present your ideas; be sure you have identified the real problem at hand.

One way to examine and cross-examine your own team's thinking is to employ the Six-Sigma technique of the "Five Whys." This practice is commonly used to get to a root cause issue, the underlying reason a problem exists. By challenging yourself to continually question why a problem exists, you will get closer to the real issue that needs to be tackled.

In the case of CSL, by thinking through the Five Whys, the root cause issue the company faces becomes much more evident. Despite CSL's rapid growth strategy, inadequate integration of communication structures to streamline centralized units had the opposite effect of fueling growth: it caused the company to lose valuable production time, delayed release of products, and lost subsequent market share. Rather than meet aggressive goals to offset acquisition costs, CSL's management team inadvertently placed the company at risk. Discovering the fifth why would get your team much closer to the goal of being able to build and structure a coherent presentation designed to move CSL's executive managers to immediate action.

# Steal Some Thunder!

As you set your audience up to follow your presentation, you will want to streamline their ability to follow your line of logic. In this case, one way to align with your audience and build a frame is to present alternatives, options, or potential oppositions. When done correctly, disclosing the reasoning behind your position streamlines the audience's understanding of the position while aligning them with your position. This strategy builds your credibility as you can disclose what other options or alternatives were considered (and why they were dismissed.) Remember to include the "no action" as a possible way to continue to frame the problem and create urgency to act in your audience.

When you anticipate the opposing viewpoint's argument and include it as a means of building your case, it is called "stealing someone's thunder." In a court of law, this is a common approach among trial attorneys. In a business environment, this provides you with the option to build credibility and take away any "arrows" from opposing viewpoints in the room, prior to those voices having a chance to raise objections. Research confirms when you bring up a point against your own recommendation, your audience will view your position more favorably than if it is raised by someone else (Williams, 1993). As discussed in the section on persuasion back in Chapter 1–2, there is an art to deflecting pushback without planting seeds of dissension.

In the case of CSL, the options presented would showcase the depth of research and results by discussing other options for consideration. When you display multiple options using accurate points of comparison (metrics) and analyzing the best fit for the audience, you provide a compelling shortcut to your position. This approach helps convince your audience you understand their issues, giving you a leg up on credibility. This is an effective framing device that helps build connection with your audience.

## FIVE WHY'S…. IN THE CASE OF CSL

**Problem: Our productivity is much lower than we anticipated after our most recent Merger and Acquisition (M&A).**

**1st Why?** Because despite staff increases in centralized QC and Marketing teams, they are unable to keep up with production cycles.

**2nd Why?** Because these are centralized units handling eight distinct units' "final" products. The release of products is not streamlined nor communicated effectively across divisions.

**3rd Why?** Because distinct cultures and productions processes were kept intact during the rapid acquisitions to minimize disruption to production cycles.

**4th Why?** Because senior management believed preserving cultures and management teams would minimize disruption to existing operations.

**5th Why:** Because CSL doesn't have a centralized communication system in place to synch the eight divisions, coordinate production, or strategically allocate the division of resources across the entire organization.

## PUT IT INTO ACTION... CSL'S OPTIONS

| | OPTION 1 | OPTION2 | OPTION 3 | OPTION 4 |
|---|---|---|---|---|
| **EVALUATIVE CRITERIA** | Set strategic communication plan that integrates goals and processes across divisions. (Recommended Proposal) | Do nothing. | Centralize communication across only new acquisitions. | Rebrand culture and build from the ground up so everyone feels included and can decide how best to share information. |
| **REVENUES** | Hit Projected Goals for Product Release within 6 months. Estimate to capture 80% of projected $1.7B— total of $1.36B. | Continue to lose market share 10% loss of Revenue. Targets at $940.5M. | Current revenue stream for 5 other divisions maintained with focus on new acquisitions with best case scenario stop the 10% loss. Holding at $950M. | Current state continues at 450M loss until new processes built and put into place. Process review and integration estimated at 1–2 years for full review, training and integration across organization. Revenue Targets at $950M with slight increase up to projected models within a year. |
| **COSTS** | $375M | Nothing | $750M | $750M |
| **RISKS** | Disclose more problems within silos. (Upside, they'll be addressed.) Causes disruption to entities. (Upside, culture integration begins.) | Do nothing. | Grows a new culture within new acquisitions not shared with umbrella organization; further misalignment. | Further market share loss, more financial hits, further product delays while systems are reviewed, selected, and trial runs considered. Conflicts surface that slows production further. (Upside, might arrive at a more cohesive environment) There are more effective and cost efficient ways to drive change. |

**Table 2**   *Options*

Once you have the audience on your side with a clear frame and focus, you are ready to begin to build your case with the most compelling evidence you can find.

# Is This Relevant? Cull Your Data

While investigating and researching possible responses to an identified problem, undoubtedly an enormous amount of information will surface. For example, in the case of CSL, your team might research "merger and acquisition best practices." Or, perhaps you examined the cycle of product releases in the educational software industry before you examined internal processes for communication. (Is there a seasonal product cycle? What are consumer patterns behind software acquisition? What about students? Faculty? You might have conducted industry analysis on CSL's competition. You could examine what sectors their competitions' products recently targeted and their success rates.) Regardless of the data unearthed, it becomes your responsibility to sift and sort through the information to identify patterns, relevant trends, and determine what is (and what is not) relevant for your audience.

It is not uncommon to gather far more information than can actually be distilled into a final presentation. Moreover, it is not uncommon to include different types of information for different stakeholders in the company. For example, when speaking to the centralized marketing team at CSL, you might include different information than if you were speaking to one of the newly acquired companies. Why? Even though your message about centralization of communication processes hasn't changed, the data these distinct audiences would need to understand and accept your message might require different data sets. Your driving message determines the most relevant information that needs to stay in the presentation.

# The Most Common Error: The Data Dump

It can be overwhelming to manage so much information and do so ethically and with coherence. This is why it is so common for individuals to want to include as much as possible in their presentation. They want to showcase their hard work AND make sure they haven't omitted anything pressing to their varying audiences. This is when it is most tempting to do the data dump. Resist this temptation. Your evidence needs to be culled and grouped with a sense of coherence. Just as it is important to avoid the data dump in your writing, it is arguably more important to avoid it in your presentations because your audience has less control over how they consume the presentation.

Audiences expect and crave an established structure. They need to understand how to move with you through the presentation. Will they challenge you and ask hard questions? If your research is solid, you can count on it. Questions are one more way of arriving at understanding. If you are lucky, they will ask questions. If they sit there with no comments, you are getting pretty clear feedback they have no idea what to do with the information you have disclosed. Don't be afraid of being wrong; be afraid of being the data dumper. Rather than take a risk and concentrate your findings, you include everything, so no piece of information is missed. This is a classic error, and it only serves to alienate the audience or open yourself up for challenges that can derail your presentation.

Think about it this way: imagine you need to make a presentation on streamlining the production of the newest model of a cell phone. For your presentation, you took apart a cell phone, all its tiny little sophisticated parts—filters, duplexers, oscillators, actuators, sensors, micro-displays, gyroscopes, etc.—and said to the audience, "Here's the problem, look at all these pieces. This is how complex it is for our company to build smartphones." You brandish a tray littered with tiny circuitry boards. Your audience would have all the disparate tiny pieces of information, but they would have no idea what *to do* with that information.

You might get some kudos for understanding all the pieces, but unless you show your audience what they need to do to accelerate or streamline the processes for building a phone, you are admitting you only have a pile of junk. You don't know what to do with what you have uncovered. Essentially, you just lost your audience. That is the fate of the data dumper.

It is up to you to collect the data, then group and analyze that data to make sure what you select to include in the presentation is relevant to the audience, supports your claims, and showcases depth and breadth of research.

You should also vary the types of data you collect to ensure you have unearthed as much information as possible. A usual sampling of data would include a healthy blend of both primary and secondary research. Additionally, your research should combine a blend of qualitative and quantitative data.

Quantitative data relates to information that can be measured and is mostly numerical. Qualitative data is largely informational or descriptive. For example, it is typical for you to use qualitative data to reinforce and deepen your audience's understanding of quantitative data. Remember, different types of audience members' communication styles and cognitive abilities will skew their preferences one way or the other; if possible, appeal to both.

Finally, the ability to show complex interrelationships between data sets is one of the most effective ways to build and sustain a message. When you explain why or how your recommendations will lead to the results they want, people find this more convincing than when you just provide evidence that your recommendations lead to desired results (Abela, 2008). Most powerfully, research shows that causal arguments or explanations are more persuasive than statistical evidence (Slusher Morgan, 1996). This means if you explain the interrelationship between your data sets and tailor them to your audience, particularly if you can show relationships between them (cause and effect), you stand a much better chance of moving your audience to adopt your viewpoint.

# Move Your Audience: Structure Their Learning

One way to think about moving your audience through this process has to do with sequencing your information. Or, as Nancy Duarte points out, "The structure to all great presentations simply moves the audience from the current state or pain of the now to the "new state of bliss" (Duarte, 2000).

You will need to consciously select information and contrast it so your audience can see the stark difference in realities. There are a number of ways to do this (see table 6–2.3), but you want to be sure that the way you organize your information is sequenced so your audience can grasp and understand the potential as well as any consequences of inaction. These types of contrasts provide your audience with a consistent way to see what is possible as they move through the presentation. This not only engages your audience but helps them become active agents in "learning" your message. When you engage your audience in this type of intellectual motion, you not only involve them directly, but you also enhance their ability to retain and recall information later. Essentially, you are improving your chances for moving your audience to buy into your ideas. In the case of CSL, it would be fairly easy to map out a presentation that took the company from its state of "current pain" and map a trajectory to "a new state of bliss." This type of sequencing of information helps the audience to learn alongside you and experience what a new route or path of information flow should look like. This is how audiences are moved, and most importantly, moved to act.

| WHAT IS | WHAT COULD BE |
|---|---|
| Alternate viewpoint | Your viewpoint |
| Past/Present | Future |
| Pain | Gain |
| Roadblocks | No Obstacles |
| Resistance | Action |
| Impossible | Possible |
| Need | Fulfillment |
| Disadvantage | Advantage |
| Information | Insight |
| Ordinary | Special |
| Question | Answer |

(Duarte, 2000)

**Table 3**  *Is vs. Could Be*

# What's Your Story?

While it may seem counterintuitive in a business presentation to tell a story, structuring your presentation so that it involves the reader in the unfolding of a story has been proven to accelerate comprehension, connection, and most importantly, retention.

Peter Gruber, Chair and CEO of the Mandalay Entertainment Group, writes:

> The power of storytelling is also central to my work as a business executive and entrepreneur. Over the years, I've learned that the ability to articulate your story or that of your company is crucial in almost every phase of enterprise management. It works all along the business food chain: A great salesperson knows how to tell a story in which the product is the hero. A successful line manager can rally the team to extraordinary efforts through a story that shows how short-term sacrifice leads to long-term success. An effective CEO uses an emotional narrative about the company's mission to attract investors and partners, to set lofty goals, and to inspire employees (Gruber, 2007).

The problem is this: No spreadsheet, no bibliography, and no list of resources is sufficient proof to someone who chooses not to believe. The skeptic will always find a reason, even if it's one the rest of us don't think is a good one. Relying too much on proof distracts you from the real mission—which is emotional connection."

-Seth Godin
*Too Much Data Leads To Not Enough Belief*

Stories are one of the quickest ways to emotionally connect with your audience. One reason we recognize stories so deeply is that as a species we are hardwired to change by watching one another's behaviors and listening to collective experiences. Stories are a way for us to deeply connect and transmit information. Thousands of years ago, we used stories to tell one another migration patterns, where danger lurked, how to plant and cultivate food. Oral traditions predate written language by thousands of years. When we listen to a story, we are invited in and anticipate useful knowledge will be transmitted. At the heart of every story is essentially a kind act: we are sharing knowledge. Nancy Duarte insists, "Stories are the most powerful delivery tool for information, more powerful and enduring than any other art form".

When we talk about storytelling in business presentations, it is more than sharing an anecdote of your own experiences, although testimony can be a powerful example. What kind of a story your presentation evokes becomes the way the audience responds to the information. There are only so many familiar plot lines (or tropes) we universally recognize. When you invoke them, the audience may or may not recognize on the surface what you are doing. As a presenter, you don't say, "This is a Quest Story." What you invoke is a familiar patterning of information that pulls us in to play a role in the story. Remember, the audience in any successfully utilized story plot plays the role of the hero in the story (not you). Your presentation story should pattern their journey and subsequent discoveries. This is the power of story: it places the audience in the central role as the star.

## Use Your Story as a Framing Device

The power of the frame statement, or the organizing principle of a presentation, is woven through every step discussed so far—from moving your audience from Think to Do, isolating the most compelling issue, establishing the criteria to examine your position, culling data, and selecting your story. Essentially, each one of these steps assists you in building a streamlined way for the audience to understand and remember.

The story you choose for your presentation is one more framing strategy. How many times have you heard, "The facts speak for themselves?" Actually, they do not. It is how you interpret and analyze the data that determines how facts will be understood. People make judgments based on the frames in which you embed your data.

**MOST COMMON ERRORS OF COACHED CEOS:**

1. Fail to frame

2. Trigger a negative frame (I'm NOT a crook)

3. Lead with facts, provide frame afterwards.

*Helio Fred Garcia*
*Power of Communication*

---

### THINK IT THROUGH…. WHAT STORY SHOULD CSL HEAR?

Consider the case of CSL, what story would you press your presentation into to convince them?

- The Quest? CSL has been on a quest to improve its outputs and it failed. How would a quest story revitalize the company and make your solutions "the holy grail"? How would you make the audience the "hero" in this story?

- Stranger in a Strange Land? Who would be the ideal audience to embrace this story? Who is the stranger in the strange land? What is the "foreign landscape"? What stakeholders would this resonate with the most? How would this help you frame certain data sets?

- From Rags to Riches. How would this frame help inspire your audience? Is there a rag to riches story already among the audience you could invoke? How can learning lessons between divisions help you tell this story? Or, is it too early to tell this story? Challenge yourself to find how this could be an effective frame.

- A Love Story (the classic M&A story?) Is there a love story here? What is the miscommunication keeping the merger from succeeding? What relationship(s) would need to be the focal point for this story to gain traction among stakeholders?

  You could probably use any one of those story structures to assemble evidence into a compelling frame for your audience. How the audience would interpret your data would be different for each story you select to tell. Challenge yourself to think of which situation and audience would yield the most fruitful match.

*Morgan, N. (2009). Trust me: Four steps to authenticity and charisma. San Francisco, CA: Jossey-Bass.*

Consider this: in 2011, Stanford University researchers demonstrated the importance of framing. Two groups were given the exact same statistics, but via different "stories" or metaphors. Both groups were given crime statistics for a sample city, Addison. The exact same statistics were delivered to both groups—a sharp increase in violent crime with an upward trend from 330 murders in 2004 to more than 400 by 2007. The first group was told that crime was a wild beast "preying on a city." The other group was told crime was a "virus infecting the city." Based on the message received, each group was asked to propose a solution. The group who had the statistics framed through the wild beast metaphor provided far more conservative and invasive responses. Seventy-four percent of the group proposed law enforcement: capture the criminals, punish them, and build more jails. The group who had crime described as a virus were twice as likely to propose solutions involving reform: investigate root causes, invest in education, and eliminate poverty. Even though the data was exactly the same, the frames led to dramatically different responses from the groups via their policy solutions. Even more interesting, the reasons given by each group were exactly the same. Whether or not law enforcement or reform was proposed, both groups cited the crime statistics as the reason why they made the recommendation. The only difference between the two groups was the dramatic implication of the frame (Thibodeau, 2011).

What is important to remember is how to use your examples to involve the audience into "experience" of the story so they fully understand the emotional connection, the forward motion, and what they need to do to make their next steps successful. Knowing how to press your presentation into the service of a good story will make your presentation stand out and be remembered.

## Make It Memorable: How Sticky Are You?

The white-hot field of neuro-marketing is a strong example of how neuroscience has reinvented entire disciplines, and the field of communication is no exception. Routinely, practitioners explore the role of memory and retention in the audience to determine best practices for shaping messages.

Most of us have heard the rule, "Your audience remembers 10% of what they read, 20% of what they hear, 30% of what they see, 50% of what they hear and see, but upward of 90% if they DO (or actively learn)." This model was originally put forward by Edgar Dale, and was called The Cone of Learning. While the research behind this theory

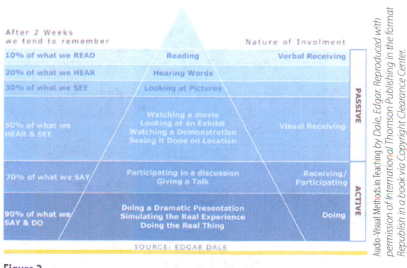

Figure 2

has been challenged, lauded, debunked, and defended, the rule continues to be widely cited and accepted into communication practices. Exact percentages and metrics are continually debated, but this fact remains: retention of information is amplified if you activate the mind's recall system.

The Heath Brothers, Dan and Chip, explored and researched the ways to activate a concept's "stickiness" and how the mind can recall certain types of information more readily than others. Their 2007 book, *Made to Stick*, was published to rave reviews. The *New York Times* and *Wall Street Journal* both listed it on their best seller lists, and the book earned accolades and awards. Eventually, it was named one of the best 100 business books of all time. Since then, it has been translated into 29 languages. The Heath brothers moved the concept of "stickiness" into a mainstream consciousness. The question they posed was relatively simple: how is it that some ideas, say urban myths, can capture the public's imagination and retain such a vivid role in our minds, when abstract information falls flat and is easily forgotten?

The fundamental principle of stickiness relies on disrupting a commonly held frame, then displacing it with a concept or idea that is concrete, credible, emotional, and couched in a story. Due to a number of factors, the concept creates a certain quality of "stickiness" that allows the concept to be retained.

The concept sounds simple enough, but think about what "sticky" information has made it into your world. What was the last urban legend you heard? Perhaps it was surrounding either the appearance of AIDS or Ebola viruses as a government plot for population control, or perhaps the oft discussed idea that the eternally youthful Pharrell Williams is a vampire. While ridiculous, these concepts have a "stickiness" that surpasses logic, lodges itself in the mind, and surfaces as oft-told stories that hold little or no credibility.

The more channels splinter and proliferate, the more stickiness seems to emerge as a force to be harnessed. The concept of "groundswell" operates on the idea of stickiness. One only needs to think of news events that spiral beyond the media and go viral to see stickiness in action. The more we can develop ideas that "stick" themselves into the audience's mind and resonate with a longer life, the better chance we have of being heard.

Many excellent presenters use "stickiness" to their own advantage. Watch any of Steve Jobs's presentations on new product launches, and you will see a master at work displaying how to build a brand and make it sticky. Jobs was a master communicator, but let's look at an example from a presenter generally regarded as less gifted and not nearly as charismatic, Bill Gates.

As one of the world's leading philanthropists, the Bill and Melinda Gates Foundation is one of the world's largest private foundations worth in excess of 38.3 billion dollars.

The mission of the foundation is to focus on improving health and alleviating extreme poverty in the world. While this is work that is sorely needed throughout the world, some issues are more difficult to raise public awareness in, and one of those is malaria. While the Gates Foundation has a substantial amount of money to direct at the root of the issue, Bill Gates took his concern to TED to spread the word on malaria.

Not known as a particularly gifted speaker, Gates' style is analytical and reserved. Worse, the topic, malaria, was not particularly interesting to his audience. Most likely, the audience was more interested in hearing from a former celebrity CEO than they were receiving information on a disease not perceived as an imminent risk.

In his TED talk, Bill Gates appeared to understand this about his audience. As he patiently explained that pharmaceutical companies spend more money funding drugs that battle baldness than on malaria

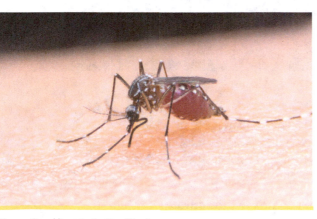

**Figure 3**  *Mosquito Sucking Blood.*

© PlotPhoto/Shutterstock.com

(a clear division of class issues), he took a moment to define what it means to be poor and have malaria. Then, in a moment that caused the video to go viral, Gates drove his point home by releasing a jar of mosquitos into the audience saying, "There is no reason only poor people should have this experience."

While the mosquitos were not infected with malaria, as they rose into the air, the audience burst into applause, an interesting confirmation of their understanding. It was at this moment when the problem was made instantly "real" and that caused the video to go viral. Why? Because the audience experienced the problem in a way that was simple, unexpected, concrete, credible, emotional, and, in a very real way, in that moment, they became a part of the story. This is stickiness at its best.

We don't recommend you release mosquitoes into your audience the next time you give a presentation, but we do recommend you find a "sticky" way for the audience to recall your presentation and align themselves with you.

## Pulling It Together

By now, you should have a clear understanding of the importance of planning a presentation. From analyzing your audience, to building a frame, finding a story and making it stick, planning a presentation is a critical step in shaping your message and being heard. Now that you have explored some of the more important critical thinking factors of presentation planning, it is time to turn the focus toward one of the most important mediums of your message: you.

# You Are the Presentation

To truly enter into a high-level conversation with the audience, you have to initiate the conversation. While this sounds obvious, it is hard to do well. If you think of the last time you attended a presentation where your mind wandered, or you ended up judging the speaker, it is probably because you didn't feel a part of the conversation. You probably felt that was someone was talking **at** you, not **with** you. One of the most common and deadly misalignments that occurs in presentation is separating yourself from your audience. This happens all the time. Perhaps you don't feel like an expert, or you are overly focused on all the points you wish to make; in either event, the more you concentrate on yourself—convincing yourself that you are a worthy and credible speaker or making sure every last point gets heard—you are missing the chance to connect with your audience. And if you miss the audience, they miss your message.

When a presentation is truly audience-centric, you (the speaker) are simply one more conduit toward fluid understanding. In essence, you become a vital piece of the presentation. How you speak, how you move, how you look all become an extension of your presentation that can make or break the final credibility of your message. Sound important? You bet it is! This chapter is devoted to a rigorous exploration of the signals we send, both verbal and nonverbal. With some self-awareness and practice, you too will be ready to move into mastery of one of the most convincing elements of your presentation: you.

## Verbal & Vocal Delivery

### Language Articulation

Most adults speak an average of 7,000 to 20,000 words per day. In casual everyday conversation, the people you interact with may not be hanging on to every word you say. However, when you are presenting in front of a group, chances are your audience is listening to each spoken word. For this reason, language articulation, or the way you put your ideas and thoughts into words, is important. Your language articulation assists the audience in understanding the thoughts you are trying to convey.

Your presentation language should be precise, concise, and fluid. Precision relates to the accuracy and exactness of the words you use, to ensure you are conveying what you intend. Concision means that you are able to provide an abundance of information clearly, using as few words as necessary. Your language articulation should be brief, but comprehensive. You also want your language to flow smoothly. As you strive for well-articulated language, work to avoid unintelligible sentences, omitted words or phrases, and wrong word choices. Advanced preparation and practice is key to attaining effective language articulation.

## Paralanguage

Paralanguage refers to the verbal elements of your delivery that are not referred to as language. Paralanguage, put simply, is not what you say but how you say it. Paralinguistic elements like tone, inflection, volume, pace, emphasis, hesitation, pausing, and other verbal noises contribute to the whole of a message (Trager, 1958). The way we say something can (intentionally or unintentionally) add an emotional or attitudinal dimension to the message. In this way, the nature of the message is altered. Take the phrase, "I'm sorry," for instance. Have you ever been told that you don't sound sorry, or that your apology lacks sincerity? Chances are paralanguage is to blame. The statement "I'm sorry" can be rendered meaningless, or even taken as an insult, if not delivered using paralinguistic cues of sincerity. Sometimes, as with sarcasm, we rely on paralanguage to convey our intended message. The phrase "way to go" is used as a hurtful message almost as often as it's employed as a congratulatory statement. The distinction lies in the delivery. The nuance of how we say our message conveys meaning.

The key to being a compelling presenter is the ability to align what you are saying with how you are saying it. With every conversation or presentation, there are actually two conversations taking place (Morgan, 2009). The first is the words or content, and the second is the non-content, yet information-rich vocal and physical communication. Aligning the words you say with your tone and gestures allows the audience to understand the meaning behind your message. Further, you may avoid sending unintended relational messages.

Albert Mehrabian, a pioneer of communication research, found that in order to decode the emotions underlying words, audiences look to cues other than the actual content. His findings concluded that people interpret meaning through the following channels and percentages:

- 55% Gestures
- 38% Tone of Voice
- 7% Content

The findings above further emphasize that our audience interprets the meaning behind our words, not by what we say but how we say them. In fact, 93% of how our audience interprets our meaning is through how we say our message. When a presenter does not align the message content with how she or he says it, we typically believe the gestures and tone over the actual words. Remember from chapter 2–1, relational meaning refers to what the message implies or means in the context of a relationship.

## Inflection and Tone

Knowing what we do about the importance of paralanguage, it is wise to consider how your tone affects relational meaning. Sometimes, speakers use an upward inflection at the end of sentences. A practical function of paralanguage, this inquisitive inflection helps communicators distinguish between a question and a statement. However, some people use this upward inflection or "uptalk" when making statements, and it can lead to a number of undesirable outcomes. When doing this, the speaker communicates a lack of confidence, and this can damage his or her credibility. Further, the heightening of frequencies may imply an inherent weakness, or subservience (Trager, 1961). It is best to reserve upward inflection for questions and keep the inquisitive "melody" out of statements or assertions.

Varying your tone to convey emphasis can help the audience stay engaged throughout your presentation. If you use a tone of enthusiasm as you emphasize key points, your audience is more likely to stay connected. Conversely, if you speak with a monotone throughout your presentation, it is likely your audience will become bored and disengage from your presentation. Keeping a lively and smooth tone throughout your presentation will show the audience that you are passionate and confident about your message.

## Volume

Using the proper volume for the audience and setting is an important aspect of successful verbal delivery. You want to ensure you are speaking at the appropriate volume throughout your presentation. You do not want to speak so softly that the audience is unable to hear what you are saying. In addition, it is equally important that your volume is inviting and not too loud. The proper volume is heavily impacted by the venue of your presentation. You may need to speak louder in a large presentation hall to be heard by everyone. Conversely, you will want to speak at a softer volume in a smaller setting to avoid overwhelming your audience.

It is a good idea to practice in the location you will deliver your presentation so that you can determine the proper volume. Remember that sound carries better in an empty room because bodies and objects absorb and prevent the reflection of sound, so you may need to increase your volume when you present in a room full of people. Volume is an easy component to regulate and alter to meet the needs of your audience members.

## Pace

The rate of your speech impacts how your audience digests your message. In most cases, you know your presentation material better than the audience. This is both a blessing and a curse. Due to the familiarity you have with the material, you may be able to speed through your entire presentation with ease. However, your audience may not be able to follow along and digest your message at the same rate you are speaking. As you present your research and rattle off facts, your audience is trying to listen and make meaning of what you are saying. It is essential that you speak slowly enough to be understood and pause briefly to check that the audience is tracking. It is also common for presenters to speak faster when experiencing mild presentation anxiety. Therefore, you may want to practice speaking at an even slower pace than you think you need to.

## Common Disruptive Errors

We want our presentations to be free of any verbal disruptive errors that may distract our audience from our main message. Common verbal disruptive errors include the use of "um," "like," "kinda," etc. Instead of inserting these words into your presentation, try to pause, be silent, and breathe. Apologizing for making a small disruptive error creates another verbal distractor. By making the apology, you actually draw more attention to your error. An audience will typically excuse a verbal distractor or two, as long as it is not excessive. The more you practice, the better you will become at avoiding verbal disruptive errors.

# Physical Delivery

## Looking the Part

Physical appearance can influence perceptions. You may have heard the adage, "dress for the job you want, not the job you have." This statement reflects the power of physical appearance in interaction. People who are well-groomed and appropriately dressed are often considered more attractive, persuasive, and likable than those who pay little attention to their appearance.

Take some time to ensure your clothes are washed and pressed, and elements like hair, skin, and nails are clean and tidy. When you attend to your personal appearance, the benefits are often exponential. When others find your appearance pleasing, they're more likely to comply with your requests. In addition, they will afford you numerous positive characteristics, even if you don't necessarily deserve them.

Observers often assume attractive people are kind, intelligent, and similar to themselves. This is called the halo effect: a perceptual bias in which we favor those we consider physically appealing (Thorndike, 1920). Whether or not it's fair, our physical appearance leaves a lasting impression. Like other aspects of our communication strategy, it requires forethought.

In high-stakes situations like job interviews or public presentations, it is usually wise to dress slightly more formally than your listeners. This demonstrates respect for your audience and communicates your attention to the occasion. Dress the part; it's a precious opportunity to enhance your speaker credibility.

**THIS SIMPLE "POWER POSE" CAN CHANGE YOUR LIFE AND CAREER**

Read about Harvard Professor and Social Scientist Amy Cuddy's Tips for Powerful Nonverbal Messaging

http://www.businessinsider.com/power-pose-2013-5?op=1#ixzz34UiciWVv

©Monkey Business Images/Shutterstock.com

**Figure 1**   *Dress for the Job You Want*

## Approaching the Stage

It is best to minimize setup in front of your audience. If possible, view your presentation space before the speaking event. Consider the environmental elements that may influence your presentation: location, size, lighting, technological resources, and other room characteristics. Avoid unnecessary surprises and make the most of your space.

Your presentation begins long before you start speaking. Therefore, your approach is a critical element in creating a desirable first impression. Approach the stage or speaking area with confidence and poise. When you take the floor, be ready to start your presentation. If you're presenting in a team, avoid last minute conversations and preparations. Look ready, even if you don't feel ready.

## Positioning Yourself for Success

The manner in which we position our bodies holds communicative value. In fact, movement is a leading instrument in the symphony of cues that constitute nonverbal messages. Start with your posture and carry yourself with confidence. Keep your head high and shoulders back; this is neither the place nor time for droopy, inward, protective stances. Project a confident image, and make it believable. Strike a power pose.

Earlier, we learned about Communication Accommodation Theory. We can converge and diverge our nonverbal behavior the same way we do our verbal messages. By **mirroring**, or matching others' nonverbal messages, we can communicate a sense of cohesion and similarity. For instance, people engaged in conversations will often face one another and model open, attentive gestures and facial expressions. You can connect with your audience through mimicry by creating positive nonverbal alignment through mirrored gestures. For example, if you want your audience to be excited, you need to show your excitement and enthusiasm. Through seeing your excitement level, the audience will begin to mirror your behavior.

Though you can't necessarily mirror an entire audience's nonverbal cues, you can model open communication through **nonverbal immediacy**. Immediacy behaviors demonstrate a speaker's regard for his or her audience and may include open gestures and posture, friendly facial expressions, and audience-centered positioning. Do not be afraid to use the presentation space. It's often refreshing to see a speaker come out from behind a desk or podium and address both sides of the room.

## Push Out the Jive, Bring in the Love

Decreasing the physical distance between you and your audience will help keep the focus on you and your message. It is hard to ignore someone or become disengaged when they are right in front of you and making eye contact. You want to be close enough to engage your audience but refrain from invading their personal space. Certainly, proximity comfort levels vary from culture to culture. Positioning your body so that you are not blocking the screen is also important.

Sometimes, there are physical barriers preventing you from moving close to the audience or positioning your body favorably. These physical barriers may include a podium or computer desk. If possible, relocate movable objects that may prevent you from obtaining a close proximity or optimal positioning to your audience before your presentation begins. In other instances, you as the presenter create a barrier by the amount of space between you and your audience. In those instances, take a few steps forward towards the audience. A few feet can make a big difference in your ability to engage and connect with them. Like most nonverbal messages, immediacy is conveyed through a mixture of several nonverbal cues.

## Using Gestures

Gestures, or hand and arm movements, serve a variety of purposes. Research indicates that gestures may aid speakers' thinking processes and help retrieve thoughts or words (McNeill, 1992). This may explain why people often gesture when talking on the phone, even though their listeners cannot see them. In addition to this function, gestures convey meaning, and when used effectively, illustrate or complement verbal messages.

| COMMON GESTURES | |
| --- | --- |
| EMBLEMS | Gestures that take the place of particular words.<br>E.g., holding one's palm out to signal "stop." |
| ILLUSTRATORS/ICONIC | Gestures that accompany speech and illustrate the speaker's idea.<br>E.g., using hands to demonstrate the size or shape of something. |
| METAPHORIC | Gestures that are symbolic representations of ideas.<br>E.g., bringing arms together when talking about group work. |
| RHYTHMIC | Gestures that punctuate or accentuate verbal messages.<br>E.g., using fingers to count off points. |

Table 1

It takes practice to develop meaningful, natural-looking gestures, and an equal or greater amount of work to break bad habits. The gestures discussed in Table 1 represent some appropriate hand movements for public presentation.

Gestures are powerful, and they are great for evoking emphasis. However, it is essential to have controlled gestures and move with purpose. When you overuse gestures, you run the risk of the audience being distracted by your gestures, rather than more attentive to your message. If you are not someone who typically speaks with his or her hands, you can start small by using gestures to emphasize your key points. On the contrary, if your hands are always moving when you are talking, work to make your movements more purposeful.

When you gesture, keep a few best practices in mind:

1. Use deliberate, purposeful gestures
2. Develop an open, neutral resting position for your hands and arms
3. Keep movements tailored and clean
4. Avoid excessive palm-up gestures (too many may signal an "I don't know" message)

## A Word on Self-Touch

Self-touch behaviors are worth noting because, in a professional context, it is best to avoid most of them. Common types of self-touching include shielding actions, cleaning actions, self-intimacies, and adaptors (Ekman & Friesen, 1974; Morris, 1971).

Shielding actions are behaviors used to symbolically shield one's self from perceived threats or potentially unpleasant noises. They tend to include actions that limit sensory input or output such as covering one's eyes or ears. Cleaning actions are performed for purposes of removing something from one's face or body—literally cleaning, but they also include preening behaviors.

Preening behaviors are actions performed for the purposes of tending to one's appearance. Hair touching, clothing readjustment, and jewelry repositioning are examples of preening behaviors. Cleaning actions are best avoided in a professional context and addressed in a private place.

Self-intimacies represent another type of self-touching worth avoiding in the work environment. These touches mimic the calming or soothing gestures usually provided by others. Leg hugging, self-embraces, and rocking motions are representations of self- intimacies. Again, these cues communicate insecurity and often distract others.

Finally, adaptors, sometimes referred to as "leakage" cues, are actions performed to expend apprehension-induced nervous energy. Body adaptors, like knuckle cracking, hair twirling, or ear pulling may redirect feelings of nervousness but reveal those insecurities in the process. Object adaptors serve much the same purpose; they simply introduce an object into the nerve-driven behavior cues.

Object adaptor-related habits include but are not limited to compulsive pen clicking, tie straightening, and overreliance on props, or visual aids. More often than not, self-touch behaviors reveal more information than necessary. If possible, monitor these actions, and do your best to limit those that indicate discomfort or weakness. Skilled communicators channel nervous energy into more effective gestures and movements.

Remember, it's important to avoid distracting gestures, movements, or self-touch and habits like:

- fidgeting, or playing with your hands
- crossing your arms, or holding hands at your stomach
- placing both hands in your pockets
- using raised shoulder and upturned palm gestures
- slumping
- swaying or shifting on feet
- touching or grabbing at clothing or jewelry
- cracking your knuckles
- unnecessarily snapping, clapping, or pounding fist into other hand

Though sometimes tempting, these are rookie moves; the type of cues that signal inexperience and a lack of professional confidence.

## Negotiating Presentation Aids

Most often, slides are used as presentation aids. Though helpful, negotiating these visual aids requires some coordination.

Whenever possible, practice with your slides to refine timing and downplay slide transitions. Consider investing in a presentation remote control—a clicker—that advances your slides. Go ahead; treat yourself. We think you are ready for the big leagues.

On rare occasions, you may have an easel, poster, or object integrated into your presentation. If this is the case, use them wisely. Just like the stealthy remote handling, you do not want to call attention to these items. In fact, if using a physical prop or presentation aid, try to conceal it until you are ready to discuss the object. Keep props and aids out of sight, then, reveal them when it counts. Audience members are curious, and rather impatient. If you put something in plain view, they are going to look at it, especially if you request they don't, at the expense of paying attention to you.

> **REMOTE CONTROL**
>
> When holding a remote, do your best to hold it with your thumb against your open palm. It should become a part of your hand. Do not hold it with two hands, spin it, shake it, flip it, or otherwise call attention to the device. Consider the remote your little secret. Good remote handling is like great acting; if done correctly, people should not notice you're doing anything at all.

When finished talking about a particular aid, return it back to its hiding place. Don't fall into the easy but unprofessional habit of holding on to visuals long after they've served their purpose. Worse still, props and visual aids can become object adaptors—a fidgeting device for nervous hands. Don't let the visual aids interrupt your purposeful, professional gestures.

## Perfecting Your Game Face

Facial expressions are complicated blends of muscle movements under the skin. Much like any nonverbal message, several cues combine to create a particular expression or message. Display rules for facial expressions and eye contact differ from culture to culture. However, there are six universally recognized facial expressions: fear, anger, disgust, happiness, sadness, and surprise (Ekman, 1972; Ekman & Friesen 1984). Even these expressions of our most basic emotions are communicated through blends. Happiness, for example, is often represented by a smile, but a smile without slightly raised eyebrows or expressive eyes does not convey the same meaning. Try smiling in a mirror without any other facial movement; you'll notice the difference.

Building awareness of your facial expressions is important to your success as a communicator. Do you know what your face says to others at any given moment? What facial expression do you wear when you're not speaking or participating in a conversation?

Remember Jaime's furrowed brow habit from Chapter 2–1? His facial default was one of displeasure, and this affected his work relationships. **Expressers** are people who seem to "wear" their thoughts on their faces. When speaking to expressers, you usually know how they feel about something before they offer a verbal response. This is because their faces reflect their real-time reactions to almost everything they encounter. If they enjoy the first bite of a sandwich, their eyes may light up. If they dislike a particular co-worker, they may inadvertently sneer when that person enters the room. In a professional context, it is best to avoid disclosing information this way; for a presenter, it is critical.

Unfortunately, many expressers don't realize their tendency to wear their emotions. If you are unsure, ask your friends and family; they can provide you with a valid measure of your expressiveness. If you are indeed an expresser, try to control the habit at work. **Masking,** or the ability to cover one's feelings with neutral facial expressions, is a beneficial skill, especially if masking negative feelings. You work hard to strategize messages, and unintentional revelations, especially those that reveal negative appraisals, can undermine your goals. Those friends and family members who exposed your expresser tendencies may be enlisted to tell you when you are unintentionally expressing. The more aware you are of this tendency, the more easily you can mask unfavorable or self-defeating facial expressions.

Facial expression is an especially powerful element of your nonverbal delivery. Control your facial expressions when speaking in front of an audience. As the gatekeeper of your professional persona, remember that your expressions can make or break your game. Develop a game face, a presentation face that says, "I'm in control, and I'm happy to be here today." If presenting in a group, add "I'm very interested in everything my teammates say."

## Eye Contact

You cannot fully engage your audience when you are reading from your slides or notes. To connect, you need to be able to look your audience in the eyes and speak to them. When you are dependent on slides or notes, you are showing the audience that you do not know the material. Furthermore, you are missing the opportunity to connect with them. Think of it as a conversation. If you were trying to talk to a friend or colleague and they kept glancing down instead of looking at you, it would be distracting and maybe even disrespectful. In order to give the audience members the attention they deserve, make proper eye contact. It is imperative to know what you are going to say so that you are confident enough to step away from your slides and notes. Do not try to remember a speech word-for-word, but be familiar enough with the key concepts you want to address so you can speak in a conversational style about them.

| SOME BEST PRACTICES FOR SPEAKER EYE-CONTACT |
| --- |
| Water the lawn—make momentary eye contact with audience members in every area of the room. |
| Keep your eyes on the action—if presenting in a group, look at the person speaking |
| Keep your eyes off your visual aids |
| Make eye contact early and often |

In American culture, many believe the proverb, "the eyes are the windows to the soul." Eye contact is valued as an indicator of honesty, credibility, and trust. Therefore, communicators are expected to maintain appropriate levels of eye contact with listeners. The duration, intensity, and frequency of eye gazes depend on the culture in which we're communicating. In an American business context, appropriate gazing behaviors include consistent eye contact with occasional momentary breaks.

Though eye contact can communicate attentiveness and interest, prolonged gazes may be threatening or awkward.

When speaking in public, it is important to make eye contact with audience members. You don't have to systematically stare at each person in the audience, but you should try to make momentary eye contact with as many people as possible. To do this, work your way around the room with your eyes: left, right, front and back. This conveys nonverbal indicators of liking, interest, and attention (Mehrabian, 1971), otherwise known as nonverbal immediacy. Eye contact is a valuable element of communication, and if you are not used to the behavior, it might take some practice. If at first uncomfortable, keep trying—it's worth it.

# Engaging Your Audience

## Charisma and Authenticity

In addition to the vocal, verbal, and physical presentation delivery strategies we have discussed, there are a few more tips for powerful presentations. Think about the factors that all great presenters have in common. Passionate, knowledgeable, and genuine are characteristics that typically come to mind. If you have passion for the topic you are presenting, your audience can feel it. When you know what you are talking about and have done the necessary research, your audience perceives you as a knowledgeable subject matter expert. When you are authentic and bring your true self to the presentation, you are seen as relatable and genuine. With ample practice, all of the traits mentioned above are attainable to the average presenter.

## "Hey You There"—Addressing Specific Audience Members and Asking Questions

In some instances, you will know your audience well, and in other circumstances, you may be meeting them for the first time. When you know the attendees, use what you know about each individual to tailor your presentation to his or her unique needs. If you have not met members of the audience, it is a good idea to arrive early and introduce yourself to people in the audience. In addition to learning their names, ask questions to understand their reasons for attending your presentation.

Getting to know a few key pieces of information about your audience will allow you to customize your presentation in the moment. For example, if you know that Jane is particularly interested in a budget for implementation, you can address her by name as you introduce the budget section. You can add value for Jane by stating, "Jane, I know the cost of implementation is important to you. Therefore, I have provided a detailed budget for you."

Addressing specific audience members and their needs gives your presentation a personal touch and lets your audience know you care about each attendee's needs. You can also ask questions of the audience to get them involved throughout the presentation. Asking questions of audience members not only keeps them engaged, but it also helps you select the information that can best meet their needs.

## Managing Public Speaking Anxiety: Feeling the Burn

Many of us experience public speaking anxiety. In fact, it is one of the top ranked fears for Americans (Croston, 2012). In order to connect with the audience, we need to appear confident and competent, even when we may be a little nervous. We want our authentic self to show through, not the nervousness we are experiencing. There are several strategies for managing public speaking anxiety. The single most important factor in overcoming your anxiety is practice.

The more you present, the less anxious you will feel about it. Take every opportunity to talk in front of others; the more familiar it becomes, the easier it will become. Another important factor is breathing. Holding your breath will make you tense up further and will actually make you more anxious. We all do it subconsciously, but when we limit the amount of oxygen we inhale, our body goes into emergency mode and starts producing stress hormones to help defend itself. Before your next presentation, take a few deep breaths to calm your nerves. You might need to check in with yourself during your presentation and consciously remind yourself to breathe. Learning to manage your anxiety will allow you to be a more effective presenter.

## Letting Your Passion Shine Through

Believe it or not, a simple smile can go a long way to connecting with and engaging your audience. A smile conveys warmth and typically evokes positive emotions in your audience. Interestingly, the act of smiling also releases stress-alleviating brain chemicals; the more you smile, the less anxious you will feel. Likewise, using an enthusiastic tone lets your passion shine. You will be better able to connect with and engage your audience with a positive disposition and facial expressions.

## Presenting in Teams

Now that you have explored presentation planning from content to delivery, it's time to move from individual to team presentations. Team presentations are a large part of information delivery in business today. Companies rely on teams of individuals with unique sets of skills to complete major projects. Preparing and delivering an individual presentation involves many of the skills and characteristics presented earlier in this chapter. However, team presentations require a group of people to collaborate, consolidate, and choreograph in order to present a unified message. The best team presentations involve regular face-to-face meetings to prepare from start to finish.

**Figure 2**   *Plan as a Team*

## Planning as a Team

From the moment you meet with your team and are assigned a project, you should begin to define the roles each person will fill. This means understanding each other's areas of expertise and interest as well as the varying work styles on the team. Taking advantage of each member's knowledge and skills will ensure better content and more enthusiasm in the delivery. Once roles are determined, however, it is important for everyone on the team to agree on every aspect of the presentation. Defining the overall objective and determining section development must be a collaborative effort.

A presentation is made up of a number of different pieces, but those pieces are all interrelated. Imagine listening to a group presentation in which each member pops up, delivers one segment of the message, and then sits down. This is followed by the next three team members doing the same thing. No one tries to connect his or her information to previous sections, nor does the next section logically follow the information being presented. In the end, you might have gained some new information, but the "Big Picture" will not be clear. If, on the other hand, the presentation is more like a continuing storyline, you will get to the end and understand how all the pieces fit together and what the next steps should be.

Collaborative planning makes for more effective group presentations. Meet often, brainstorm ideas, agree on the content needed in each section, trust one another to gather individual pieces, and come back together to complete the "puzzle."

Another reason that close collaboration is important is that you never know when you may need to present another team member's section of the presentation. If someone gets ill or there is a scheduling conflict that cannot be avoided, you may need to fill in or divide a section between two other team members. Collaboration will enable you to do this.

Once the content is finalized, collaboration must continue. If you are using Power Point, you will need consistency across all of your slides. Creating a template together is just the beginning. You will need to agree on the font, font size, and color. Remember, you want a unified message, and your visual aids can help to convey that unity. You will also want to go over finished slides together to eliminate needless repetition or to fill gaps left within or between sections. The goal is to get the slides to the point where the message flows and every team member is proud to present from his or her presentation aids.

## Rehearsing as a Team

Now that content and visuals are ready, how can a team prepare for the actual delivery? While it may be tempting to disperse and regroup just prior to the presentation, it is not advisable to do so. Yes, you can (and should) work on your individual sections until you are satisfied that you know what you want to say and how you want to say it, but then come together soon and often to rehearse. Practice out loud; record and view your presentation as a team, if possible. Look for ways to improve individual delivery and to enhance the transitions between sections.

Transitions are key to delivering a cohesive team presentation, and while there are a number of views on what each transition should consist of, keeping the presentation moving is always the ultimate goal. Topic transitions, wrapping up your section (your topic) and building a bridge to the next topic, are the best way to keep your presentation moving forward.

One speaker might conclude his or her section by saying, "This gives a clear understanding of the problem we are currently facing; now let's talk about what led up to this situation and what action we can take." The next speaker can then pick up on this cue and begin by saying, "While there may be several actions that led up to our current situation, I will focus on three actions that can be addressed immediately." This type of transition prevents unnecessary interruptions to the flow of information and allows your audience to follow your train of thought from start to finish.

Before you can build in your transitions, however, your team will need to decide on the order of information. The most important consideration is to organize the content strategically; each idea should logically follow the previous one. This may be chronological or it may be a problem-solution-based structure. Your team will have to decide how best to present the specific information so that the audience can follow the storyline and come to the same conclusion your team has.

In a professional presentation, there is one other organizational consideration to address. Since the two most memorable sections of a presentation are the beginning and the end, you want to have high-energy presenters in those positions. At the beginning, you want an individual who can convey both enthusiasm and credibility. He or she should be comfortable addressing the audience and should exhibit a genuine desire to connect with them. The opening speaker sets the stage and establishes the tone for the rest of the presentation. Of course, all members of the team should convey interest in and enthusiasm about their own segments of the message to keep the audience engaged.

Finally, most people remember the last thing they hear more vividly than any previous information. Therefore, you will want to select a final speaker who can summarize key points and "move" the audience to action. She or he must be able to win over any skeptics and motivate everyone in the room to embrace new possibilities.

## Delivering a Team Presentation

Prior to your team's presentation, you will want to be sure that you have the choreography all mapped out. This may seem more relevant to a dance troupe than a business team, but if you want to deliver your message without distractions, you have to plan and rehearse more than just the content.

One of the first things to determine is how you will handle introductions. If one person is going to do this, the names must be clearly enunciated, and it must be obvious who belongs to which name. A slight nod from each individual as his or her name is presented will suffice. If each member introduces himself or herself, you will want consistency in both content and tone.

Next, your team should consider logistics; this includes team placement and movement. You want to avoid the "sinking ship" sensation that occurs when all members are standing on one side of the room. Create a balance across the front of the room and be sure your team is situated to include all sections of the audience. Each member should then step forward when speaking to show a desire to connect with those listening. Be careful not to step in front of another team member or to block the screen if visuals are being used. Do not start speaking until you have finished taking your step forward. Another subtle yet important aspect of a team presentation is the use of strategic movement and pre-determined cues. You may need to signal a team member to change a slide for you. Rather than shouting out, "Next slide!" you should have a signal that is not apparent to the audience but is clear to the other team member. During questions from the audience, having cues can help your team look better prepared and knowledgeable.

If a question is asked to the entire team, the person who feels most confident about addressing it might move his or her foot slightly forward. The other team members can then look at that person in support instead of looking at the floor or at one another in panic mode. More on handling the question and answer portion of the presentation will be discussed in the next chapter, but having a few nonverbal cues in your team repertoire will greatly add to the smooth flow of every aspect of the presentation.

We have discussed the importance of unity in a team presentation, but there are still a few more things you can do to convey this concept to your audience. First, do not interrupt another speaker; if you feel you have something that needs to be added, you can return to that point later. Interrupting a speaker conveys a lack of trust and preparedness and will reduce your team's credibility. Another effective way of keeping the presentation unified is to refer to key points made by the other speakers. Connect your ideas with something that has already been presented; connect, don't just repeat. This will help your audience to see how all the information is linked and will enable them to see the "big" picture in every detail.

Finally, remember you are always on stage. This means that even while waiting to speak, you are engaged with the presentation, your team, and the audience. Look at the speaker, nod when something of interest is said. Look at the screen when the speaker refers to something on the current slide. Keep a watchful eye on the audience to gauge their level of interest and comprehension. Be an active member of the team at all times and avoid being a distraction. This will allow the audience to stay focused on what is being presented.

Listening to a team presentation requires the audience to take in and process much more than an individual speaker presentation does. It is vital that the message be unified both in content and delivery. From the planning stage to being "on stage," your team must find ways to present a clear and cohesive message. You will be pleasantly surprised at how much this will increase your own confidence and how it will help you and your team to achieve your objectives.

As you prepare for your next important presentation, it is helpful to make your own check-list of strengths and weaknesses. We are all works in progress, and everyone has some area of natural ability and key points for improvement. Sharing these with your team can help the team leverage differences and figure out how to position each individual for success. A key list of areas you wish to improve in both verbal and nonverbal delivery areas can really help you and your team minimize distracters and build a more credible message.

Working together toward a common understanding of what makes for successful delivery can make a big difference in your audience's levels of engagement and retention of your message. Your team should take an honest and tactful appraisal of one another's level of ability, and then coach one another toward success. Each team makes its own magic. The art of blending delivery and aligning style with message content is just one more aspect of building a message that is fluid and set up for success with your intended audience. Now that you and your team have the tools to proceed, it is a matter of practice and feedback that will unlock your success.

# Chapter 6-4

# Driving Discussion, the Art of Q&A

One of the most critical factors in any presentation is the opportunity to listen to your audience and address them in real time—to hear their questions, comments, and concerns. This is when we truly enter into conversation with the audience and can tailor our message to their perception, address points of resistance, and build agreement. The ability to listen in the moment is a skill worth developing.

Sadly, listening in general is a lost art, but being able to listen in the moment to allay a concern, or seize the opportunity to build a bridge to your audience are all possible through the art of the answer.

Remember, the goal of any successful business presentation is to move your audience from what they currently think or do to what you would like them to think or do.

This chapter explores the art of the answer. Did you know that there are different types of questions, and each one has a strategic way to respond? Understanding why people ask questions can help you unlock the best type of answer to give. Whether you are delivering a consultative style presentation (where the entire presentation is a give and take of questions) or you are engaged in a formal Q&A session, this chapter is designed to help you turn questions into opportunities to advance your message.

## LISTEN CORRECTLY TO ANSWER PROPERLY

"Everyone who tries to win in business and, in fact, everyone who tries to win in any endeavor by seeking the concurrence of other people, must avoid the fatal mistake of not listening. The remedy is a seemingly simple but deceptively counter-intuitive two-step solution:

1. Listen correctly

2. Answer properly

. . .Heed the advice of the Zen master: Empty your cup. Empty your mind of all your thoughts so that you can fill it instead with those of the questioner. Concentrate.

. . .Resist thinking of the answer and instead listen for the key issue. Concentrate. Listen for the one or two words that identify the essence of the question, the heart of the matter."

— Jerry Weissman, *In the Line of Fire: How to Handle Tough Questions. . .When It Counts* (2005)

# Rethinking Q&A: How to Turn Questions into Opportunities

As we learned earlier in this chapter, it is important to put your audience first and think of your presentation from their point of view.

## The Genesis of Q&A: Why Do People Ask Questions?

A highly skilled presenter actively encourages and manages questions with the confidence that open discussion with the audience is simply additional time to present. You should consider yourself lucky to field questions during your presentation. If you raised an eyebrow at this, we don't blame you. Many presenters fear questions like the plague because questions force them to get "off script" and cede some control of the presentation to the audience. Such unscripted conversations may expose things the presenters want to hide, such as holes in their research, errors in their calculations, or gaps in their knowledge. Savvy presenters, however, welcome questions as opportunities to engage and establish rapport with their audiences. They recognize that moving an audience requires breaking down points of resistance that keep an audience from moving in the direction the presenter would like them to go. Resistance, it turns out, is usually based on a fear of change. Asking someone to reject the status quo (what is) and work toward something new (what could be) involves changing mindsets and behaviors. Sayings such as "old habits die hard" and "you can't teach an old dog new tricks" exist for good reason.

Before they accept your solution and agree to change, your audience will want to know two things. First, why should they change? As we have learned, you will need to frame your presentation carefully and build your case for the solution you would like to implement. Second, if your audience accepts your frame and agrees with your case, they will want to know how to change, or specifically what they need to do to implement your solution. These two concepts—why and how—are at the core of most questions you will field during a presentation.

If you dig down further, you will find that both of these concepts are rooted in your audience's resistance to change. Whether based on organizational inertia, lack of understanding, insensitivity to the problem, aversion to risk, or fear of the unknown, resistance is the wellspring of all questions, and it usually boils down to a fear of change.

# Getting at the Root of the Question

Because resistance can manifest itself in many ways, questions can take a great many forms. Active listening is the key to understanding what your audience is really asking. You must listen carefully to recognize the type of question and the root of that question.

## Active Listening

In his groundbreaking work on Q&A strategy, Jerry Weissman (2005) emphasizes the importance of active listening as the fundamental prerequisite for successfully handling tough questions. While "stop, concentrate, and listen, then respond" may sound easy, it is remarkably difficult to execute in the heat of the moment. After all, you need to assess the root issue of the question, whether it is a challenging, audience member who has yet to accept you; your presentation of the problem; or your strategy for solving it. We have all had moments where we have fumbled a question. This often happens because we do not really concentrate on what the questioner is asking. We become so focused on selling our presentation to the audience that we lose sight of what the interaction is really all about—an opportunity to connect with other people and communicate an idea that will improve our lives. From this state of mind, any interruption from the audience, especially a challenge or an expression of disagreement, is an obstacle that gets in our way. If we view questions as problems that need to be solved, we stop listening as soon as we think we have the answer the questioner wants. Answer the question, put out the fire, and get back to your message, right?

Wrong. If we perceive questions this way, even challenging or openly hostile questions, we risk fumbling an opportunity to engage with the audience on an authentic level. Much of what we try to "sell" in a presentation is our own credibility, and nobody buys anything from a salesperson they don't trust, unless they have no other choice. In this context, listening is absolutely essential to building trust and moving our audience from point A to point B. Listening demonstrates that you are putting your audience first and that your interests can be aligned with theirs.

The next time you find yourself in front of an audience, whether it is a room full of people or a tabletop meeting with just one person, try Weissman's approach. When a person asks a question, resist the temptation to immediately think of the answer as they are speaking. Instead, listen for the key issue—the root—of their question. Concentrate, and listen for key words that signal what they are really asking about. The root may come wrapped up in a messy ball of string, so if you don't recognize it the first time, apologize (take responsibility) and ask them to restate the question (Weismann 2005).

### ...YOU STILL DON'T UNDERSTAND

"Remove these statements from your vocabulary:

- Let me see if I have this right. . .
- Does that answer your question?
- Is that what you're asking?

If you do not completely understand the question. . .and that means 100%, not 99.999%. . .picture a bold red line between you and your audience. Do not cross the line. Do not retake the floor. Do not answer. Do not interpret. . . .

Instead, return to sender. Do not retake the floor, leave the questioner with the floor by saying 'I'm sorry, I didn't follow, would you mind restating the question?' In doing so, you take the responsibility for not understanding, rather than pointing out that the questioner asked an unintelligible question.

What will the questioner do? He or she will rethink the question and then restate it in simpler terms. And you are off the hook."

– Jerry Weissman, *In the Line of Fire: How to Handle Tough Questions. . .When It Counts* (2005)

## Anticipating Types of Questions

Although much of successful Q&A rides on active listening, knowing the types of questions you may face will help you plan your responses to them.

### A Word of Caution

If you do plan ahead for questions—and you would be foolish not to do so—beware of the danger of scripting your answers. Having "canned" responses prepared ahead of time will interfere with your active listening. You will find yourself tuning out your audience once you think you understand what they are asking, and you may miss the root of the question entirely. Even if you provide a canned answer that is mostly right, your audience will be left feeling that you were not really listening to them. It would be like a shoe salesman trying to persuade you to buy a shoe that almost fits, just because he has that one in stock. He is putting his need to sell shoes above your need to find a pair that fits.

## Four Basic Types of Questions

With that important caveat in mind, you can proceed with planning for questions. There are four basic types of questions, each of which exhibits a different type of resistance. The four types—Query, Clarification, Confirmation, and Challenge—are outlined in the table below, organized from most friendly to least friendly (Tisdale, 2004).

| QUESTION TYPE | FRIENDLY OR UNFRIENDLY? | THE QUESTIONER'S RESISTANCE |
|---|---|---|
| Query | Neutral, Friendly | The questioner needs more information. |
| Clarification | Neutral, Friendly | The questioner didn't quite understand something you said, or she or he missed it the first time around. |
| Confirmation | Usually Friendly (listen carefully to the questioner's tone) | The questioner wants to show that she or he understands, or that she or he agrees with something you've said. These are not usually in the form of a question. Respond with a "yes" or "no" answer. If unfriendly, beware of stepping into a trap with a follow-up question ("So what you're saying is..."). |
| Challenge | Not Friendly | The questioner has concerns, or she or he flat out disagrees with you. The resistance is often clear. |

**Table 1**  *Four Types of Questions*

## How to Handle Each Type of Question

Queries, requests for clarification, confirmations, and challenge questions all present opportunities to overcome your audience's resistance and move them toward accepting your solution. Listen carefully so that you understand what the questioner is asking, and respond with the information that he or she needs.

### Queries

A query is simply a request for more information. Rejoice! This is an opportunity to discuss your topic in greater depth, and overcome the resistance that stems from misunderstanding or fear of the unknown. Use your answer to build a champion in the audience, a person who understands what you want to achieve and can relay your story to others. A nodding head is a good sign that you are on the right track.

## Requests for Clarification

In a routine, informational presentation, requests for clarification are usually easy to field. The presenter is not defensive and is, therefore, better able to listen, and the audience is not resistant. The more persuasive the presentation, however, the higher the stakes. The more resistant the audience, the more difficult it can become to recognize a request for clarification for what it really is—an admission of vulnerability. The questioner is admitting that she or he missed something or does not fully understand something you said. If you are already in a defensive posture as the presenter, you may not recognize this vulnerability.

There is tremendous benefit to handling these types of questions effectively, but even greater cost to misfiring. Woe to the presenter who makes the questioner feel stupid for asking a question. In the best case, you will only offend that person. In the worst (and more likely) case, you will offend everyone in the room and torch your credibility.

If an audience member asks for clarification, be patient and gracious—do not scold them for their lack of understanding. Your tone and body language are critical. Never, ever, make them feel stupid, or sigh and start your answer with "As I stated on slide 16, …." Simply state the answer, even if you already covered the information. A nodding head, a smile, and perhaps a genuine "thank you" from the questioner are signs that you have handled the question appropriately.

## Confirmations

Tone and body language work both ways. As critical as your tone is in handling a request for clarification, you will need to pay close attention to the questioner's tone and body language in order to determine how best to handle a confirmation. Confirmations can be wolves in sheep's clothing. Again, the more resistance you anticipate from the audience, the more likely you will be to encounter confirmations that have ulterior motives. Watch for wolves.

Consider the following question:

> "So you're telling us that we can reduce employee turnover by 15% if we make our applicants participate in a rigorous, unpaid training program in which they compete for a limited number of positions?"

If the confirmation is genuine, the questioner will likely be asking this to make sure that she understands the benefits of your recommendation. She may also look around the room to ensure that others understand this as well. If she emphasizes any part of the question, it will likely be the benefits or positive aspects, such as "reduce employee turnover by 15%," "rigorous," and "compete."

If the confirmation is not genuine, the questioner will be asking this to telegraph the costs to the rest of the audience. Listen for emphasis on the costs or negative aspects, such as "So you're telling us," "make our employees," "unpaid," and "limited." She may also raise an eyebrow when she says "15%." Watch for smirking, raised eyebrows, or notes of sarcasm, and expect a follow-up question that challenges your analysis or your expertise.

## Challenge Questions

When you get a challenge question, you will know it. The questioner has concerns, or she or he flat out disagrees with you. On the surface the resistance is usually clear; a smart audience will often challenge you or disagree with how you have done one of the following things:

1. Framed the situation (What is happening? Is this a problem or an opportunity?)

2. Defined the problem or opportunity, or analyzed its root cause (What problem are we here to solve? What is the opportunity?)

3. Established relevance, or created a sense of urgency (Why this problem? Why now?)

4. Recommended action (What is the best way to solve this problem or take advantage of this opportunity? How do we know this solution will work?)

Depending on who is asking the question and what your relationship is to that person, the tone of a challenge question can be either forceful and direct, or gentler and more indirect. Your supervisor may be asking the question to test your frame and see what you have excluded from the presentation, or a colleague from a different department may disagree with your assessment that his team is responsible for a delay in the project.

Whatever the tone, you will need to listen carefully to understand the root of the question. The resistance will likely stem from one of the following things:

- Organizational inertia (Why change something that already works, and risk failing?)

- Lack of understanding or awareness of the situation (Is this really a problem?)

- Insensitivity to the problem (I haven't seen evidence of the problem you're asking us to solve.)

- Aversion to risk, or of trying something that might not work (What if this doesn't work? We will be blamed for failure.)

- Lack of faith in you as a presenter due to insufficient credibility or trust in your motivation or expertise (Why should we believe you?)

- Fear of the unknown (We've been doing this a certain way for a long time and it has always gotten us the results we've wanted. Why fix something that isn't broken?)

---

### SELF-VALIDATORS, AKA TROLLS

"Lots of things about work are hard. Dealing with trolls is one of them. Trolls are critics who gain perverse pleasure in relentlessly tearing you and your ideas down. Here's the thing(s):

1. Trolls will always be trolling

2. Critics rarely create

3. They live in a tiny echo chamber, ignored by everyone except the trolled and the other trolls

4. Professionals (that's you) get paid to ignore them. It's part of your job.

'Can't please everyone,' isn't just an aphorism, it's the secret of being remarkable."

— Seth Godin, "Trolls" (sethgodin.typepad.com)

---

## Questions That Aren't Really Questions

While the four types of questions we have discussed so far cover the vast majority of the questions you are likely to face, you may encounter a situation in which the questioner takes the floor without an apparent question in mind. There are several terms for this phenomenon. Seth Godin refers to people who do this consistently as "trolls," but we will call them "Self-Validators."

Self-validation questions are not really questions at all. Look for the following red flags:

- They are in the form of a statement, or there doesn't appear to be a question

- They are not necessarily related to something you have covered in your presentation

- They can be either neutral or resistant, but they are rarely positive or supportive

The "Self-Validator" is simply trying to flex his muscle and demonstrate his power. She or he takes the floor to do one of the following things:

- Show her or his importance
- Demonstrate that she or he understands
- Address a hot topic that you have touched upon
- Take control of the agenda

Dealing with a self-validator is tricky. Your primary objective is to maintain your composure, hear her or him out, and do your best to get the conversation back on track as soon as possible. Take the high road by recognizing the validity of the concern, paraphrasing the statement, and wrapping it up in the form of a question that relates to what you are trying to prove. Let us examine an example of how to handle a self-validator.

Steve Jobs was a master presenter in many respects. Listening was one of his strengths, and he employed that strength to deal with self-validators of all types. During his keynote address at the Apple Worldwide Developers Conference in 1997, Mr. Jobs fielded a question from an audience member that went something like this:

©Anton_Ivanov/Shutterstock.com

**Figure 1**  *Steve Jobs Holds Forth*

*Questioner:* "Mr. Jobs, you're a bright and influential man."

Audience laughs…

*Steve Jobs:* "Here it comes."

*Questioner:* "It's sad and clear that on several counts you've discussed you don't know what you're talking about. I would like, for example, for you to express in clear terms how, say, Java, in any of its incarnations, addresses the ideas embodied in Open Document. And when you're finished with that, perhaps you could tell us what you personally have been doing for the last seven years."

Amid "oohs" from the audience, the presenter takes his seat. Calmly and eloquently, he has delivered his kill strike in front of an audience of thousands of people. Mr. Jobs remains seated on his stool and takes a sip of water, looking down and away from the audience in a brief moment of silent reflection.

*Jobs:* "You know, you can please some of the people some of the time, but…"

Pause, audience laughs uncomfortably…

*Jobs:* "One of the hardest things when you're trying to effect change is that people like this gentleman…are right! In some areas."

Clouds part and a small ray of sunshine enters the auditorium. Momentum shifts. What did he just say?

*Jobs:* "I'm sure that there are some things Open Doc does, probably even more that I'm not familiar with, that nothing else out there does. And I'm sure that you can make some demos, maybe a small commercial app, that demonstrates those things. The hardest thing is… how does that fit in to a cohesive, larger vision that's going to allow you to sell 8 billion dollars, 10 billion dollars of product a year?"

The camera pans to an audience sitting in rapt attention. Some people are on the edges of their seats. Jobs continues:

*Jobs:* "And one of the things I've always found is that you've got to start with the customer experience and work backwards to the technology. You can't start with the technology and try to figure out where you're going to try to sell it. And I've made this mistake probably more than anybody else in this room, and I've got the scar tissue to prove it, and I know that it's the case. And as we have tried to come up with a strategy and a vision for Apple…it started with 'What incredible benefits can we give to the customer? Where can we take the customer?' Not starting with 'Let's sit down with the engineers and figure out what awesome technology we have and how are we going to market that?' And I think that's the right path to take."

Game, set, and match. Can you identify the resistance? A lesser presenter would have fumbled the question; as smooth and concise as it was, the question was layered with innuendo intended to insult, infuriate, and embarrass Jobs in front of thousands of people.

But the question backfired. Rather than react immediately, Jobs paused and thought about what the questioner was really trying to say. That long pause communicated to the audience that he was really listening, that there was a genuine conversation taking place, and that they were about to hear a sincere response. Jobs started on the high road by recognizing the validity of the concern, paraphrasing the statement, and wrapping it up in the form of a question that related to Apple's higher vision, which was precisely what Jobs was there to present. The train was back on track.

## Remembering That Presentations Are Conversations

We can learn a great deal from Jobs and seasoned presenters like him. Before you retake the floor to answer a question, make sure that you fully understand what the questioner is really asking. Addressing the root of the question—*Is this really a problem? I haven't seen evidence of the problem you're asking us to solve. What if this doesn't work? Why should we believe you? Why fix something that isn't broken?*—will help disarm your audience and demonstrate that you understand their concerns.

At its core, a presentation is the most basic of human interactions, a conversation between you and someone else. As the presenter, you are telling the audience a story, and you want to inspire them to do something. The audience needs to accept you before they will follow you. They will be much more receptive to you and your idea if you demonstrate, through active listening, that you know who they are and how this problem affects them, and that you have crafted a solution that is in their best interest.

## Aligning for Q&A Success

Depending on the type of presentation you are giving—informational, persuasive, or bad news delivery—you may need to pay particular attention to how you align with your audience or craft a buffer. We discussed strategies for organizing your content based on your purpose in Chapter 1–2. This would be a great time to go back and review the direct and indirect approaches to informing, persuading, and delivering bad news. You can apply those same strategies to your presentations. Pay particular attention to how to employ the "You Attitude" and put your audience first.

## Anticipating Specific Questions

Steve Jobs made presentations and Q&A look easy. His relaxed and candid demeanor on stage belied the fact that behind the scenes, he was a relentless and driven planner, who invested hundreds of hours into practice before a live presentation like a keynote or product launch at the Apple Worldwide Developers Conference.

The time you spend practicing and planning will pay off handsomely. As you prepare for your next presentation, carve out some time to stop and think about your argument as critically as possible. Think about the way you are framing the situation, presenting the problem, sequencing your evidence, and making your recommendation. How are you building your case? How could a reasonable person object to what you have to say?

The sample questions listed above may help you think of specific questions that someone may ask. If you cannot think of at least a few questions in each category, you are not thinking hard enough. Do not walk into your presentation unprepared. Plan ahead but remember the caveat mentioned earlier about the danger of scripted answers.

## Plan Your Speakers and Transitions (Avoid the Dog Pile)

If you are preparing for a team presentation, it is important to decide who will field each type of question. Share your Q&A as evenly as possible among all teammates. When the audience asks a question, don't dog pile and have multiple presenters "add on" to an answer. Dog piling makes you look disorganized, fragmented, and unrehearsed. For each question, decide who is responsible for answering it, and practice how that person will transition back to your team's core message after they field that question. How does each specific question, and its underlying resistance, relate to your bottom line? What do you need to say to get back on track?

# Making Q&A Work for You

## Q&A Has Benefits

In this chapter, we dived deeply into Q&A strategy, examined why people ask questions, and given you some ideas for turning questions into opportunities to advance your message. There are significant benefits of planning for, and looking forward to, fielding questions from the audience. Even a tough question, or, better put, especially a tough question, can provide you with the material you need to build a bridge to your audience. To adapt a concept from Chip Heath and Dan Heath, the Q&A should be the entrée of your presentation, not the garnish (Heath & Heath, 2007). Your handling of questions, either your success or your failure at it, is what your audience will remember. It's where the magic happens.

## Q&A Is More Time to Present

Think of Q&A as more time to present. A question is an opportunity to ensure that you are providing your audience with the information they need to overcome their resistance to you or your idea. Listening carefully to each question also gives you the confidence of knowing that you are pulling the right persuasive "levers" for that particular audience. If they want more data, you can provide more data. If they prefer case studies, focus on examples of similar situations at other companies. If they want an emotional appeal, zoom back out to your company's vision and all of the people who will benefit from your proposal. If they just need to commiserate with you, acknowledge the fact that you are in a difficult situation, then pivot to how this solution may help you all work toward a better future.

## Q&A Builds Your Credibility

Relationships and trust are based on shared history. If you demonstrate active listening and a real concern for your audience, you have added a positive chapter to that history. Each individual question is a chance to build rapport with another person and become a known quantity—a real human being—to them.

## Q&A Reduces Anxiety

If you are the type of person who fights severe anxiety during a presentation, take heart. Over many years of coaching undergraduate business students, graduate business students, and professionals in the workplace, we have noticed that something interesting happens to an anxious person during Q&A. *Believe it or not, their anxiety actually subsides when they are asked a direct question.* Don't believe us? Try it. A direct question, especially a friendly or neutral question, pulls the anxious presenter out of "presentation mode," in which they are reading off a script in their mind, and puts them into "conversation mode" in which they are talking to a real person. That mental script is the source of much of their anxiety. They are so worried about "messing up" and forgetting something on their script, they freeze if they lose their train of thought. A question, especially if they answer it effectively, can be just the thing to pull them out of their heads and build their confidence.

As you move into your next presentation, see if you can find the moment of opportunity to have questions become a way to connect to your audience: take a step closer, build a bridge, and listen. True listening opens up pathways towards mutual understanding. Once you realize the tremendous power you unleash when you open the floor to your audience, you'll find that you no longer dread the inevitable Q&A. You might even save a bit more time to make sure your message if fully heard. Those extra few minutes when you can convince your audience to act, when you make it possible for them to act, can often become the distinguishing factor between your ideas moving forward and taking root, or simply becoming a fading memory.

# Presentation Aids and Visual Design

In a world that has rapidly become more visual than literate, a picture is truly worth way more than a thousand words. Worse, living in an omni-channel world means we are perpetually "on" and our senses are overloaded with imagery. Our expectations are higher for compressed meaning, and our appetite to grasp concepts visually is greater. Understanding the power of visual design and the ability to accelerate meaning through well-designed graphics has become a norm for any effective presentation. It is no longer enough now to "say it with charts"; our audiences demand complex concepts visually rendered. Information design has evolved into its own discipline, and our audiences have sophisticated expectations when it comes to graphical compression of complex data sets.

While there are many excellent online tools and sites to visit that can assist you in designing imagery, it is important to understand the basics and principles of design so you can select and develop the right visual approach to your message. Whether or not you realize it, you are already a sophisticated consumer of visual design. Simply think of your favorite brand and its associated imagery. Or think of a meme you recently "liked" or an infographic you scrolled through. To live in the 21st century means you are an active participant in the exploding field of visual literacy. This chapter will help you understand how those images work, and ultimately, guide you as you successfully "brand" your next presentation.

## Support, Don't Distract

Think about the last time you sat through a presentation; were you paying more attention to the speaker or what he or she projected on the screen? If the presentation aid was designed effectively, you should have been paying closer attention to the words the speaker said instead of whatever he or she had displayed on the screen. Visual elements of a presentation should serve to augment the message of the person or team presenting. In fact, presentation aids—especially slide decks—are best suited to highlighting specific key points that the speaker(s) can then elaborate on verbally.

Now that you are an expert on the personal and team aspects of delivering presentations, it is time to throw another element into the mix: presentation aids. The most common type of presentation aids include projected slides created in Microsoft PowerPoint, Apple Keynote, Google Slides, or Prezi (we collectively refer to these slide presentations as slide decks or just decks). Other frequently-used but less common presentation aids might include handouts of key points, executive summaries, or giveaway items. The key element common to all presentation aids, regardless of format, is that they support the presentation instead of distracting audience attention from it.

For the remainder of this unit, we will discuss effective visual design strategies.

We will also cover practical logistical tips to help you ensure that your presentations are polished, professional, and accomplish what you need them to do.

# Presentation ≠ Lecture

You are likely quite used to sitting through people standing in front of you talking while there are slides on a screen behind them. In fact, in the very class for which you are reading this textbook, you have had to sit through many such experiences this semester alone. You should not hold those experiences as the gold standard for delivering business presentations.

Just as with your writing, business presentations are different from academic presentations. In your class lectures, your instructors have a relatively limited amount of time to transfer as much knowledge as possible. Academic presentations—lectures—require their audiences to retain as much as possible and later demonstrate mastery of the topics covered. Though academic presentations tend to be longer than most traditional business presentations, they also cover more material, often in a single sitting, and need to be more thorough. In contrast, business presentations often cover only one or two topics in a sitting and should be as concise and precise as possible.

In other words, business presentations are not academic lectures.

# We Eat First with the Eyes

There's an old saying in the culinary world that applies to business presentations too: "We eat first with the eyes." When referring to the work of chefs, this aphorism means that the diner will see the dish served to them before they even smell or taste it. Though we usually associate eating with the sense of taste, the sense of sight gives us our first impression of the food we are about to eat.

The same is true of presentations. We often associate presentations with what the presenter has to say, but the audience's perception of the message will be irrevocably influenced by the visual aids used to support it. A poorly designed slide deck can hurt your credibility and lead to your audience tuning you out altogether. Incidentally, this may also help explain why you sometimes are tempted to fall asleep during an academic lecture: the visual aids that the instructor may be using are not well designed, and his speaking alone may not be enough to keep your attention. Another reason that business presentations should not be the same as academic lectures!

The following tips will help you develop visually-appealing presentation aids to engage your audience without distracting from what you are saying. This can be a delicate balancing act, but with practice you will walk that tightrope with ease.

# Keep It Simple Stu...dents

Science students are often told that the simplest hypothesis is often the most correct. Simplicity is a powerful visual design concept for the same reason: by eliminating all that is unnecessary, you are left with the most important idea. Many students have a tendency—sometimes bordering on compulsion—to load their slides with many visual elements. As we understand it, their thinking is that more is better, so providing more visual information on a slide will lead to better understanding and retention by their audience. In fact, just the opposite is true (Karia, 2012).

There is a term in engineering and music that explains the difference between your core message and everything else that distracts from it: the signal-to-noise ratio. In audio production terms, the signal is the song, composition, or broadcast message. The noise is any unwanted sound, which may come from any source, from the whirring of electronics powering your home to the honking of traffic outside your door. Audio production also takes into account the concept of self-noise, or noise created in the process of creating signal (Alten, 2005). The signal-to-noise concept applies to visual design too. In this shifted metaphor, the signal is the key message in your presentation and on individual slides, while the noise is everything else. In visual presentation terms, noise is equivalent to clutter on the slide, everything that does not relate to or support the key point. We are focused here on the noise you can control, the visual equivalent of self-noise. Just as we have told you to cut the fluff in your writing, you should also cut it in your presentations. Fluff is nothing but noise.

Recall that effective visual aids do not distract from what you have to say during your presentation. Though you may be tempted to add text on top of charts on top of images to your slides, resist that temptation! Consider the differences between these two slides:

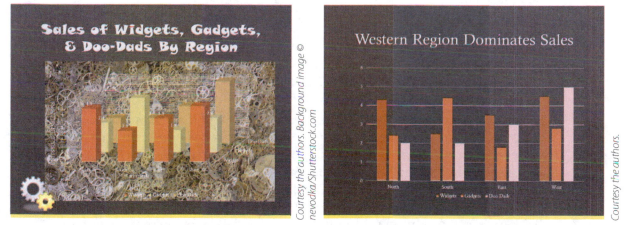

*Courtesy the authors. Background image © nevodka/Shutterstock.com*

*Courtesy the authors.*

**Figure 1**   *Overdesigned slide*          **Figure 2**   *Simple slide*

You might be surprised to learn that both slides actually present the exact same information. The first slide above may have given you a headache just looking at it. That slide is an example of what we call overdesign. Note the funny font, the busy background behind the chart, the wordy title, the use of 3D effects, excessive chart and data labels, and the extraneous clipart in the bottom left corner of the chart. If you showed this slide during a presentation, your audience would likely spend most of their time trying to decipher what those visuals mean instead of listening to you explain them.

Obviously, that first slide is an extreme example of overdesign, and you would never make a slide so busy and distracting. Fair enough, but the path to overdesign is a slippery slope: one extra font or piece of clipart can easily lead you and your team astray. It is fine to start with many elements on your slides, but you must take the time to carefully edit and simplify. Just because a slide is simple, does not mean it is boring. Remember, the star of your presentation should be you, not your slides.

The second slide above works for several reasons. By cutting down the clutter, eliminating what is not necessary, and tweaking the language, we can draw the audience's attention to the key point. Focus on that bottom line for each slide, especially when you have large amounts of data or if the information itself is complicated.

Simplicity does not just apply to the representation of hard data. Another common pitfall for many students is overloading their slides with text. Often, these text-laden slides are basically just talking points written on a slide instead of spoken off the cuff. It is fine to refer to information depicted on a slide, but you should never rely on your slides to jog your memory during a presentation. Further, you should never let your slides do the talking for you.

Consider the next two examples.

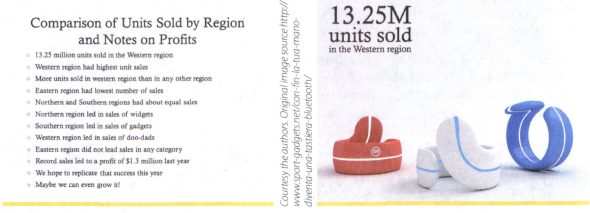

Courtesy the authors.

Courtesy the authors. Original image source http://www.sport-gadgets.net/con-fin-la-tua-mano-diventa-una-tastiera-bluetooth/

**Figure 3**   *Wordy slide*          **Figure 4**   *Non-wordy slide*

The slide in Figure 3 above is just packed with text; some of that text is redundant and some of it is not even on topic. The content of the slide might work as a list of talking points for the presenter to know before the presentation, but they only serve to distract that same presenter if displayed while she or he is speaking. While many different theories and philosophies exist for slide design, they almost universally support the concept of limiting each slide to a single topic. The slide in Figure 3 covers at least two different topics and does so in several different ways. This is confusing for the audience and damages presenter credibility.

The slide in Figure 4, on the other hand, is beautiful in its simplicity. It uses a bold image and minimal text to illustrate a single point. Note that the rest of the bullet points in the first slide could still logically be stated while the second slide is displayed. This approach has the added benefits of the audience paying closer attention to the presenter and an increased likelihood of them remembering that key point: the Western region sold 13.25 million units.

You don't have to take our word for it: there is a large and ever-growing body of research screaming for all of us to simplify our presentation visual aids. Design principles that were once the province of TED Talks are now widely accepted throughout corporate environments. In his May 2017 keynote address at Google I/O, the company's signature developer conference, CEO Sundar Pichai took 12 slides to reach a total of 40 words on screen, a milestone that most professionals, unfortunately, reach in their presentations in a single slide. Instead of words, Pichai used pictures and videos on his slides to support his speech and keep his audience's attention (Gallo, 2017).

In order to effectively simplify your slide design without sacrificing meaning, you will need a working knowledge of the theory behind human interpretation of signs and how to harness this powerful body of thought.

# Signs, Signs, Everywhere A Sign: Semiotics as Communication

Once you accept the value of simplicity in visual design, you may wonder how to consistently get your point across using less overall information in the layout. The key is to use signs and symbols to represent more complex ideas. You do this every day without realizing it; any time you read or write language, you are using signs to represent ideas. As human beings, we are prone to seek meaning in every piece of information we consume, whether that meaning was intended or not. In fact, we are likely to interpret observable data without even realizing it. As long as something experienced through one of our five senses can "signify" something else, it is interpretable (Chandler, 2007).

However, we also implicitly know that signs, though intrinsically connected to what they represent, are not the same thing as that which they are intended to represent. In his famous work usually referred to as "The Treachery of Images," the Belgian artist René Magritte painted a picture of a pipe, under which he carefully painted the words, "Ceci n'est pas une pipe": "This is not a pipe." A Magritte biographer and close friend, Harry Torczyner, reported that Magritte was often confronted about his surrealist painting and had this reply to his critics: "The famous pipe. How people reproached me for it! And yet, could you stuff my pipe? No, it's just a representation, is it not? So if I had written on my picture 'This is a pipe', I'd have been lying!"

The Betrayal of Images: 'Ceci n'est pas une pipe', 1929 (oil on canvas), Magritte, Rene (1898-1967) / Los Angeles County Museum of Art, CA, USA / Bridgeman Images. © 2017 C. Herscovici/Artists Rights Society (ARS), New York

**Figure 5** Magritte's "The Treachery of Images" is part of the collection of the Los Angeles County Museum of Art

Magritte is saying that his painted pipe may look like the real thing, but it is only a representation and to call it the real thing would be a lie. This is how signs work: they represent something else, a sort of shorthand for an audience when the real thing is not present. Some signs are straightforward—the pipe in Magritte's painting clearly looks like a pipe. From Magritte's perspective, he had a moral imperative to provide his disclaimer that his painted image of a pipe was not actually a pipe. Of course, no person viewing the painted pipe would try to stuff it with tobacco and smoke it; we all know that it is a representation of the object, not the object itself.

The use of signs gets tricky when they are ambiguous or could have many meanings. Have you ever felt that you received "mixed signals" from a potential romantic partner? Signs are not always limited to paintings and visual cues. Throughout this book, we have discussed the idea of "cues" in the communication process. Those cues can be considered types of signs. How your audience interprets your signs may be informed by their culture, level of education, past life experiences, acquired knowledge, or the sway of influencers in their lives. To be an effective business communicator, you must have an understanding about how and why your target audiences may interpret your signs.

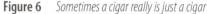

**Figure 6**  *Sometimes a cigar really is just a cigar*

On the other hand, you must also aim for simplicity in your choice of signs to save yourself time from over-thinking your audiences' potential interpretations. The father of psychoanalysis, the Austrian Sigmund Freud, is often credited with saying, "a cigar is sometimes just a cigar." Freud was well known for his theories on sexuality and the subconscious, so we will leave it to you to interpret what a cigar could signify besides tobacco wrapped in flammable paper. Suffice it to say, even Freud advised against reading too far into signs all the time.

You may be wondering at this point why we have been telling you about Belgian surrealists and Austrian analysts in a chapter about visual design. Our purpose is to energize your thinking about how you can use signs and symbols to visually streamline your business presentations. The use of signs and symbols—and how they are interpreted—lies at the center of a robust and weathered field of research.

**Semiotics** is the study of signs and how they are interpreted. This is a field that formally dates back to the 19th century and has grown to include many branches. Just as the boundaries of human knowledge have grown exponentially over the past 150 years, so too has the study of how humans make meaning from all of that knowledge. Since interpretation of signs is constant and universal, it behooves you to understand a bit more about how this interpretation works and how you can use these concepts to your own benefit. Semiotics—though useful in any form of communication—is especially helpful when preparing to communicate through visual channels, such as business presentations

In order for you to fully capitalize on the theories of semiotics, it will be helpful to understand some basic tenets of the field. There are two primary schools of semiotics, one founded by the Swiss linguist de Saussure and one founded by the American philosopher Charles Sanders Peirce. For the sake of simplicity, we will focus on Peircian semiotics in this text. Peirce developed the concept of the sign as a three-part system:

- **Representamen** is the outward appearance of the sign
- **Interpretant** is the meaning assigned to the representamen
- **Object** is that to which the sign refers

To simplify, in Peircian semiotics, a sign has three components: what you see or sense (the sign itself), what you interpret it to mean, and what it actually references. This is important to remember because in your slide decks, your audience will assign meaning to the signs you choose, and the signs you choose will represent actual objects or ideas (Peirce, 1903).

Peirce further identified three types of signs, best understood as relationships between the representamen (sign itself) and either the interpretant (meaning assigned by the viewer) or the object (Peirce, 1885). These sign types are probably more familiar concepts to you:

- **Symbols** are signs for which there are commonly shared rules for how they will be interpreted. Common symbols include languages (letters, punctuation, numbers, etc.), traffic signals, and Morse code.

*Whether Freud actually said this is disputed. Visit http://quoteinvestigator.com/2011/08/12/just-a-cigar/ for a detailed examination of this debate. Regardless of whether the quote is directly attributable to Sigmund Freud, the sentiment still rings true!

- **Icons** are signs that directly resemble or imitate the object. Familiar icons include metaphors, sound effects, scale models, photographs, and portraits.
- **Indices** are signs that indirectly indicate the object and are open to a wider range of interpretation. Index examples include smoke ("where there's smoke, there's fire"), thunder (often interpreted to mean there is a storm in the area), health symptoms (a fever usually means you have some kind of infection), signals like a ringing telephone (it probably means someone is trying to contact you), or directional signs (somebody likely wants you to follow the arrows).

All of your written communication, at least on the surface, consists of symbols. However, those symbols are open to misinterpretation if your audience is unfamiliar with the language or how you use it. If you concede that your primary job as a business communicator is to facilitate your audience's understanding of your messages, then it is clear to see that icons are the most effective type of sign among the three for achieving that goal. Symbols rely on both the sender and the receiver of the message to have already agreed upon the same set of meanings for each symbol and for how those symbols interact with each other. Indices are not exact and are open to broad interpretations that you may never have intended. Icons, however, are the hardest to misinterpret because they do not require rules to be interpreted and are direct representations of the actual object with little room for misinterpretations.

Therefore, we encourage you to use visual icons—including high-quality stock photography and pictograms—in your slide decks to minimize distractions and maximize audience understanding of your presentations. What you commonly knew as icons before reading this chapter are more correctly known as pictograms. These are small, simplified drawings that represent abstract concepts, such as time, money, art, different forms of technology, or relationships. Pictograms are powerful icons in the semiotic sense of the word because they provide you with a quick and effective shorthand version of what you want to say. Instead of using the symbols of language, which take up more space, require more time to interpret, and can be misused or misinterpreted, icons take up less space, can be interpreted nearly instantaneously, and, when carefully selected, are less likely to be misinterpreted. Pictograms are often used in "infographics," short for "information graphics," which use illustrative symbols to communicate complex data in a quick and accessible way. In addition to pictograms, infographics often include simplified charts and graphs to show trends. We will discuss selecting and representing data in the next section.

# 450 UNIVERSAL ICONS

MULTIMEDIA   ECOLOGY      FAMILY      RESTAURANT   FITNESS   MUSIC
BUSINESS     EDUCATION    MEDICAL     CONSTRUCTION  SCHOOL    SHOPPING

**Figure 7**  *Universal Icons*

© Treter/Shutterstock.com

Besides pictograms, high-resolution photographs can be engaging and effective semiotic icons. Photographs of people participating in recognizable activities fire mirror neurons in our own brains and elicit empathy. In other words, when we see people doing something, we tend to envision ourselves doing the same action. If you see a picture on a slide of a group of people arguing in a meeting, you might think of a time that you got into an argument in a meeting and pay closer attention to find out how the rest of presentation relates to that experience you shared with the people in the photograph. Even photographs of objects are effective communication tools because they are usually familiar and relatable to an audience.

The table on the following page lists online resources for pictograms, high-resolution photographs, and for creating infographics. Most of these resources are available for free.

Instead of loading up your slides with words, use icons that represent the concepts you will discuss. Remember, your visual aids should support what you say, not distract from your presentation. To that end, icons give you the most bang for your buck.

| RESOURCE TYPE | SITE NAME | URL |
| --- | --- | --- |
| Pictograms | Flat Icon | http://www.flaticon.com |
| High-resolution photographs | Unsplash | http://www.unsplash.com |
| | StockSnap | http://www.stocksnap.io |
| | Stock Up | http://www.sitebuilderreport.com |
| | Wikimedia Commons | https://commons.wikimedia.org/wiki/Main_Page |
| | RaumRot | http://raumrot.com |
| Infographics | Venngage | https://venngage.com |
| | Piktochart | https://piktochart.com |

**Table 1**   *Resources*

While icons are useful for quickly representing more abstract concepts, you will also need to accurately present hard data in visually appealing and easily understood ways during your presentations.

# Quantitative Data Visualizations

Successful businesses understand and use data efficiently. As a business communicator, you must know what data is relevant to your purpose, interpret it through the lens of your bottom line, and skillfully communicate it effectively to your audience. The starting point for crafting any visual aid is always your presentation's bottom line or value proposition. Think about what you want your audience to get out of watching your presentation. Once you have that clear goal in mind, you will likely have collected data that relates to that bottom line.

For example, you may be planning to deliver a presentation that proposes that your company expand into a new country. Your goal is to convince your audience of executives to launch that expansion. Now you must consider the types of data that would convince those executives to launch that business decision. Those executives are probably concerned about both the costs of expanding into your intended country and the size of the market for the products your company sells in that country. You will have to conduct research identify data on these and related topics. You might find concrete data on:

- What it has cost other U.S. companies to expand into this country
- The size of the market in this country
- Average income of the local population
- Competitors and their shares of the market in the country already

- Laws and regulations that govern U.S. companies operating in the country
- Industry performance in the country over time—whether the market is expanding, maintaining, or contracting

These are only some of the data points you might uncover through your research. What other types of information would you want to know if you were an executive facing a similar situation?

Once you have conducted a significant portion of your research, you will have to decide which parts of it best support your bottom line. Just as you rank and prioritize stakeholders as described in Unit 3, you also have to rank and prioritize your data. Consider your intended audience and think about the type of information that is most likely to bring them around to your point of view. In addition to the data itself, you will also want to consider the reliability and credibility of your sources.

Once you have conducted your research, ranked, and prioritized it, you will have to determine how best to present your highest priority information for your audience. Gene Zalazny, Director of Visual Communications for McKinsey and Company, a global consulting firm, says that there are five basic types of data comparisons that you can make with your data. These relationships will help you inform how you visually present that data. Table 2 briefly explains these relationships and the types of graphs that best represent those relationships.

| COMPARISON | DESCRIPTION | BEST GRAPH TO USE |
|---|---|---|
| Component | Shows the relationship between a part of a whole and the whole itself (percentage of total) | Pie charts |
| Item | Shows the rank relationship between two entities (ranking) | Bar charts |
| Time | Shows the relationship of an entity to time and how it has changed over that duration (changes over time) | Column charts<br>Line charts |
| Frequency | Shows the relationship of entities to distinct categories and how the entities are distributed among those categories (items within ranges) | Column charts<br>Line charts |
| Correlation | Shows the relationship between two variables and seeks to identify a pattern in those interactions (relationship between variables) | Bar charts<br>Scatter plots |

**Table 2**   *When to use different types of graphs*

## Pie Charts

When you want to demonstrate the relationships between parts or components of a whole, the pie chart is the way to go. In fact, this is the only reason to ever use a pie chart: when you wish to visually represent relative sizes of parts, such as the income of each division within a company. Pie charts should be used the least of any of the graphs we will discuss in this chapter because they are the easiest to misinterpret or misrepresent your data. Most data visualization systems built into office software will automatically format your data using best practices, but you still have to give these systems clean and clear data to work with.

When using pie charts, avoid having more than six data points; if your data set has more than six data points, group the smallest data points after the fifth one into one group called "other." The "slice" of your pie chart that starts in the 12 o'clock position (the ray extending from the center of the pie to the top point of the circle) is often considered the most important. Most built-in data visualization software systems will place the first data point on your list in this prime position, so make sure you place what you consider to be the most important component first.

Never use three dimensional or forced perspective in any chart, but especially not in pie charts. The whole point of pie charts is to show size relationships between parts of a whole, and three dimensional and forced perspective effects distort those relationships. You can experiment using other shapes or dividing up icons, but those shapes and icons should always remain flat if you want your audience to accurately understand the relationship you're trying to demonstrate.

## Bar Charts

Sometimes you will want to compare two items that are not part of the same whole or do not add up to 100%. In those circumstances, you probably want to use some variation of a bar chart. A bar chart uses horizontal bars whose length indicates the relative size of the items being compared to each other. The vertical axis of a bar chart is used only for labeling and does not represent an independent variable. Since there are many different kinds of relationships between data items, there are several different types of bar charts that you can use to represent those relationships:

- **Traditional bar charts** compare individual items with each other
- **Clustered bar charts** compare items within larger categories to each other
- **Stacked bar charts** compare items as components within larger categories; if the items within each category add up to 100%, you can use the variation of the stacked bar chart, the **100% stacked bar chart**

Though these variations also exist in column charts, bar charts are preferable to column charts in item comparisons for two reasons: they are less likely to be confused with time comparisons, and they afford more space for data labels.

## Column and Line Charts

Column and line charts share some properties with bar charts, as mentioned above, but are most useful for showing how items change over time or how they are distributed into various "buckets" (frequency). Western cultures generally interpret time as linear and able to be discreetly measured. We tend to like measuring changes at regular intervals, so the even distribution of data points along a horizontal axis—even as there may be wide variation in values along the vertical axis—works well for showing item changes over time.

These charts are also useful for comparing how many items fall into distinct categories. You may remember learning about histograms and histographs in your statistics class. Histograms are column charts that show frequency, while histographs are line charts with the same purpose. Either column or line charts can be used to show frequency distributions, such as the number of customers who fall within specific income ranges (e.g., customers who earn less than $25,000 annually, customers who earn between $25,001 and $50,000 annually, and customers who earn $50,001 or more annually).

A variation of the line chart is the area chart, and may be easier to read than line charts because the areas under each line are a solid color instead of matching the background of the graph. Use your discretion when determining whether a line or area chart will be easier for your audience to understand.

## Scatter Plots

While all of the preceding chart types measure one variable for each item, scatter plots are used to show two variable values per item. Scatter plots may be most familiar to you in representing supply and demand curves, in which economists show the relationships between unit prices and unit quantities either supplied or demanded. While scatter plots can be presented as a set of dots plotted on horizontal and vertical axes, data visualizers often connect the dots to more clearly show patterns in the relationships between variables for each item. Data visualizers will also often color code dot sets and their connecting lines to help their audiences differentiate between items presented.

When scatter plots are used to graph correlations between variables in a data set but the correlation is not perfect, it is impossible to connect the dots using one continuous line. In these circumstances, and if the correlation is strong enough, the savvy data visualizer will use a trend line to demonstrate the general direction or rate of the relationship between the two variables. These correlations are useful for describing the relationship between variables and the dependence of one variable on the other (e.g., as $x$ increases, so does $y$ at the same rate, or as $x$ increases, $y$ decreases twice as fast).

We live in a complex world, and there are often more than two variables at play in business decisions. You can represent tri-variate relationships using a variation of the scatter plot known as a **bubble chart**. The bubble chart begins with the same general concept of the scatter plot, but incorporates the third variable by altering the size of the dots being plotted. The larger a dot, the more representative it is of the third variable. The position of each dot is still determined by the first two variables, just as it would be in a traditional scatter plot.

# Qualitative Data Visualizations

While your business presentations should contain significant amounts of hard data, you will also have occasion to present relationships between items that are not necessarily quantifiable. As we have discussed throughout this chapter, simplifying layouts, using icons, and reducing text on your slides are the rules to live by in visual design. While it may be very tempting to list ideas in bullet points on a slide and call it a day, there is a better way.

Starting around the 2007 release of its Office suite, Microsoft introduced the SmartArt feature to help users create more visually appealing documents and presentations. This feature allows users to populate with their own content pre-designed templates that use basic geometric shapes. The templates are grouped into categories that will help you choose the model that best represents your qualitative data:

- **List**: Instead of wordy bullets to show non-related blocks of information, consider using actual blocks or other geometric shapes
- **Process**: If you are trying to show a sequence of events, consider using one of these combinations of shapes and arrows along a spectrum
- **Cycle**: While processes are non-repeating, cycles can be represented by shapes and arrows that connect in a closed pattern
- **Hierarchy**: Connections between people, departments, or items can be complex; a chart showing hierarchy helps your audience visualize the relative power dynamics between levels
- **Relationship**: No part of a business exists in a vacuum, so use a relationship visualization to show how different parts of a larger system relate to one another

- **Matrix**: If your intention is to show how different variables combine to form spectrums, matrix visualizations will help you illustrate those concepts
- **Pyramid**: For the more complex data that you need to visualize, a pyramid offers you a way to show relationships and relative importance of items

All of the data visualizations listed above can be made even more effective by incorporating icons such as pictograms or photographs. Think of it as the best of both worlds: easily identifiable imagery that also represents qualitative concepts for your audience.

It is perfectly acceptable to use whatever built-in data visualization capabilities your preferred presentation software offers, but you also might consider using some of the following online tools.

| TYPES OF VISUALIZATION | SITE NAME | URL |
| --- | --- | --- |
| Flowcharts | Lucid Chart | https://www.lucidchart.com |
| Flowcharts | Draw.io | https://www.draw.io |
| Charts, Diagrams, and Flowcharts | Cacoo | https://cacoo.com |

# The Golden Mean

Before we can discuss the obvious elements of visual design, such as fonts, colors, and shapes, we must first think about the general structure and composition of each slide. For this, we can turn to some very old, very reliable math, as described in many books, including Mario Livio's (2002) *The Golden Ratio, The Story of PHI, the World's Most Astonishing Number*.

# The Rule of Thirds

Refer back to the slide in Figure 4 earlier in this chapter; it illustrates a design concept that can be your magic weapon in creating visually appealing slides: the rule of thirds.

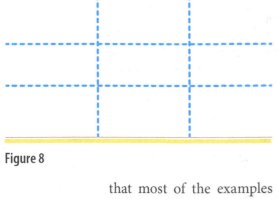

**Figure 8**

As it happens, good visual design uses math because this math makes sense to us on an innate level. This provides you a way to now visually compose your slides for maximum audience engagement and positive response.

The Rule of Thirds says that to create the greatest visual appeal in a graphic composition, place key elements in one-third of the field of the view either horizontally or vertically. Another application of this Rule says that you should leave blank at least one-third and preferably two-thirds of your field of view. You will note that most of the examples of how to apply concepts in this chapter employ The Rule of Thirds.

# A Picture Is Worth a Thousand Words

So far, we have covered the general structure and composition of your slides, but there is one visual design element that completes the picture. The most effective way to support your presentation's key message is with high-resolution images. You may search for free, Creative Commons-licensed images using the built-in online image search functionality of

PowerPoint, or you might try looking through the Flickr Creative Commons. You could also try paid stock photography websites like istockphoto.com.

Regardless of where you find your images, you should carefully select them to highlight key ideas of your presentation. We suggest that you avoid using clipart, as most clipart looks cheap, tacky, and unprofessional. Instead, search for photographic images that illustrate the key point on each slide. Imagery of people doing things is especially powerful when your presentation calls for making recommendations.

Any time you want your audience to do something, include images of people doing those same things. We do not tell you this just because we think it looks good; science supports this tactic. Humans are hardwired with mirror neurons that cause us to subconsciously mimic the activity we observe in other humans (Pentland, 2008).

Using pictures of people is most powerful when you incorporate storytelling into your presentations. This grabs your audience's attention by turning a potentially abstract concept into something concrete. By being specific, you make your presentation more relatable to your audience and encourage their retention of your key messages (Karia, 2012).

As you can see from the following two slides, the use of a picture helps illustrate the point of the slide. In Figure 9, we use the image of a laptop computer as a representative for all technology. The concept is still abstract though: how does technology improve productivity? Certainly, this slide is better for having any picture on it, but a picture with a person using the technology could drive the point home even more. Enter Figure 10. Now that's a slide that tells a story! Same words, same background, even a similar laptop, but now the laptop is being used in a specific way. The second slide is certainly more memorable.

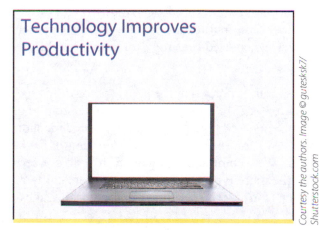

**Figure 9** *Slide with Picture*

**Figure 10** *Slide with Picture Plus Person*

There is more to visual design than just spacing and the use of images. All of the elements must work together and use time-tested principles to look professional and effectively convey meaning.

# Fonts, Colors, and Layout

Many laypeople think that just getting content in front of an audience is an accomplishment and that how the content looks is irrelevant. Nothing could be further from the truth. Every decision you make about the design of your content plays a role in both audience understanding and their willingness to support your bottom line. Every design choice you make should be conscious, informed, and strategic. This section will examine two fundamental elements of visual design: typefaces and colors. We will also give you some guidance on designing or selecting effective slide templates to help you expedite your design process.

## Serif's Up: Typefaces for Every Occasion

# Aa Aa

**Figure 11**  *Sans Serif (Century Gothic, left) vs. Serif (Times New Roman, right) typefaces*

Although we encourage you to reduce the number of words you place on your designs in favor of more iconography, text on slides is ultimately unavoidable. The content of that text is certainly important, but so too is the style. There is an entire field of design dedicated to the style of text, called typeface. Typefaces prescribe a set of common style rules for letters, numbers, and other characters. Variations on those styles can be grouped together into typeface families. When you apply a specific size to a typeface, it becomes a font.

The font you choose for your visual design does make a difference in the readability of your presentations. Some typefaces are better suited to paragraph text while others have more impact when used sparingly in headlines. There are two major varieties of typefaces: serif and sans-serif. The word serif has Germanic origins and roughly translates to "dash" or "line." A typeface with serifs is recognizable by the little hooks and tails that hang off of its letters. The most commonly recognized serif typeface is Times New Roman. In fact, serif typefaces are sometimes collectively referred to as "Roman."

Conversely, sans-serif typefaces lack any of that additional ornamentation. These typefaces are also sometimes referred to as "Grotesque" or "Gothic." A recognizable example of a sans-serif typeface is Arial. Both serif and sans-serif typefaces are often styled in different weights or line thicknesses. Those weights can range from narrow or thin, through normal or regular, to semibold, thick, heavy, and bold. The typeface itself and the typeface weight you choose in any given business communication situation will depend on what you use the text for. Just like any other tool in your business communication toolkit, use the right one for the task at hand. Heavier weights work best when used sparingly, for emphasis; thinner weights may be difficult to read.

Merriam Webster's *Manual for Writers and Editors* reports that the people who study typeface readability have found that serif fonts are easier to quickly read and understand. For this reason, use serif fonts for paragraph text. Sans-serif typefaces are better suited for short bursts: headlines, titles, and anything that allows for a larger size or shorter length. Do be careful about mixing typefaces on your slides. We recommend using no more than one serif and one sans-serif typeface per slide deck. The more typefaces you use, the more cluttered and unprofessional your presentation appears. Don't sacrifice your credibility for the sake of using an interesting or unique typeface.

For presentations, which are usually viewed on a screen from a distance, you will want to make sure that the typefaces you use—serif or not—are thick enough and large enough to be seen by audience members farthest from the screen. We have been beating the drum on being audience centered in your communication strategy throughout this text, so it should come as no surprise to you that this concept even applies to the types of fonts you choose to employ in your presentations. As you prepare your slide deck (or infographic or sign or whatever other visual aid you're working on), think about who is likely to sit in your audience. What do you know about their ages or health that might influence their eyesight? You also must consider the systems on which your visual aids will be viewed.

Generally speaking, with LCD projectors commonly found on university campuses and in large business auditoriums, the larger the screen onto which the projectors cast an image, the more diffuse the light output and therefore the more difficult to see. Some companies and schools now use LED or LCD television displays for showing visual aids during presentations. While these screens are nice and bright, the trade-off is that they usually offer a much smaller field of view.

Regardless of your audience's expected visual acuity or the display system you will be using, you should always make sure that your chosen typefaces are large, simple, and clear enough to be seen and understood by any audience member on any screen.

Whenever possible, we recommend testing your slides before your presentation on the same display system you will use to deliver your actual presentation. This is a good general rule to begin with, but is especially useful for testing your typeface choices. Once you pull up your slides during your test session, stand in the very back of the room as another team member scrolls through the slides. If you struggle to read any of your text on any of your slides from the back of the room, make adjustments, usually by increasing the size of the font. Even if you can easily read the text, try getting a second opinion. When in doubt, reduce the amount of text if you must to make the remaining text bigger.

## Color Me Impressed: Basic Color Theory and Common Color Systems

While typefaces are a critical component of good design, there are few design tools more powerful than the strategic use of color. The colors you choose to use as part of your slide design can have a surprising effect on the emotional state of your audiences, often on a subconscious level. Have you ever felt your breathing slow and a sense of calm wash over you at the sight of peaceful blue lake? Perhaps you're familiar with expressions like "seeing red" to connote anger or "green with envy" or "yellow-bellied coward." These are all examples of ways that colors have come to be associated with specific feelings, states of being, and attitudes. In addition to evoking certain emotions, color can also evoke a sense of place and of time—both time of year and time of day. This is good news for the nascent business communicator: you can use these associations to your advantage. What other color associations can you think of?

You may have learned about primary and secondary colors in your elementary school art class. Red, yellow, and blue could be mixed to form the secondary colors orange (red + yellow), green (yellow + blue), and purple (blue + red). As you might imagine, the variety of colors available to you for your presentations is much more robust than just these six. The range of visible colors has nearly infinite gradations, so it is helpful for you to understand several of the components to reproducing color. Each of these components interacts with the others to help you achieve the specific effect you seek.

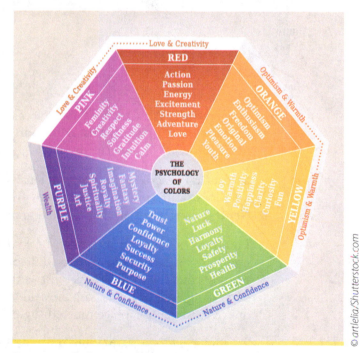

**Figure 12**  *The Psychology of Colors*

© artlelia/Shutterstock.com

**Hue** refers to the color value itself when we look at an object. The word can usually be used interchangeably with the word color. Hue is the difference between a red apple and a green one. If we place the range of hues on a linear spectrum starting with red on one end and ending with purple on the other end, we can see a map of **color temperatures**. The hues on the red half of this spectrum, including variations of orange and yellow, are considered warm

**Figure 13**

temperatures. We associate these colors with heat and sources of heat, like fire. The hues on the purple end of the spectrum, including variations of green and blue, are considered cool temperatures. We associate these colors with cold.

**Saturation** describes the relative intensity of a hue. Depending on the color system you use, hues lose saturation the farther away from the "pure" hue they get and the closer to gray. **Neutral** hues, like tans, browns, and grays, generally have very little saturation.

**Lightness** or **tone** can sometimes be confused with saturation because these words refer to how light or dark—how close to white or black—a hue may be. There are emotional qualities associated with color tone, just as there are with the hues themselves. Stories that are depressing, sad, or unpleasant are said to be "dark," while stories that are uplifting, funny, or even just neutral are considered "light."

To appreciate how saturation and tone interact for any given hue, imagine the hue in a graph. Think of saturation and tone as occurring on the horizontal and vertical axes of this chart, in which the horizontal axis represents saturation, and the vertical axis represents tone or the different shades of the hue. Graphic design software like Adobe Photoshop and most presentation software like Microsoft PowerPoint gives you the power to adjust both the hue, saturation, and tone of any element. We encourage you to experiment with these controls to see how adjusting any one component affects the meaning and mood of your design.

For a fun way to explore how these components interact and to help you choose your own color stories, visit http://color.adobe.com. This website from Adobe presents you with a color wheel, on which you can move circles to choose a color you like. Once you have done that, the website allows you to explore "color rules," or established systems for how colors may interact. Those color rules include the following.

- **Analogous** colors have the same degree of saturation and tone as the selected color, but their hue values are equidistant from each other, fanning out in both directions from the selected color. Analogous color families are pleasant because they are intuitively harmonious.

- **Monochromatic** colors have the same hue but varying levels of saturation. Monochromatic colors are useful for adding some variety to a design without making it look too cluttered.

- **Triad** colors are similar to analogous colors in that only the hues change, In the case of triad colors, there are only three, and they are each equidistant in value from the other two. Triad colors tend to clash with each other because they are quite literally as different as can be.

- **Complementary** colors are opposites on the color wheel. They are said to complement each other, but may also seem to clash because they literally oppose each other.

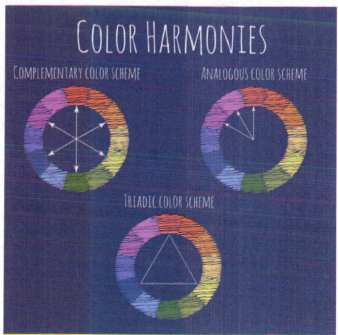

**Figure 14** *Color Wheels*

- **Compound** colors use a complicated algorithm to calculate a set of colors that should be harmonious with each other, even if the hues vary significantly. If you want to appear sophisticated in your use of color, try a set of compound colors.

- **Shades** keep the hue the same but adjust the tone of that hue. Shades are very similar to monochromatic colors.

One of the advantages of exploring colors with the Adobe tool is that it will not only calculate the exact colors using each rule's specific formula, but it will provide those color values as recipes that you can plug into your design or presentation software using one of several color systems. Color systems are structures created to consistently reproduce colors from one location to another. Designers have long known the power of color and have sought to faithfully replicate their deliberate color choices to maintain the meaning and intent of their designs. We should note that most of the common color systems offer designers far more variations than what healthy human eyes can perceive; as a species, we can each detect roughly 10 million variations in color (Judd and Wyszecki 1975). Table 3 describes the five most well-known and widely-used color systems: RGB, CMYK, Hex, HSV/HSL/HSB, and Pantone.

| COLOR SYSTEM | PRIMARILY USED FOR | HOW IT WORKS |
|---|---|---|
| **RGB** | Screens and print | RGB stands for the primary colors of light: red, green, and blue. Old-style cathode-ray tube televisions used groups of red, green, and blue pixels that could be triggered in various degrees of saturation to reproduce a full spectrum of hues. Each of the three hues can be adjusted to levels ranging from 0 to 255 (so 256 levels each); the higher the level value, the more saturated and lighter that hue. When all three level values are at 0, the resulting hue is black; when all three level values are at 255, the resulting hue is white. An easy way to remember this is to recall that RGB represents light, and the more light you add, the brighter an object gets. |
| **CMYK** | Screens and print | CMYK stands for the primary colors of ink printing: cyan (a light blue hue), magenta (a purple-ish red hue), yellow, and black. If you have ever owned a color printer and had to pay for ink cartridges, you may already be familiar with how this system works. Each of the four hues can be adjusted as a percentage of its total possible value (between 0% and 100%). The higher the percentage, the more saturated and lighter the hue. However, something interesting happens when all the level values are at 0: in contrast to the RGB system, CMYK values at 0% produce white and values at 100% produce black. An easy way to remember this is to recall that CMYK represents ink printing, and the more ink you add to a printed picture, the darker it gets. CMYK has the capacity to show more subtle variations than RGB; whereas RGB has 16,777,216 possible combinations ($256^3$), CMYK has 100,000,000 ($100^4$). |
| **Hex** | Screens | Hex stands for hexadecimal and is a color system created exclusively for computer screens. Hex is widely adopted and used in web programming and is named for the fact that it uses six digits to classify colors. Every two digits equals one byte of data, so every color point sent through the internet to your computer is three bytes long; for higher resolution screens, with more pixels per square inch, that's a lot of data! Hex calculates color in a very similar way to how RGB does so. In Hex, the first two digits are used to calculate the value for red, the middle two digits for green, and the last two digits for blue. The digits can each be occupied by numbers 0 through 9 and by the letters a through f. 99 is the highest numerical value available, but then the letters add more information, with f being the highest and most saturated. Each byte can use any combination of numbers and letters to fill its two digits. Since there are 16 possible options (ten numbers and six letters) per digit, Hex offers an elegant way to recreate RGB colors for a system that is limited to two places for all 256 gradations. |
| **HSV/HSL/HSB** | Mostly print | HSL, HSV, and HSB are virtually interchangeable color systems that allow for control of color through adjustments to the individual components of hue (H), saturation (S), and tone (represented by "value," V, "luminosity," L, or "brightness," B). In this color system, you can alter any one component independently of the others. This is useful when creating monochromatic color rules or shades. The hue value can be set from 0 (red) to 280 (purple), and the other two values can be set from 0 to 100. The higher each of the second two values gets, the more saturated and closer to white the color becomes, respectively. Some website and software implementations of this system offer the same number of variations as the RGB or Hex systems, only through changing the independent component values instead of hue values. In some software implementations, however, HSV/HSL/HSB may offer the fewest distinct color options, with "only" 2,800,000 possible variations, but in exchange, it offers designers the most precise control over the three variations that compose color. |

*(Continued)*

| Pantone | Screens and print | Pantone is unlike any of the other color systems described above. It is proprietary, developed by a company of the same name, though it is an industry standard for graphic designers. Unlike the other color systems, which originated as ways to faithfully recreate colors selected by designers, Pantone was developed as a way to faithfully recreate colors already found in nature. Legend has it that naturist and birdwatcher Robert Ridgeway created one of the first color guidebooks with his 1912 Color Standards and Color Nomenclature (Lewis 2014). As a birdwatcher, Ridgeway would have had to develop a keen eye for the subtle variations in hue, saturation, and tone in the feathers of his flying friends. By 1964, the New Jersey-based company had acquired the rights to publish Ridgeway's color classification system. The Pantone system continues to grow as they add more colors. Pantone has even recently entered the zeitgeist, selecting an annual "color of the year" to capture the color it sees as the representation of current events and culture at that moment in time. Pantone colors are widely used because of their consistency across platforms and because they offer a common language to designers across industries. |
|---|---|---|

**Table 3**  *Color Systems*

We could continue discussing color at length; in fact, there are entire textbooks about how to use color effectively in graphic design. For our purposes, we will ask you to consider how color can both subtly and overtly affect your audience's perception of your presentation—and make strategic and deliberate color choices accordingly. Color can play a key role in the building blocks of your presentation, the slide template.

## Don't Be Basic: No-Limits Layouts

We are about to lay down some truth for you that we hope you will find freeing: you do not have to stick with the boring slide deck templates that come with Microsoft PowerPoint, Google Slides, or Apple Keynote. In fact, we encourage you to flex your creative muscles and branch out! Those stock templates may save you some time in the preparation of your slides, but they are virtually guaranteed to put your audiences to sleep. Those templates also tend to limit what you can do on your slides because they are often cluttered with useless elements like random shapes or lines that do nothing to add visual interest or enhance audience understanding. In case you cannot tell, we intensely dislike built-in templates.

If you or a team member has a flair for creativity or just want to try your hand at altering or creating your own templates, this can be easily accomplished. In PowerPoint, click on the View tab, then select Slide Master. This will take you to the slide master view, which is where you can create or edit the current template. Any changes you make to the master slides will automatically propagate across your content slides when you exit from slide master view (a large red button found on the now-visible Slide Master tab at the top left of your screen).

Slide master view provides you with the ability to customize slides for specific types of layouts, such as title or subtitle slides, title-and-content slides, two-content slides, title-and-picture slides, and even blank slides. If you want to adjust your template and have those changes flow through all of your various layouts, just make the changes on the very top "parent" slide in slide master view and the changes will automatically ripple through all of the layout slides. This can be handy for placing automatic slide number or text macros on all slides without having to copy and paste to every slide in your deck.

Of course, we fully understand that creating a deck template from scratch requires time and at least a moderate eye for design, both of which may be in short supply on your team. Fortunately for you, there are plenty of online resources for slide deck templates that are more visually interesting than those that come pre-packaged with your presentation software. Some of our favorites are in the chart below.

| DOWNLOADABLE FORMAT | SITE NAME | URL |
| --- | --- | --- |
| **Google Slides** | Slides Carnival | http://www.slidescarnival.com |
| **Adobe PDF (free), PowerPoint (premium)** | Canva | https://www.canva.com |
| **PowerPoint** | AllPPT | http://www.free-powerpoint-templates-design.com |

Now that you have a better sense of the basic building blocks of good graphic design and the freedom to explore new template options, let's explore some best practices for slide layout.

# A Load of CRAP

In his 2008 book, *Presentation Zen*, presentation design and delivery expert Garr Reynolds lays out four specific design principles that are both simple and effective. Contrast, repetition, alignment, and proximity are easy to remember and put into practice, and will improve the CRAP out of your presentations when used effectively together.

## Contrast

Things that are different are inherently more interesting. In design, we use contrast to create interest and to make the important information stand out. Contrast can come in many forms, from the relative size of elements on the page, to differences in color and tone, to contrasting fonts.

As a general rule, you should always have light text against dark backgrounds or dark text against light backgrounds. Black and white provide the most contrast, but you can also play around with color. Just bear in mind that not all projectors are created equally, and what you see on your computer screen will not necessarily show as crisply and with as much contrast when projected onto a bigger screen.

Contrasts in size are an effective way to show relationships between objects, words, or concepts. The more variation in size, the larger the difference in relative value of the items being compared.

Here are some illustrated examples of contrast in action:

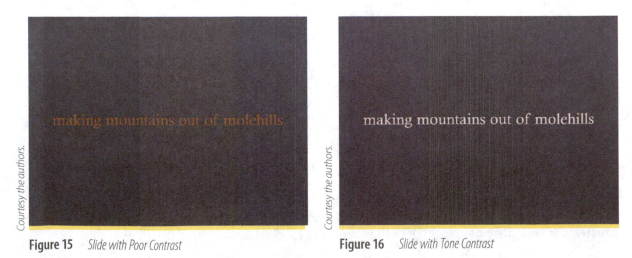

**Figure 15**  *Slide with Poor Contrast*

**Figure 16**  *Slide with Tone Contrast*

Note how difficult it is to read because of the dark text on a dark background.

By changing the text from a dark color to a much lighter version, the slide becomes instantly easier to read.

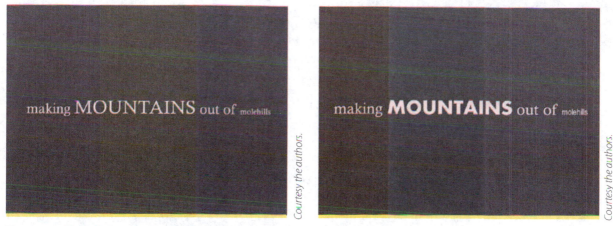

**Figure 17**   *Slide with Contrast in Font Sizes and Cases*

**Figure 18**   *Slide with Contrasting Fonts*

Mountains are large objects, so we made the font in which that word is written bigger than any of the other text and made it all caps. Conversely, we made the word "molehills" small to emphasize their difference from mountains.

Here we have further altered the words "mountains" and "molehills" to further emphasize their differences. We used a bold, sans serif font (one without decoration) to emphasize the strength of mountains and a narrow font to emphasize the weakness of molehills.

Finally, we change the colors of the key words of text to further draw audience attention to those words. Due to the changes in size, face, and case of the word "mountains," it can now support a darker tone without hampering readability. Compare this slide to the slide in Figure 15 and we think you will agree that this one is much more visually interesting.

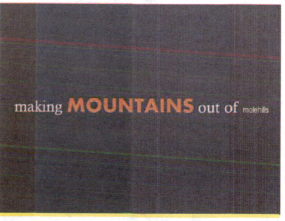

**Figure 19**   *Slide with Color Contrast*

There are other ways you can show contrast visually: through shapes, textures, ages, and even metaphors. Another way to think about contrast is through the stories you tell. Differences are interesting, and they grab an audience's attention (Reynolds, *Contrasts Are Compelling*, 2011). Contrasts invite comparisons, which engage the audience. Besides being an effective visual design tool, contrasts are also an effective storytelling tool; after all, no great literary hero is ever the same at the end of his journey as he or she was at the beginning.

## Repetition

While contrast is about drawing attention and generating interest by strategically highlighting differences, repetition is about satisfying your audience's inherent desire for stability by making your presentation aids consistent. If this sounds familiar, it may be because repetition in this context sounds like the concept of branding. In a unified brand, all materials produced by a company have the same look and feel. This is the essence of repetition in visual design. PowerPoint, Keynote, Google Slides, and Prezi all make this easier for you to achieve through the use of design templates. These templates provide unified color, font, and layout schemes so that all of your slides will be consistent.

Repetition can extend beyond just the basic overall look and theme of your slides. You may decide to add creative touches for particular emphasis on some slides. For example, you might add imagery that looks like a scrap of paper attached to your slide with a paper clip to introduce a joke or humorous anecdote about some topics in your presentation. When you use and repeat this visual cue a few times, your audience will then be conditioned to know to be prepared to laugh when they see that paper clip, even before they read the "scrap paper."

Here are two examples of repetition of this motif in action:

**Figure 20**

**Figure 21**    *Repetition of a design element.*

In these two slides, we repeat the motif of a handwritten scrap of paper "attached" to the slide with a paper clip. Note the use of black bars to give the appearance of the scrap paper and paper clip extending beyond the edge of the slide in presentation view.

Incidentally, and because we cannot say it enough, repetition is also great advice for you when it comes to rehearsing your presentations. Practice your presentation delivery and then practice it again and again until they become second nature. Lather, rinse, repeat.

## Alignment

**Figure 22**    *Same Slide, Different Alignments. Which of the above slides is the most attractive to you? We think the top right slide is =the most appealing.*

The elements of your visual design do not exist in a vacuum. There should be some clearly-defined relationship between each element on the slide. The concept of alignment extends beyond the left-center-right or top-middle-bottom paradigms. Those paradigms are powerful though and should serve as a starting point when considering how to use alignment to your best advantage.

In the English language, we read text on a page from left to right, then top to bottom. This is how native English speakers will also automatically read your slides. Most of us who were born and educated in the United States will naturally first look at the top left corner of a slide to start, then read across, then scroll down (Weissman,

2008). Therefore, if you plan to present important information, you should try to place it as close to the top left corner of your slide as possible.

The converse of this advice is also true. If you really want to call attention to something, you might align it on the slide in an unconventional or unexpected place. Use this approach sparingly, however, as it can be jarring and off-putting for your audience since it is so anathema to how we usually read or view material.

## Proximity

Just like its cousin alignment, proximity is all about establishing relationships between visual elements. Proximity relates to how near or far apart two or more items appear on your slide. The smaller the physical distance between lines of text, the more likely those lines of text are in some way connected. Proximity applies the concept of "chunking"—keeping like information together—to your presentation aids and visual design.

If you absolutely insist on using bullet points on your slides, you should make sure that information for each bullet point appears to be grouped with its sub-bullets. Equidistant spacing is the enemy of audience comprehension. By keeping related information physically closer together, you will dramatically increase the likelihood that your audience will retain that information.

Consider these two examples:

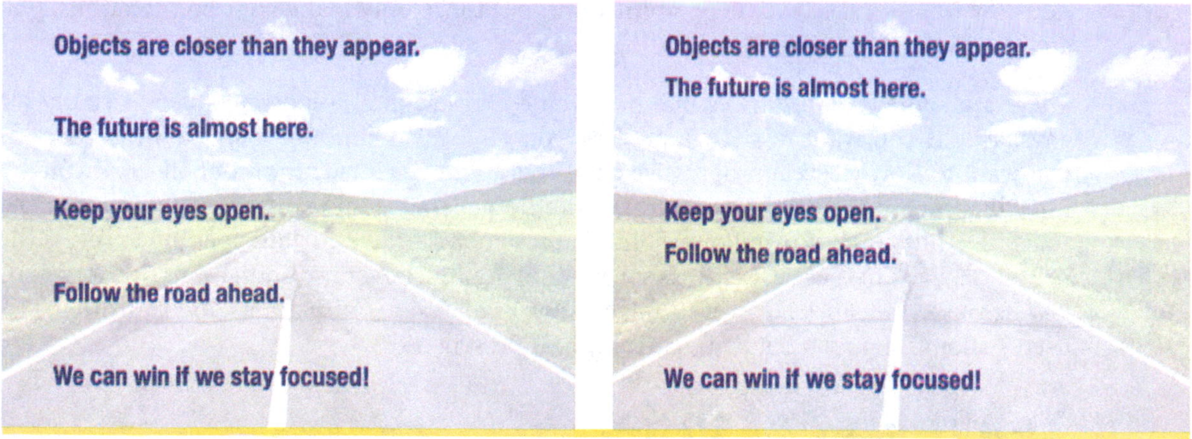

**Figure 23**  *Slides with and without Good Use of Proximity*

*Courtesy the authors*

In the slide on the left, all of the lines of text are equidistant. For all the reader knows, each line of text is equally related to all other lines of text on the slide. In the slide on the right, we have grouped, or chunked, lines of text that belong together. One way we can tell that those chunks make sense is that each chunk is in parallel form. The top two sentences start with a subject, while the second two sentences begin with a verb and are commands. It is not only easier to understand the themes of the slide, but it is also more visually appealing.

We have been careful to explain each of the CRAP concepts—contrast, repetition, alignment, and proximity—separately so as to make each concept understandable on its own in your mind. However, these four concepts work best when they work together. Consider how the slides above could be improved by employing the additional concepts of contrast, repetition, and alignment:

**Figure 24**   *Slide Using the Concepts of Proximity, Alignment, and Contrast*

With the background image looking down a country roadway, it makes sense to align the text to the center of the slide. Note that the size of the text increases as the words get closer to the bottom of the slide, also mimicking the forced perspective of the roadway extending to the horizon. Different colors and fonts help emphasize important words or concepts.

When used smartly, CRAP can significantly improve the visual appeal of your slides. This will help you both maintain audience engagement during your presentations and improve audience retention of your key points. Added benefit: now you can be proud when someone tells you that your slides are full of CRAP.

## Animations and Transitions

We generally advise against using animated slide transitions or effects in your professional presentations. They tend to look unprofessional, and they can waste valuable seconds that would be better spent presenting your arguments. If you do choose to use slide transitions or animations, keep them as short and subtle as possible. PowerPoint is filled with ostentatious (or what it calls "exciting") animations, but those only make your presentations look amateur.

There are some circumstances in which you could use animations effectively, usually for emphasis. If you want to show a process, you might use a motion path or wipe effect. If you want to slowly reveal progressive data, you might use a fade in or out effect. If you are unveiling a new product or service and want to generate some fanfare, you might use the "curtain" slide transition in PowerPoint that resembles a stage curtain opening to reveal the next slide. Each of these use cases is specific and limited; never use animations or transitions just because you can. Like everything else in visual design, animations and transitions—if used—should support, not distract from, your presentation.

## You're Out of Order!

How you sequence your slides is just as important as their content. Just as with the presentation itself, your slide deck should follow a logical progression from one idea to another.

## Say Cheese!

First things first, though. The very first slide of any deck should be a title slide with names and photos of all the people presenting. This can be a group photo of all presenters, or individual photos of each presenter; just ensure that the order of your names as listed corresponds with the order of appearance in the photo or photos.

We recently watched presentations for a case competition to provide feedback on presentation delivery. One of the presenting teams did not even include their names on the title slide, nor did they verbally introduce themselves at the start of the presentation. This resulted in their individual delivery feedback being addressed to "woman in blue blouse" and "guy in patterned tie." Your name is valuable, so use it. Don't be just another guy in a tie.

# One-Click Navigation

No matter how thoughtful the construction and sequencing of your slides, you will inevitably have to move through slides out of the order that you had originally intended to display them. Fortunately, we offer two tips for navigating nonlinearly in both directions through your presentation.

# Presentation Trackers

When you read a book, there is often a book title on even pages and a chapter title on odd pages. This helps you keep track of where you are in the book. You should similarly consider using what we call a slide tracker on each of your slides. A slide tracker serves several purposes: they help highlight your progress during a presentation, they tell the audience what was covered and what will be covered next, and they provide a convenient method of jumping to nonlinear slides without clicking through most of your presentation to get there. In addition to the tracker, we strongly suggest adding the name of the person presenting each slide somewhere on them, usually close to the tracker.

# Index Slides

Instead of ending your presentation with a slide that simply says "thank you," or even worse, with the dreaded "questions?" use an index slide. An index slide contains text hyperlinks back to every other slide (or major section heading) in the deck. This way when you call for questions, you can quickly and professionally jump directly to the slide with the relevant content instead of repeatedly pressing the backspace or left arrow key. You will come off as more polished, professional, and savvy. The index slide also provides a convenient gateway to hidden slides. You can add hyperlinks to any slide using the method described above, except you will not need to use the Master View to do so.

# Preventing "Gotcha" with Hidden Slides

When you research and create presentations, chances are you will have more information than you have time to cover it all. All is not lost! You can still include all that rigorously researched data. Particularly if you had to edit in the interests of time and space, you face the strong likelihood your audience will still have questions about that data. Hiding slides is an effective way to have the data readily available without getting lost in the details during the presentation proper.

## HOW TO ADD A SLIDE TRACKER

The easiest way to add a slide tracker to every slide so that it appears in the same place in each slide is to add it to the master slide. In the latest version of PowerPoint, choose the View tab, then click on Slide Master. Insert a text box on the very top slide to appear here and type in the name of each of your major slides. You will have to do some whittling to get your tracker down to five or fewer entries.

Do not try to insert your tracker into an existing element on the Master Slide, such as the pre-existing Footer; PowerPoint does not allow you to hyperlink text in these elements. Note that if you are placing your tracker along the bottom of your slide, PowerPoint adds slide controls in the bottom left corner of the screen during slideshow view, so you will not be able to access hyperlinks in roughly the bottom left third of the screen. Therefore, avoid placing links on that region.

To turn your static text into hyperlinks, highlight just the words that you want to link to a specific page in your document, hover your cursor over the highlighted text, and right click. In the pop-up context menu, click on "Hyperlink. . .." On the left side of this pop-up box, you will see a list of items under "Link to:." Choose the "Place in This Document" item; the list directly to the right now displays every slide in your presentation.

Simply choose the slide you want to jump to when that link is clicked and click OK. Repeat this process for all of your other tracker items. When you are done, make sure you are on the Slide Master tab and click "Close Master View." Now your slide tracker will appear on every slide, in the same place on every slide. More importantly, you can now click on those links on any slide to jump easily back and forth to your selected slides.

## HOW TO HIDE A SLIDE

To hide a slide in PowerPoint, locate it in the slide list on the left of the screen, then right click on the slide you wish to hide and choose "Hide Slide." The slide will now appear dimmed and there will be a line through the slide number in the list. You can still preview and edit the slide, but it will be skipped during a slideshow. You can also still hyperlink to the slide and it will be displayed during a slideshow in that case. You can also hide slides without hiding them in the way described above by simply placing them at the end of your presentation, after your index slide.

Regardless of which option you choose, hidden sides are a useful way to both include extra information and especially to answer potentially hostile or challenging questions. Sometimes, you will face an audience that just does not like your message and is looking for holes in your arguments. You can counter these attacks by jumping to a hidden slide that fills in those gaps. Of course, you will have to plan your presentation strategically and anticipate where those questions might arise so that you are sure to include hidden slides.

# Check Your Deck

Always test your presentation on the computer on which it will be presented before the actual presentation. If that is not feasible, at least try to learn what the computer platform and software version your slides will be played on and find another comparable computer on which to test your deck.

There are few worse feelings than getting up in front of a room of people after rehearsing diligently, and then having something not work as you rehearsed it. This is especially true of slide transitions and animations—one more reason to avoid using them. You must test every aspect of your presentation aids before you use them in a presentation. Don't be caught unaware because a computer is set to run a different font or the bulb on the projector in the room you wish to present turns the colors on your presentation darker or lighter, often resulting in slides that don't look the way you designed them.

Use that old motto—to be early is to be on time. Arrive early, set up and run through the deck you intend to use. Allow yourself enough time to do any advance damage control. Worst case scenario, you can get out ahead of any errors. Best case scenario: you are in full control of the room as your guests begin to arrive, setting perceptions off the bat that your presentation is ready to roll, and you are ready to rock.

# Conclusion

Well-developed public speaking and presentation skills will set you apart from other professionals in your field. The ability to inform or persuade an audience is an enviable attribute; especially if you can take the presentation from the organization stage all the way through to stellar delivery. The more speaking you do, the more comfortable you will become—or at the very least, the more comfortable you will seem. Do not discount the latter. Look and act the part; the rest will follow.

Presentations are living entities. Their creation is an iterative process of applying many skill sets to craft an effective message for a specific audience. The tools you choose to help you convey meaning can either help you win over your audience or create unnecessary artificial distance between you. If used correctly, the visual design tools and tricks described above will help you narrow the alignment gap between you and your audience. They will help you focus on, rather than distract from, your key messages.

# Unit 6 References

Abela, A. (2008). *Advanced presentations by design.* San Francisco: Pfeiffer.

Alten, S. R. (2005). *Audio in media* (7th ed.). Belmont, CA: Wadsworth.

Boettinger, H. (1969). *Moving mountains.* NYC: Macmillian Publishing.

Croston, G. (2012). The real story of risk. NYC: Prometheous Books.

Chandler, D. (2007). *Semiotics the basics.* New York, NY: Routledge.

Duarte, N. (2000). *Resonate.* Hoboken: John Wiley & Sons Inc.

Ekman, P., & Friesen, W. V. (1974). Nonverbal behavior and psychopathology. In R. J. Friedman & M. N. Katz (Eds.) *The psychology of depression: Contemporary theory and research* (pp. 203–32). Washington, D.C.: J. Winston.

Ekman, P. (1972). Universals and cultural differences in facial expressions of emotion. In J. Cole (Ed.) *Nebraska symposium on motivation* (pp. 207–83). Lincoln, NE: University of Nebraska Press.

Ekman, P., & Friesen, W. V. (1984). *Unmasking the face* (2nd ed.). Palo Alto, CA: Consulting Psychologists.

Gallo, C. (May 23, 2017). Google's CEO doesn't use bullet points and neither should you. *Inc.* Retrieved from https://www.inc.com/carmine-gallo/how-googles-ceo-creates-brain-friendly-presentations.html.

Green, D. M. (1979). *Form in formal music: An introduction to analysis* (2nd ed.). United States of America: Holt, Rinehart and Winston.

Gruber, P. (2007). The Four Truths of Storytelling. *Harvard Business Review.*

Heath, C., & Heath, D. (2007). *Made to stick: Why some ideas survive and others die.* New York: Random House.

Judd, D. B., & Wyszecki, G. (1975). *Color in Business, Science and Industry.* Wiley Series in Pure and Applied Optics (3rd ed.). New York: Wiley-Interscience.

Karia, A. (2012). *How to deliver a great TED talk: Presentation secrets of the world's best speakers.* CreateSpace Independent Publishing Platform.

Lewis, D. (June 24, 2014). How red is dragon's blood? *Smithsonian Magazine.* Retrieved from http://www.smithsonianmag.com/arts-culture/how-red-dragons-blood-180951822/?no-ist.

Livio, M. (2002). *The golden ratio: The story of phi, the world's most astonishing number.* New York, NY: Broadway Books.

Mehrabian, A. (1971). *Silent messages.* Belmont, CA: Wadsworth.

Morgan, N. (2009). *Trust me: Four steps to authenticity and charisma.* San Francisco, CA: Jossey-Bass.

Morris, D. (1971). *Intimate behavior.* New York, NY: Random House.

Peirce, C. S. (1899–1900 [c.]). *Notes on topical geometry.* MS [R] 142.

Peirce, C. S. (1903). *Syllabus: Nomenclature and Division of Triadic Relations, as far as they are determined.* MS [R] 540.

Pentland, A. (2008). *Honest signals: How they shape our world.* Cambridge, MA: The MIT Press. Reynolds, G. (2011). Contrasts are compelling. In *The naked presenter: Delivering powerful presentations with or without slides.* Berkeley, CA: New Riders.

Reynolds, G. (2008). The big four: contrast, repetition, alignment, proximity. In *Presentation zen: Simple ideas on presentation ideas and delivery.* Berkeley, CA: New Riders.

Slusher Morgan, A. C. (1996). Using causal persuasive arguments to change beliefs and teach new information: The mediating role of explanation availability and evaluation bias in the acceptance of knowledge. *Journal of Educational Psychology* , 110.

Thibodeau, P. A. (2011). Metaphors we think with: The role of metaphor in reasoning. *PLoS One (6) 2* .

Tisdale, J. (2004). *Effective business presentations* (NetEffect Series). Prentice Hall.

Torczyner, H. (1979). *Magritte: Ideas and Images.* Harry N. Abrams, Inc.

Trager, G. L. (1958). Paralanguage: A first approximation. *Studies in Linguistics, 13,* 1–12.

Trager, G. L. (1961, January). The typology of paralanguage. *Anthropological Linguistics, 3(1),* 17–21. http://www.jstor.org.ezproxy2.library.arizona.edu/stable/30022290

Weissman, J. (2005). *In the line of fire: How to handle tough questions when it counts.* Upper Saddle River, NJ: Pearson Prentice Hall.

Weissman, J. (2008). *Presenting to win: The art of telling your story, updated and expanded edition.* FT Press.

Williams, D. (2013, September 9). Leading like Jeff Bezos: Words are more important than numbers. *Forbes.*

Williams, K. D. (1993). The effects of stealing thunder in criminal and civil trials. *Law and Human Behavior,* 597–609.

Zelazny, G. (2001). *Say it with charts: The executive's guide to visual communication.* McGraw-Hill.

# UNIT 7:
## Advanced Strategic Communication

# Stakeholder Analysis

**B**y now, you should understand the importance your audience plays in the way you strategize your messages. In Chapter 1–2, we touched on tailoring your messages to meet the needs of various stakeholders. As a reminder, a stakeholder is anyone who can *impact* or *be impacted* by a particular decision or situation a business faces. Another way to think about a stakeholder is anyone who has a stake in the decision, situation, or outcome. In this chapter, we will discuss stakeholder analysis in more detail.

Every business decision or situation has many stakeholders, and each stakeholder has varying expectations. As public interest becomes increasingly embedded in business decisions, it has become more important for decision-makers to understand who is impacted by the decisions they make and who can impact the decision. Conducting a stakeholder analysis will allow you to determine all of the people involved in a particular business decision or situation, understand what each stakeholder's wants and concerns are, prioritize which stakeholders are most important to your cause, and plan the best communication for each stakeholder in order for your message to obtain your intended results. Knowing how to engage the right people in the right ways will allow you to be a successful businessperson.

As students of business, you may want to jump straight to developing solutions to the business problems you encounter. However, without taking the time to properly analyze the current situation and the people who can impact or be impacted by the challenge you are facing, your solution may not produce the intended results. A stakeholder analysis allows you to look strategically at a situation and gives you the information you need to craft appropriate communication to reach all of your audiences and secure their support. Successful businesses use stakeholder analyses to assist in making strategic and effective decisions. Stakeholder analysis has been well studied and refined over time to further assist business people in making well-informed business decisions. The four-step process below will assist you in successfully conducting stakeholder analyses.

# Stakeholder Analysis Four Step Process

Conducting a stakeholder analysis is a straightforward process:

1. Identify Stakeholders
2. Understand Stakeholders
3. Prioritize Stakeholders
4. Plan Communication with Stakeholders

## Step 1: Identify Stakeholders

The first step in this analysis is to identify the stakeholders. Identifying the pertinent stakeholders will ensure that you understand all of the people involved in your particular decision or situation. When you analyze a given situation, there are often many more individuals or groups of people who can impact or be impacted by the situation than you originally thought. All of these people are stakeholders.

During this step, it is important to think about all of the stakeholders both within and outside your company. Internal stakeholders are people within the company who could impact or be impacted by your decision. Conversely, external stakeholders are those individuals outside your organization who can impact or be impacted by your decision. Some stakeholders will be obvious and easy to identify. However, other stakeholders may take some thought before you can identify them. The questions below are designed to help you identify potential stakeholders:

- Who could be positively impacted by the decision or situation?
- Who could be negatively impacted by the decision or situation?
- Who holds official positions relevant to what you are doing?
- Who has been involved in any similar decisions or situations in the past?

Another common way to identify stakeholders and differentiate between internal and external stakeholders is by using a stakeholder wheel, a visual representation of internal and external stakeholders. An example stakeholder wheel is found below. In this example, the internal stakeholders have been identified as employees, management, and shareholders. The identified external stakeholders in the example are the community, competitors, media, customers, regulators, and suppliers. Each of these stakeholders could impact or be impacted by the business decision or situation you are facing. However, it is unlikely that each of the stakeholders you have identified wants the same outcomes from your decision or situation.

Once you have identified all of the potential stakeholders, you will want to understand each stakeholder better so that you can determine how best to communicate with each.

## Step 2: Understand Stakeholders

Now that you have identified your stakeholders, the second step is to understand them. In this step, your goal is to find out as much as possible about each stakeholder group so that you can better understand them and what drives them. You should ask yourself questions like:

- What are the critical issues for this stakeholder group?
- What are the concerns of this stakeholder group?

- What does this stakeholder group care about?
- What does this stakeholder group want?
- What does this stakeholder group need?

**Figure 2**   *Stakeholder Wheel Example*

The answers to the questions above will help you understand what each stakeholder group values. This information will be critical in helping you plan your communication with stakeholders in step four. But first, you must determine which stakeholders require more of your attention.

## Step 3: Prioritize Stakeholders

Now that you have identified the stakeholder groups and have a better understanding of their critical issues, the third step is to prioritize them to determine the key stakeholders you need to communicate with. One model for prioritizing stakeholders is the Salience Model developed by Mitchell, Agle, and Wood (1997). In the Salience Model, stakeholders are prioritized based on Power, Legitimacy, and Urgency. A stakeholder's power is determined by how much influence that person has to impact the decision. Legitimacy is the extent to which the stakeholder has a legitimate relationship to the decision. Urgency is the degree to which the stakeholder calls for immediate attention.

### Salience Model

Using the Salience Model allows you to prioritize stakeholders into the following categories based on the level of power, legitimacy, and urgency each has.

1. *Definitive* stakeholders have power, legitimacy, and urgency. Therefore, you need to provide focused attention to these stakeholders. Definitive stakeholders must be communicated with. These are the key stakeholders whom you should seek to understand and plan to communicate with first.

2. *Dominant* stakeholders have both power and legitimacy, giving them strong influence. You should manage dominant stakeholders closely. However, since the urgency is low, they are ranked below the definitive stakeholders and do not need to be communicated with immediately.

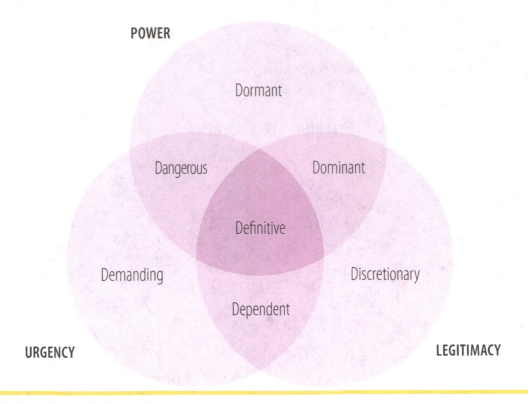

**Figure 3** *Salience Model*

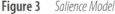

3. ***Dangerous*** *stakeholders* have power and urgency, but lack legitimacy. This makes them a threat. Dangerous stakeholders often emerge as an individual who holds a senior role within your organization. That individual is classified a dangerous stakeholder when he or she tries to force his or her views on the outcome of your project, even though the individual is not really part of the project. You should keep dangerous stakeholders appropriately engaged and satisfied.

4. ***Dependent*** *stakeholders* lack power but have urgency and legitimacy. You should manage dependent stakeholders to ensure they align with your decision. Since they have no real power, they should not require as much of your attention as the first three stakeholder groups.

5. ***Dormant*** *stakeholders* have the power to influence the decision. However, since they do not have legitimacy and urgency, their power remains dormant. Due to their power, you should keep dormant stakeholders informed and prudently manage them.

6. ***Discretionary*** *stakeholders* have high legitimacy but low power and low urgency. Due to their legitimacy, you should try to communicate with them occasionally to provide them with updated information.

7. ***Demanding*** *stakeholders* have urgency, but neither power nor legitimacy. Be careful not to invest too much time in keeping demanding stakeholders up to date, as there are more important stakeholders to communicate with.

After you have prioritized your stakeholders, you will want to develop a plan to communicate with each of them.

## Step 4: Plan Communication with Stakeholders

In the first three steps, you identified your stakeholders, determined what their critical issues are, and prioritized communication with each stakeholder group. In this last step, you will use the information you previously gained to plan your communication with each stakeholder. Your communication plan will be based on the critical issues you identified in step two and the prioritization you established in step three. The communication plan you develop will speak to the wants, needs, and concerns of each stakeholder so that your message will achieve its intended results. An easy way to plan stakeholder communication is by using a series of charts similar to the ones used in the practice and application exercise below.

**Figure 4**   *Stakeholders*

# Stakeholder Analysis Practice & Application

Now that you have an understanding of stakeholder analysis, let's put your new skills into practice using the Mylan case study on the supplemental website to this textbook. Please read the Mylan case study before you move through the four-step stakeholder analysis exercise below.

1. *Identify Stakeholders*

   In this step, we identify all of the potential internal and external stakeholders who are impacted by or could impact the situation outlined in the Mylan case. The key internal and external stakeholders are listed below:

| INTERNAL STAKEHOLDERS | Employees, Shareholders |
|---|---|
| EXTERNAL STAKEHOLDERS | Customers, Media, Government Officials, Competitors |

## 2. *Understand Stakeholders*

In step two, we determine the critical issues of each of the stakeholders we have identified above.

| STAKEHOLDER | CRITICAL ISSUES |
|---|---|
| Employees | Concerned about job stability since the EpiPen is a major source of Mylan revenue. |
| Shareholders | Concerned that the value of Mylan stock may go down due to the PR crisis surrounding the EpiPen. |
| Customers | Concerned about the drastic price increase of the EpiPen. |
| Media | Reporting the Mylan news story to the public. |
| Government Officials | 1. Concerned about the classification of the drug in regards to the rebate program.<br>2. Alarmed by the large number of constituents who are concerned by the Mylan price increases-80,000 people who signed the EpiPen price gouging petition and the more than 121,000 people that sent letters to Congress. |
| Competitors | Since Mylan has a dominant market share of 90%, smaller competitors could try to gain a larger market share during the Mylan turmoil. |

## 3. *Prioritize Stakeholders*

In this step, we use the salience model to identify the definitive stakeholders who
have power, legitimacy, and urgency.

In the Mylan case, the definitive stakeholders are customers and government officials.
Both of these stakeholder groups have power, legitimacy, and urgency. Therefore, it is
imperative that we communicate with them as soon as possible.

POWER

URGENCY

LEGITIMACY

Customers
Government
Officials

## 4. *Plan Communication with Stakeholders*

Now that we know who our key stakeholders are, what their critical issues are, and have prioritized customers and government officials, we need to plan effective communication with them.

| STAKEHOLDER | PRIORITY | CONCERNS | RECOMMENDED COMMUNICATION |
|---|---|---|---|
| Customers | High | High price of EpiPen product | Assure that the safety of customers and products is a top priority for the company, explain new pricing strategy, reiterate company's mission to make high-quality medicines available to everyone who needs them. |
| Government Officials | High | 1. Concerned about the classification of the drug in regards to the rebate program 2. Alarmed by the large number of constituents who are concerned by the Mylan price increases | 1. Agree to pay $465 million to the Department of Justice and other government agencies over the way we classified the EpiPen in the Medicaid Drug Rebate Program. 2. Make them aware that we are working to create a generic medication that will be offered at a lower price. |

## Summary

Using the four-step stakeholder analysis process to identify, understand, prioritize, and plan your communication with stakeholders will assist in your decision-making and communication-planning processes. Using this process will ensure that you consider all of the relevant stakeholders that will be impacted, understand their needs, prioritize communication with them, and craft a communication strategy to address their concerns and secure their buy-in. Performing a stakeholder analysis will help you understand who needs to be addressed and the most effective ways to communicate with them. After performing a stakeholder analysis, you will want to reference Chapter 1–2 to assist you in drafting your messages to the key stakeholders.

# Client Communication

In this chapter, we will explore client communication, starting with an overview of consulting basics followed by an exploration of the consulting process. Strategic and effective client communication is at the heart of good consulting services. A successful consultant communicates with her clients and conveys valuable ideas that help them improve their businesses. All types of businesses and organizations hire consultants to help them better achieve their goals.

**Figure 1**  *Various Clients*

©Rawpixel.com/Shutterstock.com

## What Is a Client?

A client is a person or organization that hires a consultant for a specific purpose. In consulting, the specific purpose is often referred to as a project or engagement.

## What Is a Consultant?

Consultants are business professionals who are experts in certain fields and provide advice related to their areas of expertise. Consultants are problem solvers. They look at situations with a new perspective and offer solutions. Consultants are exposed to a wide variety of experiences and are taught how to apply lessons learned from other situations to the one at hand. Consulting is the art of making connections with people and ideas. Consultants communicate frequently by listening to clients, explaining concepts, and presenting findings.

# Types of Consultants

There are many different types of consultants. Some consultants are independent, and some consultants work for a consulting firm. Some consultants specialize in a specific area while other consulting firms offer assistance in multiple areas and industries. The role of consultants is always expanding to keep up with the ever-changing needs of business. Some of the most common types of consultants are listed below.

### Strategy/Management Consultants

Consultants in strategy and management work to improve the structure, management, processes, and profits of an organization.

### Financial Advisory Consultants

Financial consultants provide advice on financial issues such as compliance, capital budgeting, valuation, and risk management.

### Information Technology (IT) Consultants

IT consultants design and implement IT systems and develop better IT practices.

### Human Resources (HR) Consultants

HR consultants recruit, hire, and train employees and manage compensation and benefits programs.

Even though the types of consultants vary greatly, all consultants have a common goal in helping their clients solve problems. In order to effectively solve problems, consultants typically follow proven processes.

# The Consulting Process

Each consulting process is different based on the client, the consultant, and the project. Below is an outline of a general consulting process that can be adapted to meet the needs of any consulting engagement.

1. Initial Client Research
2. Needs Assessment Meeting
3. Establishing the Project Scope
4. Creating a Project Plan
5. Project Progress Updates
6. Presenting the Final Deliverable
7. Implementation

Typically, consultants will follow the steps above to successfully complete a consulting project for their client. The steps are described in detail below.

## 1. Initial Client Research

A key role of a consultant is information gatherer. It is important that you show the client that you are capable of conducting robust research and analysis. The information you gather before you meet with the client to discuss the project is critical in preparing you for your client needs-assessment meeting. In this phase, you should conduct initial research to identify background information on your client organization. If you know a few details about the potential project, you can conduct initial research on industry best practices around those project components. The goal of this phase is to find out as much information on your client organization as possible to allow you to be prepared for your first meeting with them. Researching the information below on your client organization is a good place to begin:

- its industry or industries
- its products or services offered
- its target market(s)
- its local competitors and/or similar organizations across the nation
- best practices for items articulated in initial project discussions

After you have a good understanding of your client organization, you are ready to schedule a meeting to better understand their needs regarding the consulting project.

## 2. Needs-Assessment Meeting

Understanding the client's needs is necessary to ensure that you are a successful consultant. After you have a firm understanding of the client organization, you should set up a needs-assessment meeting. The client needs-assessment meeting is a chance for you to meet with the client to better understand their expectations and to ensure you can successfully complete the project.

**Figure 3** *Maintaining collaborative communication with clients is the key to consultant success*

©Dusan Petkovic/Shutterstock.com

The needs-assessment meeting is a crucial information-gathering phase. Consultants must ask the right questions, listen intently, and analyze the conversation in the moment to determine what the organization needs. The information exchanged during the needs-assessment meeting will assist you as a consultant in the next phase of establishing the scope of the project. Each needs-assessment meeting will be different based on the client and project. Consultants should consider the questions below as a start to the conversation.

- What is the problem or challenge you are trying to solve?
- Have you tried to solve this problem or similar problems in the past?
- What is the project seeking to achieve?
- What would you like the final project deliverable to look like?
- Who is the project seeking to influence?
- What is the optimal time frame for the project to be completed?
- What resources are available for the project?

These questions will help the client talk through the project needs with you. Sometimes, you and the client may discover previously undetected needs through your conversations. Ensure that you are taking detailed notes throughout the meeting so that you can reference them as you draft the project scope in the next phase.

## 3. Establishing the Project Scope

Since clients hire consultants for a specific purpose, it is important that the project purpose is clearly articulated. The project scope is a formal document that captures and defines the tasks, activities, deliverables, and timeline for the project. It is a detailed description of what will be achieved at the end of the project. The project scope is an important tool because the scope determines the boundaries of the client project. Occasionally, some clients may try to add new tasks or objectives after you have mutually agreed to the scope of the project; in these circumstances, having the scope in writing can be useful to help keep your task as a consultant manageable so as to avoid "scope creep." It can also be used as a communication tool during the course of your project. Taking the time to capture the right information and clearly define the scope of work will help you properly plan and manage your client project.

## 4. Creating a Project Plan

Once you and the client have agreed upon the scope of the project, now it is time to develop a clear sense of how you will execute your consulting project by establishing a project plan. Your project plan will determine how you plan to go about solving the problem you have been tasked with by your client. The project plan will include key information on when and how you will accomplish the project scope. Obviously, your plan may change slightly as you uncover new information, but you should do your best to create a realistic work plan. You should create a coherent project plan that covers the following elements:

### The Problem/Opportunity

In this section, state the root of the problem or opportunity you have identified. This shows that there is a real need for the project.

### The Project Scope

Summarize the scope of the project as outlined in the full project scope description.

### Pertinent Stakeholders

Discuss the people and/or groups that can impact or will be impacted by your project. (For additional information on stakeholder analyses, please see Chapter 3–1)

### Relevant Situational Variables

Include the factors that can impact or be impacted by your project. While stakeholders are the people who impact or can be impacted by your project, situational variables are "things" that impact can be impacted by your project. Often this will include financial, human resources, time, or other resource constraints.

### Research Plan

Establish a research plan to gather and analyze the information and data that you will need to complete the project. The first step is to develop research questions to drive your inquiry. A research question is not simply a question that could be answered by your client or another person. It is a question that can only be answered by actual research. To develop your research question, key areas of research, and research methods, complete the two steps below:

**Research Areas**

Develop three to five driving research questions that you plan to research and answer throughout the project. Start by brainstorming all of the questions you will need to answer to solve the problem you have identified. Then group the questions into categories. These categories of questions are your driving research questions and your key areas of research.

**Research Methods**

Think about how and when you will gain answers to the research questions you have developed. Create an action plan for each research question, including the information you need to research, resources you plan to use to obtain the answers to your questions, deadlines to complete the research, and the person responsible for each research area.

## Project Timeline

In this section, you should clearly articulate the internal and external deadlines to complete the project.

## Budget

Outline all of the monetary resources necessary to complete a consulting project. This budget should not include implementation costs; only the costs to conduct the project scope itself are included in this budget.

A realistic and detailed project plan is the key to a manageable and efficient project. The project plan can also be used to benchmark your progress throughout the project.

# 5. Project Progress Updates

Throughout your project, the client may ask you to provide an update on the status of your project and the work you have completed on your project to date. The purpose of a progress update is to keep your client informed of the progress you have made on the project. You should update your client in accordance with the process and deadlines outlined in the project scope.

> **TWO TYPES OF RESEARCH**
>
> **Primary Research** involves collecting information directly from a source. Examples of primary research methods include surveys, interviews, and focus groups.
>
> **Secondary Research** involves collecting information from sources who have already conducted, analyzed, and published their own findings. Examples of secondary research sources include books, journals, and databases.

©dotshock/Shutterstock.com

**Figure 4**  *Developing a project plan should be a collaborative process*

Project updates allow the client to evaluate your work before the project is complete. Updates highlight the progress you have made and provide an opportunity to bring forward problems and concerns in time to be corrected. Your project updates should be concise yet provide a comprehensive analysis of the research you have conducted and the findings you have uncovered. Think about the information that is important to your client and the best way to structure your progress to meet the client's needs. Though your project updates rightfully give clients an opportunity to redirect you if they feel you have gotten off course, it is your responsibility as a consultant to ensure that their requested course corrections do not significantly alter or amend the agreed-upon project scope. Each update should contain the four main sections below:

## Introduction

This section frames, forecasts, and provides an overview for your client.

- Highlights the bottom line of the project progress (on-track/off-track)
- Reminds the client of the problem you are solving
- Reminds the client of your project scope
- Forecasts the key information that will be addressed in the update

## Present Progress

This section informs the client of the progress you have accomplished and outlines work to be completed during the remainder of the project. You should discuss an analysis of your initial research and findings. The client is interested in understanding the research you have conducted and initial conclusions you have drawn based on your research. Depending on your project and client's priorities, you may choose to break down your progress using the task method or the time method.

### Task Method

Focus on providing information about specific tasks your team has completed. This method works well if your project consists of several tasks that are being completed concurrently.

### Time Method

Focus on your timeline and what you have accomplished. Grouping tasks into categories of "completed," "in progress," and "to be completed" is an effective approach. This works well if your project tasks build on each other and follow a linear timeline.

## Address Problems/Concerns (Only if Applicable)

This section is necessary only if you have had to make changes to your team's project scope or project plan. Clearly state any problems or concerns you have encountered or anticipate based on your initial research. Your client expects the project to progress smoothly but understands that it will not be flawless. Keeping your client aware of necessary changes will increase their confidence in you. Be sure to describe how you have tried to solve the problem(s) you encountered, or how you plan to address future problems. This is not a time to gripe about insignificant hurdles but is your opportunity to provide additional context for your client if you anticipate those hurdles delaying or impeding your successful completion of the project.

## Conclusion

This section provides a summary of the main points discussed and highlights work to be completed during the remainder of the project.

Keeping your client updated throughout the project will increase the chances that your final deliverables will meet expectations.

## 6. Presenting the Final Deliverable

At the end of a consulting engagement, the consultant typically presents the final deliverable to the client in both a written report and an oral presentation. The report and presentation highlight the work that has been completed over the course of the project and provides the next steps for implementation. A best practice for consultative reports and presentations is to use the SBARR organizational structure outlined below.

Situation: Remind the client of the problem you are solving and your project scope. Highlight the bottom line of the project and forecast the key information that will be addressed in the report/presentation.

Background: Present the key research that your team conducted and your key findings. This is the section in which you describe the individual pieces of the puzzle that, once assembled, will solve your client's problem.

Analysis: Provide a detailed analysis of your research findings for your client based on your anticipated recommendations. The analysis is the section in which you interpret your findings (as discussed in the background section) and assign meaning to that information. This is the section in which you describe how the puzzle pieces relate to each other and can fit together. Your analysis lays the foundation for the justification of your recommendations in the next section.

Recommendations: Provide actionable recommendations and justification for what you identify to be the key solution(s) for the problem the organization is facing, and how best to address the issue.

Response: This section provides a process for the organization to implement your recommendations. Include a timeline, budget, and specific steps to implement. Clients often appreciate a high level of detail in these step-by-step instructions for implementing your recommendations.

## 7. Implementation

Many people have the misconception that consultants are only hired to conduct research, diagnose a problem, establish processes, and make recommendations. However, consultants are not only hired to plan and advise, but they are also hired for implementation. In the implementation phase, consultants work alongside the organization employees or lay leaders to execute the recommended strategies.

To further assist you in understanding the consulting process, examples from each phase in the consulting process are included below. Since every consulting engagement varies, this project example may be similar to or different from the consulting projects you may face.

# Example Consulting Deliverables

The example deliverables in this section are based on a consulting engagement with *The Center*, a national network of nonprofit community centers. The Center has more 100 locations throughout the United States, including a 100,000-square-foot facility located in Tucson, AZ. The Tucson Center offers diverse programs in the areas of arts, fitness, sports, wellness, early childhood education, special needs services, and after school enrichment classes. These examples are adaptations of actual student submissions and are therefore realistic but imperfect.

**Figure 5** *The Center*

# Example Initial Client Research

## Industries

Due to the variety of services The Center offers, it can be categorized in various industries including Civic, Social & Youth Organization, Indoor Sports Facilities Management Organization, and After-School Program Providers.

### Civic, Social & Youth Organization

According to IBISWorld, the Civic, Social & Youth Organizations industry is a 16.5 billion-dollar industry. However, revenues are expected to shrink over the next five years. The Civic, Social & Youth Organization industry is comprised of nonprofit social clubs, alumni organizations, community support groups and other societies and organizations outside of religious congregations. Like other organizations in this industry, The Center collects government grants, membership fees, and donations from individuals and corporations.

### After-School Program Providers Industry

As reported by IBISWorld, about 18% of American children are enrolled in after-school programs. That number is expected to grow in the next few years. The after-school care industry is a mature industry that is growing after a recovery from the most recent recession. The majority (59.1%) of the industry market is concentrated on children in kindergarten through 5th grade.

### Indoor Sports Facilities Management Industry

According to IBISWorld, some of the programs offered by the indoor sport facilities management industry are indoor swimming, indoor basketball complexes, and general sport facilities. The Tucson Center houses all of these programs and more. The industry is in a quality growth stage with opportunities for evolution against traditional fitness centers. The draw of a community center is the variety of facilities and programs offered.

## Services

The Center offers a variety of services, including programs in the following areas:

- Special Needs
- Early Childhood Education
- Arts
- Youth Camp
- After School Enrichment Classes
- Fitness
- Aquatics
- Sports and Recreation

## Target Market(s)

The Center targets people of all ages. Young families with children make up the primary users.

## Local Competitors and/or Similar Organizations Across the Nation

### National Competitors

According to IBISWorld, there are more than forty thousand Civic, Social & Youth Organizations in the United States. This medium competition level stems from the low barriers to entry in the market. Although there are many national competitors, three main competitors stand out: The Boys and Girls Clubs, Boys Scouts, and YMCA.

### Local Competitors

The Center competes with the three larger national organizations outlined above and various local Civic, Social & Youth Organizations. After-school care is a very competitive field in Tucson. Many elementary schools partner with either the YMCA or Boys and Girls Clubs for their after-school programs. Based on the Arizona Center for AfterSchool Excellence database, there are about eight competitors in a three-mile radius of The Center, but they are much more limited in their program offerings.

### Best Practices for Items Articulated in Initial Project Discussions

Internal research conducted nationwide by The Center suggests that two key indicators of membership retention are 1) members' informal conversations with staff and 2) member participation in at least three programs per year. This data indicates that regular communication with staff and involvement in multiple programs increases the chance of membership renewal and retention at The Center.

## Example Project Scope

With membership growth during the past three years, The Center would like to shift its membership focus from recruitment to retention. The consultants will develop a membership retention communication plan for The Center. National data suggests that two key indicators of retention are 1) members' informal conversations with staff and 2) member participation in at least three programs per year. This data indicates that regular communication with staff and involvement in multiple programs increases the chance of membership renewal and retention. The consultants will explore the following questions throughout the project:

- *Retention strategies and measurement*: What are the best strategies to retain members? How can The Center track which strategies are working to retain members?
- *Communication with members*: What are the best points of contact, mediums, methodologies, and types of conversations to have with members to increase retention?
- *Transition points*: How can The Center better promote members to use and transition between its various programs? The Center would like to better retain members as they transition out of one program by introducing them to new programs. For instance, the majority of the children enrolled in the early childhood education program do not transition to additional programs at The Center after their pre-school years.
- *Training for staff*: How can The Center train its staff members to promote retention among its members?
- *Celebrating its long-time members*: How can The Center recognize and celebrate individuals and families that have been long-time members?

The membership retention communication plan must align with The Center's focus on bringing members a long-term sense of community, belonging, and family. The project process is outlined in the chart below.

| | |
|---|---|
| **PHASE 1** | • Obtain an in-depth understanding of The Center<br>• Conduct best practices research of similar organizations locally and across the nation<br>• Benchmark best practices research with the Center |
| **PHASE 2** | • Conduct in-depth research and analysis into the exploration questions<br>• Develop recommendations, justification, and a plan to increase membership retention at The Center |
| **FINAL DELIVERABLE** | Recommendation report and presentation for membership retention communication plan |

# Example Project Plan

## Introduction

This project plan outlines our strategy to develop a solution for improving The Center's retention rates. Our approach requires research on member-to-staff interactions and increased programs participation. This document will also provide an analysis of the stakeholders and situational variables, our research plan, timeline, budget, and expected final deliverable.

## Challenge

The Center has been successful in their recruiting efforts of the past few years, raising membership to an all-time high. The Center would like to pivot their attention towards a retention effort that is focused on growing the retention rate among its members from approximately 70% to about 80%.

## Project Scope

Internal Center data shows that members who have informal conversations with staff have a higher likelihood of renewing their membership. Given this information, we plan on developing a solution to increase informal communication skills by the staff to create a more welcoming environment for the members. Center data also indicates that members who participate in more programs are more likely to renew their membership. Our team will focus on measures that encourage increased member participation in community center programming. In addition, we will provide strategies for increasing member involvement in multiple programs.

## Key Stakeholders

There are several stakeholders who will be impacted by the recommendations we make in our final plan. These stakeholders must be considered throughout the research and development process so that their needs are fully met by the retention plan. The key stakeholders fall into two groups, described below.

### Members

Members will be influenced by any retention strategies we develop. We will conduct ample research to understand what drives members to renew their membership in a community center and we will develop our retention methods accordingly.

### Employees

These stakeholders will be the front-line personnel in the retention effort. The employees are responsible for informal communication methods, with the goal of increasing membership retention. Employees will also be responsible for promoting increased program participation. The effectiveness of our solution will be determined by employee acceptance of our proposed strategies.

## Situational Variables

In addition to key stakeholders, there are certain situational variables unique to The Center. These factors will have an effect on the effectiveness of the solution that we will develop. The key situational variables are described below.

### Part-Time Workforce

The Center has a high number of part-time employees, with roughly 70% working less than full-time. These employees are the most likely to come in contact with members, meaning that they are the most crucial employees in the informal communication effort.

### Membership Fees

Since the Center offers various programs above and beyond a typical fitness center, it has a higher membership cost. If current members are price sensitive or do not see the value in The Center's services, it may be harder to retain them.

Given these stakeholders and situational variables, we have developed a research plan that will guide us in building our solution for The Center.

## Key Research Areas

In order to provide the best solution for The Center to retain its current members, we have identified three key research areas:

### Increasing Informal Conversations

An important opportunity The Center has is the ability for staff to interact with members on a daily basis. Informal conversations serve as a platform to retain members. Through our research, we will explore the best practices for training staff to increase their informal conversation rates.

### Encouraging Member Involvement in Multiple Programs

One key metric to research for this area is program usage rates. This number ultimately reflects the usefulness of The Center and its programs to its members, and therefore is a large indicator of retention rates. The key focus of this research is to understand the best ways to increase program participation, in order to make The Center more relevant to its members.

### Increasing Community Atmosphere

This research area involves the culture at The Center, and the overall atmosphere the community maintains. This research will include elements that bring the community together, as well as what types of incentive members desire. This research area should focus on the wants and needs of the membership.

## Research Methods

We will conduct numerous types of research before creating an overarching retention plan. The main purpose of our research is to determine how the members and staff perceive the current retention efforts of The Center. In addition, we want to gain a better understanding of the abilities of the Customer Relationship Management (CRM) software. Upon collecting this data, we will analyze how the various feedback factors interact and develop a plan for retention that is better tailored to the needs of the members and the abilities of the organization's staff. There are three research methods that we will use:

### Best Practices (Secondary Research)

We will research the best practices for retention at competitors and similar community centers both locally and nationally.

### The Center Data (Secondary Research)

The Center has provided our team with raw user data based on information collected from the members. This information acts as a starting point and a guide to formulating questions for the primary research we will conduct. We will analyze the following data provided by The Center:

- Member Demographic Information
- Programming Schedule
- Employee Training Manual
- Past Benchmarking Surveys

### Focus Groups (Primary Research)

We have arranged two focus groups at The Center in order to ask members and employees key questions that will give us a firsthand account of how these groups experience the organization. This primary form of investigation is valuable because it allows us to obtain insight into how individuals perceive the organizational structure and how they feel it could be improved. Our questions will be organized into the following categories:

- Staff Questions
  - Employee Performance
  - Programming
- Member Questions
  - Employee Satisfaction
  - Programming
  - Participation Profile

### CRM Software Research (Secondary Research)

Understanding the nature of the CRM software that The Center is initiating is crucial to the application of our retention efforts. We will learn how the CRM platform operates and also understand how other organizations have implemented and utilized it most effectively.

## Timeline

The projected project timeline is included below to enable our team to complete our project in a timely and efficient manner.

| DATE | TASKS TO BE COMPLETED |
|---|---|
| February 1 | Conduct best practices and The Center data secondary research |
| February 15 | Develop questions for focus group |
| March 1 | Conduct focus group |
| March 15 | Analyze secondary and primary data to identify areas to add to the employee training procedures |
| March 15 | Analyze secondary and primary data to identify underutilized programs |
| April 1 | Develop new employee training procedures |
| April 1 | Identify which programs to promote to members |
| April 1 | Research CRM system |
| April 15 | Develop new strategies and procedures to promote retention |
| May 1 | Final client presentation and report |

## Final Deliverable

Our final deliverable will be a membership retention plan that includes all of the information collected throughout our primary and secondary research. We will develop strategies to enable The Center to train its staff to keep its members satisfied. We will create a plan to increase member participation in The Center programs. Additionally, we will provide recommendations for using data within informal communication and the CRM system to allow employees to better serve the needs of members.

We will utilize the information discovered through our research to formulate a retention plan for The Center. This plan will take into account the relevant stakeholders and situational variables that may affect the efficacy of our plan, and the solution will be tailored with The Center's overall goal of providing a sense of community to its employees and members. The recommendations will be well suited to benefit The Center in retaining its members for years to come.

## Example Project Update

This project update provides you with our progress in developing a solution to improve The Center's retention rates. We are currently on schedule with our research plan and have found good information through our secondary research.

### Completed Task

- Through our secondary research, we found that The Center offers over 125 programs per week. This number is much higher than its local competitors.
- Through secondary research, we found that most community centers offer quarterly training for employees.
- Based on our secondary research, we developed our focus group questions.

### Upcoming Task

- Focus group at The Center on March 1st

We are on track and ready for our primary research focus groups next week.

# Example Executive Summary for Final Deliverable

## Overview

The Center recently shifted its focus from recruiting new members to retaining current members. This report will provide The Center with recommendations for a successful membership retention plan. Enhancing employee training to include strategies for members to staff informal conversations and promotion of program participation will enable The Center to achieve its goal of an 80% member-retention rate. By utilizing its CRM software effectively, The Center will see the 10% increase in retention rates it desires. These two recommendations will facilitate improved, tailored employee and member interactions and permit members to learn about programs to fully engage in The Center.

## Program Promotion

In order to develop effective recommendations, we conducted secondary and primary research. Our secondary research indicated that abundant programs are available to members at a variety of times. After reviewing The Centers offerings, we determined that there are more than 125 free weekly classes that are well staffed. Since these programs are not being fully utilized, an opportunity exists for The Center to improve in program promotion.

## Staff Training

Through our primary research focus groups, we determined that employees could benefit from additional training in information conversations and program promotion. Employees expressed their discomfort with interacting with members. They two key reasons for anxiety came from not knowing the members well enough to start a conversation with them and not knowing enough about The Center programs to provide useful information.

## Recommendations

Based on our research and analysis we developed the following two recommendations:

1. Employee Training

   Facilitating increased interaction with members will require employees to be comfortable in their positions. Enhancing the employee training and the employee training manual will prepare staff for informal communication tactics. In addition, employees need to be made aware of all programming so that they can promote programs effectively to members.

2. Utilization of CRM Software

   The Center should continue with its plan to implement its CRM software. The usage of CRM software will provide knowledge about members that staff can use to start conversation and tailor interactions with members. This will help staff to be less apprehensive about informal conversations and allow them to provide meaningful program suggestions.

## Implementation

We have provided a timeline for The Center to implement our recommendations at the end of the report. We have broken down the process into simple steps that should be implemented over the next three months. Over time the process will become a routine element of employee behavior and company culture. The Center will continue to be a valuable organization for its members by implementing enhanced employee training and advanced utilization of its CRM to aid in member engagement and retention.

# Summary

Like all successful business communication, consultative communication is tailored to meet the needs of your audience. Your client communication will change with each new client and consulting engagement. Now that you have an understanding of client communication and the consulting process, you can master the art of advanced strategic communication in all of your consulting endeavors.

# Unit 7 References

Hollaren, K. (March 2016). *IBISWorld Industry Report* OD5884. After-School program providers in the US. Retrieved March 27, 2017 from IBISWorld.

Hollaren, K. (October 2016). *IBISWorld Industry Report* 81341. Civic, social & youth organizations in the US. Retrieved March 27, 2017 from IBISWorld.

Mitchell, R., Agle, B., & Wood, D. (1997). Toward a theory of stakeholder identification and salience: Defining the principle of who and what really counts. *Academy of Management Review*, 22(4), 853.

Rivera, E. (September 2016). *IBISWorld Industry Report* OD4647. Indoor sports facilities management in the US. Retrieved March 27, 2017 from IBISWorld.

# UNIT 8:

# Intercultural Communication: Global Business Insights and Strategies

As students of Business, you will inevitably encounter global issues. Whether it's working with international students on a team or researching overseas expansion opportunities for a company in a particular industry, you'll quickly learn that culture and communication norms differ from country to country. One way to deal with these differences is to insist that your way is the only "right" way. A more effective strategy, however, is to increase your understanding of how others live, think, and communicate so that you can become a more adaptable and successful communicator. This is not only true while you're studying toward a business degree, but it will also be true throughout your career.

Commerce today does not operate in a one-country environment. A striking example of global impact is that of China's economy and how it affects the economy in the United States and around the world. After a rapid rise to being one of the greatest economies of the world, China began to experience a slow-down between 2011 and 2014. The country's GDP growth rates fell steadily, and its stock market stagnated. This economic slow-down had rippling effects around the world.

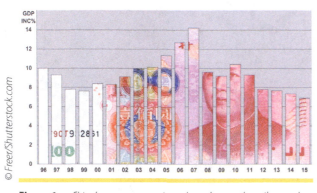

**Figure 1** *China's economy experienced steady growth until around 2011, when its economic growth started to slow.*

In the United States, for example, this was felt in the sale and pricing of commodities such as steel and copper, which had skyrocketed due to Chinese demand in previous years, but now would experience a significant decrease in sales. Luxury goods would also feel the effects. Take for instance, brands like Louis Vuitton and Tiffany. China and its Asian neighbors had made up around a quarter of Tiffany's sales, but with reduced GDP in China, these sales could not be sustained. Louis Vuitton saw its sales in China, Macau, and Hong Kong fall by 10% as China's economy faltered. While you may not relate these industry losses to everyday life in America, consider the effect on mutual funds and retirement accounts as major industry stock prices plummeted (Mansharamani, 2015). What happens halfway around the world, does not stay halfway around the world.

Now let's consider the number of U.S. companies that have expanded to countries that have become the economic leaders of the world. The BRIC nations, as they were officially coined in 2010, are Brazil, Russia, India, and China. As these nations emerged as economic powerhouses, companies around the world took notice. Many determined that to continue to be relevant in their respective industries, they could not ignore the call to expand into these countries. And so, the rush began.

Many companies that you know well are now flourishing in some of these countries but are faltering in others; consider McDonald's and Walmart to name just two. Both are prospering in China but took hits in India and Brazil. Other companies have not fared well at all in China. Best Buy entered China in 2006, purchasing a majority stake in Jiangsu Five Star Appliance Co, with plans to open its own name brand stores in major cities over the next few years. In 2011, however, it retreated, closing nine Best Buy-branded retail stores in China, choosing to focus its attention only on its acquired Chinese Five Star chain in the country. Then, in 2014, Best Buy sold off Jiangsu Five Star Appliance Co and exited the country for good (Burkitt, 2014).

This begs the question: what contributes to a company's success and/or failure when expanding overseas? This will be the focus of chapter 1 in this unit. Once we have explored global concepts on an industry level, we'll turn our attention to a cross-cultural skillset that you, as business students, can adopt. In chapter 2, you will learn strategies for equipping yourselves to succeed in a continually growing global marketplace. Get ready to gain new insight and to increase your intercultural competency. After all, this skillset is in growing demand at the very companies where your dream jobs await.

# The Global Challenge: Why Companies Succeed or Fail Overseas

**W**ith any new business venture, in-depth research and strategic planning are necessary. This especially applies to international expansion. It is important for a company to both evaluate the driving forces behind a move into another country and to analyze its own preparedness for such an initiative. It will be important to have a firm foundation on which to grow long-term operations in a new culture. So, let's take a look at these two criteria in detail.

## Motivations for International Expansion

Several factors play a part in a company making a strategic decision to expand abroad. The first question that should be answered is, "Why is this a good decision for the company?" In order to justify both the expense and the disruption involved in such a significant undertaking, the motivation must be solid.

The following chart provides three aspects to consider in this analysis:

**Figure 1**    *Do you know what it takes to effectively communicate with people from other countries?*

©kirill_makarov/Shutterstock.com

341

| | |
|---|---|
| **A VIABLE MARKET** | Here you would research the GDP and analyze consumer purchasing trends in the target country. You should also consider the popularity of the product and of U.S. brands among the population. |
| **STAKEHOLDER DEMAND** | It is important to listen to those who will be impacted and who may impact the success of a venture like this. Investors may see this as an opportunity to increase stock value and remain competitive. |
| **COMPETITIVE THREAT** | A company must keep up with trends in the industry, or it may find it has acted too late. In some cases, being ahead of the game will benefit a company; at other times, it may be smart to watch and learn. |

These and other factors must be closely scrutinized to determine if there is a strong and convincing driving force moving the company in an international direction.

# Company Preparedness

Once the motivation has been verified, the next step will be to look at the company's infrastructure to confirm it has the resources needed to survive and succeed in a new culture. We'll call this *Company Preparedness*, which includes both resource stability and operational integrity.

| | |
|---|---|
| **RESOURCE CAPABILITY** | There will always be financial investment and risk involved with any new ventures. So, a company must determine what it is willing and able to risk, and balance this against projected gain. Short-term and long-term risks should be closely examined. Staffing, logistics, and other resources must be considered in addition to finances. |
| **OPERATIONAL INTEGRITY** | The key to assuring success when operating in a new country is adapting to the norms of the culture without compromising the integrity of your business. Protecting intellectual property and maintaining safety and ethical standards may be challenging. Knowing what to watch for in a specific country will help navigate gray areas. |

Many consulting firms have tools for analyzing and documenting factors that contribute to a company's decision making when it comes to international expansion. It is wise to find or create a template for conducting this type of assessment. Technomic Asia is one such consulting firm, which has generated a comprehensive assessment tool for preparing to expand a company into China (Ganster, 2005). These tools are useful in determining the feasibility of an international expansion; however, strategic research is critical to the success of any foreign enterprise.

Providing a company conducts a comprehensive analysis of its motivation and readiness to expand into a new foreign market, there is a good chance of success. At the very least, it will instill confidence in and garner support from key stakeholders, preparing the way for more detailed research into the feasibility and potential profitability of an international expansion. The following sections will explore additional areas of research that are needed to understand the specific country into which a company seeks to expand.

# Legal and Political Requirements

Before a U.S. company considers an international move, there must be a clear understanding of the type of foreign investment permitted and the regulation being enforced by the government of that country. While many countries provide incentives to foreign companies to come in as wholly-owned foreign enterprises, some set restrictions on the type of ownership or percentage of ownership allowed in a new foreign venture. This will influence the decision-making process both in financial terms and in principle. Let's consider the government regulations surrounding foreign investment opportunities of a few potential foreign markets.

# Openness to and Restrictions on Foreign Investments

The following excerpts provide examples of what a company should know about foreign direct investment (FDI) opportunities in three different countries (Openness, 2016).

| COUNTRY | SINGAPORE | SOUTH AFRICA | CHILE |
|---|---|---|---|
| **OPENNESS TO FDI** | • Foreign investors are not required to enter into joint ventures and may maintain managerial control.<br>• Local and foreign investors are subject to the same basic laws.<br>• The judicial system upholds the sanctity of contracts, and decisions are transparent and effectively enforced. | • The government's openness to foreign investment stems from a desire for economic growth.<br>• Most business sectors are open to foreign investment.<br>• Government approval is not required to invest, and there are few restrictions on the form or extent of foreign investment. | • Sound, market-oriented policies create significant opportunities for foreign investors in the country's steady economic growth.<br>• Business climate is generally straightforward and transparent.<br>• Foreign investors receive treatment similar to locals, and no economic strategies or policies discriminate against foreign-owned investments. |
| COUNTRY | SINGAPORE | SOUTH AFRICA | CHILE |
| **RESTRICTIONS ON FDI** | • Government restrictions are enforced in the areas of telecommunications, broadcasting, domestic news media, financial services, legal, and other professional services, and in property ownership.<br>• Articles of Incorporation may also place limitations on ownership in major corporations by foreign individuals. | • Government approval for foreign participation is required in some sectors, including energy, mining, banking, insurance, and defense.<br>• A lack of urgency from national government to support foreign investment deals.<br>• Foreign entities experience trouble accessing senior decision makers.<br>• Lack of conviction about the importance of Foreign Direct Investment to South Africa's growth and prosperity. | • Foreign investors have access to all productive activities, except for a limited number of restrictions in sectors such as maritime and air transportation and the public media.<br>• International reciprocity restrictions exist for fishing.<br>• Chile does not restrict the right to private ownership or establishment, except for some strategic activities such as nuclear energy and mining. |

**Table 1**   *Foreign Direct Investment*

# So, What Should a Company Do with This Knowledge?

A full understanding of government allowances, restrictions, and incentives is needed before a company considers expanding into a foreign market. It is imperative to know the legal requirements, but it is also important to know the political climate and general openness to foreign investments. Details to get started on this are available at the World Trade Organization's website and other credible sources. However, a company would be wise to hire a knowledgeable legal advisor from the country itself to ensure smooth entry and successful operations. Having a reputable corporate attorney will also be helpful in understanding the amount of capital required to get started and the tax code structure to stay compliant.

Once the political and legal climate has been analyzed, and it has been determined that the pros outweigh the cons, the company can explore the business structures and practices of the new country. This is important to be sure these align with the company's own values and to see what adaptations are needed.

# Business Organizational Structures

When doing business in another culture, there may be confusion about what is expected or why potential business partners are behaving in a certain way. Confusion can lead to misunderstandings and even resentments that will ultimately sabotage any business relationship. So, it is important to understand business structures and expectations as much as possible before approaching the cross-cultural bargaining table. It is necessary to understand the various organizational structures and what is behind them in order to avoid misguided and game-ending conflict.

This brings us to another question: what types of business organizational structures exist around the world? The two dominant structures are hierarchical and democratic, but there is more to this distinction than what the names may imply. An increasing number of U.S. corporations are run as democratic entities, in which the management style embraces input from all employees, regardless of their positions. Of course, many U.S. companies still operate more as hierarchical organizations where decisions are clearly made and enforced from the top down. In most other countries, the latter is more the norm, but the extent of this style will vary from culture to culture.

# Five Dimensions of Culture

Geert Hofstede, a Dutch social psychologist and former IBM employee, is most noted for his dimensions of culture model. This theory has had various applications and is used extensively in the area of international business relations. He developed five dimensions of culture that are relevant to doing business in various countries. The five dimensions of culture that he introduced are power distance, uncertainty avoidance, collectivism vs. individualism, femininity vs. masculinity, and long-term vs. short-term. Let's take a brief look at these dimensions and their relevance to business.

## HOFSTEDE'S CULTURAL DIMENSIONS

| | |
|---|---|
| **POWER DISTANCE** | The Power Distance index measures the degree to which individuals of every segment of society are allowed to be or are comfortable with influencing change upward. In business, it is exemplified by the relationship between boss and employees and involves how accessible the communication channel between them is made. |
| **UNCERTAINTY AVOIDANCE** | The Uncertainty Avoidance index measures how people cope with ambiguity. The higher the uncertainty avoidance, the more regulations are put in place. In business, a low uncertainty avoidance may result in more openness to change, greater innovation and inclusiveness, and more of a comfort level with risk-taking. |
| **COLLECTIVISM VS. INDIVIDUALISM** | The Collectivism vs. Individualism index measures how personal goals and group goals are prioritized. In a high-collectivist society, people make decisions based on what is best for the whole. In more individualistic societies, people make decisions based on what is best for him/herself. In business, the latter tends to show more initiative. |
| **FEMININITY VS. MASCULINITY** | The Femininity vs. Masculinity index measures how societies view assertiveness versus modesty. Masculine countries tend to place value on status and achievement, while those considered feminine value relationships, consensus, and quality of life. Though based on gender role stereotypes, one must consider the work environment that each style produces in business. |
| **LONG-TERM VS. SHORT-TERM** | The Long-Term vs. Short-Term index measures the length of time people are comfortable with taking to achieve results. In a long-term society, value is placed on hard work and perseverance. The focus is on the future. Short-term societies are concerned with the present and past. They value tradition and fulfilling social obligations. |

**Table 2**  *Hofstede's Cultural Dimensions*

Each of these dimensions tells us something about the culture in which we live and work. They also help companies anticipate cultural differences as they consider international expansion. While it may not be necessary to understand everything about a new culture, especially in scientific terms, knowing a few basics may prevent needless misunderstandings and allow a company to move forward after conflict, instead of retreating.

# Cultural Insights and Considerations

In this section, we will look deeper into the core values of a culture in order to help us resist the tendency to form assumptions, draw conclusions, and adopt beliefs based on shallow observations. As you learned in chapter 2–3, making inferences based on limited information can be dangerous.

The Cultural Iceberg theory was introduced by Edward Hall in 1976. Hall was a world-renowned anthropologist and cross-cultural researcher, whose publications have influenced many fields, including education and business. His idea of the Cultural Iceberg helps us see that there is much more below the surface of any culture that needs to be considered if we are ever to fully-understand people in other countries. By learning about the core values of a society, we become aware of what drives people's attitudes and perceptions and what leads to the way they behave and expect others to behave. On this level, you begin to engage with the new culture and communication style, not simply try to imitate verbal and nonverbal behavior.

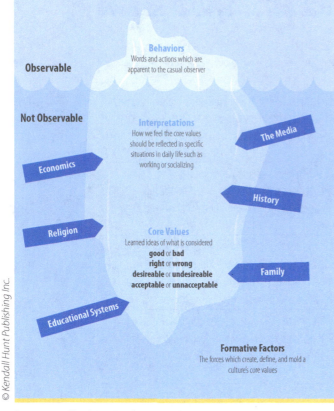

**Figure 2**   *The Cultural Iceberg*

Core values are the very fabric of a culture. They are formed by a number of different forces and experiences. Core values may be rooted in religious beliefs and teachings, others are necessitated by economic events, and still others are developed over the unique history of a country. Wherever they originate, core values are deeply instilled in the people of any given culture. They determine what we believe to be good and bad, right or wrong, desirable and undesirable, and acceptable and unacceptable. Consider the ramifications to conducting business in another country without understanding the core values of that culture.

The core values of a culture form people's attitudes about life and relationships. This, in turn, causes people to interact in culturally acceptable ways and to expect others to conduct themselves likewise.

# An Illustrative Business Scenario

Based on one of Hofstede's Five Dimensions and on Hall's Iceberg theory, let's consider a cross-cultural business scenario: a U.S.-based clothing company is looking for a manufacturing partner to produce lower-priced zippers. They turn to a company in Sri Lanka. Let's compare Power Distance in the two countries

## Sri Lanka

With a high score of 80 on the Power Distance index, Sri Lanka is a relatively hierarchical society. This means that people accept a hierarchical order in which everybody has a place and nobody questions any inequality this might entail. It also means that it is expected that a business deal will be handled by high-level executives on both sides and that those on the production line have no say in the final decision.

## The United States

The United States, on the other hand, scores around 40 on the Power Distance index. One quality of this is that in American organizations hierarchy may be established for convenience, but superiors are accessible, and managers rely on individual employees and teams for their expertise.

There are two distinct value systems in play here, but how might that discrepancy affect the business relationship between the American clothing company and the Sri Lankan zipper manufacturer? The following is one possible way this scenario could work out.

## The Situation

The COO of the U.S. clothing company has his team locate a company in Sri Lanka. He places a phone call, and after several attempts speaks with the CEO of the zipper manufacturing company. A visit to the manufacturing plant is arranged. The COO of the clothing company is not an expert on manufacturing plants, and he trusts his design team to make an informed decision once they have seen the operations in Sri Lanka and negotiate the terms of the agreement. In fact, they are given full authority to revise and sign the contract before returning home.

When the design team arrives in Sri Lanka in blue jeans and polo shirts, they are met by the CEO himself and two other high-level executives, who are wearing suits and ties. Once it is established that these are indeed the representatives of the clothing company, the CEO asks when the COO will be arriving. The team looks slightly embarrassed but insists that they are fully authorized to discuss the deal and to finalize the agreement. Out of courtesy, the Sri Lankan hosts take the team to the hotel and buy them dinner. There is no discussion of the deal over dinner, just small talk. The next morning, a car arrives to take the team back to the airport. New flights have been arranged, and no explanation is given as to why the negotiations will not be held.

**Figure 3**   *Understanding cultural norms will make you a more effective negotiator.*

What happened? What was the cultural disconnect that derailed what should have been a simple purchasing arrangement? The American team and their COO should have realized the importance of hierarchy in a collectivist society. Sending presumably low-level employees to conduct the negotiation was considered rude by the Sri Lankan executives. The American team returned home befuddled, told their boss about the strange events of the past 48 hours, and began a new search for another zipper manufacturer...

# Business and Negotiation Practices

Now, had the U.S. clothing company made it to negotiations with the Sri Lankan manufacturing plant, they would have had new challenges to face. By this time, you understand the importance of doing one's homework in order to be better prepared for each new phase of international expansion. Since business is conducted through a series of negotiations, it is important for us to explore several aspects of culture and business practices around the world that play a part in the negotiation process.

Negotiations in one's own country are challenging enough. A company sends in a representative with experience and authority to arrive at an agreement that serves both parties' interests. Of course, each side has its own idea of what will serve its interest best. Each side determines in advance what it is willing to give and what it must receive before a settlement is reached. Some negotiators believe in achieving integrative, win-win outcomes, while others believe in achieving distributive, zero-sum outcomes. While challenging and potentially fraught, it is at least a familiar procedure.

Intercultural negotiation adds several more layers to the challenge. However, with a clear understanding of the cultures involved and a willingness on both sides to adapt to the other's practices, a profitable and long-term partnership can be established. The following are steps in the intercultural negotiation process (Chaney & Martin, 2014).

## Preparation

Several of the topics we've already looked at will be useful in preparing for international negotiations. It is advisable to consult with someone who is from the target country or who has lived there for an extended length of time. This person will help maneuver through the culture, the beliefs, the business and social etiquette, and the language of the foreign country.

Deciding where to hold the negotiations will be an important consideration. If the business will be conducted in the foreign country, the negotiations will be expected to take place there as well. Even the appropriate room arrangements must be researched, especially in hierarchical cultures, where status must be recognized. Whether a round table or a rectangular one is preferred in the host country, the person in the highest position should always be seated farthest away from and facing the door to signify respect and honor.

## Team Selection

As we learned in the Sri Lanka scenario, it is important to select the right negotiating team. In most countries, people in executive positions will be expected to conduct the meeting; others may attend, but should serve in support roles. Those selected should have the expertise necessary to field questions and present clear and valid explanations.

It may also be necessary to follow the customs of the host country regarding women in the workplace and in positions of authority. In a country where women are not welcome to act in leadership roles, the U.S. company may have to decide if this goes against their own ethical standards, to weigh the pros and cons of the deal, and to decide whether to move forward or pull out of the deal.

## Relationship Building

In the United States, it is common to get down to business with minimal small talk. However, in many other cultures, time is built into any negotiation process for socializing and building trust. It would be wise to plan for an extra day both before and after negotiations to establish a relationship with the host partners. For example, there is a concept in China called *Guanxi*, which denotes a type of social networking designed to build trust before entering into a business relationship. There are similar expectations in Latin countries, where the subject of business is off-limits until after a meal and sufficient time to talk about family, sightseeing, and any number of topics meant to create a bond.

## Opening Talks

Once it is time to start the negotiations, it is still important to know how to approach the discussion. In Scandinavian countries, meetings start promptly and follow a strict agenda. In other countries, small talk is expected, and an agenda is seen as an aggressive move meant to gain control. In some Arab countries, an agenda stifles the natural progression of the discussion, since they prefer to talk about more than one issue at a time. While most cultures appreciate a genuine smile, using humor is not always considered appropriate, so know your audience and keep jokes and innuendos to a minimum.

## Discussions

Expect delays! Even with people in senior positions at the negotiating table, final decisions may need to go through government officials or other important partners. So, don't expect to walk away with a contract signed after the first discussion. In fact, insisting on having a contract signed too soon can reduce your company's credibility and destroy the trust you have started to build with your foreign partners.

U.S. businesses answering to government and corporate regulations will need a contract. You may need to explain this at some point. Show that both sides want the same thing: to establish trust. Then explain that in the U.S., a signature on a contract is a promise and a sign of trust.

## Agreement

Reaching an agreement is a momentous occasion in international negotiations. Once ready to review the contract, be sure it includes a few vital details. Dates and responsibilities should be locked down. Timeline and costs should be made clear. Protection of patents and trademarks should be clearly established. Information reporting and degree of exclusivity must be agreed on. It would be wise to include assumptions at the end of the contract that will allow the other party to feel there is room for discussion and change in certain events. This will make it easier for them to sign a contract without feeling manipulated (Chaney & Martin, 2014).

Negotiations are a challenge whether in one's own country or abroad, but success is possible with proper knowledge and careful preparation. Let's conclude this chapter with a few considerations of global business etiquette that will be helpful to understand during the negotiation process.

# Global Business Etiquette

At the negotiation table, each culture has its own customs that foreign partners will be expected to follow or at least be aware of. These behaviors reflect deeper perceptions and values of the given country, and they will color the impression your international partners have of you and your company.

## Greetings

In one of the bestselling guides to doing business abroad, Terri Morrison and Wayne Conaway (2006) present insight into one of the most basic actions in any professional setting. The name of their book is *Kiss, Bow, Or Shake Hands,* and it discusses greetings, among other topics, in more than 60 countries. The range of appropriate gestures and behaviors is very detailed and specific to each country. Of course, most Western countries, and more and more countries around the world greet each other with a handshake. However, even the handshake has a variety of "acceptable" forms.

©Rawpixel.com/Shutterstock.com

**Figure 4**   *Every culture has its own rules for everything, including how we greet each other.*

### The Handshake

A handshake in the United States is firm; it is accompanied by eye contact and a smile and lasts only a few seconds. In France, a handshake is common, but it is gentler and never involves a strong grip. While someone from the United States would have the impression that the French person is weak, the French person would draw the conclusion that the American is aggressive. Handshake customs vary from country to country and even from region to region in some cases. In Indonesia, a person might clasp your hand in both of theirs and hold it for 10–15 seconds. Shaking hands with women may have its own protocol. In some Middle Eastern countries, it would be strictly forbidden; however, even in some European countries, it is wise to let the woman extend her hand first (Morrison & Conaway, 2006).

### The Kiss

The kiss is a form of greeting that you won't see in a traditional U.S. boardroom meeting, but it is still prevalent in several countries around the world. Today, most cultures have adopted the Western style handshake; however, as the relationship grows, a kiss is still standard protocol. In Brazil, for example, greetings are more lavish than in the United States. A handshake is common during the first encounter, but this progresses to an embrace and kiss on the cheek, thereafter (Morrison & Conaway, 2006).

The number of kisses also varies from country to country. In Croatia, it is standard to kiss three times on alternating cheeks. One of your (female) co-authors relates this story of her own experience in this southeastern European nation:

> "On a business trip to Zagreb, I got fairly close to a group of women colleagues and adapted to their greeting style. Once, however, I went in for a fourth kiss and was stopped abruptly. 'Only three kisses,' I was reprimanded by my new friend, Mia. I didn't get a clear explanation; I was only told that it wasn't done that way in Croatia."

The rules can be just as strict in other parts of the world, too. In Brazil, two kisses are customary, but a single woman may be kissed a third time for "luck" in finding a husband. Even the smallest of gestures can be traced to the core values of a country. Commitment to family is among the strongest values in Brazilian culture (Morrison & Conaway, 2006).

### The Bow

Finally, we come to the bow. You may wonder if any culture still practices the bow in business settings today. The answer is yes! Although the handshake is used in Japan, especially with foreign guests, the bow still holds traditional relevance and specific rules of etiquette. When bowing, the eyes are lowered, and palms are held flat against the thighs. If you are ever in Japan, and someone bows to greet you, take notice of how far they bow and return the bow with the same depth. This reflects the status of an individual and the relationship between the two parties.

India is another country with a unique bow when greeting someone, either socially or professionally. The Hindu population of India has a traditional greeting in which the person says the word *Namaste* (*literally translated, the light in me honors the light in you*), and with palms pressed together under the chin, bows slightly. This is also the recommended greeting for foreigners in India. It prevents any misunderstanding when a Western businessman greets an Indian woman or when a Western business woman greets an Indian man (Morrison & Conaway, 2006).

Learning the basic greeting in the country to which you are traveling will help improve the impression you make on others as you move into business meetings and negotiations. A common adage states that a person forms an opinion of you in the first seven seconds of meeting you. As discussed in chapter 2–1, much of those first impressions are based on the nonverbal cues you produce. In fact, Carol Kinsey Goman of Forbes elaborates on what happens during that brief moment in time. She says, "First impressions are more heavily influenced by nonverbal cues than verbal cues. In fact, studies have found that nonverbal cues have over four times the impact on the impression you make than anything you say" (2011, p.1). So, while knowing an appropriate phrase to greet your international partners is highly recommended, it is even more important that you know the proper non-verbal etiquette to use when meeting new business partners. Doing your homework will pay off in dividends that go beyond simply closing the deal!

## Business Card Exchange

Most business students are just beginning to think about business cards. Many students and business professionals haven't considered the etiquette involved in business card exchange around the world. When someone hands you his or her business card, what do you do with it? You probably put it in your pocket and say thanks, but in some countries, that would be considered rude.

In most Asian countries, business cards are exchanged upon meeting someone or as a meeting is getting underway. The card is presented with both hands, and the receiver is expected to accept it with both hands (a slight bow may or may not accompany the exchange). One should study the card for a moment and mention something significant from the information on the card.

For example, you might say, "As the CEO of the company you must be very busy this time of year." Then, when you sit down, the card should be placed in front of you on the table to refer to throughout the meeting. This is very different from the way we exchange business cards in the United States. It will take a few extra steps to ensure you make a good first impression and that you do not offend a potential business partner.

Other countries have their own business card etiquette, too. In Scandinavian countries, a company is expected to have the year it was established on its business cards. This is a way to gain credibility, as the longevity of a business proves its success and trustworthiness. In Arabic countries, it is vital to remember one important rule when accepting or passing a business card (or anything else for the matter). Never use your left hand in the exchange. This has to do with hygiene more than anything else, but also holds spiritual significance in some countries.

**Figure 5**  *Believe it or not, there are even cultural rules for how you exchange business cards!*

## Superstitions and Taboos—No, Not Tattoos, Taboos!

You might have associated some of the customs we have discussed to superstitions, and you would not be wrong in many cases. No matter how developed a country is, it still has residual superstitions and behaviors that are considered taboo. The United States is not immune to this phenomenon either. After all, the number 13 is still considered unlucky here in the United States! Some high-rise buildings do not have a 13th floor, and some airlines skip the number 13 when numbering the row of seats.

Other superstitions dealing with numbers exist around the world. Do you remember the date of the Beijing Olympics? If you said August 8, 2008, you were correct. The number 8 represents—and to some ensures—success and good fortune, so selecting 08/08/2008 was no coincidence. What number is considered unlucky in China, you might ask? The number 4, because its pronunciation is the same as the word for death. What does this have to do with business negotiations? Imagine the impression you would leave on your Chinese clients if you were to request a meeting or suggest a grand opening on April 4th.

As far as taboos are concerned, there are many, but let's focus on common gestures in this discussion. Even something as seemingly innocent as beckoning someone by bending your index finger toward you is considered extremely rude in some Asian and African countries. The proper way to motion for someone to come in Thailand is with your arm extended in front of you, palm facing your body, and all fingers being waved toward you. Otherwise, you may be calling someone a dog or worse. Yes, gestures can get you into trouble, as one did for then-Vice President Richard Nixon during a trip to Brazil. The political meetings had been successful, so as he was boarding the plane, Nixon turned to the throngs of Brazilian citizens and high-level political figures and gave the OK symbol (thumb and index finger joined to form a circle and the rest of the fingers held high). That gesture, in Brazil, is considered extremely vulgar and offensive, so as the Brazilian peopled gasped in horror, the rest of the world shook their heads in disbelief. An international incident could have been easily avoided if only someone had done a little homework and educated the Vice President.

## Gift Giving and Bribery

The topic of gift giving and bribery is loaded with potential dangers for U.S. companies conducting business in foreign countries due to the varying concepts of ethics as they are observed around the globe. It is crucial to explore the important balance a company must maintain when doing business abroad. Remember, the challenge and the goal of international expansion is to adapt as necessary without sacrificing the integrity of the company. That said, let's look briefly at various opinions on bribery around the world (Chaney & Martin, 2014). The callout "Rules for Gift Giving Around the World" presents a few facts on the subject of bribery and gift giving.

With these guidelines in mind, it is easy to see that ethical lines can be difficult to draw. However, it is here that a company must stay true to its core values and the laws governing it in its own country. While bribery may not be officially sanctioned in the countries above, it is common practice and expected, at least from local businesses. Bribery may also be disguised as "tipping." In Indonesia, people are accustomed to giving a tip to an agent in order to obtain a driver's license. One view that Indonesian contractors hold on bribing government officials is that it saves a lot of time. Rather than going through lengthy channels to be awarded a government contract, a bribe cuts through the red tape (Hodge, 2000).

Studying the various business practices of any country with which you plan to do business is absolutely necessary to avoid finding yourself and your company in an awkward and/or compromising position. All stakeholders must be taken into consideration, but bottom line, a company must stay true to its own values.

### RULES FOR GIFT GIVING AROUND THE WORLD

**United States**

The most restrictive laws against bribery

**Italy, Germany and Japan**

Companies may deduct amount of bribes on taxes

**Middle East or Brazil**

They would think you were crazy for not offering a bribe…

**East Asian countries**

Gift giving is expected and follows strict protocol

# Chapter 8-2

# Increasing Your Intercultural IQ

In this chapter, we will move into practical ways for you to increase your Intercultural Competency or Cultural IQ. We will begin by looking at the most common division of countries and cultures, as designated by E. T. Hall in 1990. Then we'll move on to the stages of culture shock you might experience should you spend extended time in a foreign country. Finally, we'll explore the basics of communicating across cultures. With this information, you will gain a greater awareness of cultural differences and begin to develop strategies for bridging the gap between cultures.

## Social Contexts: High- & Low-Context Cultures

Through extensive research, Hall (1990) designed a framework for comparing the major cultures around the world. He classifies them as either high-context cultures or low-context cultures. The table below outlines the key characteristics of each category, which we will elaborate on further in this section.

| HIGH CONTEXT | LOW CONTEXT |
|---|---|
| • Implicit communication | • Explicit communication |
| • Non-verbal emphasis | • Verbal emphasis |
| • Collective initiative | • Individual initiative |
| • Humanistic work relationships | • Mechanistic work relationships |
| • Reliance on intuition | • Reliance on facts |
| • Circular reasoning | • Linear reasoning |
| • Spirit of the law | • Letter of the law |

**Table 1**  *High-context and Low-context Cultures*

# High-Context Cultures

High-context cultures are known for their more indirect communication style with a greater emphasis on nonverbal cues for a true grasp of any conversation or discourse. In these cultures, people are more sensitive to the body-language and intonation others use in their communication. In other words, they're good at reading the context of the situation and interpreting meaning from unspoken signals. This is not to say they don't hear your words; they simply look for non-verbal cues to assess what's behind your words.

High-context cultures have a collectivist mindset when it comes to both social and workplace behavior. They consider the group more essential than the individual. Therefore, they will often sacrifice their own recognition to work for the greater good. This is true in both family and work relationships. An interesting fact in a high-context work environment is that individuals are often treated with greater regard because of this group mindset. Companies will keep an employee longer due to their loyalty and will bring new employees on board if they have established a good relationship with (or are related to someone in) the company. Loyalty is a deep-seated value in high-context cultures (Hall & Hall, 1990).

The way different cultures reason and support ideas differs across both high-context and low-context cultures. However, in general, high-context cultures favor more of a reliance on intuition and principles than on hard facts and statistics when justifying a decision. Religious tenets, a predominant philosophy, or government mandates may all override scientific proof that doesn't serve higher purposes. Due to the implicit style of communication—implying meaning through reading contextual clues—it is rare for people in a high-context culture to come right out and say what they mean. In fact, when doing business in some of these cultures, don't expect a straight "yes" or "no" on an important choice. There may be considerations beyond the boardroom that are not easily recognized or presented. Thus, the answers you might get to a direct question may seem to "beat around the bush."

A final characteristic of high-context cultures is that of an adherence to laws "in spirit." For any organization or government to be viable, there must be regulations in place. However, these are subject to more practical or valuable concerns. In some high-context cultures, it is common to have an employee miss work because of a family celebration or milestone. This could be a birthday, an anniversary, or a sporting event; regardless, family takes precedence over work. In developing countries' cultures, laws may be disregarded if they seem impractical.

One example is India's traffic laws. While living and working in Bangalore, India in 2012, one of your authors was astonished by the traffic on major roads through the city. In one lane, you could have an automobile, a tuc-tuc (a small local taxi), half of a city bus, a motorcycle and a cow all trying to occupy the same space as they slowly moved to their destinations. When she asked her driver why people didn't use the lanes that were clearly marked on the streets (her own value system rearing its ugly head), the driver simply told her that the white lines are mere suggestions and that it would not be practical to drive single-file in a city so congested with vehicles. Other of your authors have experienced similar cultural attitudes toward traffic in Buenos Aires, Argentina. The photo below illustrates the situation.

This was a brief overview of high-context cultures. We will look at some specific countries in this group after we have discussed low-context cultures and their characteristics. In the meantime, you might try to identify the countries you think belong in each category.

## Low-Context Cultures

Low-context cultures are those with a distinctive direct style of communication. Verbal (and written) communication are absolutes in many ways. You may have heard someone say, "my word is my bond." In high-context cultures, we expect to believe what we hear and read, and this is never more evident than when

**Figure 1** *The rules of the road are less rigid in high context cultures!*

preparing business contracts. They need to hear "yes" or "no," get it in writing, and have a signature to seal the deal. This can cause a great deal of stress when working with people in a high-context culture.

In 2016, one of your authors traveled to Shanghai to teach a class for students and conduct training for faculty members at Shanghai University of Finance and Economics (SUFE). She had met with the director and a faculty member first in the U.S. where the collaboration had been set in motion. After they met a few times and established the scope of the project and dates involved, the SUFE representatives returned to China, and the U.S.-based instructor dutifully created a "contract" or Arrangement Letter. She sent it off, and it was received with an unspoken acceptance and an "oh, this is very comprehensive…"

As the instructor and SUFE representatives continued to communicate by email over the next few months, items were adjusted to include new arrangement and changing dates, all of which the instructor documented carefully and sent to SUFE in a new version of the Arrangement Letter. Once in Shanghai, she met with the administration and reviewed the letter page by page. The SUFE representatives agreed on every aspect, then concluded the meeting by saying, "This has been very successful. Shall we go to lunch?"

The instructor thoroughly enjoyed teaching the classes and meeting the faculty members of SUFE. They took excellent care of her, inspired her, and compensated her fairly; she couldn't have asked for more—except perhaps a signature on the contract! On the final day of her trip, as she arrived back to the SUFE offices, the SUFE director asked, "So, do you still need us to sign the contract?" The instructor simply smiled, and said, "No." She had come to understand a little more about the term Guanxi (the concept of networking to build trust before entering into a business relationship) when doing business in China.

Low-context cultures place emphasis on a strong individual initiative, and this is also evident in workplace decisions. Even from a young age, people are encouraged to "look out for themselves." Students compete in spelling bees and debates, which end with one winner. Of course, teams are a necessity in endeavors such as business and sports, but even then, individuals strive to stand out. When a college player is recruited by a national team, he or she is selected based on individual stats, not team stats. In company hiring and retention of employees, an individual is kept or terminated based on individual performance. The decision is more mechanistic than humanistic in that productivity takes precedence over loyalty (Hall and Hall, 1990).

In low-context cultures, policy making is (preferably) driven by proven facts and statistics. Research is key whether in academics, business, medicine, government, and so on. No matter how enticing a new idea might be, if it cannot be supported by credible research, it won't be taken seriously or find investors to take it very far.

In communicating ideas, people in low-context cultures follow a linear thought system. They will go from A to Z, tackling one item at a time. We will revisit this idea when comparing cultural thought patterns at the end of this section.

Finally, let's consider the attitude toward laws in low-context cultures. In these countries, the law is taken literally and is followed precisely. No matter who the person might be, poor, rich, powerful or weak, everyone is expected to play by the same rules. Even when it seems impractical, the law is enforced. When an international student (who was from a high-context culture) was asked what he had found strange about American culture, he said the traffic laws. He stated that he had been walking past a four-way stop intersection. He said that although there were no cars coming in any other direction, a man in a vehicle stopped at his designated stop sign before proceeding. Responding to quizzical looks of those listening to his response, the student asked, "Why did he stop?" The response he received: "Because it's the law." Yes, as you might have guessed, the United States is a low-context culture.

Have you thought about what other countries fit into either the high-context or low-context culture categories? Bear in mind that all countries basically fall into these two sets; however, where they fall on the continuum varies.

The image below shows where some major countries fall on this continuum. As you can see, the United States is not the most extreme low-context culture; Germany and Scandinavia reflect these characteristics even more. On the other end of the spectrum, many Asian countries represent the most extreme of the high-context cultures, although this varies across the many Asian countries. Whether you plan to travel to another country or are working with people from another country, knowing the context of that country will help you anticipate characteristics that might differ from your own. Then, you can practice flexing your own style to adapt. You'll be surprised how much you grow as you try to see things from different perspectives.

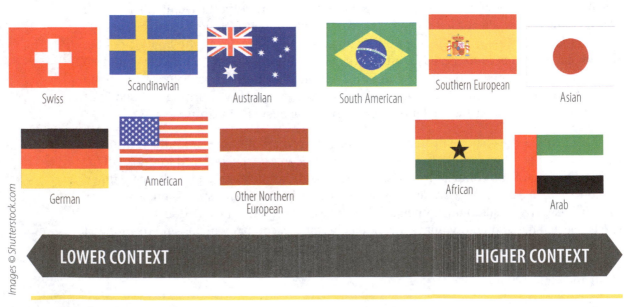

**Figure 2**   *Continuum of cultural contexts*

Now to return to the idea of thought patterns or reasoning. Robert Kaplan sketched an informative view of the various thought patterns incorporated around the world. Have you ever interacted with someone from another country, and thought to yourself, "that's just not logical?" Well here's an important reality check: **every country has its own logic!** In the image below, you'll see five such styles of logic.

Kaplan explains each of these styles in more detail in his 1966 article on Cultural Thought Patterns in Intercultural Education. As we have already discussed the most direct of these styles is in the English-speaking world. We are taught to stay on point, one point, and develop it fully. Then and only then, do we move on to the next point. Other language groups are not as linear in their discussions (or negotiations).

In the Semitic languages (Arabic and Hebrew), several points may be in play during any part of the discussion. The logic is that there are several aspects of any given topic that need to be considered along the way.

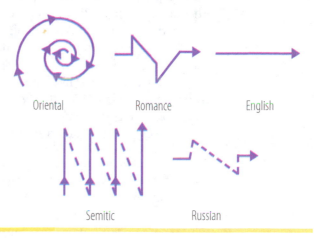

**Figure 3**  *Logic patterns of various language families*

The Asian (or Oriental, as it was called in the 1960s) language patterns follow a circular logic. Although they have a point, they will not come right out and tell you what it is. Instead, they will trust that their listener will pick up on any number of subtle nuances in their discourse and come to the same conclusion they have.

Romance languages, such as Italian or French, follow a logic that will eventually come to a point. Along the way, however, one can expect a number of digressions. These digressions may come in the form of an illustrative story or a fact that has some relevance (although, not always clear at first) to the point being made.

And, finally, the Russian language is much like that of the Romance language groups, but the logic appears more fragmented, and the digressions may be longer (Kaplan, 1966).

In every thought pattern, the logic of the discourse is clear to the speaker and to the listeners, as long as they are from the same group. Communicating across cultures, therefore, requires understanding and patience no matter where you may call home. Understanding the logic of discourse is the first step to successful communication across cultures.

# Understanding Intercultural Language Issues

Today, most international business is conducted in English; however, if you have ever spoken to someone from another part of the world in English, you have observed difference and developed strategies for ensuring proper understanding. When a language is adopted as a common language between speakers whose native languages are different, we call this the *Lingua Franca*. The parties in each of the two countries will likely have various levels of proficiency and speak with an accent that isn't familiar to the other. Even if English is the first language of a country, there may still be differences in vocabulary and level of formality from another English-speaking country. A few guidelines will, therefore, help you to prepare for better cross-cultural communication.

# Forms of Verbal Interaction

One of our favorite illustrations of differing forms of verbal interaction came from a student from Japan who was studying in the United States. She told us that she had observed a difference in the conversational style of people in the United States and people in Japan. She used an analogy to describe how she viewed a conversation between two Americans. She said that it was like they were playing table tennis (ping pong). When asked to elaborate, she stated that much like the ball in table tennis, the conversation between two people in the United States could never stop; it went back and forth, seemingly endlessly. When asked what a conversation in Japan was like, she both demonstrated and explained. After a 10-second pause, index finger on her chin and eyes averted, she said, "It is more like playing chess." What you might have considered uncertainty or shyness, or worse, an inability to understand and reason, is likely actually a cultural behavior based on the values of thoughtfulness and respect.

This difference, sometimes referred to as linear and non-linear language, can cause problems in intercultural communication. Imagine a multi-cultural team where both styles of conversation were "in play." What would the dynamic be? What would the different team members' perception of each other be? Who would have the most opportunity to speak, and who would be left out of contributing their ideas? It would be like trying to play ping pong with someone who thinks they're playing chess!

The advice that both groups would need to follow to make it work is to understand and adapt. Low-context cultures, with more of a direct communication approach and little tolerance for silence, would need to draw their teammates out by asking for their input and being patient. High-context cultures, characterized by people who are accustomed to deferring to others in a conversation or to taking time to think through their response before answering, would need to pick up the ping-pong paddles, and start "getting into the game."

Left: © sakkmesterke/Shutterstock.com;
Right: © View Apart/Shutterstock.com

**Figure 4**    *Don't play ping pong with someone who thinks they're playing chess!*

# Written Communication Insights

We discussed *Lingua Franca* earlier. Being aware of the variations of English spoken around the world, especially in business, is even more important in written communication. Remember, in spoken communication, you have the chance to read signals from your audience and reword a statement if you observe confusion. It is also possible to ask for clarification and receive it immediately. In writing, however, your recipient might muse over a line in your text and even look up specific terms but still have no guarantee he or she has grasped your intended meaning. Writing back and asking for clarification, even in an email, is awkward and can seem embarrassing, so the result will be a break in communication.

Guidelines for "internationalizing' the English language have been developed and adapted since the 1980s. Beginning with Riddle and Lanham (1984–1985) with their journal article entitled, "Internationalizing Written Business English: 20 Propositions for Native English Speakers," researchers have presented practical guidelines for effective written communication across cultures. In 2005, Weiss fine-tuned his colleagues' propositions in his book, *The Elements of International English Style*. The following guidelines are further adapted for our purposes and give you 10 tips that will improve your written communication with any English speaker and avoid confusion, regardless of his or her first language.

1. *Use only standard vocabulary (avoid words that are stylistic or jargon)*
2. *Select words with only one meaning (**point** = verb: to point your finger at someone, noun: the main idea or the sharp end of a pencil)*
3. *Avoid redundant and wordy expressions (honest in character -> honest)*
4. *Avoid two- or three-word verbs (take into account -> consider)*
5. *Be aware of alternative spellings (organisation = organization)*
6. *Avoid slang or idiomatic expressions ("a real zinger" or "step up to the plate")*
7. *Remember that numbers are sometimes punctuated differently (3,000 = 3.000)*
8. *Conform to rules of grammar (avoid run-on sentences or fragments)*
9. *Use more short, simple sentences (avoid compound-complex sentences with more than two clauses)*
10. *Use a more formal tone (most countries prefer this in business)*

The idea of tone is something we should consider for a moment. In many high-context cultures, it is seen as rude to begin a correspondence directly, as business people do in the United States. A "buffer" of sorts is expected whether the communication is presented directly or indirectly. For example, in Japan, a common way to begin a letter is to comment on the weather or seasonal changes. In most Islamic countries, a message starts and ends with "God willing" (Inshallah). Knowing and using these changes in tone will help you to make a better impression and to accept your foreign partner's style (Chaney & Martin, 2014).

# Non-Verbal Communication Issues

Since much of our communication comes through nonverbal channels, it is wise to consider how these differ from country to country. It is easy to make a mistake in another culture that could cost you a personal relationship or a business deal.

Perhaps you are already familiar with hearing what someone is saying, but receiving very different non-verbal signals. A person might say, for example, "I'm very glad to be here today." Then, you observed his somber facial expression and slumped posture and have trouble believing what you heard. You can refer back to Jaime's story from Chapter 2–1 for more examples of misalignment between verbal and non-verbal cues. This type of mismatch between verbal and nonverbal cues happens everywhere, but the extent is heightened when you are communicating across cultures.

While there are many aspects of nonverbal behavior that warrant our attention, we will be focusing on just three in this text: proxemics, oculesics, and kinesics.

## Proxemics

The study of proxemics deals with personal space. Various cultures tend to tolerate closer distances between them and someone else when they are speaking than others. Standing too close to someone in a culture that requires a larger personal space may give the impression a person is aggressive or rude. Conversely, standing too far away from someone in a culture accustomed to close proximity may give the impression a person is distant and cold. This varies in social and professional settings, of course, but there are still protocols that will help you adapt to any international setting. Let's look at a few examples.

In the United States, people are most comfortable standing approximately 18 inches apart when they are speaking. If someone invades that personal space, you might notice them backing up or crossing their arms in front of them as a "blockade" of sorts. Another aspect of proxemics is how we arrange seating for a discussion. In the United States, people prefer face-to-face conversations, and they feel most comfortable when there is a table between them and others.

In Latin American countries, personal space may seem non-existent, at least to someone from the United States. People in Mexico and South America may stand less than 12 inches with no sign of discomfort. In fact, touching someone's arm or shoulder during a discussion, professional or otherwise, is quite common. Most Latin Americans are familiar with the need for other cultures to have a greater distance between them, but it still feels awkward and aloof to them.

In Asian countries, the distance is even greater than in the United States except in certain situations. The Chinese are most comfortable at around 24–36 inches apart as they speak. This is similar in other Asian countries. In most cases, they are accustomed to holding discussions side-by-side, so a round table is preferred. An important exception to the proxemics rule in Asia is when using public transportation or standing in line for a public attraction. One of our South Korean students once showed the contrast between proxemics in the United States and her culture on public transportation. She showed two photos much like the ones below to demonstrate the difference. In South Korea, there is actually a job called "pushers" who pack the subway cars at tight as possible by pushing people in as the doors are closing. In the United States, people prefer some distance and may even place a backpack or purse on the seat between themselves and a stranger if space allows. One retired American businessman told us that he wasn't claustrophobic until he rode public transportation in Japan for the first time!

*Left: © EORoy/Shutterstock.com;*
*Right: © Tupungato/Shutterstock.com*

**Figure 5**   *Japanese vs. United States Public Transportation*

## Oculesics

The study of oculesics deals with eye contact and the various meanings that are conveyed through it. In many low-context cultures, such as Canada, Great Britain, and the United States, making eye contact with someone while you are speaking with them is a sign of respect and attentiveness. In fact, if someone does not make eye contact during a conversation, people in these countries might even question that person's trustworthiness.

There are two common expressions related to eye contact that you might be familiar with. You're your grandmother speaks to you and your eyes wander, she might emphatically say, "Look at me when I'm talking to you." You know she means business and probably immediately comply! If you don't believe something a younger sibling said to you growing up, you might have challenged him with, "Look me in the eye and say that." This was a sure-fire lie detector in many of our minds, and it usually works. While eye contact has a mostly positive connotation, prolonged and unbroken eye contact can create a feeling of uneasiness even in low-context cultures.

In many high-context cultures, eye contact may have very different connotations. People in China, Japan, or Indonesia are taught to lower their gaze to show respect. Looking into someone's eyes can convey disrespect and even aggression. In many African countries, people also will avert their eyes from someone with whom they are speaking as a sign of respect. However, in some Arabic speaking countries, eye contact can be prolonged and sometimes unsettling to someone from a different culture, even though no ill motive is intended. It is also important to consider variations in eye contact in some countries when speaking with women or even with someone in a different caste system.

## Kinesics

The study of Kinesics has to do with body movement and posture; for our purposes, we will discuss facial expressions and gestures in this section.

### Facial Expressions

People convey their emotions differently from country to country. Some of the most emphatic cultures are those connected with Romance languages. The Italian culture tops the list with their animated gestures and their vivid facial expressions. One never has to guess what an Italian person's feelings on a subject are; just watch and you'll know. A country much farther down on that list would be China. People rarely show their emotions through facial expressions; in fact, it can be seen as a weakness to display one's emotions openly. This is an area where people must have an understanding of the cultural norms and be willing to adapt if you want to be taken seriously.

### Gestures

We addressed the challenge of gestures when we talked about Nixon's embarrassing blunder in Brazil. However, knowing correct gestures for a particular country does more than just protect you from humiliation; it can also go far in uniting you with your cross-cultural business partners. Below are a few common gestures and their meanings in different countries. These will give you a good start on seeing the usefulness of knowing these gestures as you work with people from various cultures.

### The Chin Flick

In France, this gesture expresses disinterest or may even be used to tell someone to get lost. In Italy it is a bit stronger, expressing extreme disinterest.

### Nodding/Shaking the Head

In many countries, nodding the head means yes and shaking the head means no. However, in Greece it is just the opposite; the head nod means no and a head shake means yes.

### The OK Sign

We know that in Brazil this gesture is offensive; yet in the United States, it is a sign of agreement and approval. In Japan, it has yet another meaning; it is used to represent the idea of money.

### The Head Bobble

In India, there is a unique gesture, commonly called the head bobble. It is done by moving the head in a circular yet back and forth motion. We once asked a young man from India what this meant. He told us it could be used to express yes, or no, or uncertainty. When asked how you would know the difference, he said "Oh, you would know from the situation." We have since worked with hundreds of students from India and still cannot interpret the head bobble accurately.

Can you identify these other gestures? Do a little research and find out what they mean in other countries.

Images © Shutterstock.com

**Figure 6**  *Gestures*

As this unit wraps up, take a few moments to reflect on what you've learned. Yes, there are challenges and potential for miscommunication when dealing cross-culturally. However, there are also significant rewards. Learning about other cultures is not only very interesting, but it can also expand your horizons significantly. Increasing your intercultural competency will position you for success as you work on multi-cultural teams in your business school and also prepare you for even greater success as you explore your career options for the future.

# Unit 8 References

Burkitt, L. (2014). Best Buy to exit China, *The Wall Street Journal*. Retrieved from http://www.wsj.com/articles/best-buy-to-exit-china-1417678576

Chaney, L., & Martin, J. (2014). *Intercultural business communication*. Sixth edition. Pearson Education.

Ganster, S. (2005). *The China ready company: Using the China readiness assessment to prepare your company for China*. China Pathways LLC. Aurora, IL

Hall, E. T., & Hall, M. R. (1990). *Understanding cultural difference*. Yartmouth, ME: Intercultual Press.

Hodge, S. (2000). *Global smarts: The art of communication and deal making anywhere in the world*. New York: John Wiley & Sons.

Kaplan, R. (1966). *Cultural thought patterns in intercultural education*. Language Learning. University of Southern California.

Kinsey Goman, C. ( February 13, 2011) *Seven seconds to make a first impression*. Forbes.Com https://www.forbes.com/sites/carolkinseygoman/2011/02/13/seven-seconds-to-make-a-first-impression/2/#4462a8b04f08

Mansharamani, V. (August 27, 2015). *Three ways China's economic slowdown will affect your finances*. PBS News Hour. Retrieved from http://www.pbs.org/newshour/making-sense/3-ways-chinese-slowdown-will-impact/

Openness to and Restrictions on Foreign Investments (2016) Export.gov. International Trade Administration. U.S. Department of Commerce. Retrieved from https://www.export.gov

Riddle, D. I., & Landham, Z. D. ((1984-1985, Winter). *Internationalizing written business English: 20 propositions for native English speakers*. Journal of Language for International Business.

Weiss, E. H. (2005). *The elements of International English style*. Armonk, NY: M. E. Sharpe.

# UNIT 9:
## Mastering Virtual Communication

# Welcome to the Virtual World

**N**o matter where your career takes you, your ability to write, present, and collaborate through screens will set you apart as an effective communicator and valued teammate. In this unit, we will examine how written, verbal, and interpersonal communication present unique challenges in a virtual environment.

With advances in cloud services and video conferencing technologies, it's becoming more and more common for companies to be virtual, meaning the majority or entirety of their team telecommutes 100% of the time.

(Shin, 2016).

We will follow our protagonist, Betina May, through the onboarding phase of her internship at Sax Global, Inc., a multinational consulting firm, which will challenge her to build upon her existing communication skill set and manage her credibility in a fast-paced virtual team. Betina has been added to a Data Analytics team as part of her company's Leadership Development Program, or LDP. The LDP is where the company carefully evaluates high-potential recruits. These new recruits are encouraged to introduce themselves to their new peers through the LDP online message board, which connects the geographically dispersed interns. We meet Betina in the following post.

Post #1: Meet Betina

What challenges does Betina expect to face during her LDP rotation?

What does she hope to accomplish?

# What Is Virtual Communication?

Virtual communication means using technology to communicate across distances such as space, time, and organizational boundaries. While they may be located in the same office, virtual teams are just as likely to collaborate across the country or across the world, and they may rarely—if ever—meet face to face (Berry, 2011). By this definition, you have likely already participated in a virtual team through your team's use of technology to communicate. When you share space and work schedules with your co-workers, you generally communicate synchronously; conversely, most virtual communication is asynchronous because interaction is not necessarily immediate.

# Why Do Companies Use Virtual Teams?

Since the 1980s, companies have taken advantage of technology to communicate with employees who work remotely. While these remote workers, also called telecommuters, do not account for all virtual communication, their numbers are representative of overall trends. And their numbers are growing dramatically.

Experts project that within a few years, more than 1.3 billion people will work virtually.

(Johns & Gratton, 2013)

According to Gallup's annual Work and Education Poll, 37% of U.S. workers said they telecommuted in 2015, up from 30% the previous year. It is interesting to note that this is much more common among college graduates, 55% of whom have telecommuted.

What is driving this trend toward telecommuting? The answer, simply put, is that workers demand flexibility, and companies generally benefit from empowering employees to work remotely. Adam Kingl, director of learning solutions at the London Business School, argues that flexibility is the number one reason that Millennials are attracted to a workplace (Vanderkam, 2014).

These trends are not new, however, and Millennials are not the first generation to crave flexibility. In fact, Tammy Johns and Lynda Gratton have identified three main waves in the evolution of work models, beginning in the early 1980s with the advent of email (Johns & Gratton, 2013). The following table summarizes their research and highlights some of the pros and cons of virtual work, both for employees and employers.

| WAVE ONE: VIRTUAL FREELANCERS | Untethered work on a large scale began in the early 1980s when a "freelance nation" of virtual workers using nascent email networks emerged. It enabled marginalized talent—stay-at-home parents, caregivers, retirees, students—to enter the labor market. |
|---|---|
| WAVE TWO: VIRTUAL CORPORATE COLLEAGUES | Despite its benefits, the first wave required compromises. For workers, the big concession was that in embracing the freedom of contributing remotely, they had to give up formal connection to a company and all that went with it—from health and retirement benefits to leadership development and career progression to equipment and tech support. |
| WAVE THREE: VIRTUAL CO-WORKERS | As the second wave gained momentum, organizations began to realize that virtualization was compromising some traditional workplace benefits they had taken for granted. Hoping for teamwork, they realized that too much division and distribution of labor meant less natural collaboration. Workers shared these concerns.<br><br>Somewhat paradoxically, then, a new wave of complex, global virtualized work has surged, as many workers physically reunite and re-tether to specific spaces. A major focus of the third wave's new technology is to give workers the feeling of being in a shared environment. |

Table 1    *Adapted from Johns & Gratton, 2013*

In this third wave of virtual work, it would appear that virtual communication has come full circle. Co-working spaces, where professionals can have a sense of being in a shared environment, do much to address one of the major disadvantages of remote work: isolation.

But what if you don't telecommute? What if, like most professionals, you find yourself in a more traditional office environment? Sara Sutton Fell, CEO of FlexJobs, explains it this way:

> In most white-collar jobs, I'd say 99% of people are already working remotely in that they take work home. It creeps into our work style already. I think it's just not formalized by either the employer or employee. If remote work means that you check email on Sunday night then congratulations! You already have a work-from-home job. (Vanderkam, 2014).

Whether you telecommute or work in a corporate office, you need to be prepared to communicate virtually. The good news is you have probably already begun to develop your skills in this area. The rest of this unit will help you develop these skills more deliberately, so you can be the catalyst your team needs to succeed.

# How Are Communication and Collaboration Different in a Virtual Environment?

In Unit 2 of this book, you learned that teamwork presents some of the biggest challenges you will face in your professional career. It also provides some of the greatest rewards. You have probably grappled with many of these challenges already.

At their best, teams are synergistic and collaborative, producing work that surpasses the abilities of individuals working independently. At their worst, teams are dysfunctional and limiting, and they can produce work that falls short of expectations while causing considerable stress for all involved. This is because teams have a way of amplifying both the strengths and weaknesses of their members. Strengths, if not properly harnessed, can become weaknesses. As a professional, your challenge is to harness your team's strengths and be a catalyst for positive collaboration.

Never has there been a greater need for this type of catalyst. We live in a time when the nature of teamwork is changing rapidly. Although teams are a ubiquitous part of how work gets done in almost every organization (Berry, 2011), the definition of a team as a co-located, synchronous entity is evolving. Some teams do share office space and meet face to face, but you are entering a world in which more and more teams do most of their work—and their communication—virtually.

To succeed in this environment, you will need a fully-fledged set of skills to communicate and collaborate with colleagues at a distance. The first step in developing your virtual communication skill set is to recognize the differences between teamwork across two major dimensions—distance and time. The graphic below illustrates the major differences between traditional teams, which tend to work in co-located, synchronous environments, and virtual teams, which must adapt to dispersed, asynchronous environments.

We use the word "More" below to underscore the fact that "Traditional" and "Virtual" are points along a spectrum—they are not discrete categories. The more traditional your team is, the more you can rely on workplace encounters such as face-to-face meetings, ad-hoc work sessions, serendipitous "water cooler" conversations, and phone calls. Your team can connect and get on the same page rapidly, which allows you to respond to change and navigate ambiguity fairly quickly.

**MORE TRADITIONAL**

**Co-located teams** share an office or work space. These teams meet face to face and benefits from serendipitous collaboration.

**Synchronous teams** communicate and work on projects in real time and are usually in the same time zone. Team members reply to one another's emails, messages, or phone calls immediately.

**MORE VIRTUAL**

**Dispersed (also called "remote" or "virtual") teams** do not share the same office space. One or more members are located in different offices or work spaces. These offices can be in the same city, but they are often located in different cities, states, or countries.

**Asynchronous teams** do not communicate in real time and are usually in different time zones. Teammates rely on written messages, such as emails, and usually reply within one business day.

*Image © Sauers, et al. 2017*

**Figure 1**  *Traditional vs. Virtual Teams.*

But as researchers and practitioners like Johns, Gratton, and Fell have observed, 100% co-located, 100% synchronous teams are far from the norm and haven't been for decades. Most teams incorporate elements of remote work and must, therefore, learn to communicate and collaborate virtually.

One of your authors once supervised a team of employees who were dispersed between seven different locations within the same city. At one point during his tenure with this company, he gave up his own office space and became a remote worker, both commuting between these seven locations and regularly telecommuting from home and coffee shops around town. He had to develop a culture of accountability among his staff while also exercising great discipline to be able to effectively manage and support each team member. Besides regular use of telephone and email conversations, his team adopted new-to-them technology platforms that provided other options for more information-rich synchronous communication.

**Figure 2** *Remote collaboration tools are abundant and many are free*

Think for a moment about your own experience on teams. Chances are you have already experienced what it is like to work in a virtual environment. Consider, for example, the tools you use to collaborate with your teammates on a regular basis. How many of the following have you used in your career?

These are some of the most popular online collaboration tools used to communicate, share files, and receive immediate updates from their teammates (Chadha, 2015). These tools share several characteristics that promote widespread adoption:

- **Free, low cost, or already included** in the suite of tools provided by organizations
- **Ubiquitous**, so most individuals have experience with them before joining work teams
- **Easy to use and reliable**, requiring little to no troubleshooting and virtually no downtime
- **Cloud based and platform agnostic**, providing ample storage and similar usability for all users regardless of whether they use Apple, Google, or Microsoft devices.

Of course, there is usually a learning curve when a company or its employees adopts new technology. Team members come to the workplace with a diversity of experiences and comfort with various technologies, and some will adopt and learn those technologies faster than others. Let's check in on Betina's latest discussion board post to see how she is adapting to SGI's use of collaborative technology.

Post #2: So Many Screens, So Little Time

How are communication and collaboration different in Betina's new work environment?

How has she responded to the demands of working at SGI?

Dear SGI Intern Community:

During my first few days on the job, I have focused on getting up to speed with the technological platforms we use at SGI. I still haven't met anyone on my team in person, but I have made sure to study the technology involved in and the expectations for the software my team will be using. Some of the tools didn't work right off the bat, so I submitted support requests with IT to make sure I had the right tools to succeed.

I'm curious—how has technology helped or hindered your onboarding process? None of us wants to be the person who balks at learning a new software, isn't fluid in joining in online chats or face-to-face conferences, or doesn't understand the best practices their virtual team is already using to get the job done. First impressions count, and we will be rewarded if we demonstrate agility and learn new programs quickly.

While I think that I have a handle on this new technology, I'm not so ready for my next challenge —learning how to write for my team on screens. You may be surprised that someone would admit to this, so let me explain.

At my previous organization, I worked in a small enterprise that required me to work closely with my manager. Every single document I generated was read closely and proofread by my boss, then went through an editing review before it was released to either internal or external stakeholders. We had specific formats for reports, email exchanges, even regular team updates at traditional meetings. This isn't the way things work at SGI.

Over the past several days, I have been surprised at how quickly my team moves. Since we use a tool that allows everyone to view and edit documents at the same time, my teammates jump on my document and begin editing while I am still working on it. Things get really crazy at deadline time: my phone buzzes nonstop as messages fly around between team members, and the IM chat window on my laptop pings constantly. Sometimes I feel like I can't focus on the document itself because I'm constantly responding to messages!

I'll admit to being overwhelmed at times, and even paralyzed by inaction worrying how my work will be perceived in different formats and by varying audience members. This is problematic because I know how I will be perceived if I don't participate in the process.

So, LDP community, I'm open to suggestions. What are you doing to manage your workflow and build credibility through all of these screens, when you're more than once removed from your audience?

Best regards,
Betina.

===
Betina May
LDP Intern, Sax Global Inc.

Betina's confession has profound implications. Her biggest hurdle is moving from a traditional to a virtual workplace. She cannot rely on a face-to-face meeting, ad hoc work session, or to catch up to a flustered co-worker in the break room. She had to figure out how to connect with her team in writing, through a screen.

You may find your experience mirrors Betina's when you work virtually. Whether it takes up your desk, rests on your lap, or fits in your pocket, your screen is your lifeline to your team. Even if you share an office with your teammates, your virtual persona and screen presence—the value of what you type or say through a screen—will make a lasting impression and will likely determine your career progression. This is true whether you know the audience with whom you're virtually communicating or if they're "meeting" you for the first time through your online presence.

As with many virtual teams, getting a handle on how to best meet your team's needs means starting at the beginning with the basics on how to write on screens and meet so many conflicting expectations. In the rest of this unit, we will examine what this means and how you can thrive in this environment. We will begin by examining the concept of virtual distance, and how virtual distance poses challenges for teams. Then, we will dive into the three fundamental types of communication—written, verbal, and interpersonal—to help you prepare for the challenges of writing, presenting, and collaborating through screens.

# The Difference Is Distance

As you have already learned, most of the information we send in a given message is nonverbal. We convey nonverbal information through cues like body language, tone, and context. This is a function of how human beings evolved to communicate—in relatively small, co-located, familiar groups that shared a common context—and it is an essential part of the message. Without it, the recipient may misunderstand the true meaning of the message. This can, of course, vary from culture to culture; as you learned in Unit 4, different cultures rely to different degrees on context to communicate.

Regardless of their native cultures, however, both the sender and recipient must share a common understanding of what each facial expression, hand gesture, or vocal inflection means in order for the nonverbal cues to be effective. The less of this context they share, the more difficult it is to communicate effectively. Think of the last time you tried to share an inside joke with someone outside your circle of friends. A shared joke between friends often falls flat outside of that circle—a certain vocal inflection, facial expression, or cultural reference may be the key to "getting" the joke. We often give up, saying, "You had to be there."

This same rule applies to the workplace. Individuals with similar backgrounds working on co-located teams usually find it easier to communicate than individuals with different backgrounds working on dispersed teams. And the more physically dispersed the team is, the harder it is to communicate.

Ironically, the tools we have created to bridge the physical distance between people can, on their own, create a special type of distance called "virtual distance." These tools are imperfect substitutes for face-to-face communication, and they can leave individuals feeling isolated. They also have a tendency to magnify, or at least draw attention to, the differences between people. Let's examine the isolation problem by looking at the factors that create virtual distance on teams.

# Understanding Virtual Distance

In 2004, Dr. Karen Sobel Lojeski founded a consulting practice to help companies tackle what she referred to as virtual distance, which can be defined as the perceived distance created by too much interaction with technology like email, text messaging, instant messaging, and other electronic channels. The more time we spend communicating through a screen, the more distant we tend to feel from our colleagues. This perceived distance can undermine trust, lead to feelings of isolation, and may stress the fabric that binds teams.

Betina's internship at SGI's Leadership Development Program illustrates the types of distance inherent on virtual teams. As we revisit her in the next post, Betina has just returned from a national leadership conference for LDP interns. This experience was a bit intimidating since so many of the other LDP interns were exceptional, and she got a very real sense of the level of competition between her peers. In addition to her primary work team, Betina is also on four other work teams, and only one of them is made up of solely other interns. She is co-located with only one of the 27 team members represented on all of her work teams. Her immediate supervisor is in another city but in the same time zone.

Post #3: Betina Meets Her Team

Dear SGI Intern Community:

It was great to meet so many of you at SGI's national leadership conference in Boston last week. I came away from the conference with a deeper understanding of the many challenges we face as new interns here at this company, and a renewed commitment to use this discussion board as a platform to connect with and learn from all of you.

Someone had a great idea during one of our breakout sessions in Boston: Since we are all on dispersed teams, why don't we each post a description of the core members of our primary team and how we communicate with them? Doing so might help us see how our teams are connected, and how they are similar or different. This should also yield insight into the common challenges we face as interns so we can collaborate to overcome them. So here goes—here's my team:

**Madeline Lee** is my immediate supervisor. Madeline keeps a wide variety of team projects functioning, while she also provides guidance for me. One thing I really admire about Madeline is her boundaries. She has made it clear as a new working mom she values her work life balance. She really only expects to have a weekly update from me and her other interns, which we file via email. She lives in San Francisco, but makes it to my office in Houston about once every six weeks. Madeline is a rising star in the company, and while she is committed to my success, it takes place along with everything else. Our relationship is limited to weekly email reports, phone calls, and a face-to-face meeting every month or two.

**Jackson Benioff** is the lead for my most important work team in Data Analytics. He is co-located in the same Houston office, but he is a manager for a division. Jackson is on a different floor and is on the road traveling a lot of the time, so it can take time to get on his calendar. Jackson is a results-oriented manager, so he prefers to track my contributions through my work team's results. He took me out to lunch on my first day and made some introductions. Other than that, the only feedback or input I have received from Jackson has been through overall team reports and feedback collected from conference calls or submitted in writing. Things seem to be going well for the team, but as an intern, I am aware that I may be protected from what real perceptions of team results are. So far, our team is on track for our assigned project.

I'm sure most of you know **Rishab Chaudhary**, the regional coordinator for the LDP program. He works out of our Boston headquarters. He is an important stakeholder for all of us, since all offers and training opportunities pass through his office. Rishab takes pride in grooming the talent pipeline, and the LDP program is his brainchild. While he is a very busy executive in the HR Department, he takes the time to check in with his interns on regional conference calls, Skype sessions, and tries to periodically create connections within organizations and with other interns. I had the chance to meet with him and attend a focus group on the LDP program last week in Boston, but other than that, I have only attended a few Skype calls and some webinars to give Rishab updates on my experience and the projects I am working on. These meetings were always attended with at least five other LDP interns.

What types of virtual distance exist on Betina's team?

How can she bridge the gaps, and communicate effectively with each of her colleagues?

## Physical Distance

The first type of distance is easy to understand. Geographic distance, temporal distance, and organizational distance contribute to the physical distance that a team must bridge. If you work in a different building, city, state, or country than the rest of your team—or even on a different floor in the same building—you may experience a sense of isolation from your teammates. This can be compounded if you work in different time zones or have different work schedules (temporal distance), and compounded even further if you work in different departments or report to different managers (organizational distance).

> Physical distance makes it difficult for teammates to be in the same place at the same time. This poses challenges to scheduling meetings and collaborating in real time.

The *geographic distance* alone limits a team's ability to call an impromptu meeting or work on projects or rehearse presentations.

How about *temporal distance*? Team members may all live in different time zones, with very different work schedules. Even if the entire team work in the same time zone, they may still have different work schedules depending on their needs and the employer's flexibility. Competing workplace commitments, varying work schedules, and conflicting responsibilities also make regular meetings difficult to schedule.

The third type of physical distance, *organizational distance*, arises when teammates have different organizational affiliations. Most professionals today work on cross-functional teams and often serve on several project teams with colleagues in other business units, departments, or organizations. Each team, business unit, department, and organization has its own workflow, schedule, and deadlines, not to mention context and work culture, which can place competing demands on busy professionals.

We most often think of virtual collaboration in terms of physical distance, but Dr. Sobel Lojeski points to two other important types—operational and affinity distance—which, combined with physical distance, contribute to the overall sense of isolation you may experience in the workplace. Let's examine operational distance next.

# Operational Distance

Operational distance refers to all of the technical or habitual issues that can get in the way of effective communication and collaboration on the team. The mix of channels we use to communicate, the number of other projects we are working on at the same time, and any technical malfunctions that occur with our collaboration tools are three of the most common types of operational distance.

Think back to the tools we discussed earlier, such as the Google productivity suite, email, and GroupMe, which many individuals use to collaborate with teammates. These channels empower users like never before, enabling teams to communicate via text, voice, and video, and collaborate on projects in real time.

With so many channels at their disposal, though, it can often be difficult for teams to know which one is the most appropriate for a given task. On your team, for example, you may open a Google document and begin brainstorming a project via a face-to-face conversation during a meeting, and then switch to GroupMe when the meeting is adjourned. Your GroupMe conversation will probably evolve in fits and starts as you and your teammates chime in at different times; not everyone is willing or able to participate in a meaningful text conversation while they're tending to other responsibilities at work or at home.

If you have ever checked your text messages or a shared Google document after a few hours of downtime, you know how frustrating it can be to try to catch up, especially when the conversation has evolved beyond a certain point. If your teammates made decisions regarding the project while you were offline, you may feel uneasy about inserting yourself back into the conversation and recommending a different approach. Conversely, if you have spent several hours chatting with a subset of your team via GroupMe and working on a shared Google document, you may find it frustrating to loop an absent teammate back into the conversation.

> Operational distance makes it difficult for teammates to use communication channels consistently and effectively. Day-to-day collaboration can become a real challenge, as teammates are often not on the same page.

Whether you are the absent teammate or trying to loop that person back in, you are out of sync with your teammates and are probably experiencing a sense of isolation. This is due to the *communication distance* that results from the variety of channels we use to communicate with a dispersed team. The more channels we use, the more likely it is that the shared context we rely on to make decisions is spread unevenly across multiple channels. In other words, each person can be on a different page depending on when they were available to join the conversation and which channels they used to communicate. Add technical glitches and multitasking into the mix, and you have a recipe for operational distance on your team.

Operational distance compounds the virtual distance you may already experience due to the physical distance—the geographic, temporal, or organizational factors—we discussed earlier. Physical and operational distance can present significant challenges to virtual teams, even if those teams see each other face to face regularly and only have a few members. Even so, teams can overcome these challenges once they become aware of them, have identified the root causes, and are motivated to do so.

This last component of successful teams—motivation—is absolutely critical to bridging the types of distance we have discussed. The third and final category of distance, though, undermines that motivation and can render a team incapable of overcoming physical or operational challenges. This pernicious category is called Affinity Distance.

# Affinity Distance

Affinity distance refers to the depth of the relationships between members of a team, or the affinity they have for one another. If affinity distance is high, teammates do not feel emotionally connected to one another, which can make it very difficult to motivate them to work harder, adjust their behavior, or adopt new practices for the benefit of the team. Affinity distance can arise from cultural, social, relationship, and interdependence distance.

The first source of affinity distance is *cultural distance*, which occurs when people do not share the same values or communication styles. We often see cultural distance arise between people who hail from different countries, especially if one person was raised in a high-context culture and the other is from a low-context culture. Cultural distance may arise if one of your teammates is from another country, but beware of limiting yourself to an oversimplified definition of culture. Refer back to Unit 4 for more tips on managing cultural distance.

> Affinity distance refers to the depth of the relationships between members of a team. If affinity distance is high, teammates do not feel emotionally connected to one another. This undermines their willingness to work harder, adjust certain behaviors, or adopt new practices to benefit the team.

Culture is a complicated concept, encompassing all of the knowledge, beliefs, morals, laws, customs, and any other habits that people have as members of a particular group or society. While you could observe cultural distance between members of your team who come from different countries, you may also see it arise between people who come from different parts of the country or socioeconomic backgrounds, practice different religions, or have distinct ideas of what "hard work," "respect," "compromise," or "teamwork" mean.

The second source of affinity distance is *social distance*, which occurs when there are differences in social status that cause people to feel as though there's a gap between them and others on the team. These differences can be based on formal or informal social status. Teams will occasionally develop social distance when some members form tight bonds with each other and, as a result, are perceived to exclude other team members in social activities or frequency of communication.

The third cause of affinity distance, *relationship distance*, is particularly common among incoming students who are new to a particular institution, professionals who have recently been hired on to a company, or professionals who are brought in from other departments to serve on cross functional teams. If you have ever been the new person on a team, you know what this feels like. Relationship distance exists when teammates do not have a preexisting relationship, meaning they have never worked together before or do not know any of the same people.

This type of distance can be resolved through a deliberate orientation process, but there usually is not much time for orientations, especially on teams that have been assembled rapidly to manage time-sensitive projects. Often, we take for granted that everyone is as comfortable as we are on a team, leaving some members feeling disconnected or isolated.

Teams that have been assembled to deal with time-sensitive projects or projects that have predetermined end dates are also particularly vulnerable to the fourth and final cause of affinity distance. *Interdependence distance* arises if individuals do not feel as though their futures are connected, or their success is dependent on their teammates.

Going back to Betina's team, we can see many possible examples of potential for all these types of distance to surface. In all likelihood, Betina is experiencing some sense of isolation, yet realizes she must bridge the divide and start to find ways to add value and connect with her team if she is going to succeed. She can choose to "tough it out" and just concentrate on her work, but she puts herself at risk. While she needs to get results to report out on, she needs to think about ways to lessen the gap. If she persists in feeling isolated and not "connected" she is jeopardizing her own team's ability to succeed, as well as her mobility within an interconnected fast-moving work culture.

Virtual distance exists on all teams. If it is too high, it breeds isolation, undermines trust, and stresses the fabric that binds teams. Properly managed, however, teams can form even stronger relationships as they identify the root cause of the distance and work to close the gaps. Virtual environments create opportunities for professionals who can navigate distance. These individuals are adept at minimizing distance, building trust and creating communities by engaging in meaningful communication with colleagues and teammates.

# Writing for Screens

In the previous chapter, we asserted that the major difference between traditional and virtual communication is the extent to which that communication happens on a screen. Whereas traditional teams can take advantage of face-to-face meetings, ad-hoc work sessions, and serendipitous "water cooler" conversations, virtual teams must rely on more deliberate communication through technology.

More often than not, this means communicating in writing. In fact, writing is so important to companies that rely on virtual teams that many of them make hiring decisions based on a candidate's writing skills. Take Basecamp, for example:

> *If you are trying to decide between a few people to fill your position, always hire the better writer. Assuming your candidates are fairly equally skilled and qualified overall, always hire the better writer (Ciotti, 2016).*

We have structured this chapter to build on what Betina has learned so far at SGI. Betina's tips reflect much of the current thinking about written communication for virtual teams. In her latest post, Betina offers her fellow interns her discoveries about what it takes to communicate effectively in writing for screens.

Dear SGI Intern Community:

Does anyone else feel like they are drinking from a firehose? I thought I had a good handle on business writing, but this internship has caused me to question some assumptions about how my writing affects my professional persona here at SGI.

At the risk of sounding naïve, I thought I'd share some of my recent "ah ha" moments. I certainly wish someone had pulled me aside and given me some of these tips earlier. Here goes:

1. I didn't realize how important emails were, or how many I would need to write.
2. My teammates had an impression of me before they ever saw my face. My writing became my avatar.
3. My emails weren't getting read, even though I had filled them with so much important information!
4. I didn't know how to ask for clarification without sounding stupid.
5. Wait, other people are reading my emails?
6. Sometimes you just need to pick up the phone.
7. Most of my emails were being read on the fly (on small screens).

Has anybody else discovered any of these challenges? How have you dealt with them?

Best regards,
Betina.

===

Betina May
LDP Intern, Sax Global Inc.

> "I didn't realize how important emails were, or how many I would need to write."
>
> "My writing became my avatar."

# Email Isn't Going Away. Get Good At It.

In 2016, business professionals worldwide sent and received more than 116 billion emails, which amounted to roughly 55% of total email traffic. This number is about 3% higher than the 112 billion they sent and received in 2015, but less than the 120 billion we are projected to see in 2017.

Let's think about this number for a moment: *One hundred and sixteen billion business emails*. According to the Radicati Group, a market research firm based in Silicon Valley, this works out to about 123 emails per person per day—90 emails received, 33 emails sent. While many emails only take a minute or two to read and answer, the average U.S. worker spends about 6.3 hours per day checking email, 3.2 hours of which is devoted solely to work emails and 3.1 hours to personal messages.

> Get settled in, because email isn't going away anytime soon. Many top professionals won't even check their office voicemail messages anymore, as they expect important requests and announcements to come to them in the form of an easily archivable and retrievable digital message.
>
> (Asghar, 2014)

Even with the rise of other forms of written communication such as texting, instant messaging, and posts on social media, email usage is projected to increase steadily into the foreseeable future. This is especially true for virtual teams, who rely on email for the vast majority of their communication. With so much time spent on email, it's a skill worth mastering.

# You Are What You Write. Be Clear, Concise, and Compelling.

In a virtual environment, your writing is your avatar. Your virtual teammates will read something you've written before they see your face or hear your voice (if they ever do). On some teams, your emails and IMs may be the only part of you that your teammates ever see.

For these reasons, it is critical to demonstrate audience awareness and establish relevance as quickly as possible. Your writing will create a portrait of you in your audience's mind. What does your writing say about you? Hopefully, it says that you understand your audience, respect their time, and have something valuable to say.

# Say What Needs to Be Said, but No More (TL;DR).

To ensure your writing makes the right impression, keep it as short as possible and put the most important information up front. Demonstrate audience awareness by putting your bottom line on top (BLOT), removing extraneous information, and eliminating unnecessary commentary. Show respect by saving your audience time; edit your email and focus on the information your audience needs to move forward.

In internet slang, "TL;DR" stands for "Too Long; Didn't Read." Keep in mind that most busy professionals don't read every word of an email, and nothing is worse than opening a message and seeing a wall of text.

Sites such as three.sentenc.es have arisen in protest to lengthy, rambling emails. While the three sentences rule may sound extreme, you may want to give it a try. If you need more (or less) of a challenge, there is also two.sentenc.es (or four, or five.)

# Use Language That Everyone On Your Team Understands.

By their nature, virtual teams are usually cross-functional, meaning they comprise people from different departments, business units, or locations within an organization. It is tempting to assume that everyone who works for a company speaks the same language and shares a common vocabulary, but this is often not the case. According to authors Chip and Dan Heath, the Curse of Knowledge refers to the phenomenon of the communicator automatically assuming her audience has the same content knowledge that she does. It is all too easy to fall victim to this curse!

The reality is that professionals on dispersed teams spend most of their time in separate contexts, coalescing briefly around a particular project before moving on to other tasks. They may use different language—or jargon—for each context. Differences often include the following:

- Acronyms or other shorthand
- Unit or department-specific jargon
- Technical terms
- Names of relevant third parties

Communicating in a virtual environment, particularly when that communication is in writing, demands that we question our assumption that the entire team is fluent in the same jargon.

Why is writing different? In a face-to-face meeting, it is easy to ask for and receive clarification of an unfamiliar term. You can ask the speaker to pause and clarify, or turn to the person sitting next to you for clarification. If you are the speaker, it is also easy to check if your teammates understand you. A verbal check or quick look around the table will tell you if your audience is on the same page.

In writing, however, the game is different. Neither the sender nor the receiver has the benefit of nonverbal cues to alert them to miscommunication. The sender cannot look around the table or do a quick verbal check, and will plow forward unless someone asks for clarification. The request for clarification may not come. In a virtual environment that relies mostly on email, receivers must ask for clarification in writing. Therein lies the rub.

As human beings, we are loath to admit ignorance, especially in situations where we do not know our counterparts very well, such as virtual teams. We are especially hesitant to broadcast our ignorance in writing. Admitting ignorance risks damaging the credibility we work so hard to build. Doing it verbally during a meeting requires a sense of psychological safety and trust in your teammates, both of which can be in short supply on a virtual team. Writing the words "I don't understand what you mean by X. Would you please clarify?" can be very difficult if we are trying to impress an audience we don't know very well.

It may sound silly, but think about it. When was the last time you asked for clarification in writing, other than emailing your professor or TA? Are you more likely to ask a friend, someone you know and trust? If you are like most people, the answer is yes.

So how can we tackle this problem? The best time to build a common lexicon is early in your team's collaborative process when the team is still in its learning phase. If you initiate an email conversation, check the content of your email before you send it. Consider your audience—are you using any acronyms, unit-specific jargon, or technical terms that others might not understand? Are you referring to anybody who is not on the team, perhaps an office mate, co-worker, higher-level manager, or client? If so, there is a good chance that not everyone on your virtual team will be familiar with those terms or know that person. Remember that dispersed teammates spend most of their time in contexts separate from yours.

If you are unsure about the content of your email, you may want to define key terms or briefly describe people the first time you mention them. Consider this example:

> Option A: "We need a SOCO before we take this to Kim."

> Option B: "We need a clear Single Overriding Communication Objective (SOCO) before we meet with Kim Overton, our client's Media Relations Manager, at next week's client meeting. She will want to approve it before we proceed with the full ad campaign."

In Option A, you are making the assumption that everyone on the team is familiar with the term SOCO, knows who Kim is, and understands why you need her approval on this project. The term "SOCO" means very different things depending on the context in which it is used. Is it an oil and gas exploration company? A spider? A crime scene? An American liqueur? Go ahead, Google it. A teammate may be too embarrassed to ask what SOCO means. And who wants to write, "Who is Kim?" when they reply to your message?

In Option B, you eliminate any confusion surrounding the term SOCO. Anyone who is still unfamiliar with the term can research it to learn more. By introducing Kim, you ensure that everyone on your team understands that she is a key stakeholder in this project and that you need her approval before you proceed. You have anchored your team on key terms, shored up its common vocabulary, and clarified workflow all by considering your audience before you hit "send." While this added context makes your message longer, the added benefit of eliminating ambiguity far outweighs the few extra seconds it will take your team to read the message.

# Beware of Unintended Audiences. You Don't Want Your Message to Go Viral.

This tip is pretty straightforward. Don't put anything in writing that you wouldn't want your audience to forward. People forward messages all the time, and you don't want something you crafted in haste to be the next trending topic of conversation. If you are not sure whether to include something in a message, don't write it. Think it over and send a follow-up message if it is really important. The fact is, you never know where your messages will be forwarded or who will end up seeing them; better safe than sorry.

# Don't Hide Behind Your Email. Know When *Not* to Write.

Written communication channels, such as email, have their limits. As you rise through the ranks of your organization and take on more responsibility, you will need to respect the limits of each channel and use them appropriately. Knowing when to write and when to make a phone call or meet face to face will make you a more effective manager and bolster your credibility.

The key to determining whether written communication is appropriate is to understand the concept of media richness. Media Richness Theory, or MRT, was originally proposed by Richard Daft and Robert Lengel in 1986. Daft and Lengel ranked a variety of communication media by how reliably each medium reproduced the information sent over it. The resulting spectrum, which ranges from leaner media to richer media, is a useful way to think about the appropriate use for each medium. The diagram below illustrates this spectrum.

**Figure 1** *Illustration of Media Richness Theory*

In order for a medium to be considered "rich," it must accurately transmit most, if not all, of the information that the sender wants to transmit. Remember that the vast majority of information we send in any given message is nonverbal. Human beings are wired to communicate using a full range of subtle verbal and nonverbal cues.

Face-to-face communication, which captures vocal and visual cues, allows for all of these cues to transmit from the sender to the receiver. As we move away from face-to-face communication into video conferencing, we start to lose visual and audio quality. We also may lose other nonverbal cues that are present in face-to-face communication. For example, if the other person is nervous and starts to sweat subtly, we might pick up on the olfactory cue in a face-to-face conversation. Unpleasant, perhaps, but undeniably useful information that doesn't come through in a video conference. By the time we get to telephone calls, we have lost all but auditory cues, which is difficult when we do not know the other party well enough to tell when they are serious, joking, or being sarcastic. Job candidates, for example, often dread phone interviews because they find it difficult to judge how well they performed during the interview.

Strip away visuals and vocalics, and we are left with the written word, whose effectiveness depends on the skill of the writer. While it goes without saying that the written word can be immensely powerful on its own, it takes on a whole new life when it is read aloud or performed, as it is during book readings, poetry readings, and stage performances. Unfortunately, we rarely have cause to create artful messages in the workplace; our purpose is usually more transactional than inspirational.

> The harder the conversation you expect, the richer the required medium. If you find yourself needing to have a hard conversation with one of your colleagues, you will be more effective—and stand a better chance of earning their respect—if you use the richest medium available.

This brings us back to the purpose of this section of the chapter, which is to encourage you to choose the medium for your message carefully. Hard conversations are part of daily life as a business professional. The harder the conversation you expect, the richer the required medium. If you find yourself needing to have a hard conversation with one of your colleagues, you will be more effective—and stand a better chance of earning their respect—if you use the richest medium available in that situation. While a face-to-face meeting may not be possible in a virtual environment, get as close as you can. If you send a text message or email when the conversation warrants a phone call or meeting, your audience will interpret that as a form of hiding.

# When in Doubt, Write for Small Screens.

This tip is a tough one, but it is worth the effort to find out how, when, and on what device your audience reads their messages. When in doubt, craft your messages for small screens.

While many professionals still do most of their writing on a computer, more and more of us are moving to smaller screens, such as smart phones and tablets, that allow greater flexibility in time and place for consuming emails and IMs. Unless you know that your audience is likely to read your email on a large computer screen during office hours, you may assume that he or she checks email on a phone or tablet. If this is the case, you will need to adjust your writing strategy accordingly.

The illustration on the following page shows the amount of content that will fit on two different screens. The screen on the left is an email application window on a 13-inch laptop screen. The screen holds about 214 words before the user needs to scroll down. The screen on the right shows that same email on a smart phone. Notice how little content the mobile device accommodates—only about 88 words—and how much space those few words take up. The whole second paragraph, outlined in red, is missing from the mobile screen.

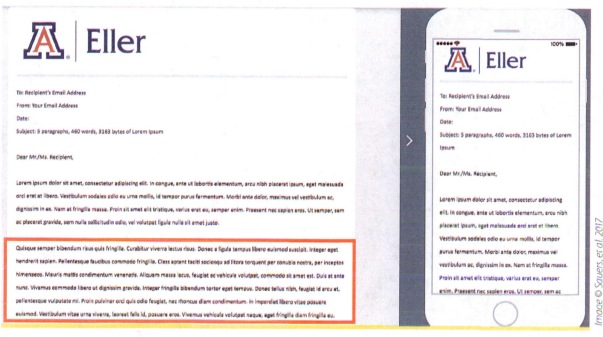

**Figure 2** *Big Screens vs. Small Screens.*

If you were to send an email like this to someone reading on a laptop, your audience could read your entire introduction and second paragraph before needing to scroll down. This would make it much more likely that they would actually read—or at least skim—that material, especially if you incorporated a few visual design strategies to make your message more skimmable.

The mobile reader, by contrast, would face a wall of text that would quickly fill up their entire screen. They would need to scroll down a few times just to reach the end of the second paragraph, at which point they would be unlikely to read the rest of the email.

Luckily, the best practices you have already learned—concision and document design—can help you craft more effective messages for small screens. Shorter, more impactful sentences and paragraphs, visual design cues like section headings, bullets, and numbering, and BLOT all result in messages that are perfectly tailored for mobile devices and tablets. And bonus: these habits make for more effective messages on large screens, too.

# Presenting through Screens

In our discussion of Media Richness Theory in the previous chapter, we learned that communicating in a virtual environment forces us to make tradeoffs that affect the quality of communication. As we seek to reap the benefits of working with talented professionals who are geographically distant from us, we are forced to use channels that do not carry as much information as co-located, face-to-face communication.

Most of the communication you will do in a virtual environment will be in writing. You will spend the bulk of your time drafting emails, text messages, brief reports, and project updates. Occasionally, though, you will need to use a richer medium, such as video conferencing, to conduct a synchronous meeting with your team.

## Preparing to Present: Understanding the Technology

Video conferencing tools abound. The illustration below shows some of the most commonly used applications today. These tools attempt to bridge the geographical distance between dispersed workers so that they can meet, present, and collaborate in real time.

**SKYPE FOR BUSINESS**

**GOOGLE HANGOUTS**

**CISCO WEBEX**

© Shutterstock.com

**Figure 1**  *Commonly-Used Video Conferencing Software.*

The ultimate goal of video conferencing design is to make participants feel like they are physically in the same room at the same time, just as they would be if they were having a face-to-face conversation. Doing so would enable participants to use their full range of verbal and nonverbal cues to communicate effectively.

To achieve this, the most useful video conferencing tools, like Skype for Business, Citrix GoToMeeting, Cisco WebEx, and Adobe Connect offer suites of features, which include most or all of the following:

- International phone number calling support
- Multi-language support
- Whiteboard tools
- Desktop sharing
- Mouse and keyboard sharing
- In-app chat and private chat
- Calendar integration
- Audio and video recordings
- Social media integration
- Cloud storage for audio/video recordings and shared files

While not all applications offer all of these features, the most useful apps enable dispersed teams to enter an immersive environment that simulates being in the same room at the same time. Seeing one another's faces, hearing each other's voices, sharing a desktop or presentation screen, and chatting via in-app chat windows significantly helps facilitate communication during a virtual meeting or presentation. By facilitating communication, this mix of visual, verbal, and auditory media builds trust on virtual teams. Teammates become more "real" to each other and feel a greater sense of connection.

If you are new to this technology or have limited experience with it, it may help to look at an example. Consider the screenshot below:

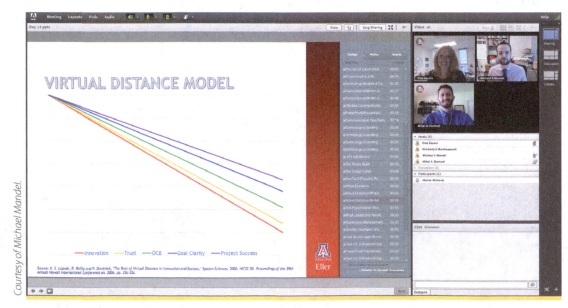

Courtesy of Michael Mandel.

**Figure 2**   *Adobe Connect Meeting Center*

The screenshot above captures the basic features of a video conferencing application. The application captures much information simultaneously, so let's walk through what we see on this screen. We will focus on the most important features—layout, desktop and file sharing, video and audio streaming, chat, and recording. Though the example shows one of the platforms listed earlier in this chapter, the features we are about to describe are common to almost all modern video conferencing platforms.

- **Configurable layout**: If this were your meeting, the window above would likely occupy your entire computer screen during the meeting (although you could make it smaller). As you can see, there is a large space on the left to share your desktop and files, and smaller tiles on the right for live video streaming and chatting. These spaces and tiles are usually configurable, so you can adjust their sizes and positions to meet your needs.

- **Desktop and file sharing**: One of the most important features of a video conferencing application is the ability for participants to share their desktops and files. This gives the presenter control of the meeting, allowing him or her to load and navigate presentation slides, Word or Excel files, Internet browser windows, or anything else the other participants need to see. File sharing allows participants to collaborate on shared files in real time and keeps everyone on the same page (literally,) cutting down on the time spent sending files back and forth between teammates.

- **Live video streaming**: Live video streaming is another critical feature of these tools. Using your computer's webcam, the application streams live video of you to other meeting participants' screens. The other participants' webcams stream the same way, and they appear below your image, although this can change depending on who is talking.

- **Audio streaming**: Most video conferencing applications use a Voice over IP (VoIP) connection to transmit audio content, although some do allow users to connect via telephone. This is important because it underscores the necessity of a robust and reliable Internet connection. The audio stream and video stream synchronize to give participants the experience of communicating in real time. To capture audio reliably and minimize echo, participants are often encouraged to use headphones with built-in microphones rather than their computers' speakers or microphones. Many external webcams now include good-quality microphones, reducing the need for a separate set of headphones.

- **Chat:** In the bottom right corner of the screenshot, you will see an area marked "Chat." The chat and private chat functions are useful features for jotting notes, logging questions, and holding side conversations, as long as they are used judiciously (more on this later). The chat function, however, becomes a lifesaver when a meeting participant loses audio or visual connectivity. Participants can often communicate and troubleshoot via chat when nothing else works.

- **Recording**: Finally, the ability to record a meeting or presentation is an invaluable way to share that event with a teammate who may have been unable to attend or who may have lost connectivity during the meeting. Recording a meeting, however, should only be done with the consent of those participating.

With the ability to capture, transmit, and record so much information simultaneously, video conferencing applications are rich mediums that have changed the way dispersed teams work. They do much to bridge the gaps between dispersed teammates, and when they work properly, they facilitate communication, improve collaboration, and build trust.

While these applications empower virtual teams to collaborate in ways that were not possible until recently, they rely on skilled users to fully leverage their potential. In the next few pages, we will examine the skills you will need to present successfully in a virtual environment. As with writing for screens, presenting for screens builds on the skills you have already learned for co-located presentations. Let's check in on Betina as she debriefs with her peers on her first virtual presentation.

Post #5: The Progress Presentation

Dear SGI Intern Community:

We have reached the midpoint of our first rotation of this LDP. I hosted my first virtual meeting this week—a progress presentation to my team. While I'm pleased to report that the content was solid (I'm right on track with my project and supporting analysis) the presentation itself did not go as smoothly as I would have hoped.

Here's a quick recap:

- I bought a new headset with a built-in microphone for the meeting, but didn't think to test it ahead of time

- I set the meeting to begin at 1:00 p.m. EST (lunchtime here in Houston) and checked in about 5 minutes early

- I ran the meeting from my desktop computer here at the office

- My slides were packed with information, but no text smaller than 14-point

Can you guess what went wrong? Pretty much everything. Since the meeting, I've followed up with each of my team members for feedback on my progress thus far. Rishab, Madeline, and Jackson were supposed to provide this feedback during the meeting, but unfortunately, the technological glitches, background noise, and text-heavy visuals resulted in a lot of questions during the meeting, which chewed through most of our time.

How did your progress presentations go? Please tell me I'm not the only one who botched this one. . .

Best regards,
Betina.

===
Betina May
LDP Intern, Sax Global Inc.

What probably went wrong during Betina's presentation?

How could she have prevented losing so much time during the presentation?

# Learn to Troubleshoot

We are still in the nascent stages of virtual collaboration; the technology that enables it demands that users be able to troubleshoot and work around its limitations. In much the same way that motorists in the 1920s, 30s, and 40s were expected to know the basics of automotive repair in case their cars broke down (which they often did), users of video conferencing applications need to be able to troubleshoot when the technology gets buggy (which it often will).

To be an effective virtual presenter, you cannot assume that the technology will work every time you fire it up, or that it will work for all participants at the meeting. Video conferencing applications are large, complex systems that receive inputs from a variety of sources, not all of which work perfectly all of the time. You may log in to the meeting to find that your headphones or microphone, which worked the last time you logged in, don't pick up your voice, or that one of the meeting participants is unable to see your video stream.

Whatever the problem may be, virtual environments create opportunities for people to distinguish themselves by their ability to troubleshoot and solve problems in the moment. The time you spend learning the system before you present—by attending trainings offered by your service provider, watching online tutorials, and reading the instructions—will pay off when you have to resolve a technical glitch during your presentation. Establishing your expertise in an important workplace technology builds your credibility. More importantly, solving a problem on the fly can make the difference between delivering a successful presentation and having to reschedule one.

# Show Up Early

This basic rule is incredibly important in a virtual environment, whether you are hosting, presenting, or simply attending a meeting. If you are simply attending a meeting, you cannot just walk into the room and take your seat. You will need time to log in to the application, ensure that your video and audio inputs work, adjust your settings, and verify that you have access to the shared files your team will be discussing. If you have difficulty with any of these items, you will need time to troubleshoot before the meeting begins. *Don't be the person who chews through the first 10 minutes of the meeting trying to get set up!*

We have had many experiences of running virtual case competitions that get increasingly behind schedule because the team member with the slide deck shows up just on time and did not leave any time to check their technology first.

If you are hosting the meeting or presenting, you will need to log in even earlier. Arrive early enough to welcome participants as they log in, and troubleshoot with anyone who needs help.

# Design for Small Screens

Design any visuals, such as PowerPoint slides, for small screens. While participants can configure their layouts to view your presentation full screen, most participants prefer to see your face and the video feeds of other participants while you present. This means that you only have about 50% of your audience's screen for any visuals (see the screenshot we discussed earlier.) Design high-quality, high-impact visuals that are easy to read and understand in a smaller format.

# Remember Your Limits

For all their capabilities, video conferencing applications are still not as rich as a face-to-face communication. Variations in each participant's Internet speed or bandwidth, headphone, microphone, and webcam quality limit the range of verbal and nonverbal cues you can transmit reliably through this medium. Often, the poorest connection sets the pace for the entire presentation. Regardless of how good your connection is, you may find yourself slowing down, repeating yourself, or otherwise adjusting your delivery to accommodate a teammate (or supervisor or instructor!) who is experiencing technical difficulty.

Fewer cues mean more scrutiny on those that remain. With limited audio and visual cues, your audience will pay more attention to what they can actually see and hear.

Savvy virtual presenters know this and adjust their webcams, microphones, backgrounds, and wardrobes accordingly.

Fewer cues mean increased scrutiny on those that are visible. With limited audio and visual cues, your audience will pay more attention to what they can actually see and hear. Savvy virtual presenters know this and adjust their webcams and microphones accordingly. You will want to pay particular attention to the following items:

- **Your webcam**: Adjust your webcam so it sits level and points straight at your face. Don't angle your webcam so it points up from below or down from above. You don't want your audience to have the impression that they are sitting on the floor looking up at you, or towering above you looking down. You want to be eye-level with your audience as if you were sitting across a conference table from them. If you are using a laptop with a built-in webcam, you may need to prop your laptop up on a book (or two) until the webcam is level with your eyes. While taking selfies from a high angle yields more flattering pictures, it is not appropriate in professional settings. Check your video stream and adjust accordingly.

- **Your background**: This is particularly problematic for inexperienced virtual presenters. What does your background say about you? Check your video stream and make sure that what your audience sees behind you enhances your credibility, rather than detracting from it. Refrigerators, bedroom walls, bed headboards, open closets, cluttered workspaces, concert posters, and totally blank walls make poor backgrounds. Consider tightening the frame of your webcam so your face and shoulders take up most of the screen.

- **Your wardrobe**: Since your audience can only see you from the waist up, what you wear establishes your professionalism. Excessive jewelry can interfere with your microphone; wrinkled shirts, three-day stubble, unkempt hair, and plunging necklines affect your credibility. Remember to dress for the job you want!

- **Background noise**: If you work in a noisy office environment or share a home office with a dog or children, you will need to mute your microphone when you are not speaking. Background noise damages the audio quality for everyone in the meeting and can create the impression that you are distracted. If possible, find a quiet place for the meeting.

# Don't Assume You Have Your Audience's Full Attention (But Give Them Yours)

Virtual environments are full of opportunities for distraction. Unlike co-located presentations and meetings, in which you can easily see if someone is texting or working on a different task while you are speaking, a video conference leaves plenty of space off-camera to hide a phone, and plenty of space on screen to multitask.

This unfortunate reality puts the ball in your court in two important ways. As the presenter, it is even more critical to craft a presentation that is concise, engaging, and invites audience participation through in-stream questions and discussion. As an audience member, it is your responsibility to keep your eyes on the task at hand. Your eyes are the most noticeable feature on your face, and the other participants will be able to see them wander off screen. Letting your eyes wander can be quite disruptive, so keep them locked on the application window.

# Collaborating through Screens

No matter where your career takes you, your ability to write and present through screens will set you apart as an effective communicator and valued teammate. So far in this unit, we have examined how written and verbal communication present unique challenges in a virtual environment. We have followed our protagonist, Betina May, through the onboarding phase of her internship at a multinational consulting firm, which has challenged her to learn new ways of writing and presenting. In this chapter, we shift our focus to the third pillar of communication—interpersonal communication—which challenges us to apply what we have learned about writing and presenting, and questions our assumptions about what makes virtual teams work.

## How Virtual Is Your Team?

Recall that virtual teams are defined by the degree to which they are dispersed and asynchronous. Let's take a quick look at these terms again before we move on:

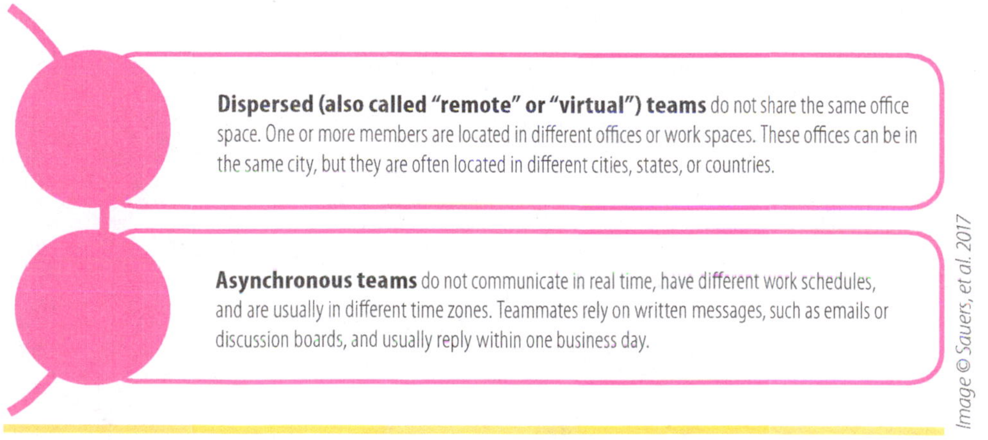

**Dispersed (also called "remote" or "virtual") teams** do not share the same office space. One or more members are located in different offices or work spaces. These offices can be in the same city, but they are often located in different cities, states, or countries.

**Asynchronous teams** do not communicate in real time, have different work schedules, and are usually in different time zones. Teammates rely on written messages, such as emails or discussion boards, and usually reply within one business day.

*Image © Sauers, et al. 2017*

**Figure 1**  *Characteristics of Virtual Teams.*

While very few people work on teams that are 100% dispersed and entirely asynchronous, most professionals work on teams that are at least partially virtual. Interactions with colleagues in these virtual environments occur in one of four scenarios. In each scenario, the sender and receiver must bridge physical distance, temporal distance, or both. Each scenario also uses different media and carries with it a unique set of expectations:

1. **Same time, same place.** This situation is similar to a face-to-face interaction. The sender and receiver are in the same office building, but decide to communicate via telephone, text message, or instant message to "check in" or share ideas in real time. Senders expect immediate replies to their messages in this scenario.

2. **Same time, different place.** In this scenario, the sender and receiver are in the same time zone but in different locations. The sender, located at corporate headquarters, may send a text message or email to a colleague who is away on business in another location. The sender expects the receiver to reply within the same business day, but usually does not expect an immediate reply.

3. **Different time, same place.** In some cases, it is impractical or impossible for co-workers to communicate in real time. They may have different work schedules or find themselves in separate meetings during the day. In these cases, the sender will often use email or a team discussion board. Receivers are expected to reply within one business day.

4. **Different time, different place.** This last scenario is the most virtual because it involves both temporal and physical distance. Teams that work across both distances rely on a suite of robust communication technologies that often include email, discussion boards, file sharing, shared calendars, and video conferencing tools. Teams use these tools, or media, to communicate and work toward common deadlines. Messages sent through each medium carry different expectations in terms of response time; these expectations are often clarified during the team's norming process.

Communicating effectively in each of the four scenarios requires that senders and receivers have a clear understanding of how and when to use each medium. Users must also have a common understanding of the proper response times for each type of communication they receive.

If this sounds simple, it isn't. Anchoring an entire virtual team on a common set of expectations takes significant time, patience, and effort. This is further complicated by the fact that today's workers are unlikely to serve on just one virtual team—most professionals serve on several—and each can have its own rules, norms, and expectations. It's time for Betina to report back on the feedback she received on her virtual progress presentation.

Dear SGI Intern Community:

I've had a chance to debrief my progress presentation via a series of follow up conversations with Rishab, Madeline, and Jackson. Each of my supervisors used a different medium:

- Jackson called me by phone
- Rishab sent a short series of text messages
- Madeline crafted a crisp, concise email focused on the bottom line and next steps

In her email, Madeline presented me with my next challenge for this LDP rotation, which is to recruit one or two new members for my virtual team to help me complete this project. To do this, I will need to: 1) assess my strengths and weaknesses, 2) identify my role on that team, 3) recruit people who complement my strengths and shore up my weaknesses, and 4) identify best practices for virtual collaboration that I will use to anchor my team.

I realize that to be successful in this task, I'm going to have to be more proactive. I need to do some research to get out ahead of this rather than learning by making mistakes. As I've begun researching, I've discovered that I am not the only one trying to figure this out—far from it. A mountain of research, both academic and popular, has piled up over the years as experts have tried to get to the heart of what makes virtual teams work.

Trends have emerged rather quickly—best practices center on one of three things: people, process, and technology. Wish me luck as I consider my options and embark on my challenge to build a virtual dream team!

Best regards,
Betina.

===

Betina May
LDP Intern, Sax Global Inc.

> What strengths do you possess that would help you succeed on a virtual team? What would make working in a virtual environment difficult?
>
> What types of people would you need to recruit?

# Making Virtual Teams Work

Writing for the Harvard Business Review, Keith Ferrazzi offers a useful frame for organizing and understanding all the elements that create successful virtual teams. While we might be tempted to think that technology—the hardware and software that enables co-workers to communicate and work together over long distances—plays the pivotal role, it doesn't. In fact, technology's impact on virtual teams is far from primary. Two other elements that all teams share—people and process—are more important. To understand why this is true, let's examine each element in turn.

> [V]irtual teams are hard to get right. . . .[I]n our research, we've discovered that most people consider virtual communication less productive than face-to-face interaction, and nearly half admit to feeling confused and overwhelmed by collaboration technology.
>
> (Ferrazzi, 2014)

# Find the Right People

Betina's next challenge is to recruit one or two new teammates to help her complete her project. She will need to recruit people who can be successful in a virtual environment. According to Ferrazzi, the most successful virtual workers share a handful of important traits. These are:

- **Good communication skills**
- **High emotional intelligence**, or the ability to recognize other people's emotions and use that information to guide thinking and behavior
- **Ability to work independently**
- **Resilience**, or the ability to recover from mistakes or technological glitches (recall "Learn to Troubleshoot" from the previous chapter)
- **Cultural sensitivity**

Communication skills, a strong work ethic, and resilience are fundamental to succeeding in the virtual workplace (or any workplace, really.) You may be surprised, though, to see emotional intelligence and cultural sensitivity ranked among those other universal qualities. Why might this be? It's not that these traits are unimportant in co-located and synchronous teams, but they have special importance on teams that use leaner media to bridge greater distances, communicating and collaborating in a way that builds trust. *In other words, in an environment with less face-to-face communication, you need people who can do more with less.* You also need people who can decipher cues and build understanding with colleagues from other cultures.

People who flourish in virtual environments were either born with these traits, or more likely, had to cultivate them through significant effort. Two types of people—inspirational leaders and biculturals—are particularly effective at doing more with less, and using their skills to galvanize virtual teams. Consider the author we mentioned in chapter 5–1 who used to supervise a dispersed team and used technology to try to improve collaboration; he had been using computers from a very young age—even before the internet existed! The organization was in the nonprofit sector, too, which is the embodiment of the concept of "doing more with less."

## Inspirational Leaders

In their work on dispersed teams, Joshi, Lazarova, and Liao focus on the special role that leaders can play in these environments. Much of what we know about leadership is based on the assumption that leaders can influence followers based on close, sustained, and personalized contact. As we have learned in this unit, however, new organizational realities involving remote teams challenge this assumption. Individuals who work from home or a satellite office, or who spend a lot of time on the road, often do not identify strongly with a work group or collective organizational entity. That author who supervised a dispersed team and worked 100% remotely himself bristled any time the organization hosted a pot luck staff gathering. The lack of physical proximity, fewer possibilities for face-to-face interaction, and competing demands from other work teams can undermine an individual's connection to the team.

As Betina has learned from her internship, managers in these contexts rely on infrequent and technology-mediated communications to motivate their teams. Exceptional managers, though, transcend the limits of technology and become more "real" to their teammates.

These managers become inspirational leaders, bridging distances to form meaningful relationships with their teammates, and inspire trust, loyalty, and a sense of belonging. They do this by becoming the "missing link" on virtual teams, drawing on socialized relationships to forge a collective identity for the team. The illustration below highlights how they do it.

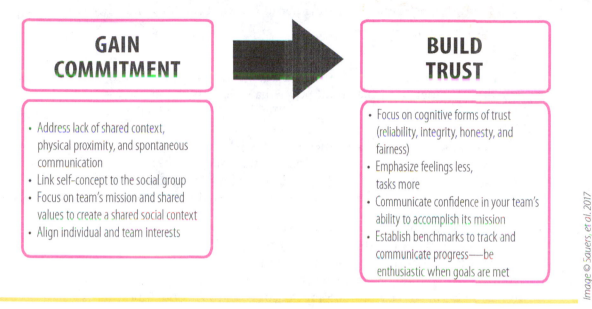

**GAIN COMMITMENT**

- Address lack of shared context, physical proximity, and spontaneous communication
- Link self-concept to the social group
- Focus on team's mission and shared values to create a shared social context
- Align individual and team interests

**BUILD TRUST**

- Focus on cognitive forms of trust (reliability, integrity, honesty, and fairness)
- Emphasize feelings less, tasks more
- Communicate confidence in your team's ability to accomplish its mission
- Establish benchmarks to track and communicate progress—be enthusiastic when goals are met

*Image © Sauers, et al. 2017*

**Figure 2**    *Adapted from Joshi, Lazarova, and Liao (2009).*

Rather than shy away from it, inspirational leaders address the distance on virtual teams head on. They gain commitment by focusing on what the team has in common—its mission and shared values—to align individual interests and get everyone on the same page. They build trust by focusing less on feelings than on tasks, tracking and measuring progress toward shared goals. This may sound counterintuitive. When the team achieves a goal or accomplishes a task—even a minor one—the leader celebrates the accomplishment. Since human relationships are based on shared history, this process builds trust organically by establishing a track record of successful collaboration on the team. In this way, inspirational leaders create more cohesive teams whose members feel like they are working together and can rely on one another.

## Bicultural People

As companies expand internationally to tap the best talent available, teams become more multicultural. While multicultural teams have the potential to be more effective in a globalized and diverse workplace, they must first overcome affinity distance—and specifically cultural distance—that creates divisions among team members. Problems on multicultural teams can take many forms, including the following:

- Structural gaps, or fault lines, among cultural groups
- Conflicts across members' national cultural boundaries
- Direct versus indirect communication
- Trouble with accents and fluency
- Different attitudes toward hierarchy and authority

Managers can tackle the problems on multicultural teams in a variety of ways. Common solutions include the following:

- **Adaptation** (acknowledging cultural gaps openly and working around them)
- **Structural intervention** (changing the shape of the team or reassigning roles)
- **Managerial intervention** (setting norms early or bringing in a higher-level manager)
- **Exit** (removing a member)

While these tactics can be effective, they tend to overlook one of the latent benefits of multicultural teams, namely, that there may be someone on the team who has a high degree of bicultural competence. Bicultural people have deep, personal knowledge of the values, norms, and beliefs of at least two cultures. People who are bilingual, such as immigrants or children of immigrants, often fall into this category, though be careful not to assume that people are bicultural only because they are bilingual. Bicultural people often navigate two or more different cultures on a daily basis, and they are fluent in the languages of both cultures. For example, they may speak one language and follow the norms of one culture when they are at home, but then switch to another language and culture at school or in the workplace.

The true value of a bicultural person lies in her or his ability to bridge cultural distance on a team. As we discussed earlier in this unit, teams suffer when members misinterpret messages or behaviors that arise from differences in their cultural backgrounds. If there are two dominant cultures on a team, such as a Korean company with a satellite office in Los Angeles, a person with bicultural competence (and strong communication skills) in Korean and American culture can span boundaries and mediate conflicts to promote knowledge transfer.

While the example of a Korean-American bicultural person working for a Korean company in Los Angeles is rather obvious, bicultural people can use their skills even if they don't hail from one of the dominant cultures on the team. Research shows that if someone is fluent in two cultures, he or she will find it easier to assimilate to a third, applying what he or she already knows about navigating cultural distance. For example, if the Korean company engages a team of software developers in Denmark, our bicultural team member could use her cultural sensitivity to improve communication and collaboration on a team comprising members from all three countries.

The more bicultural individuals are given the opportunity to play boundary-spanning and conflict-mediating roles, the more effective multicultural teams will be. The challenge is to recognize and understand bicultural people and their ability to increase the effectiveness of a multicultural team.

# Establish Clear Roles and Effective Processes

Inspirational leaders and bicultural people have unique skills that can bridge distances and bring virtual teams together. While these individuals can be important catalysts to galvanize teams, the most important characteristics are the ones we mentioned at the outset of this chapter: good communication skills, high emotional intelligence, cultural sensitivity, an ability to work independently, and an ability to bounce back and troubleshoot when things don't work.

Beyond cultivating these skills, effective virtual teams establish clear processes for getting work done. While a team's process depends on the project and the industry in which it operates, team members should know exactly what their roles are and how they fit into the process. This is especially important if members work on multiple teams, as they may have different roles on each team.

The graphic below illustrates three critical process-oriented roles that should be clear on virtual teams. The team should have a project coordinator to initiate communication and facilitate collaboration, multiple implementors to evaluate ideas and generate content, and one completer-finisher to synthesize material and take responsibility for submission.

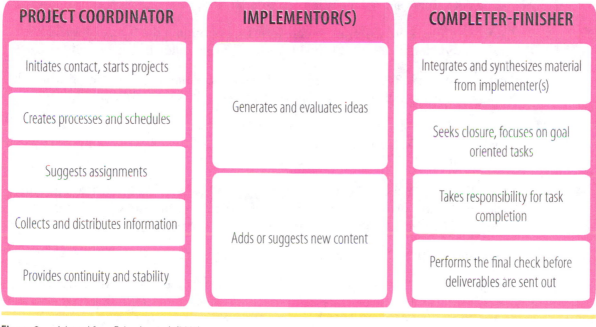

**Figure 3**    *Adapted from Eubanks, et al. (2016).*

# Looking Ahead: Excelling on Virtual Teams

Whatever your role is on a team, virtual environments are full of opportunities to build connections with others, demonstrate your skills in communication and collaboration, and enhance your credibility. It is relatively easy to sit back and passively accept the distances inherent in these types of teams. Sadly, many people do.

We hope this unit inspires you to do the opposite. By understanding the driving forces behind the virtual workplace, you can more easily diagnose the root causes of problems you encounter and work to solve them. As you do so, you will create trust and synergy on your teams, and your reputation as a valued teammate and colleague will grow. We look forward to your success in the virtual world—see you out there!

# Unit 9 References

Asghar, R. (2014, June 13). The art of the effective business email. Retrieved February 03, 2017, from http://www.forbes.com/sites/robasghar/2014/06/12/the-art-of-the-effective-business-email/#7f1fe612290a

Berry, G. R. (2011). Enhancing effectiveness on virtual teams. *The Journal of Business Communication*, 48(2), 186–206.

Chadha, S. (2015, October 23). Student voice: What collaboration tools do students prefer? Retrieved November 25, 2016, from http://edtechtimes.com/2015/10/23/student-voice-what-collaboration-tools-do-students-use/

Ciotti, G. (2016, April 23). How remote teams are becoming the future of work. Retrieved January 09, 2017, from https://www.helpscout.net/blog/virtual-teams/

Daft, R.L., Lengel, R.H. (1986). Organizational information requirements, media richness and structural design. *Management Science*. 32 (5): 554–571.

DuFrene, D. D., 1954, & Lehman, C. M. (2012; 2011). *Managing virtual teams* (1st; 1 ed.). [New York, N.Y.] (222 East 46th Street, New York, NY 10017): Business Expert Press.

Eubanks, D. L., Palanski, M., Olabisi, J., Joinson, A., & Dove, J. (2016). Team dynamics in virtual, partially distributed teams: Optimal role fulfillment. *Computers in Human Behavior*, 61, 556–568. doi:10.1016/j.chb.2016.03.035

Ferrazzi, K. (2014). *Getting virtual teams right*. Boston: Harvard Business Review.

Hong, H. (2010). Bicultural competence and its impact on team effectiveness. *International Journal of Cross Cultural Management*, 10(1), 93–120. doi:10.1177/1470595809359582

Johns, T., & Gratton, L. (2013, February). The third wave of virtual work. Retrieved November 22, 2016, from https://hbr.org/2013/01/the-third-wave-of-virtual-work

Jones, J. M. (2015, August 19). In U.S., Telecommuting for work climbs to 37%. Retrieved November 21, 2016, from http://www.gallup.com/poll/184649/telecommuting-work-climbs.aspx

Joshi, A., Lazarova, M. B., & Liao, H. (2009). Getting everyone on board: The role of inspirational leadership in geographically dispersed teams. *Organization Science*, 20(1), 240–252. doi:10.1287/Orsc.1080.0383

Martinez, J., & McLaughlin, M. (n.d.). The best video conferencing software of 2016. Retrieved February 11, 2017, from http://www.pcmag.com/article2/0,2817,2388678,00.asp

The Radicati Group, Inc. (2015, March). *Email Statistics Report*, 2015–2019. Retrieved from http://www.radicati.com/wp/wp-content/uploads/2015/02/Email-Statistics-Report-2015-2019-Executive-Summary.pdf

Reaney, P. (2015, August 26). U.S. Workers spend 6.3 hours a day checking email: Survey. Retrieved from http://www.huffingtonpost.com/entry/check-work-email-hours-survey_us_55ddd168e4b0a40aa3ace672

Shin, L. (2016, March 31). At these 125 companies, all or most employees work remotely. Retrieved November 21, 2016, from http://www.forbes.com/sites/laurashin/2016/03/31/at-these-125-companies-all-or-most-employees-work-remotely/#50f350984d94

Sobel Lojeski, K. (2016). Virtual Distance International website. Retrieved from http://www.vrtualdistance.com

Vanderkam, L. (2014, August 14). Will half of people be working remotely by 2020? Retrieved from https://www.fastcompany.com/3034286/the-future-of-work/will-half-of-people-be-working-remotely-by-2020

# Index

# D

# H

Halo effect, 262
Handshake, 349–350
Head bobble, 362
Headings, 126
Helper seeker role, 225
Hichert Partner's International Business
    Communication Standards (IBCS), 7–8
Hidden slide, 307–308
High-context culture, 353, 354–355, 358
High stakes conversation, 219–222
    delivery of bad news in, 220–221
    diversity in, 221
    dynamics in, 221
    feedback in, 219–220
    timing, expectations and culture in, 221–222
    understanding in, 222
Hofstede's cultural dimensions, 344, 345
Hue, 297–298
Human resource (HR) consultant, 322

# I

Icon, 289
Illicit ingratiation, 205
Illustrative gesture, 263
Images, 126, 289–290
Imagination, 4
Implementor role, 399
Index slide, 307
India, 338
Indices, 289
Indirect bad news message, 114–117
    body, 116
    conclusion, 116–117
    direct benefits and deflection, 102
    introduction, 115–116
    sample scenario, 117–118, 119–120
Indirect informational approach, 28–29
Indirect message, 22, 23
Indirect persuasive approach, 101–104
    AIDA, 101
    body, 102
    conclusion, 101–102
    introduction, 101

Individualistic role, 225
Industry report, 164
    student example, 165–170, 171–180
"Industry Report: Correctional Facilities" sample,
    171–180
Inflection, 260–261
Infographic, 289–290
Inform, 22
Informal message, 21
Informal presentation, 241
Informal report, 57–60, 62
    research summary sample, 59–60
    strategy summary sample, 62
    types of, 58
Informational message, 24–26
    body, 25–26
    conclusion, 26
    direct approach, 24
    introduction, 24–25
Information analysis, 4
Information design, 4, 7–8, 10–11
Information gathering, 53
Information technology (IT) consultant, 322
Informative message, 85–93
    defined, 85
    direct, 26
    organizational patterns for, 88–93
    prewriting, 87
    structure, 87–88
Ingratiation, 205
Initial client research, 322–323
Initiative, 4
Inspirational leader, 396–397
Instrumental objective, 204
Integrity, 206
Intercultural communication, 338–339, 341–352,
    353–363. *see also* Global business
Intercultural competency, 353–362. *see also* Cultural
    IQ
Intercultural negotiation process, 347–349
    agreement, 349
    discussions, 348–349
    opening talks, 348
    preparation, 348
    relationship building, 348
    team selection, 348
Interdependence distance, 377
Interference, 201